Reading Romans after Supersessionism

Series Preface

The **New Testament after Supersessionism** (NTAS) is a series that presents post-supersessionist interpretations of the New Testament. By post-supersessionism, we mean "a family of theological perspectives that *affirms God's irrevocable covenant with the Jewish people as a central and coherent part of ecclesial teaching.* It rejects understandings of the new covenant that entail the abrogation or obsolescence of God's covenant with the Jewish people, of the Torah as a demarcator of Jewish communal identity, or of the Jewish people themselves" (spostst.org). Although the field of New Testament studies has made significant strides in this direction in recent years, the volumes in this series, written by Jewish and gentile believers in Jesus, seek to advance the conversation by offering post-supersessionist readings of the New Testament that address the question of ongoing Jewish particularity, and the relationship of interdependence and mutual blessing between Jew and gentile in Messiah.

SERIES EDITORS

J. Brian Tucker
  Moody Theological Seminary, Plymouth, MI

David Rudolph
  The King's University, Southlake, TX

Justin Hardin
  Palm Beach Atlantic University, West Palm Beach, FL

PROJECTED VOLUMES

New Testament After Supersessionism, Introductory Volume
  —Justin K. Hardin, David J. Rudolph, and J. Brian Tucker

Reading Matthew After Supersessionism
  —Anders Runesson

Reading Mark after Supersessionism
  —Vered Hillel

Reading Luke-Acts after Supersessionism
  —Mark S. Kinzer and David J. Rudolph

Reading John after Supersessionism
  —Wally V. Cirafesi

Reading Romans after Supersessionism
  —J. Brian Tucker

Reading 1 Corinthians after Supersessionism
  —Kar Yong Lim

Reading 2 Corinthians after Supersessionism
  —James A. Waddell

Reading Galatians after Supersessionism
  —Justin K. Hardin

Reading Philippians after Supersessionism
  —Christopher Zoccali

Reading Ephesians and Colossians after Supersessionism
  —Lionel Windsor

Reading Hebrews after Supersessionism
  —David M. Moffitt

Reading 1 Peter after Supersessionism
  —Kelly D. Liebengood

Reading Revelation after Supersessionism
  —Ralph Korner

New Testament after Supersessionism, Supplementary Volume
  —edited by Justin K. Hardin, David J. Rudolph, and J. Brian Tucker

Reading Romans after Supersessionism

THE CONTINUATION OF
JEWISH COVENANTAL IDENTITY

J. Brian Tucker

CASCADE *Books* · Eugene, Oregon

READING ROMANS AFTER SUPERSESSIONISM
The Continuation of Jewish Covenantal Identity

New Testament after Supersessionism 6

Cascade Books
An Imprint of Wipf and Stock Publishers
199 W. 8th Ave., Suite 3
Eugene, OR 97401

www.wipfandstock.com

PAPERBACK ISBN: 978-1-4982-1751-4
HARDCOVER ISBN: 978-1-4982-1753-8
EBOOK ISBN: 978-1-4982-1752-1

Cataloguing-in-Publication data:

Names: Tucker, J. Brian, author.

Title: Reading Romans after supersessionism : the continuation of Jewish covenantal identity / J. Brian Tucker.

Description: Eugene, OR: Cascade Books, 2018 | Series: New Testament after Supersessionism 6 | Includes bibliographical references and index.

Identifiers: ISBN 978-1-4982-1751-4 (paperback) | ISBN 978-1-4982-1753-8 (hardcover) | ISBN 978-1-4982-1752-1 (ebook)

Subjects: LCSH: Romans—Criticism, interpretation, etc. | Paul, the Apostle, Saint—Relations with Jews | Judaism—Relations—Christianity | Jews in the New Testament | Gentiles in the New Testament | Judaism (Christian theology) | Paul, the Apostle, Saint

Classification: BS2665.52 T827 2018 (print) | BS2665.52 (ebook)

AUGUST 8, 2018

To Bill, Kathy, and Mark

Table of Contents

Acknowledgements xi
List of Abbreviations xiii

1 Introduction 1
2 To the Jew First 28
3 The Fatherhood of Abraham 62
4 The Validity of the Law 85
5 Israel's Present Covenantal Identity 115
6 Christ Fulfills Torah 153
7 Israel's Future Covenantal Identity 172
8 The Weak and the Strong 197
9 A Doxological Social Identity 221
10 Conclusion 244

Bibliography 249

Index of Ancient Sources 273
Index of Modern Authors 289

Acknowledgements

My interest in Romans extends back to two early Romans courses I took, one as an undergraduate with William A. Simmons and one in seminary with Gregory Couser. They raised numerous questions about the traditional reading of Romans that needed answers, ones I wouldn't be able to pursue fully until the completion of my PhD studies at the University of Wales, Lampeter. While researching under the supervision of Dr. William S. Campbell, I started to see the way many of the questions raised by Drs. Simmons and Couser might be answered. This book then serves as my response to questions that have been floating around in my head since 1989. A couple of years ago I presented a paper with content reflected in this book at a scholarly society and both of them were in the audience; that was unnerving but also rewarding. Their gracious and helpful feedback encouraged me to continue to pursue the ideas presented. The book you are reading builds on my earlier work on 1 Corinthians that focuses on the way existing gentile identities continue in Christ but seeks to apply some of its key findings to Romans, addressing the way Jewish covenantal identity also continues in Christ and the relevance this has for gentiles. This present volume offers a different view of many of the key hermeneutical points that result in supersessionist readings of this letter and argues for the continuation of existing identities in Romans. Of course there is more to say; this volume seeks to address many of the objections to a post-supersessionist reading of Romans yet recognizes that many of these points require further validation—hopefully a new generation of researchers will do just that!

The majority of this book was written during my 2016 sabbatical leave, and thus I owe a debt of gratitude to my colleagues and the administration of Moody Theological Seminary, especially Dr. John Jelinek and Dr. Larry Davidhizar, for helping make this sabbatical possible. I want to thank Dr. Matthew Novenson for inviting me as a guest of the Centre for the Study of Christian Origins at the University of Edinburgh

(New College) and to Dr. Tom Breimaier for his hospitality and research assistance during my time in Edinburgh. The staff at the Greek Bible College in Athens, Greece, were particularly helpful during the past two summers, and Samuel Spatola, the Dean of the Saints Bible Institute in San Lorenzo, Italy, provided excellent support and interaction during my stay there. In particular, I want to thank the Rev. Dr. Laura Hunt for her careful reading, suggestions, and editing of this book. Thanks also to the students in my Seminar on the Old Testament Use in the New Testament, Exegesis of the Greek New Testament, and Romans courses who raised provocative and insightful questions while going through earlier versions of this material.

I want to thank the staff at Wipf and Stock for their continued support. Dr. Robin Parry provided encouragement and insight throughout the process and has been a keen supporter of *The New Testament after Supersessionism* Series from the very beginning. I want to thank Dr. David Rudolph particularly since his continued efforts to clarify, revise, substantiate, and reconsider parts of this book have made it much better than it would have been otherwise, though I realize I am responsible for all the shortcomings that remain. Also, Ryan Heinsch who was and continues to be a helpful colleague and dialogue partner in all things Pauline. Thanks to those who discussed these ideas with me over the past few years: Dr. William (Bill) S. Campbell, Dr. Kathy Ehrensperger, Dr. Mark Nanos (the three to whom this book is dedicated), Dr. Justin Hardin, Dr. Joel Willitts, Dr. Chris Zoccali, Dr. Lionel Windsor, Dr. Robert Foster, Dr. Mark Kinzer, Dr. David Woodall, Dr. John Goodrich, Henri Goulet, Zach Johnson, Dan Thorpe, Bruce Henning, James Bryde, and Aaron Robinson. Their influence is seen throughout. I want to thank my family for their patience throughout this process: Amber, Ashley and Matthew Doyle, Alexandria and John Bodkin, Annaliese, and Abigail. To our parents Joseph and Ann Tucker as well as Richard and Carol Goode, thank you for your commitment to our extended family through the years.

J. Brian Tucker
June 2018

Abbreviations

ABBREVIATIONS FOLLOW THE RULES recommended by the Society of Biblical Literature, according to Billie Jean Collins, Bob Buller, and John F. Kusko (eds.), *The SBL Handbook of Style for Biblical Studies and Related Disciplines* (2nd ed. Atlanta: SBL, 2014). These rules include standard abbreviations for biblical books, early Jewish and Christian literature, and classical literature. The abbreviation standards found in the *SBL Handbook* for secondary sources such as journals, series, and standard reference works are also followed throughout this book. The following abbreviations are not mentioned in *The SBL Handbook of Style*.

CD	Karl Barth, *Church Dogmatics*. Translated by G. T. Thomson et al. Edinburgh: T. & T. Clark, 1936–77.
CD	The Damascus Document from the Cairo Genizah.
GGBB	Daniel B. Wallace, *Greek Grammar Beyond the Basics: An Exegetical Syntax of the New Testament*. Grand Rapids: Zondervan, 1996.
LSJ	Henry George Liddell, Robert Scott, and Henry Stuart Jones, *A Greek-English Lexicon*. 9th ed. Oxford: Clarendon, 1996.
MM	James Hope Moulton and George Milligan, *The Vocabulary of the Greek Testament: Illustrated from the Papyri and Other Non-Literary Sources*. 1930. Reprint. Peabody, MA: Hendrickson, 1997.
NETS	Albert Pietersma and Benjamin G. Wright (eds.), *A New English Translation of the Septuagint*. Oxford: Oxford University Press, 2007.

NIDNTTE	*New International Dictionary of New Testament Theology and Exegesis.* 5 vols. Edited by Moisés Silva. Grand Rapids: Zondervan, 2014.
TDNT	*Theological Dictionary of the New Testament.* Edited by Gerhard Kittel and Gerhard Friedrich. Translated by Geoffrey W. Bromiley. 10 vols. Grand Rapids: Eerdmans, 1964–76.

1

Introduction

PAUL WAS NO SUPERSESSIONIST. He was part of a Jewish mission to the nations, designed to declare God's gospel and bring about the obedience of faith among the gentiles (Rom 1:1, 5). This mission developed from within the traditions of the Jewish people, but as an ever-increasing number of non-Jews responded to the gospel, cultural tensions arose between groups that had been and continued to be different.[1] The intersection of these social identities and the way they are transformed in Christ became the focal point of much of the content of Paul's letters. Romans is no different, even though it was written to a Christ-group he did not found. Clearly, I am not the first interpreter of Paul to recognize this; identity and the relationship between the Christ-movement and Judaism have been a regular focus of scholars. However, the dominant paradigm that emerges from their work has a problem: it is supersessionist. This calls for a new reading strategy, a post-supersessionist one. Such an approach would maintain two key ideas: the irrevocability of God's covenant with the Jewish people and a continuing role for Torah as a demarcator of the Jewish people and their identity.

Paul's Identity-Forming Work among the Romans

This study sets out to investigate several verses from Romans that impinge on these two claims: Israel has a continuing covenantal identity and Torah has continuing validity within the Christ-movement. While

1. Throughout this book "non-Jews" and "gentiles" will be used as synonymous terms. The primary reason I use non-Jew is to make it explicit that there is no one ethnic group determined via the use of the term "gentile." The idea is that non-Jew reflects a broad idea, anyone not understood to be Jewish. See further on this beginning on page 19.

one could argue that the entire letter would need to be exposited in order to establish a post-supersessionist reading, I do not intend this book to answer all the questions that might be raised, but rather to interact with key discussions, laying out alternative understandings in order to add to the conversations about the letter as a whole.

This book is written from within the current of scholarship loosely referred to as the Paul-within-Judaism paradigm.[2] I have become convinced that Paul specifically, and the Christ-movement generally, is best understood within prevailing Jewish patterns of life, informed by their ancestral traditions, since the parting of the ways between Judaism and Christianity was yet to occur. This study is also informed by contemporary identity research, especially Tajfel and Turner's social identity approaches.[3] Social identity—that part of an individual's self-concept that derives from his or her membership in a group, along with the emotional attachment experienced from that membership—guides this research in terms of the identity-based groupings evident in Romans.[4] While these approaches inform the exegesis in this book at key points, they do so in the role of background technology and not as a dominant framework. They function primarily to make my theoretical approach and assumptions accessible to the reader.[5] The first-century Roman Empire was replete with differing ethnic groups, languages, and religious traditions all unified, according to the political elites, under the peace of Rome.[6] This environment presents an ideal setting for the role of social identity to be brought to bear. Thus, this study will be guided by three ideas: (a) the interpretive advances of the Paul-within-Judaism approach, (b) the understanding of group-based problems from Tajfel and Turner, and (c) the way the Roman Empire functioned as an outgroup for Christ-followers in Rome.

This study builds on my earlier work on Paul, even though most of that has focused on 1 Corinthians.[7] Those books explored the way

---

2. See Tucker, "Paul within or without Judaism," 37–41; Nanos and Zetterholm, *Paul within Judaism*; Zetterholm, *Approaches to Paul*.

3. Tajfel, "Social Categorization," 61–76; Tajfel and Turner, "An Integrative Theory," 33–47; Tajfel and Turner, "Social Identity Theory," 7–24.

4. Tucker and Baker, *Handbook to Social Identity*; Tucker, *Reading 1 Corinthians*, 40.

5. Clarke and Tucker, "Social History," 56.

6. Stegemann, "Coexistence," 3–23; Tucker, *You Belong to Christ*, 89–128; 181–93.

7. Tucker, *You Belong to Christ*; Tucker, *Remain in Your Calling*; Tucker, *Reading*

existing aspects of the Corinthians' Roman social identity was adversely affecting their communal life in Christ. Their civic identity was functioning too highly in their identity hierarchy, and thus Paul needed to remind them of two key ideas: (a) they belonged to Christ and (b) they were to remain in their calling with God. This suggests that the problem was not one between Judaism and the Christ-movement, a Torah-informed versus Torah-free pattern of life; rather, existing civic identities were hindering the salience of the Corinthians' in-Christ identity. Thus, Paul was not seeking to dissociate them from Judaism but to get them to reprioritize all aspects of life under Christ's lordship. Further, he actually sought to maintain a connection with Jerusalem via the collection (1 Cor 16:1–4). Paul does something similar with the Jerusalem collection in Romans 15:23–26; in-Christ gentiles are to remain connected with Israel and the Jewish people.[8] Another important finding from my earlier work that continues to be relevant is that Paul's "rule in all the congregations" is that ethnic identities are to continue as a matter of calling (1 Cor 7:17–24) and that Torah-informed praxis applies to both Jews and gentiles, though with different implications (1 Cor 9:19–23).[9] For Paul what matters is "keeping the commands of God" (1 Cor 7:19), which suggests that he has halakhic guidance for his audience. Paul does something similar in Romans, especially at the beginning when he lets his audience know that part of his apostleship is "to bring about the obedience of faith among all the Gentiles" (Rom 1:5).[10] Paul is, for one thing, instructing them on the social implications of the gospel, implications that differ for Jews and gentiles, and other socially relevant groups within the congregation in Rome (Rom 14:3, 5; 15:7). Much, then, of what Paul addresses in Romans

1 Corinthians. See Zoccali, "Paul," 105–14, for a major review of the first two books listed.

8. Tucker, "The Jerusalem Collection," 52–70; Campbell, *Paul and the Creation*, 48, 50, 78, 123.

9. I am not the only one who holds this view; there is a long line of scholars, some of whom have influenced my thinking in significant ways. For example, on 1 Cor 7:17–24, see Rudolph, "Paul's 'Rule," 1–23; Runesson, "Paul's Rule," 214–23. On 1 Cor 9:19–23, see Rudolph, *A Jew to the Jews*, 173–208; Nanos, "Paul's Relationship to Torah," 52–92. On Torah praxis generally, see Oliver, *Torah*; and on the Jewishness of Paul in comparison to Acts, see Oliver, "The 'Historical Paul,'" 51–80; Thiessen, *Paul*, 161–69. More broadly see Fredriksen, *Paul*; Ehrensperger, *Paul at the Crossroads*; Campbell, *Paul and the Creation*.

10. The translations in this book will follow the NRSV unless the context calls for a different translation to retain the nuance reflected in the author's discussion, in which case I have inserted my own translation of the Greek text.

has little to do with a desire to separate from Judaism, or with conflicts between his mission praxis and that of those from Jerusalem; rather, his concerns are with the normal group-based challenges that occur when individuals with differing social identifications gather for a common purpose and mission. These questions, along with the challenges of translating the gospel discourse, a set of ideas sourced in the Jewish symbolic universe, account for much if not all of the issues Paul addresses. Thus, the imposition of the idea that Paul had a problem with Judaism that needed fixing is not required. This study aims to show that Paul did not have such a problem but rather remained faithfully within the Jewish tradition even as he sought the formation of an in-Christ identity among the nations (Rom 16:26).

Supersessionist Interpretations of Romans

As mentioned above, the dominant pattern of interpretation of Romans is supersessionist; a new approach, a post-supersessionist one is needed.[11] Several key interpretive choices combine to produce a supersessionist understanding of Romans. What follows highlights some of these crucial choices and provides a quick orientation to ongoing debates within Romans scholarship. It highlights tension points between much of the dominant scholarship and the view put forth in this book in relation to the continuation of Jewish covenantal identity in the messianic age, especially as it relates to the social implications of Paul's gospel.[12] It also

---

11. The definition of post-supersessionism listed in the series preface for this book serves as a basis for my understanding of the term: "a family of theological perspectives that *affirms God's irrevocable covenant with the Jewish people as a central and coherent part of ecclesial teaching*. It rejects understandings of the new covenant that entail the abrogation or obsolescence of God's covenant with the Jewish people, of the Torah as a demarcator of Jewish communal identity, or of the Jewish people themselves."

12. The definition of Jewish covenantal identity used throughout this work follows that of Nanos: "[T]he adjective 'Jewish' is used both to refer to those who are Jews ethnically and to the behavior generally associated with the way that Jews live, albeit variously defined, such as by different interpretations of Scripture and related traditions, different views of who represents legitimate authority, and different conclusions about what is appropriate for any specified time and place. The behavior can be referred to by the adverb 'jewishly', and as the expression of 'jewishness'. In colloquial terms, one who practices a Jewish way of life according to the ancestral customs of the Jews, which is also referred to as practicing 'Judaism', might be called a 'good' Jew" ("Paul's Non-Jews," 27–28). My understanding of Paul's gospel in Romans follows that of Bird (*Evangelical*, 52); the gospel is "the announcement that God's kingdom has come in the life, death, and resurrection of Jesus of Nazareth, the Lord and Messiah, in

challenges interpreters to overcome both supersessionist and implicit supersessionist tendencies in their work.[13] One goal of this book is to highlight several interpretive moves that produce supersessionist readings of Romans. In one example of a supersessionist conclusion, Herman Ridderbos writes: "The church, then, as the people of the New Covenant has taken the place of Israel, and national Israel is nothing other than the empty shell from which the pearl has been removed and which has lost its function in the history of redemption."[14] While most interpreters craft more nuanced statements in the post-Shoah context, their interpretive moves still result in supersessionist readings.[15] This book highlights several such results, even though some of the scholars in question deny such implications to their work. Consequently, a post-supersessionist reader will be able to consider more fully the implicit supersessionism evident in certain scholars' arguments.

---

fulfillment of Israel's Scriptures. The gospel evokes faith, repentance, and discipleship; its accompanying effects include salvation and the gift of the Holy Spirit."

13. One of the problems here is a lack of precision in the use of the term "supersessionism," which is properly understood as the interpretive stance that maintains that the church (in-Christ Jews and non-Jews) has fulfilled or replaced Israel in God's plan. There are some difficulties in defining the church institutionally at this early stage, but what is important is the recognition that there are at least three nuances to supersessionism that impinge on Israel's continuing covenantal identity: economic, punitive, and structural. The economic nuance suggests that Israel's identity was transitory and preparatory, designed to prepare the world for Christ's coming, and that now that he has come, this identity ceases to be relevant. Punitive supersessionism addresses the covenantal framework more precisely; in this understanding Israel has lost its covenantal identity since it rejected Israel's Messiah and his gospel message. Structural supersessionism also addresses the covenantal framework but focuses more on the way the canonical narrative is read, i.e., Israel's scriptures and the apostolic writings reveal a plot in which Israel's story collapses into the story of Christ and has no continuing relevance. These three nuances often combine to formulate an interpretive trajectory that sees no continuing covenantal identity for Israel (Soulen, *The God of Israel*, 30–33).

14. Ridderbos, *Paul*, 354–55; see further Donaldson, "Supersessionism," 1–32; Willitts, "Jewish Fish," 1–5.

15. Dunn, *Theology*, 338: "Post-Holocaust theology could no longer stomach the denigration of historic Judaism." Ehrensperger, in *Mutually Encouraged*, 16–19, describes the hermeneutical consequences that emerge from a post-Shoah theology. These include: (a) recognizing the scriptures as still those of the Jewish people; (b) abandoning any form of displacement theologizing concerning Israel; (c) acknowledging differing interpretive methods; and (d) exposing elements of anti-Judaism in the history of interpretation in order to overcome the resulting bias they produce. She concludes with this helpful reminder: "Christians have to seek to formulate their identity in a new and different way without using Judaism as a negative foil" (19).

Supersessionism is not only a problem among contemporary inter-preters; it finds adherents in the second century. Justin and Irenaeus are two early examples. Justin writes: "As, therefore, Christ is the Israel and Jacob, even so we, who have been quarried out from the bowels of Christ, are the true Israelite race," while Irenaeus contends: "For inasmuch as the former [the Jews] have rejected the Son of God, and cast Him out of the vineyard when they slew Him, God has justly rejected them, and given to the Gentiles outside the vineyard the fruits of its cultivation."[16] While they are writing in a different context than Paul, they used his writings to buttress their claims. So, getting Paul right historically and socially on Israel and the continuation of Jewish identity will contribute to a better understanding of the way these later supersessionist interpreters misun-derstood him.[17] This book, however, will not address this later period in the development of Christianity. These two quotations are offered to alert the reader to the way supersessionism was established in Christian theol-ogy at an early period.[18] With those qualifications, let's turn to some of the interpretive choices that lead to supersessionist readings of Romans.

16. Justin, *Dial.* 135.3; Irenaeus, *Haer.* 36.2. See the helpful work of Tapie, *Aquinas*, 85–108.

17. This task has been done by others in relation to the later setting, see Vlach, *Has the Church*.

18. For example, this book is not about debates between covenant theology and dispensationalism; thus it seeks to marshal a different type of argumentation. It may then contribute to dislodging some of those arguments, but it is not designed primar-ily with that in mind. Again, others who have done so could be consulted (see the previous footnote). These debates occur primarily in conservative evangelical North American settings. Two possible alternative paradigms to the standard supersessionist interpretive stance seem to be (a) evangelical non-supersessionism or (b) post-super-sessionism; both of which would be appropriate for evangelicals to hold. These two closely related approaches reflect attempts to read the canonical narrative in a manner that does not presume the fulfillment or abolishment of Israel's covenantal identity. These approaches are not coterminous with the dual covenant or *Sonderweg* under-standing of Paul, though they are often misconstrued as such. Post-supersessionism maintains a christological necessity but recognizes an ecclesiological diversity. Evan-gelical non-supersessionism likewise argues for a christological necessity but is less diverse with regard to ecclesiology. Thus, these two views may be differentiated by noting that evangelical non-supersessionism affirms that Israel maintains its identity outside the *ekklēsia*, while post-supersessionism holds that Israel maintains its identity outside and inside the *ekklēsia*. Both approaches, however, share the contention that Israel maintains its covenantal identity and that God has not abolished that relation-ship. Jennings, *The Christian Imagination*, 159–61, is helpful in pointing out that several contemporary theological and social difficulties find their source in superses-sionist theology found early on in Christian theologizing.

Paul's letter to the Romans provides strong evidence for the continuation of Israel's covenantal identity. At the same time, it seems to interpreters like Eisenbaum and Harink to offer conflicting declarations about Israel's salvation: calling on Jesus's name is prerequisite (e.g., Rom 10:13), yet "all Israel will be saved" without an appeal to Christ (11:26).[19] This is precisely the difficulty when dealing with Israel in Romans; there is tension between Paul's reflections on the salvific necessity of Jesus and the way diverse patterns of life might emerge within the *ekklēsia* of Jews and non-Jews. Because of the first, scholarly debates often focus on the uniqueness of God's work through Jesus and its universal application.[20] Yet, what is the nature of the unity of the Christ-movement and the degree of acceptable diversity present there? Bilateral and variegated ecclesiology are two closely related approaches to this diversity that seek to resolve the inherent tension in Romans with regard to the continuation of Jewish and non-Jewish identities within the movement.[21] While these approaches are in the minority there is an increasing acknowledgement that Paul has no critique for a continuation of the Jewish calling in Christ; rather, it was his expectation that such a calling continued within the *ekklēsia*. What is crucial to recognize is that the christological (soteriological) and ecclesiological categories are different, and scholars need to be clear as to which is being debated.[22] The conflation of these two issues

19. Eisenbaum, *Paul*, 242, 247; Harink, *Paul*, 151–207; for a critique of this, see Tucker, "Paul between Supersessionism," forthcoming. Further, see Vanlaningham, *Christ*, 1–17, for an overview of the *Sonderweg* and bi-covenantal approaches.

20. The word "universalistic" is used throughout this book to refer primarily to the idea that Paul's gospel is for both Jew and gentile, and not exclusively for gentiles. The word "particularistic" refers to the understanding that different social implications emerge for each group from accepting Paul's gospel.

21. See Kinzer, *Postmissionary*, 151–79, for bilateral ecclesiology, and Rudolph, "Paul's 'Rule,'" 1–24 and Tucker, *Remain in Your Calling*, 62–88, for variegated ecclesiology.

22. Hardin ("If I Still Proclaim," 162–63) picks up on this as he highlights the role of 1 Cor 7:17–24 where "Paul expects Jews to continue living as Jews." In concluding his essay, he states "None of the above theses mitigates against the view . . . either that Paul remained a Torah-observant Jew subsequent to his apostolic call or that he assumed as normative Torah observance among Jewish believers in Jesus." Hardin (126 n. 54) offers an extensive list of contemporary Pauline scholars who see Paul as Torah-observant in his mission to the nations. He ("Equality," 233) argues that this doesn't remove the "full equality between both groups" since both Jews and gentiles are transformed "through the life, death, burial, and resurrection of Jesus the Messiah." Hardin's work is quite helpful in balancing these ecclesiological issues: full equality and the continuation of ethnicities in the body. Though it can't be pursued here, Romans 12:3–8 may clarify this even further.

often leads to supersessionist readings. Thus, they will be distinguished at key points in this book for interpretive clarity.

The coming of Jesus the Messiah has at times been used to question the continued existence of God's historic people, either unchanged or redefined.[23] The organizing framework of salvation history is sometimes used to answer these questions. In this approach, God is seen to be working throughout history for the purposes of salvation for humanity. This line of reasoning generally concludes that Israel's scriptures and Judaism were somewhat preparatory and now that Christ has come their primary purpose has been served. Thus, Israel's scriptures are still important, but the apostolic writings are the appropriate successors to these earlier works. In a similar fashion, what became known as the church is rightly understood as a successor to the religious expressions evident in various forms of Second Temple Judaism.[24] Though there are more extreme forms of replacement theologizing evident in the salvation-historical approach, many simply interpret the leaders in the Christ-movement to be arguing that their understanding of God is more correct than other Jewish understandings of their ancestral religion; the Qumran covenanters viewed themselves similarly in comparison to the Jerusalem establishment.[25] Ei-

23. Longenecker ("Salvation History," 66) frames the issue this way: "At the heart of all this lies a single question: to what extent should Paul's analogy of the olive tree in Rom 11:17–24 stand as the testimony to Paul's view of salvation history in general? In the olive tree analogy, Gentile Jesus-followers seem to be depicted as 'grafted into' the salvation history of the Jewish people." He refers to this as "the expanded-covenant model of salvation history." However, later in the article he contends that Paul doesn't maintain this throughout Romans, e.g., in Romans 4, "the notion that Gentile Jesus-followers are participating in the ongoing salvation history of the Jewish people is nowhere in Paul's field of theological vision." I will suggest, however, in chapter 3 of this book, that this theological vision is present in Romans 4 as well. This is based on the anomalous τοῖς and the continuation of the land promise.

24. Zoccali (*Reading Philippians*, 2 n. 7) is quite concerned about such a definition. For him, what supersessionism "does not mean is that the 'church' has replaced 'Israel' as God's people. Despite the popularity of this definition in both popular and scholarly discussions, this definition makes absolutely no sense of the sociocultural and theological context from within which the Christ movement arose." While Zoccali's concern is helpful, as mentioned in n. 13 above, the focal point for the approach in this book is God's plan rather than God's people. In that sense, Zoccali and I are addressing different aspects of the supersessionist paradigm. My understanding of the *ekklēsia* that avoids the concern highlighted by Zoccali may be found in Tucker, *You Belong to Christ*, 81. It is important to distinguish a grouping of first-century in-Christ Jews and non-Jews from the later institutional church.

25. Wright (*Paul and the Faithfulness of God*, 1415) makes such a comparison: "Think of Qumran, where the scrolls bear witness to a sect which saw itself as 'Israel'

ther way, it is difficult to maintain a salvation-historical approach without engaging in inherently supersessionist discourse if Jewish identity and continuity are all de-emphasized.[26] One way forward, highlighted in what follows, is to emphasize a specific Davidic messianic nuance along with a political restoration for Israel in Romans.[27] Envisioning a future or consummation component for Israel's covenantal identity will be helpful in addressing potential weaknesses in the salvation-historical approach.

The second organizing framework used to describe the status of God's historic people before and after Christ is apocalyptic.[28] In its Barthian garb, this approach sees a significant rupture in time now that Israel's Messiah has come. The new creation that emerges from his coming results in complete discontinuity with what came before.[29] One can easily

---

while 'Israel' as a whole was apostate. The covenant had been renewed! This was what the prophets had foretold! The exile was over—at least in principle, with this group as the advance guard of the coming new day. All that, uncontroversially, is what the leaders and members of the sect believed. Was this 'replacement theology'? Was it 'substitution'? Was it even 'supersessionism'? One could use words like that, but that was not of course how the sect saw itself, and the words would carry none of today's negative overtones." For a better way forward see Stendahl, "Qumran and Supersessionism," 397–405.

26. Again, Wright (*Paul and the Faithfulness of God*, 1415) would demur: "Torah and prophets had foretold a coming time of renewal, a righteous remnant; . . . was it unJewish, or anti-Jewish, to claim that this was now happening? Of course not. It might be wrong. It might be a false hope. Time would tell. But it was not, in any sense we should consider meaningful today, 'supersessionist.'" Charlesworth ("Wright's Paradigm," 228) would agree that Wright is not a supersessionist: "Can Wright be charged with emphasizing Paul's genius, his concept of fresh revelation, and a new hermeneutic defined by Jesus Christ so that he is guilty of supersessionism? NO!" However, against this understanding of Wright, see Tapie (*Aquinas*, 22), who points out that Jewish ethnicity requires the observance of the Jewish law for it to continue. See also Willitts ("Jewish Fish," 4) who points out that ethnicity in the first century wasn't only genealogical but also involved a pattern of life. Willitts's approach may suggest Wright is at least supersessionistic by implication, or so it will be argued throughout this book.

27. Willitts, "Davidic Messiah," 150–52; Rudolph, "Zionism," 171–77. The political restoration relates to, as noted by Reasoner ("Romans 9–11," 89), "the idea of the Roman occupation of the land and subjugation of the Jewish people as well." The link is between Romans 8:18–25, with its evident renewal, and "the political salvation for Israel and its land." Novenson (*The Grammar of Messianism*, 82–88) provides nuance and caution as it relates to the tradition of Jesus's ancestry from David and the messianic implications from that claim.

28. Martyn (*Galatians*, 104–5) contends that God's apocalyptic in-breaking in Christ is such that all things are radically new and thus salvation history is no longer. New creation is the result with a vast rupture between life before Christ and after it. So, similarly, Barth, *Romans*, 364.

29. See the studies in Gaventa, *Apocalyptic*; Gaventa, *When in Romans*. Dunne

see how this leads to supersessionist readings. In the apocalyptic conceptualization, often described by the interpretive framework of "creation/new creation," the presence of the new creation removes the vestiges of the old.[30] Pre-existing identities have no place in the new creation at all, since they are part of that which has been done away with now that Christ has come. Jewish (as well as other) identities have, in this view, lost their fundamental significance.[31] Romans 3:22 and 10:12 are often thought to support this organizing framework. Sometimes, the rupture between creation and new creation in Galatians—which, especially in Gal 6:15, seems to negate the continuation of Israel's covenantal identity, and, in fact, erase all identity distinctions—undergirds interpretation in Romans.[32] There is, however, another approach to apocalyptic that does not rely on Barthian thought. A more Jewish understanding of apocalyptic allows for more continuity between the epochs, between creation and

---

("Suffering," 1–15) offers a corrective to the Barthian apocalyptic approach, arguing that it lacks historical precision and is not properly Jewish based on the suffering and the covenantal hope that is evident in the Jewish apocalyptic texts, topics overlooked by the Barthian-influenced interpreters; see also Rom 8:17–23.

30. See my discussion in Tucker, "Paul's Eschatological Anthropology," 122; Tucker, *Remain in Your Calling*, 2–7.

31. Gaventa ("Thinking," 240) does offer an important nuance as one writing from within this perspective: "Paul's letter strenuously affirms the inclusion of gentiles and rejects the false conclusion that gentiles have displaced Jews as God's beloved, but it does far more than that." After highlighting the cosmic portions of Romans, she concludes: "Romans belongs squarely under the heading of apocalyptic theology." While this is a helpful train of thought, the Barthian apocalyptic approach maintains that all things are displaced before Christ. Thus, her conclusion that "it does far more than that" actually highlights the complete cosmic reordering of all things in Christ. So, her conclusion may not be as probative as it seems at first in relation to Jews and non-Jews/gentiles.

32. Martyn, *Galatians*, 565, 570; Hubing, *Crucifixion*, 229–45.

new creation.[33] This approach, along with a nuanced salvation history framework, will inform the arguments put forth in this book.[34]

Debates over salvation history and apocalyptic often focus on whether or not the covenantal framework has any continuing significance for Israel's identity.[35] This raises more acutely the issue of supersessionism or replacement theologizing. It is likely appropriate to see covenant as a key guiding principle for the combined Jewish and apostolic writings. But does all Israel still maintain a covenantal identity or has that covenantal identity shifted to the *ekklēsia*, Jews and gentiles in Christ? While some scholars suggest that Israel's covenantal identity remains intact and non-Jews relate to the God of Israel in Christ (and thus are not in a proper covenantal relationship), others see in the establishment of the new covenant a reframing of God's people such that ethnic identities have now been transcended and are no longer relevant or at best indifferent.[36] Supersessionist interpreters often take Rom 9:4, with its plural "covenants," and Rom 11:27, with its promise of the removal of "sins," as evidence that with the arrival of the new covenant the existing covenantal relationship has been set aside or universalized via gentile inclusion (Isa 59:21; Jer 31:33). These interpretive moves open up possibilities for changes in the covenantal relationship, obviating it with Israel since it is assumed that existing identities are no longer relevant in Christ. What if Paul, however, thought in the framework of one covenant with multiple blessings

33. Macaskill (*Union*, 170–71), after discussing the way temple discourse helps with understanding union with Christ, concludes: "this scriptural exegesis serves to ensure that the eschatological temple is understood in the context of the covenant and the various prophetic writings that speak of the renewal and transformation of that covenant. Over against the 'apocalyptic' approaches to the New Testament that tend to deemphasize this element of continuity with the narrative of Israel, this ensures that the story of the church is taken into the story of Israel, not as a replacement theology or a supersessionism and certainly not effacing the identities of Jew and Gentile, but as part of a messianic reality understood to fulfil the intentions of God in its globally redemptive orientation." See further Stuckenbruck, "Some Reflections," 137–55.

34. In Tucker, *Remain in Your Calling*, 186–226, I describe further this re-contextualized approach to apocalyptic in Paul. However, Macaskill's statement above summarizes quite nicely the key points, i.e., Israel's story continues and existing identities are not obliterated in the in-breaking of the Messiah.

35. Campbell, *Paul's Gospel*, 70. Martyn (*Galatians*, 455) rejects the idea that Paul thought that the covenant and the law were related.

36. Campbell, *Paul and the Creation*, 130–32; Wright, *Paul and the Faithfulness of God*, 774–1042; Esler, *Conflict*, 54–61; Barclay, *Paul*, 396–97. One point often overlooked is that because of the nature of the debate, the only identity that has actually been obliterated is Jewish identity.

flowing from it? What if he also thought that Israel's covenantal identity was a present reality and part of the gifts and calling of God that are irrevocable (Rom 11:29)? Furthermore, what if the covenant mentioned in the composite quotation in Rom 11:27 simply reflects the eschatological hope of Israel's salvation which now the nations experience through the agency of the Spirit (Rom 11:26; Isa 59:21; Ezek 36:27; Rom 8:9)? The nations being brought near (gentile inclusion) does not require the removal of Israel's covenant relationship. Answers to these questions provided later in this book help to reframe the nature of the confirmation of God's promises amid appearances to the contrary (Rom 9:3; 11:1, 28–29; 15:8).[37]

The eschatological application of Israel's covenantal identity among the nations raises important concerns with regard to the nature of this shared covenant identity and whether Paul had historic Israel as his consistent referent when using terms such as Israel, Israelites, Jews, the circumcision, or the seed of Abraham (Rom 2:28–29; 4:11–12; 9:4, 6; 11:25–26; 15:7–13). In other words, if Paul uses these words and phrases in a multivalent manner then, to at least a certain degree, his discourse could be understood as supersessionist.[38] Some scholars have maintained that Paul's use of Israel (Ἰσραήλ) has a consistent referent to ethnic Israel; others suggest that Paul uses the same broad ethnic referent even though various meanings for the term may be contextually determined (e.g., an elect subgroup identity). Finally, still others see a shifting sense beyond the ethnic boundary to include Christ-followers from the nations.[39] This last group is most problematic in that if Israel (Ἰσραήλ) has lost its historic meaning for Paul then it has been superseded by a "new" or a "true" Israel in his thinking.[40] This approach does not seem controversial to some because they understand the nature of the identity in question to be only theological. However, identity questions precede theological

37. Thus, it would be wrong to propose two different covenants, one for the Jews and one for the nations. However, the nations relate to the God of Israel in terms closely associated with God's covenant established with the patriarchs (Rom 9:7–12; 15:8–9). This relationship is not formed by the removal of Israel's covenantal identity; rather, it is fashioned in the context of a reaffirmation of it while at the same time the nations are brought near to the God of Israel (so similarly Eph 2:13, 17). With regard to the one covenant and multiple promises, this was originally suggested by Roetzel ("Διαθῆκαι," 377).

38. Lodge, *Romans 9–11*, 213; Zoccali, *Whom God*, 174.

39. Campbell, *Paul and the Creation*, 135; Whittle, *Covenant Renewal*, 70 n. 62; Wright, *Paul and the Faithfulness of God*, 1241–46.

40. For example, Cottrell (*Romans*, 391–96) sees just such a group emerging in Rom 11:1–5.

ones. Yet, in order to discern identity questions in Romans an additional set of exegetical tools are needed. An identity-critical analysis will uncover new options often not considered by previous interpreters. Paul uses group-based terms like Israel, Jews, gentiles, the circumcision, the uncircumcision, and the seed of Abraham to maintain the social identity salience of his addressees in relation to relevant comparison groups. The continuing distinction between Jews and non-Jews is crucial to overcoming supersessionist tendencies among Romans interpreters and is central to the argument of this book.

It is likely that Paul's Torah discourse in Romans contributes in a significant way to supersessionist understandings of the letter.[41] One example will suffice. Paul writes in Rom 10:4 that "Christ is the end (τέλος) of the law so that there may be righteousness for everyone who believes."[42] Supersessionist interpreters recognize the centrality of Torah in the formation and maintenance of Jewish identity and thus find it difficult to accept the claim that Jewish identity or Israel's covenantal identity could continue in any meaningful sense in the context of statements that seem to indicate that the law has ended now that Christ has come.[43] Yet this conclusion assumes that the primary purpose of Torah was salvific and that the use of τέλος here suggests "end" and termination. However, even though now that the messianic age has begun there is clearly an interpretative change with regard to Torah, there may be more continuity with the previous age than some interpreters allow.[44] Romans 10:4 does suggest that Paul's view of Torah was similar to that adopted by other Jewish writers (Matt 5:17–19). Based on Jesus's revelation, the written Torah, while not redundant, is contextualized within the Christ-following community; in this way Christ is the law's τέλος.[45] This approach preserves Torah as a continuing demarcator of the Jewish people; for gentiles it becomes primarily an ethical guide for life. Thus, as will be seen, it is unlikely that Paul repudiated the law in the manner often put forth by interpreters; rather, he seems to be working out his "rule in all the con-

41. While there would be some benefit to distinguishing between law, Torah, Law, or Law of Moses, I will use the terms interchangeably.

42. Other key verses seeming to set Torah aside include Rom 6:14–15; 7:4, 6.

43. See the important nuance for this debate from Donaldson, *Paul*, 175–76.

44. I have in mind here the transformation of the law of Moses as it is taken up in the hand of the Messiah Jesus (1 Cor 9:21; Gal 6:2); see the discussion in Tucker, *Remain in Your Calling*, 110–12.

45. Roetzel, "Paul," 126–27. See also Cranfield, *Romans*, 2.852–53, who argues that Paul did not think that Christ had abrogated the law.

gregations" that Jews were to maintain their life as Jews as a matter of calling (1 Cor 7:17–18, 20).[46] Gentiles, in line with the Jerusalem agreement in Acts 15:29 and 1 Cor 7:19, follow Christ in ways that align with Torah-informed praxis, or so it will be argued below. This interpretation allows for my view that the Christ-movement continued to relate to the broader synagogue community. A brief word is in order, therefore, on this component of the Romans debate.[47]

Jewish Community in Rome in the First Century

The Jewish community in Rome was loosely organized and lacked an "ethnarch" of the kind it had in Alexandria. The primary leadership group was the "assembly of elders" along with the various heads of the local congregations.[48] This loose structure may have contributed to the expansion of the Christ-movement within the broader synagogue community. On the other hand, the social implications of the gospel were such that there may not have been significant differences in the day-to-day lived experiences between those who had come to accept Jesus as the Messiah and those Jews who were yet to be convinced. This is actually one of the primary points of contention between the traditional reading of Paul and the Paul-within-Judaism approach. The first assumes significant social discontinuity while the second maintains more continuity between the groups at this early stage.

The earliest Christ-following community in Rome is described in a fourth-century CE document that reads:

> There were Jews living in Rome in the times of the apostles, and ... those Jews who had believed [in Christ] passed on to the Romans the tradition that they ought to profess Christ but keep the law. ... One ought not to condemn the Romans, but to praise their faith; because without seeing any signs or miracles and without seeing any of the apostles, they nevertheless accepted faith in Christ, although according to a Jewish rite (Ambrosiaster).[49]

46. See Longenecker, "On Israel's God," 33.

47. The term "Romans debate" is a way to describe the constellation of prolegomena issues foundational for the study of Romans; see the following: Das, *Solving*; Donfried, *Romans*; Longenecker, *Introducing Romans*.

48. Nanos, *Mystery*, 47.

49. Nanos, "The Jewish Context," 283. This quote comes from the prologue of

This suggests that the earliest gatherings had a strong Jewish influence on them. Two phrases are particularly important here: (1) "profess Christ *but keep the law*" and (2) "accepted faith in Christ . . . *according to a Jewish rite.*" If these two statements are brought to bear in our reading of Romans, it suggests that this community did not see Jewish identity as incompatible with in-Christ identity. However, the question here is: did Paul see this as a problem? Or did Paul accept Torah-informed praxis as a way of life for Jewish Christ-followers but not for gentile ones? If so, how could these disparate ways of life exist together?

While it is not particularly controversial to suggest that the earliest Christ-movement in Rome was heavily influenced by key aspects of Jewish identity, the broader Roman imperial cultural context impinged on this situation as well. Suetonius, as is well known, writes with regard to events occurring in 49 CE that "since the Jews constantly made disturbances at the instigation of Chrestus," Claudius "expelled them from Rome."[50] There are several debates concerning this passage: (1) does the common use of the name Chrestus suggest that Christ was not actually in view and (2) to what extent was this expulsion imposed—did it extend

---

Ambrosiaster's Romans commentary. Hvalvik ("Jewish Believers," 187) contends that "even if this text is very late, it is interesting because it conveys the impression of how one early Christian imagined the origin of the Roman church: it was the result of Jewish believers in Jesus proclaiming their faith *and* Law observance."

50. Suetonius, *Claud.* 25.4. The edict was allowed to expire when Nero ascended in 54 CE. Nanos (*Mystery*, 372–87) offers a thoroughly convincing argument against the large-scale expulsion of the Jews from Rome, especially supposing this was in response to conflicts with Christ-followers. He shows the way contemporary Paulinist scholars assume too much in their reconstructions. A couple of important points he raises include: Luke's description in Acts 28:21–22 of the reception of Paul's message by the Jewish leaders in Rome highlights only an awareness of his message but not an alienation of the Christ-movement from the broader synagogue community in Rome. Further, the kinds of tensions evident in Romans are exactly the kinds one would expect to see among closely related communities, especially as a smaller subgroup develops in terms of social influence. Foster (*Renaming*, 89–95) also rejects the traditional expulsion hypothesis. His main concern, not completely absent from Nanos ("Paul's Non-Jews," 26–53), is that the gentiles in view in Romans "held Jewish customs and religious practices in high regard" (95). Nanos's nuance concerning negative attitudes by gentiles in Rome towards Jews focuses on those situations in which non-Jews are not accepted by Jews on the gospel terms (because they do not share the gospel terms). The reconstruction here follows Nanos closely and recognizes that Foster's perspective advances the conversation, though in ways that will be queried at later points in this book. Gentile boasting over the Jewish people and an attraction to Jewish patterns of life may coexist, and Paul addresses just such a liminal experience in his invention of gentile identity in Christ.

to all Jews in Rome or simply to key Roman leaders?[51] While there is no room to address all aspects of those historical debates here, Thielman's conclusion seems to reflect the general understanding and interpretive use of Suetonius:

> [T]he disturbances were probably created by the preaching of the gospel within Rome's various synagogues, and Suetonius's term *constantly* probably means that they had been taking place for a lengthy period prior to the expulsion.[52]

I agree that the preaching of the gospel had likely been occurring for some time within the various synagogues. I would add, however, that it is not clear that this created an uproar among the community that would lead to an expulsion. It seems more likely that Claudius's action was an attempt "to protect the *religio* of Rome from foreign *superstitiones* which had become potential threats to Rome's well-being and integrity."[53] In this way of reading the text, the problem shifts to one of Roman policy and domination rather than an incipient problem between Judaism and the Christ-movement.[54]

Ian Rock has made a particularly strong case for nuancing this historical reconstruction as it applies to the letter.[55] First, he questions the way in which Suetonius is normally used, i.e., that the wholesale expulsion of Jews from Rome resulted in a gentile-dominated congregation that rejected all things Jewish. For example, he points to the fact that Claudius, earlier in his *imperium*, had already taken action to curtail the various expressions of Jewish life:

> As for the Jews, who had again increased so greatly that by reason of their multitude it would have been hard without raising a tumult to bar them from the city, [Claudius] did not drive them

51. Rock ("Another Reason," 75) suggests Chrestus refers to an "*impulsor*" to Claudius. Further, he notes that it is unclear whether Claudius, or one of his advisors, could have discerned the nuances between Christ-following and non-Christ-following Judaism at this early stage, and thus, if there is an element of concern here, it is to Judaism and its practice in Rome.

52. Thielman, *Paul*, 163.

53. Rock, "Another Reason," 76.

54. Tucker, "Paul's Economics," 1–18.

55. Foster (*Renaming*, 85–95) also rejects the standard reconstruction in relation to Claudius. He contends that Suetonius can't be used to prove that all the Jews left Rome and offers another translation that highlights only the ringleaders were sent away: "He expelled from Rome the Jews constantly making disturbances at the instigation of Chrestus" (91).

out, but ordered them, while continuing their traditional mode of life, not to hold meetings. He also disbanded the clubs, which had been reintroduced by Gaius.[56]

This piece of evidence should be read in concert with Suetonius. Second, the influence of Acts 18:2–4 continues to hold sway over interpreters; however, when one reads the context of Suetonius there were five other groups impacted by his edict.[57] However, Acts 18:12, with its reference to Gallio's proconsulship in Achaia, does not align with Paulus Orosius's claim that "Josephus reports, 'In his ninth year the Jews were expelled by Claudius from the city.'"[58] So, there is at least a potential dating issue that needs resolution.[59] Further, Acts 18:2 does not state that Aquila and Priscilla were Christ-followers, only that they were Jews who were part of those "Claudius had commanded . . . to leave Rome." Rock suggests that Paul, Aquila, and Priscilla were all part of the same *collegium*, or voluntary association, and that Aquila and Priscilla likely accepted the gospel after meeting Paul.[60] Third, Rock highlights Claudius's direction for Polybius to translate the *Aeneid* into Greek as an important piece of evidence that brings to the fore the actual issue involved in the expulsion.[61] A significant amount of Claudius's political activity occurred around 49 CE, when he sought to reinstitute the policies of Augustus.[62]

56. Dio, 60.6.7.

57. Suetonius, *Claud.* 25.4–5. Rock ("Another Reason," 75) notes that the "Lycians, Rhodians, Trojans, Germans, and the Druids" were affected by this policy and that it was part of a larger imperial policy to protect the Roman cult and thus not primarily directed towards the intramural debates within the broader synagogue community.

58. Paulus Orosius, *Historiarum* 7.6.15.

59. Foster (*Renaming*, 91 n. 25) reminds interpreters that "Luke of course reports that Claudius commanded all Jews to leave, but even if correct it does not mean that they all actually left. In other instances draconian banishments of whole groups from the city were legislated but not enforced (see e.g., Tacitus, *Ann.* 12.52)."

60. Rock, "Another Reason," 75. *Pace* Thielman, *Paul*, 163. For further explanations of these ancient voluntary associations and their institutional importance for a post-supersessionist understanding of Paul's letters see Korner, *Origin*, 46 n. 111.

61. Seneca, *Polyb.* 11.5: "Turn, now, to those poems which the efforts of your genius have made famous and which you have turned into prose with such skill that, though their form has disappeared, they, nevertheless, retain all their charm (for you have so performed the most difficult task of transferring them from one language to another that all their merits have followed them into the foreign speech)" (Basore, LCL; cf. Seneca, *Polyb.* 8.2). For a discussion of Greek translations of the *Aeneid*, see Hunt, "Jesus Caesar," 227–31.

62. Cf. Suetonius, *Claud.* 3.2; 11.2; Dio, 60.5.2; Seneca, *Apol.* 9.5.

Thus, his concern related to the way Roman imperial ideology would be understood, and the *Aeneid* served as the primary discursive marker for Claudius's policies. This is a more plausible historical context for the community in Rome in the mid-first century: Claudius expelled several groups from Rome in order to reinforce his own political vision of Augustan Rome as described in the *Aeneid*.[63]

If the expulsion of Jews in 49 CE is decoupled from disputes within the Jewish community over Jesus, what does this suggest for the idea that is often put forth by interpreters that in the five years while the edict was in force, the Roman Christ groups became predominantly gentile and were no longer associated with the broader Jewish synagogue community? For one thing, it suggests that the outgroup for the community is an imperial Roman one rather than a Jewish one. Much of Paul's letter makes sense in light of challenges associated with civic identity and the way it is transformed in Christ.[64] The decoupling of the Jewish expulsion from the interpretation of Paul's Letter to the Romans also suggests that there remained a Jewish presence among the Christ-following group. This would provide a more concrete setting for some of the social conflict evident in Romans 14–15. A continued Jewish presence may also hint that gentile boasting over the Jewish people was a more broad concern in the letter. This will be developed further in subsequent chapters.

Because of disagreements with regards to these historical events, a significant debate continues with regard to the audience for Romans, and thus a comment is in order. Andrew Das has put forth a rather robust argument that the letter was written to gentiles.[65] This approach rejects the idea that it was written to a mixed audience of Jews and gentiles, the more standard view.[66] The letter does explicitly identify gentiles as the audience (Rom 1:5–6; 15:15–16). Furthermore, in 11:13 Paul addresses gentiles directly. Mark Nanos has provided further detail on this issue noting the difference between the encoded and the implied audience.[67] This significant nuance, writing to gentiles about Jews, accounts for the Jewish concerns like the nature of Israel and the role of Torah (cf. Rom 2:17; 7:1; 15:7).[68] Thus, Paul may be described as one writing to gentiles

---

63. Rock, "Another Reason," 76–78.

64. Tucker, "Paul's Economics," 3–8.

65. Das, *Solving*, 2, 264.

66. Gadenz, *Called*, 6.

67. Nanos, *Mystery*, 83.

68. See further Matera, *Romans*, 7.

about issues that would concern Jews as well as gentiles, especially if some of this group is loosely identified as former god-fearers but more precisely as, according to Runesson, "Christ-fearers."[69] This does not require institutional separation between Jews and gentiles, however, especially the absolute separation suggested in the work of Francis Watson.[70] The addressed gentiles in Romans, rather, could be part of the larger synagogue community in Rome. This configuration assumes the more complex institutional organization called a semi-public synagogue.[71] There were, in this view, several assemblies around the environs of Rome which would be organized as a voluntary association while maintaining a loose connection with the public synagogue community, made up of Christ-following and non-Christ-following Jews.[72] It is into such a diverse context that Paul writes to gentiles concerning the continuation of Jewish covenantal identity as a crucial social implication of the gospel, one that is vital for the formation of a salient in-Christ social identity. That seeming complex identity configuration is the focus of Paul's social entrepreneurship in Romans.

The Existence of Gentile Identity in the Earliest Christ-Movement

Terry Donaldson has brought to the fore an important concept that influences the way scholars conceive of early Christian origins, especially with regard to the problematic category of "Gentile." Identity salience for in-Christ gentiles could create problems when this identity performance developed in a way that sought to replace Jewish covenantal identity.

69. Runesson ("Inventing," 73) contends that "Christ-fearers" is a group label "indicating their relationship to Apostolic Jews. Although not Jews, they would think of themselves as members of the people of God as defined by Apostolic Jewish theology." Campbell, *Paul's Gospel*, 185–87. Rodríguez (*If You Call*, ix) thinks the readers are gentiles and that even the figure in Rom 2:17 is also one. For him, Paul's interlocutor is consistently a gentile, not a supposed Jew. Thorsteinsson, Thiessen, Rodríguez, "Paul's Interlocutor," 1–37.

70. Watson, *Paul, Judaism*, 51–53; for a significant critique on Watson on this issue see Longenecker, *Introducing Romans*, 119–20. Runesson ("Placing Paul," 66) places the Christ-movement within the synagogue institutional setting, i.e., "deeply embedded in a Jewish Diaspora culture" as well as the "wider Graeco-Roman association culture."

71. Runesson, *Origins*, 64, 395–400; Runesson, "Jewish," 247–49. Korner, *Origin*, 146–47.

72. Richardson, "Synagogues," 103. Nanos, *Mystery*, 25, 31, 285.

Donaldson's study of so-called "Gentile Christianity" is clearly significant for the arguments of this book.[73] For example, could something continue in the first century, if, as he claims, it really did not exist in the first place? So, it will be helpful at this juncture to engage with his approach.

First, it is accurate to point out that there really was no Gentile (big "G") Christianity in the first century.[74] Part of the problem is that the underlying term, τὰ ἔθνη, represents a somewhat ubiquitous concept that no one in the first century would use for *self*-identification. However, as we will see, such a conclusion must be nuanced.[75] Donaldson is correct that the term "Gentile Christianity" in the research framework of F. C. Baur and those that follow his lead is problematic. There never was a single "Gentile Christianity" that was identifiable from a gentile perspective in the everyday experience of Christ-followers that could function as the polemical partner to so-called "Jewish Christianities."[76]

73. My understanding of gentile Christianity follows Boyarin (*Border Lines*, 29), who defines it "in a sort of subtechnical sense to refer to Christian converts from among non-Jews (and their descendants) who have neither a sense of genealogical attachment to this historical, physical people of Israel (Israel according to the flesh), nor an attachment (and frequently the exact opposite of one) to the fleshly practices of that historical community." Cited also in Willitts, "Paul and Jewish Christians," 144.

74. Mitchell, "Gentile Christianity," 105. Here I'm in agreement with Donaldson's four categories of usage for the term. Donaldson ("Gentile Christianity," 20) notes that "several senses of ἔθνη are present in the NT (and other early Christian literature): [1] 'nations,' used in a generic sense that includes Israel; [2] nations other than that of the Jews; [3] non-Jewish individuals; [4] what non-Jewish Christ-believers were before but are no longer." I would, however, expand it to include one more, a term describing a group's existing identity and the transformation that should be occurring to that identity in Christ.

75. Elliott (*Arrogance*, 46) doubts Romans would have referred to themselves this way, reserving the term for nations they had defeated. On the other hand, for Jews, ἔθνη could simply refer to non-Jews. Nanos ("Paul and Judaism," 130 n. 38) notes that the term "gentile" contains a sense of "not-ness," i.e., "non-Jewish (and non-Israelite)." He suggests translating ἔθνη as "member[s] of the nations other than Israel." An inference from Nanos's argument is that gentiles in Christ could be described as "honored non-Jews." This may be a way forward but remains to be fully developed. Lopez (*Apostle to the Conquered*, xii, 4) points out that the word could also refer to a non-Roman. BDAG 276 cites Appian, *Bell. civ.* 2.26.99; 2.28.107, as an example of the way a Roman could use the term to refer to a foreign people group.

76. Paget, "Definition," 48–52. From the perspective of communities of Jewish followers of Jesus, there was a clear differentiation between their community and gentile communities. Also, even Paul talks about the "churches of the gentiles" (Rom 16:4) which suggests a distinction of some kind, perhaps only demographic but the demographics would naturally translate into culture and praxis. I am grateful to David Rudolph for these distinctions.

The local expressions of Christ-movement social identity were simply too diverse.[77] So, calling into question the uncritical use of the label "Gentile" as a way to refer to non-Jewish expressions of Christ belief is quite an important reminder for those writing on early Christian origins. Furthermore, based on Donaldson's survey of Roman texts, "Gentile" could, for Romans, refer to non-Romans as well, though it would seem that the Jewish foil would be determinative for the NT usage, and the Roman foil for issues of cultural translation.

Second, one problem is that "gentile" functions today for English speakers as a term that defines the non-Jewish part of humanity, and a better term is unlikely to emerge. Central to Donaldson's inquiry into the use of ἔθνη is that the idea of "nation" is present but often occluded in translations, especially with the English gloss "gentile."[78] To substantiate this claim, Donaldson provides a brief survey of the way Roman authors used τὰ ἔθνη for their ideological purposes. This brings to the fore an interesting point with regard to cultural translation and the way this discourse would have originally been interpreted. For example, as mentioned by Lopez, the Romans could use τὰ ἔθνη to reinforce the defeated status of those whom they had subjugated.[79] This is most evident in *Res gestae divi Augusti*.[80] Thus, though τὰ ἔθνη functioned, for some Jewish authors, as a way to organize humanity, it appears that the Romans could use it in this way as well.[81] However, if non-Jewish members of the Christ-movement heard its Jewish leaders referring to them as τὰ ἔθνη, and if they also were aware of similar discourse by the Romans, they might wrongly infer that they were only being included within the Synagogue community as subordinated peoples.[82]

Even though there are questions as to whether the non-Jewish members of the Christ-movement would have referred to themselves

77. Horrell ("Pauline," 185–203) has even called into question the use of the label "Pauline Christianity" in that it is not fully clear that those local assemblies that were founded by Paul could in any significant way be seen as Pauline (i.e., embodying a social identity formed by Paul's rhetorical constructs).

78. Donaldson, "Gentile Christianity," 21, 23, 27.

79. Lopez, *Apostle to the Conquered*, 22–25; 88–113. Dio, 51.20.6–8; Pliny, *Nat.* 3.20.136–37.

80. *Res gestae divi Augusti* 3.25–33. Cf. Hunt, "Jesus Caesar," 332.

81. A few examples include: Gen 49:10; Exod 33:13; Deut 4:19; Rom 3:29; 9:30–31; Eph 4:17; Tob 1:10–12; Jdt 4:12; 1 Macc 1:11–15; 2 Esd 4:23; 9:7; T. Sim. 7:2.

82. Wrongly because Paul "argued that these uncircumcised non-Jews were full and equal member of the family of God" (Nanos, "Paul's Non-Jews," 31).

as τὰ ἔθνη, the term could still be functioning as a subgroup label for them, especially since later Christ-followers did use it for themselves.[83] One possibility is that the continual use of this group identifier for them by others may have caused them to eventually adopt it for themselves.[84] It is likely, then, that ἔθνη became at least a secondary group identifier describing those who were worshipping the God of Israel without becoming Jews.[85]

The same could be said for the term Χριστιανοί. It initially served as a group designation for early Christ-followers in Antioch, although it was not used for any kind of monolithic embodiment of a Christ-following way of life, but encompassed a plurality of approaches.[86] Eventually, the term was internalized and "owned" by the broader movement. Townsend, however, contends that the (early) use of οἱ τοῦ Χριστοῦ in 1 Cor 15:23 and Gal 5:24 functioned as a self-description specifically for "Gentile Christians."[87]

Casey refers to eight Jewish identity factors during the Second Temple period; the absence of these would indicate the degree to which a person would be considered a non-Jew. These eight include: "ethnicity, scripture, monotheism, circumcision, Sabbath observance, dietary laws, purity laws and major festivals."[88] He suggests that "anyone who scores 0/8 is clearly a Gentile, and would be universally perceived as Gentile in the ancient world."[89] If we consider Casey's framework for identifying

83. See 1 Cor 3:23, Runesson, "Inventing," 84–88. Ignatius, *Magn.* 10.2–3; Justin, *Dial.* 47.

84. Sherman, Hamilton, and Lewis, "Perceived," 92–93, cited in Hakola, "Social," 272.

85. Brewer and Silver, "Group," 154–55. See Fredriksen, "How Jewish," 193–212.

86. On Antioch and the influence of Latin on Χριστιανοί see further Hunt, "Jesus Caesar," 95–96.

87. Townsend, "Who Were," 215–16, 223. Thus, even though the Latin term *Christiani*, was imposed from the outside, it was based on the non-Jew's own self-identification. This line of research also suggests further nuancing the use of "Christianity" with regard to the "-ity" as a way to describe social (and religious) identity prior to the parting of the ways.

88. Casey, *From Jewish*, 12. See Donaldson (*Jews*, 90–93) on gentiles in John, but also, on identities in the Johannine trial narrative, Hunt, "Jesus Caesar," 328–63. Garroway (*Paul's Gentile-Jews*, 1–14) expands this list to twelve and applies this approach outside of the Gospel of John.

89. Casey (*From Jewish*, 12–13) continues "it would make no difference to this if such a person wrote a *midrash* or contributed to a collection for the poor in Jerusalem." While Casey may be overstating the way in which gentile identity would have

gentile identity, combined with Luomanen's "indicators of Jewish Christianity," then it is likely that some of the non-Jewish Christ-followers did think of themselves as gentiles since they were part of a community that: worshipped the God of Israel, followed a person who identified himself as Israel's Messiah, in some cases were instructed by a person who claimed to be their (as members of the nations [Gal 1:15–16]) unique apostle (and addressed them as such [Rom 11:13]), or more broadly were taught by Jewish leaders of the Christ-movement who made a distinction between Jew and non-Jew even if they meant different things by the bifurcation.[90] It would seem that this chronic social identification would have given rise to an identity node, a micro-identity, described as an in-Christ gentile.[91] So, Donaldson, while correctly wanting to set aside the label "Gentile Christianity," should consider keeping "gentile Christ-followers" as a salient social identity category, one that was open to local identity configurations in the mid-first century.[92]

By suggesting this I am not arguing for a universalistic understanding of in-Christ social identity (i.e., the multi-ethnic national Roman discourse described in Donaldson's paper).[93] I am arguing for the opposite, that the existing social identities of all the members of the Christ-movement

---

been universally recognized, he does bring to the fore "lived" or everyday experience as a means for discerning identity, rather than only conceiving of these terms as linguistic categories.

90. Luomanen, "Ebionites," 84. It is not clear that Paul shares the same division of humanity into binary categories that is evident in other "pre-Christian Jewish usage" (Donaldson, "Gentile Christianity," 20). This sounds counter-intuitive since Paul appears to divide humanity into two categories: Jews and gentiles. However, building on Stanley ("Paul," 119), it is not fully evident that "Paul conceived of 'the nations' in monolithic terms." Second, first-century Jews did not "routinely divide humanity into two camps without remainder." Third, Paul's ethnic discourse was "too varied and creative to support the assertion that he unreflectively adopted the worldview and terminology of his Jewish peers." So, while the distinction between Jew and gentile remains, Paul is inventing aspects of the gentile side of this binary in new ways, including a subgroup identity within the Christ-movement.

91. Woolf ("Afterword," 196) notes the presence of a microidentity in Tacitus, *Germ.* 39: "Tacitus figured his Germani as just one variety of barbarian; they included the Suebi, themselves represented as some sort of super-tribe, which in turn included nested within it groups such as the Semnones, who were themselves divided into one hundred *pagi*."

92. As a group, their differing ethnic identities continue to be salient. They recognize themselves as part of the Jewish symbolic universe, yet writers and leaders are describing them as a unique social group from the nations (see Zetterholm, "Will the Real Gentile-Christian," 373–93).

93. Donaldson, "Gentile Christianity," 29–33.

continued to retain their fundamental significance (at least in the first century). Thus, Jews continue to relate to the God of Israel *as Jews*, and non-Jews *as non-Jews*. The application of this rule from 1 Cor 7:17–24 would result in diverse expressions of both Jewish and non-Jewish in-Christ social identity.[94] If we downplay the continuing significance of non-Jewish social identities within the Christ-movement, it would likely contribute to a downplaying of Jewish identities as well—thus reinforcing Baur's view or the dominant contemporary supersessionist interpretive tradition that sees no place (during the first century) for existing social identities in the so-called *tertium quid* of Christianity.[95]

Donaldson is correct that there was no single "Gentile Christianity" in the mid-first century and scholars should discontinue the use of that term so that they do not perpetuate this misunderstanding.[96] The Christ-movement at this stage was a form of Judaism (i.e., Apostolic Judaism), existing within the synagogue community and Jewish sacred space, with local differentiations recognized.[97] However, τὰ ἔθνη did

94. Runesson ("Inventing, 85) describes this as "Proto-Christianity." See also Runesson, "Jewish," 244–47; Runesson, "Placing Paul," 58–65.

95. It is also likely that the use of the label τὰ ἔθνη moved the Christ-movement along a parallel ideological path that contributed to its eventual alignment with the political power (or diminishing power) of Rome. Donaldson ("Field," 137) elsewhere considers Paul's contribution to the development of an *oikoumenē*, which similarly describes the "church as a trans-local fellowship," something "constituting a third race."

96. See Tucker, *You Belong to Christ*, 3, for related concerns about the existence of "Christianity" in general at this early stage, and the terminology associated with its institutional setting. Runesson, "Inventing," 59–92; Runesson, "Placing Paul," 43–67. Runesson is particularly helpful in addressing the institutional genesis of Christianity.

97. Korner, *Origin*, 81–149. See Runesson, "The Question," 61 n. 14, on issues relating to the anachronistic use of the category religion as it relates to Judaism and Christianity. Judaism as used in this book really has Jewish patterns of life in view. For other assemblies that were similarly integrating others living according to Jewish patterns of life, see Josephus, *War* 2.463; 7.41–62; Nanos, "Paul's Non-Jews," 33–34. Hedner Zetterholm ("Alternative Visions," 129–30 n. 10) points to later, non-Rabbinic, forms of Judaism that could include gentiles within the group but not require circumcision for the males, while at the same time could expect them to keep the Jewish law, or parts of it. See *Didascalia Apostolorum*, the Pseudo-Clementine *Homilies and Recognitions*, for texts that she argues "represent Jewish identity that includes adherence to Jesus." The Torah-observant, Jesus-focused communities in these texts open up the idea of the existence of various Jewish patterns of life in the mid-first century, ones in which gentile Christ-followers could join the group but maintain Torah observance in ways different from its Jewish members. "Judaism for gentiles" was suggested by Runesson ("Placing Paul," 44–67). He points out there really isn't a third option for these gentiles who are living according to norms formulated by Jews as part of their ongoing pattern of life.

exist as a distinct social identity for members of the defeated nations, and there were constant reminders of this identity in the urban context.[98] Their subaltern status would have contributed to the development of an identity node that a term like τὰ ἔθνη could uniquely encapsulate and mutually reinforce. So, do we set aside the term "Gentile Christianity" or the closely related term "Christianity"? Yes, if by it we mean a monolithic social identity and set of practices clearly discernible and separate from the larger Jewish community in the first century; no, if by it we mean the continuation of localized expressions of social (even "national") identity (and sets of practices), a microidentity nested within the macroidentity of being in-Christ.[99] The various uses of τὰ ἔθνη created an opportunity for non-Jews (as members of the nations defeated by Rome) to create for themselves unique expressions of an in-Christ social identity in the spaces between Jewish and Roman discourses. It also allowed Paul to shape gentile identity in Christ in ways that cohered with his vision and vocation (Rom 1:5; 16:26).

Survey of Contents

With some of the introductory material outlined, what follows is a brief summary of the argument of the book. Chapter 2 argues that Paul sought to overcome gentile boasting in relation to Israel and that he was convinced that there was to be a continuing social identification with Israel as an implication of the gospel. He offers circumcision as one way to understand the nature of Jewish identity in Christ, both for those who possessed it and as an influence on those who did not. In this way, Paul does not seek to make redundant Jewish identity; rather he supports its continued salience and thereby upholds Torah.

Chapter 3 contends that Abraham continues to be the father of the nation Israel. He has not been removed from Israel and given to the nations. The gentiles in Christ are part of God's family but key aspects of Jewish eschatological and political hope continue; this is seen most

98. Revell, *Roman*, 36–39.

99. Since this is one of the most explicit mentions of "nation" from my point of view rather than Donaldson's, it should be noted that I follow Richter (*Cosmopolis*, 18) who describes it "in its most basic and limited sense of a community based upon *natio*: lineage and descent. The discursive practices of the nation are local insofar as they insist upon the cultural, linguistic, ethnic, and political discontinuities within the human community." Avidov (*Not Reckoned*, 177) notes that for the Romans the practices are the issue rather than the ethnic identity.

explicitly as Paul reflects on the land of Israel. Finally, Paul presents Abraham as the father of both groups since he serves as the bearer of promise and a keen prototype of the diverse ways of life that Paul expects as an implication of his gospel.

Chapter 4 addresses one aspect of the larger debate concerning Paul and Torah. If the law of Moses has been made redundant, then Jewish identity has been eviscerated of much of that which holds this pattern of life together. Paul is not seen to be addressing Torah by itself, but his rhetorical purpose is to help gentiles in Christ understand the ongoing import of Jewish identity for their own identity. The chapter then compares prepositional phrases that are all too often conflated, i.e., *under* the law, *in* the law, and *from* the law. After a brief discussion of the *Shema*, Klyne Snodgrass's spheres-of-influence approach is offered as an organizing rubric for discussing Torah more broadly.

Chapter 5 engages with Robert Foster's work and offers interpretive insights into Paul's theologizing about Jewish covenantal identity in Romans 9. In this section of the letter, Paul seeks to make clear the way he thinks gentiles should view Jewish identity. First, Jewish identity has a covenantal context that renders it important as part of the emerging identity within the Christ-movement in regards to its past, present, and future. Paul's anguish is evident in that some of his kin do not agree with his view of the way God is working through Christ. So, Paul addresses a subgroup identity within the larger group of Israelites. Even here, Paul does not inscribe in-Christ gentiles with the label Israel. He reserves that only for Jewish ethnicity. Some have challenged this idea because Paul seems to write gentiles into the promises God made to his historic people, so this chapter concludes by showing the way Paul maintains the differences between Jews and gentiles in Christ even as these gentiles share in the blessings of God through Christ.

Chapter 6 revisits Paul and Torah in relation to the latter's christological contextualization. The focus here is on whether Paul thinks Torah has been rendered inoperative in the messianic age. The three major views of Christ and the law, i.e., end, goal, or end-goal/fulfillment are discussed with the latter being seen as the slightly more probative option in light of Paul's contextualization. The chapter will spend time on Rom 10:4 because 10:5–6 have recently become an interpretive crux with regard to the idea of the existence of a righteousness of the law. Paul's approach to Israel's scriptural tradition was discussed in chapter 5 of this book; it is revisited here in order to model one post-supersessionist approach.

The result of this study is that Torah is not a problem for Paul, but Torah observance, without trust, is. The idea of obedience that springs from faith then becomes Paul's argumentative position.

Chapter 7 builds on the findings of the two previous chapters in order to show the way Paul thinks Israel's covenantal identity survives the Christ-event and thus, as expressed in Romans 11, has a future component to it. Paul begins to point out to his audience that the continued salience of Israel in the messianic era has crucial implications for their own social identity. The chapter builds on some of the findings of Mark Nanos's reading of the first part of the chapter and then addresses the difficult question of the identity of the "all Israel." It concludes with a discussion of the way Paul construes the gifts and calling of God as irrevocable.

Chapter 8 highlights the social implications of Jewish covenantal identity continuing for the gentile Christ-followers. The weak and the strong are discussed in such a way that Jewish covenant or Torah-informed praxis are not erased. Next, David Rudolph's work provides an entry point into the discussion of the food laws in Rom 14:14 and 14:20. These two verses are often highlighted as places where Paul deletes key aspects of Jewish life within the Christ-movement. However, that is not the only way to understand them. More likely, Paul is providing halakhah for gentiles in Christ. This chapter highlights one first-century implication of Jewish covenantal identity continuing for gentiles while chapter 9 opens up another.

Chapter 9 argues that Rom 15:7–13 presents a doxological social identity for in-Christ Jews and gentiles in which each group's differences abide in the Messiah's welcome. This argument develops in conversation with Joshua Garroway's claims that the service Jesus performs is only directed towards the gentiles. After seeing the continued relevance of Jews, the chapter provides an Israel-centric reading of the citations (Rom 15:9–12), critiquing Colin Kruse's arguments that they are only focused on gentile inclusion. In the process of this critique, the chapter offers a description of Paul's identity-forming work as a doxological one, in which his vision of Israel and the nations worshipping together responds to Rome's claims of glory and the unification of disparate peoples. In so doing, it provides a sustained eschatological reason for the continuation of existing identities. There is a future for Israel, which therefore continues in Paul's universalistic gospel. The book then closes with a conclusion.

2

To the Jew First

Introduction

Gregory Tatum has recently argued that Romans should be understood as a defense of Jewish privilege; the approach offered in this chapter builds on his work in this regard.[1] Not surprisingly, the scholarly consensus aligns more closely behind the idea that Paul is attacking Jewish privilege in this letter generally and specifically in Romans 1–4.[2] For example, Dunn concludes that "the principal focus of critique is Jewish self-assurance that the typically Jewish indictment of Gentile sin (1:18–32) is not applicable to the covenant people themselves."[3] In this understanding, Jewish self-confidence was based on God's election of the nation of Israel in distinction to the other nations. In a significantly different manner, the older interpretation of boasting understood it to be focused on obedience as foundational to a relationship with God. Gathercole concludes that neither of these two approaches is quite right and that some combination of the two is closer to the mark.[4] However, in what follows I will show that it is somewhat more likely that Paul is defending Jewish privilege against gentile boasting.

In Romans 1–4, Paul establishes a positive basis for Jewish privilege and a concomitant critique of gentile boasting, based on his understanding of circumcision, Torah, Abrahamic descent, and the possession of the

---

1. Tatum, "To the Jew," 275.

2. Cf. Elliott, *Rhetoric*, 190; Stanley, *Arguing with Scripture*, 145–46.

3. Dunn, *Romans*, 1.51. For a critique of Dunn see Stowers, *Rereading*, 27–29.

4. Gathercole, *Where*, 263.

divine oracles.[5] These ideas will be unpacked somewhat in this chapter and more extensively in subsequent ones. Here we will focus on (a) the problem of gentile boasting, (b) Paul's expectation of Jews continuing to identify as Jews, (c) the purpose of the no-distinction texts in 3:22 and 10:12, (d) his belief that circumcision is a continuing sign of Jewish identity and vocation, and (e) the way Paul thereby upholds Torah.

First-Century Supersessionism—Proto-Marcionism and Gentile Boasting

One of the reasons Paul establishes a positive basis for Jewish privilege in Romans is because he thinks there are some in Rome who believe that in-Christ gentiles have replaced Israel as God's people. This group thinks that Jewish identity is expunged from the emerging Christ-movement. This would explain the implicit connotations of the later anti-Jewish heretic Marcion of Sinope, especially as it relates to his claim that Paul sought to break away from Judaism, to radically bifurcate the identity of Israel's God, and to set aside Israel's scriptural tradition.[6] N. T. Wright picks up on this interpretive possibility; he writes that Paul's "argument is aimed at the proto-Marcionism he suspects may exist in the Roman church, an attitude which really would deserve the name 'supersessionism,' a belief according to which God has effected a simple transfer of promises and privileges from Jews to Gentiles, so that Jews are just as shut out now as Gentiles were before."[7] This quote from Wright is crucial since he will be discussed throughout this book. First, he is correct to note that some in-Christ gentiles are boasting over the Jews, and Paul will have none of that. Second, Wright does not think his own approach to Paul amounts to supersessionism. This is because for him the issue is soteriology, and, as he notes, being a Jew does not bar one from experiencing salvation.[8]

---

5. So, Tatum, "To the Jew," 280.

6. Grieb, *Story*, 108: "It would be fewer than one hundred years before Roman Christianity in the form of Marcion would attempt to define a non-Jewish Christianity for an all-Gentile church. Paul's gospel does not allow such a move, as he shows clearly in 11:13–15."

7. Wright, *Paul in Fresh Perspective*, 127. He further notes that this would be "a very convenient thing to believe in Rome in the middle or late 50s after those unpopular Jews were allowed back again upon Nero's accession." On this see further page 15 n. 50.

8. Wright, *Paul in Fresh Perspective*, 126–27: "the promise Paul holds out for at present unbelieving Jews is not that they are actually all right as they are, but *that they*

However, the question that is being asked here is does Jewish ethnicity (and the divine calling attached to this ethnicity) survive Paul's universalistic gospel discourse? In other words, is there a vocational element that continues? I would say there is, and this assertion constitutes the difference between Wright and the argument of this book.

Neil Elliott picks up on the proto-Marcionism as well. However, he also notes that this discourse is not simply aligned with what became known as a heretical position within early Christian teaching but that it also finds a comfortable place within the more broadly accepted teachings as well. For Elliott, the focal point of the letter to the Romans is chapters 9–11 and specifically 11:13–32 in which Paul exhorts in-Christ gentiles "not to 'boast' over Israel." Thus, there is no need to reconstruct a deficient Jewish theology; rather, "*we most profitably read the letter as directed against a nascent anti-Judaism among the predominantly Gentile congregation in Rome.*"[9] So, Paul then seeks to confront the boasting among this group especially as it relates to their assumption that they are in ascendancy at the expense of Israel. This issue is not only theological but also social; it is a combination of cultural boasting and unscriptural thought patterns that are in need of transformation among those who follow Christ.[10]

In Romans, Paul thinks that boasting in its various forms should be overcome. The strong are not to gather together with the weak for "the purpose of passing judgment on their opinions" (14:1). Nor should the weak "judge the one who eats" since each person will give an account to the Lord (14:3–4). Both of these exhortations imply a level of boasting in one's sense of normative practice. Earlier in the letter the καυχ- word group occurs in the context of differing expectations of practices related to received understandings of one or another's ancestral traditions (2:17, 23). In those verses, the problem appears to be an inordinate boasting

---

are not debarred, in virtue of their ethnic origin, from coming back into the family, their own family, that has been renewed in the gospel, and from which they are currently separated because it is marked out solely by faith, and they are currently in 'unbelief.'" For Wright there is a crucial connection between "all Israel will be saved" (Rom 11:26) and the earlier statement, "all who call on the name of the Lord shall be saved" (Rom 10:13), since the latter properly addresses his concern that "the Israelites . . . may be saved" (Rom 10:1) at which point, if they believe, "God is able to graft them in again" (Rom 11:23).

9. Elliott, "Romans," 197, emphasis original.

10. Elliott, *Arrogance*, 20. See Tucker, *Remain in Your Calling*, 168, on unscriptural thought patterns and cultural boasting.

about that which is good and proper (God and Torah) or a boastful proclamation without the accompanying practice. In the same context but somewhat earlier, Paul, as a way to discourage boasting, highlights stereotypical aberrant behaviors that groups of people exhibit (1:18—2:29, see especially 1:30; ἀλαζόνας "boastful"). As a result of these behaviors, Paul claims "that both Jews and Greeks are all under sin" (3:9). While in 1 Cor 1:31, Paul does not seek to obliterate boasting but to reprioritize it and detail the acceptable ground for boasting, here in Romans he seems to obliterate it when he states: "Where then is boasting (καύχησις)? It is excluded" (3:27).[11] However, he then goes on to point out that proper boasting is "in our hope of sharing the glory of God" and the one who has given them "reconciliation" (Rom 5:2, 11). In the midst of this reorientation of the group's boast, he points out that in Christ one should boast in "suffering" since it may produce "endurance" (5:3). Further, he thinks that boasting is a problem in a general fashion in that it results in a lack of concern for unity among the various members of the body of Christ (12:1–21, see especially 12:3). Finally, there is one particular form of boasting that is illustrative of the argument of this book: in-Christ gentiles boasting over the status of Jews (11:13–14, 25–26). The starkest warning concerning gentile boasting is in this section of the letter; Paul warns them specifically: "do not boast (κατακαυχῶ) over the branches. If you do boast (κατακαυχᾶσαι), remember it is not you who support the root, but the root that supports you. . . . So do not become proud (μὴ ὑψηλὰ φρόνει), but fear; for if God did not spare the natural branches, he will not spare you, either" (11:18, 20b–21). This verse raises several important questions for a post-supersessionist reading of Romans but here is the main point: Paul reminds these gentiles that the group they are currently boasting over actually supports them in their spiritual vitality.[12]

Paul's concern with gentile boasting highlights a difference with the letter to the Galatians. In that letter he was concerned that gentiles be accepted into the Christ-movement as gentiles while here in Romans he seems to be counteracting a perceived threat to the full acceptance of Jewish identity. Further, Paul takes a rhetorical step further and argues for a continuing covenantal identity even for non-Christ-following Jews. Philip Cunningham has picked up on this and what follows highlights

---

11. See Tucker, *You Belong of Christ*, 173–77, for a discussion of Paul's critique of cultural boasting and the implications of the gospel for this.

12. See further the discussion of this passage starting on page 180.

his main points.[13] Gentiles should stop boasting over Jews because all rely on God's generosity, grace, and mercy (Rom 3:9; 11:6, 30–33). As mentioned above, in-Christ gentiles are supported in their salvation by the Jews generally, and the agency of the "remnant" specifically is highlighted (11:5–6, 16). The gentile branches also bear fruit as they are connected to the cultivated olive tree (11:17–24). In-Christ gentile identity does not stand alone. It finds its salience in the continuing story of God's faithfulness to Israel. More controversially, God has used the preexisting disposition of some Jews who resist the gospel in order to redeem gentiles (11:25). This statement reveals Paul's pathos as he tries to maintain Israel's continued election in the context of his equally held belief in the necessity of Christ-faith.[14] Further, gentiles in Christ should not boast over non-Christ-following Jews, i.e., "branches who were broken off" (11:19), since they can more easily be grafted back in than can gentiles who are not part of their ancestral tradition.[15] Instead, gentiles should live in a manner so as to make Israel "jealous" (11:11). The need for this argument implies that gentiles were doing the opposite and thus adversely affecting their mission effectiveness. Finally, gentile boasting over Israel is excluded within the Christ-movement since "all Israel will be saved" (11:26a).[16] Thus, Paul succinctly states his hope: "God has not rejected his people" Israel since his "gifts and callings are irrevocable" (11:1, 29). This means that gentiles should thank God for his faithfulness to Israel and worship him with them rather than boast over his seeming rejection of them (15:10). Even in the midst of a "partial hardening," Israel's covenant identity remains intact (9:4–5; 11:25, 28–29). This permanent gifting and calling also means that in-Christ gentiles should include petitions for mercy within their worship practices and, in response to God's mercy,

---

13. Cunningham, "Paul's Letters," 1–20.

14. See Cunningham, "Paul's Letters," 9 n. 26.

15. On the problems with the NRSV translation "broken off," see further page 178.

16. Cunningham, "Paul's Letters," 10. Cunningham points out the following: "Jews not in Christ are, for Paul, apparently in some sort of 'theological limbo,' to use Daniel Harrington's phrase. Although currently 'broken off' from the mainstream of God's covenantal actions, they are irrevocably destined for inclusion in God's salvation because of God's faithfulness to divine promises (11:28–29). All Israel will be saved (11:26). Jews not in Christ have 'stumbled' in order to make way for the Gentiles, but they have not 'fallen' into perdition (11:11). Paul hopes to 'save some of them' from their blindness (11:14), but the inevitable Jewish recognition of God's actions in Christ will mean nothing less than life from the dead (11:15)." See Harrington, *Paul*, 55, 81. Some of this will be tempered and corrected beginning on page 184.

develop a doxological social identity (11:30–36; 15:8–13).[17] With a fresh awareness of Paul's critique of incipient boasting by some gentiles over Israel, key parts of Paul's gospel discourse may be read in a fresh light. One of the first of these is part of the letter's thesis statement in Rom 1:16, "For I am not ashamed of the gospel: it is the power of God for salvation to everyone who has faith, to the Jew first and also to the Greek." Here we will only focus on the last phrase, "to the Jew first and also to the Greek."[18]

To the Jew First in Romans 1:16

Paul uses the phrase "to the Jew first and also to the Greek" as a way to indicate the continued salience of both Jewish and Greek identities in his gospel discourse. The focus of this section is to address the differing interpretive suggestions for why Paul maintains a Jewish priority in his gospel since it might appear somewhat out of place in his otherwise universalistic outlook. This sub-section is restricted to addressing this one issue since it is most germane to a post-supersessionist reading of Rom 1:16. It will therefore address the following approaches: history/temporal, salvation-historical, mission strategy, and continuing social identification.

The historical or temporal approach simply sees Paul describing a set of historical events or processes in Rom 1:16c. For example, Robert Mounce thinks that the phrase "first for the Jew, then for the gentile" emphasizes the universal nature of salvation as it was worked out historically through Israel and now has gone to the nations.[19] Similarly, C. K. Barrett argues that the Jews were the first to hear the gospel (especially as encoded in the prophetic tradition) but once they rejected Paul's message he moved to the gentiles.[20] Two problems may be noted with regard to this approach. First, as suggested by Campbell, "For Paul, the entire

---

17. Cunningham ("Paul's Letters," 10) ends this section similarly but with a different emphasis. On the formation of a doxological social identity, see further below beginning on page 221.

18. Some of the issues highlighted in this verse in relation to the gospel and salvation will be discussed when dealing with Rom 3:21–22 (beginning on page 40) since the overlap between these verses is significant.

19. Mounce, *Romans*, 71; Käsemann, *Romans*, 23.

20. Barrett, *Romans*, 29; for a critique of the use of the term "gentile," see Magda, *Paul's Territoriality*, 187–92.

argument of Romans presupposes the faithfulness of God to his people."[21] Yet both of those scholars intimate a moving away from Israel to the gentiles in their construal of the verse. Second, the context suggests more than a historical recounting.[22] This is especially true when Rom 2:9–10 is considered, which twice repeats the same Jew and Greek binary categorization.[23] In those verses both judgment and promise are extended "to the Jew first, then to the Greek." For Paul, Jewish priority is more than just a historical detail; it is a matter of election (cf. Deut 7:6; Rom 11:26, 29).[24]

Closely aligned with the historical or temporal approach is the salvation-historical understanding of Rom 1:16c.[25] Hultgren, while recognizing that the temporal understanding has some merit, is concerned that it ignores the salvation-historical issue. An ongoing precedence for the proclamation of the gospel to the Jews is proper since the gospel was "promised beforehand through [God's] prophets in the holy scriptures" (1:2).[26] Kruse, however, thinks more than a simple recounting of Paul's mission strategy is in view.[27] Building on Rom 3:1–2; 9:4–5 and 11:28–29, he concludes: "Paul's understanding of Jewish priority rests upon the place God himself had given them in his plan of salvation by his sovereign choice of the Jewish people, his covenants with them, his promises to them, and the way he was working out his purposes through them,

---

21. Campbell, "Divergent," 206. For a full description of Campbell's approach and legacy in Pauline studies, see Tucker, "Diverse Identities," 139–52.

22. So similarly Moo, *Romans*, 69. See also Hvalvik, "To the Jew," 3.

23. This is a central part of Hvalvik's argument in "To the Jew," 4–5.

24. Hvalvik, "To the Jew," 6. Hvalvik concludes that "Israel has a prerogative which is based on God's gracious election, an election which holds good because 'the gifts and the call of God are irrevocable.' This prerogative means a promise of salvation for the Jewish people as a whole. But this prerogative does in no way abolish the gospel." This is not to be construed as a two-covenant approach but will be elucidated further below.

25. I am adopting here the definition of this term that comes from Roy Ciampa: "The expression 'history of salvation' or 'history of redemption' therefore does not refer directly to the facts of world history or to the facts/reports of God's intervention in history as though they were self-interpreting, but to particular ways in which the biblical authors interpreted key events in the history of the relationship between God and his creation/people by way of the narrative-theological structures that they used or assumed" (Ciampa, "The History of Redemption," 255).

26. Hultgren, *Paul's Letter*, 74; so similarly Fitzmyer, *Romans*, 257, but without an explicit reference to Paul's mission strategy.

27. Kruse, *Romans*, 69.

culminating in the sending of Christ."[28] Two problems are evident in the salvation-historical approach. First, it is not clear that a salvation-historical understanding would have been communicative in the first-century Roman context. Second, even if one grants the salvation-historical framework, the way it is configured by these scholars is supersessionist. What is needed is a post-supersessionist approach to salvation history, such as that put forth by Kendall Soulen.[29]

It is clear, as noted by Grant Osborne, that Paul still defines those who believe as falling into the categories of Jews and Greeks, but why he does this "is difficult to understand."[30] Similarly, Leander Keck notes that the motive for Paul prioritizing the Jews is "puzzl[ing]" today just as it likely was to those who originally received the letter. Keck hints that Rom 3:1–8 should be considered when discerning Paul's rationale.[31] This solution appears on target since Paul's "secondary argument" in Romans 1–4 is that "circumcision is of great value and is a sign of faith," an argument that goes against the grain of traditional Paulinism.[32] This broader argument will be discussed below; however, the mission strategy and an identity-critical variant of it need to be outlined, both of which provide an interpretive approach to Rom 1:16c that is not inherently supersessionist.[33]

28. Kruse, *Romans*, 69. Based on this conclusion, Kruse still focuses on the necessity of the offer of the gospel to the Jews by Paul. See also Jewett, *Romans*, 140; Moo, *Romans*, 68–69. Hvalvik ("To the Jew," 5) argues for a comparative understanding that reinforces a salvation-historical understanding of the phrase, though with different implications than Moo.

29. Soulen, "They Are Israelites," 497–504. The normal creation, fall, redemption, and consummation model expands to become creation, fall, Israel, redemption, and consummation. In addition, the God who acts is the God of Israel, not some abstracted Greek or Roman deity. He is the creator God of Israel's scriptural tradition.

30. Osborne, *Romans*, 41.

31. Keck, *Romans*, 51. The significance of at least Rom 3:1–2 will be discussed below beginning on page 56.

32. Tatum, "To the Jew," 276. The significance and defense of this claim will be developed in the chapter on Abraham beginning on page 62. Nanos (*Reading Paul*, 10) defines Paulinism as follows: "when NT scholars speak of Paul's religious life and values, of Paulinism or *Pauline* Christianity, with its 'Law-free Gospel,' most mean to signify that Paul taught and practiced a *Judaism-free* way of living based on his belief in Jesus Christ."

33. Hvalvik ("To the Jew," 1–8) does put forth a type of salvation-historical approach that is not supersessionistic, as does Brindle ("To the Jew," 233), who concludes that "Israel's election by God is permanent and determinate for salvation history." Both Hvalvik and Brindle can achieve this based on their reading of Romans 9–11.

The phrase "to the Jew first and also to the Greek" (Ιουδαίῳ τε πρῶτον καὶ Ἕλληνι) may be understood to reflect Paul's mission strategy. This approach is often present among missiologically-oriented works but is surprisingly scarce among commentators.[34] Nanos contends that "to the Jew first" describes Paul's "two-step pattern," one that is also described in Acts where Paul is seen as "going to the Jews first before turning to the gentiles" (e.g., 17:1–2).[35] He continues: "Romans reveals Paul as the champion of Israel's restoration, and his prioritizing phrase 'to the Jew first and also to the Greek' was descriptive of his missionary pattern to which he was committed, and for which he was willing to suffer immensely in order to ensure the salvation of the Jewish people, first and last."[36] Dunn, on the other hand, rejects this idea and thinks that the phrase is not "indicative of Paul's missionary strategy, since he saw himself as first and foremost 'apostle to the Gentiles' (11:13; 15:16)."[37] However, Paul's mission to the nations proceeds in the context of Israel's story, and his identity as an apostle to the gentiles does not exclude his continued mission among other Jews. Further, Dunn assumes a sectarian approach to Paul's mission that has been called into question.[38] Finally, if Paul's description of his mission in 1 Cor 9:19–23 is considered, along with Luke's description of Paul as one who "welcomed all who came to him" (Acts 28:30),[39] there is no significant reason to maintain such a social dichotomy in Paul's mission.[40]

Building on Nanos's two-step pattern approach, Paul may be using the phrase "to the Jew first" as a way to describe the continuation of Jewish privilege or covenantal social identity. A similar approach is anticipated by Gregory Tatum; however, he does not develop the social identity implications of this view.[41] In this approach, Paul ascribes a social identity

34. Fruchtenbaum, "To the Jew," 189–216; Bjoraker, "To the Jew," 110–16; but see Magda, *Paul's Territoriality*, 175–79.

35. Nanos, *Mystery*, 247; see further 239–47, especially 239 n. 1.

36. Nanos, *Mystery*, 15.

37. Dunn, *Romans*, 1.40.

38. Campbell, *Paul and the Creation*, 48–50.

39. Rudolph (*A Jew to the Jews*, 188) also notes that the Western textual tradition expands this verse to include "(both) Jews and Greeks."

40. It is possible that commentators are hesitant to affirm this view because of their desire to work with Paul's letters primarily and Acts secondarily (if at all). See on this Nanos, *Mystery*, 239 n. 1.

41. Tatum, "To the Jew," 275. There is a tendency to interpret Paul's discourse

by his use of both of these terms. This, by itself is not very controversial; however, some scholars question the continued use of these labels within the Christ-movement.[42] Campbell is one scholar who picks up on the self-designation possibilities of the term "Jew."[43] This way of describing humanity provides a basis for Paul's continued commitment to, and positive view of, "Israel according to the flesh" (1 Cor 10:18).[44]

Some scholars construe Paul's emphasis here as being on "the Greeks" rather than "the Jews." Byrne takes the argument of the whole letter and considers a salvific reversal to be evident in Rom 11:11–12, 15, 30–32. He therefore concludes that "the stress falls upon the inclusion of the Gentiles."[45] The debate revolves around the emphasis being on either "first" (πρῶτον) or "and" (καί). However, the presence of "both" (τε) used in combination with "and" (καί) argues against relativizing the Jew under the Greek. The presence of "first" (πρῶτον) does suggest, on the contrary, that Paul's emphasis is on the Jew (Ἰουδαῖος).[46] His anthropological theologizing continues to be Israel-centric and, as Zoccali notes, *the Christ event belongs to Israel first* (cf. Rom 4:1; 9:4–5).[47]

Paul's continued identification of the privilege of the Jews (Ἰουδαῖοι) raises a question with regard to Paul's understanding of the Greeks (Ἕλληνες). Commentators often point out that Paul uses Ἕλλην rather than ἔθνος and that he considers these to be generally synonymous.[48]

---

solely in theological terms and to overlook its social significance. See similarly Brindle, "To the Jew," 226.

42. For erasure language (Gal 3:28, etc.), see Trebilco, *Self-Designations*, 1–4, who does not study these terms in his work on self-designations within the early Christ-movement.

43. Campbell, *Paul and the Creation*, 122. He sees it most obviously in 2:17.

44. See on this verse below beginning on page 121.

45. Byrne, *Romans*, 57.

46. Cf. Brindle, "To the Jew," 223; Tatum, "To the Jew," 227. This does not mean that Paul's social categorization here socially distances the Greeks; rather, it highlights his social identification with Israel according to the flesh in the context of the presence of gentile social identities within the Christ-movement (Rom 11:11–12). See Fitzmyer, *Romans*, 257.

47. Zoccali, *Whom God*, 149. This is not meant to downplay the theo-centricity of Paul's theologizing in general. See on this Ehrensperger, *Paul and the Dynamics*, 182 n. 13. Nor do I mean by this that Paul has a systematic and fully developed anthropology. See further page 123 for a discussion of these verses. Cf. further Kinzer, *Postmissionary*, 140.

48. Cf. Moo, *Romans*, 68–69; Dunn, *Romans*, 1.40; Schreiner, *Romans*, 62. Jewett (*Romans*, 140) rejects the claim that these are synonymous in this context.

However, it is more likely that the choice of the term Ἕλλην rather than ἔθνος was purposeful (and not just stylistic) and that Paul has in view real Jews and Greeks (embedded in the Roman Empire) rather than merely rhetorical categories.[49] This insight brings to the fore the contextual nature of Paul's argument and the way he continues to think about ethnic and social identities. He defines his mission and those that are targets of that mission in the context of their existing identities rather than to the exclusion or erasure of them (cf. Rom 1:14).[50]

The mention of Jews and Greeks in 1:16c describes nested subgroup identities within a superordinate identity here called "the believing one(s)" (τῷ πιστεύοντι).[51] Trebilco classifies believers as one of the seven self-designations widely evident in the NT. He outlines the use and significance of this ingroup label and contends that it was a term of self-reference that emphasized faith as a key marker of early Christ-movement identity. Especially in Romans, Trebilco sees this label creating, for gentiles, a new boundary between insiders and outsiders.[52] It helpfully replaces circumcision, which would not distinguish these early Christ-followers from non-Christ-believing Jews, especially if they were all still part of the broader synagogue community. In fact, Trebilco contends that this term originated as one of the self-designations among Jewish Christ-followers under the influence of the stone discourse found in Isa 28:16 (אמן with ὁ πιστεύων in the LXX and in Rom 9:33).[53] However, what Trebilco overlooks is that existing social identities continue to be relevant. It may be more precise (at least in the case of Rom 1:16) to describe these individuals as Jewish-believers-in-the-gospel and Greek-believers-in-the-gospel. This may sound like an unnecessary and pleonastic intrusion

---

49. Stanley, "Neither Jew nor Greek," 101–24. The significance of this will be developed below. Scott (*Paul*, 123–24) suggests a mission reason for the use of Ἕλλην.

50. Jewett, *Romans*, 140. He also notes that it was politically astute of Paul to avoid the use of the term "gentile."

51. The other option here would be cross-cutting subgroup identities. This will be discussed further in relation to Romans 14–15.

52. Trebilco, *Self-Designations*, 81–82. Note that the focus is on gentiles and does not address the continued role of circumcision for Jews.

53. Trebilco, *Self-Designations*, 105. Two further observations should be noted. First, Trebilco is undoubtedly correct in his argument that believing is both something that occurs at conversion and is a component of new life in Christ. Second, it may be too stark to claim that Acts 22:19 supports the idea that believing functions as a cipher for distinguishing Christ-followers from synagogue attendees (more on this below).

into Paul's argument, but his claims in Romans 9–11 and 14–15 are predicated on just such a continuation of existing identities in Christ.[54]

An understanding similar to this has been put forth by Philip Esler. He contends that Paul's gospel has the power to save all those who believe, a group further described as "a category comprising two subcategories, Judeans and Greeks."[55] Furthermore, those who hear the gospel in the context of these identities experience a sense of belonging since their previous identities are not excluded. However, is "the believers" a transcending identity designed to eventually replace either of these existing subgroup identities? What needs further clarification is (a) the degree of identity transformation that Paul expects for non-Jews in Christ; (b) what changes, if any, need to occur with regard to Jewish identity, and (c) Paul's understanding of his role as a bi-cultural mediator between these complex social contexts.[56] The particularistic approach taken here is quite similar to Esler's, and the differences are more with regard to degree. For example, his transcending view conceives of a scenario in which the particularities of existing social identities would become less salient while, with a few exceptions noted, I would maintain that they are designed to continue as an expression of Gen 1:31 (and in the case of Jewish identity, an expression of covenant faithfulness and continuing Jewish privilege).[57] The argument being put forth here is that the use of the phrase "to the Jew first but also the Greek" is an example of the way Paul continues to view as salient both Jewish and non-Jewish social identities. However, doesn't Paul think that these identities are no longer relevant within the Christ-movement, since he says in Rom 3:22 and 10:12 that there is no distinction between Jews and gentiles? To that question, we now turn.

54. On Romans 9–11, see Campbell, *Paul and the Creation*, 121–39; Ehrensperger, *Mutually Encouraged*, 181–94.

55. Esler, *Conflict*, 140. See the later discussion of Paul's gospel discourse and the significance of Jesus's descent from David, the promised messianic line (Rom 1:3–4), beginning on page 236.

56. Each of these are addressed in other parts of this book. See page 141 for the transformation of gentile identity, page 176 for putative changes to Jewish identity, and page 200 for Paul's identity as a bi-cultural meditator.

57. For an analysis of Esler's transcending view, see Tucker, *You Belong to Christ*, 67–69. See below for a discussion of whether this approach runs afoul of Rom 3:22 and 10:12, both of which claim that there is no distinction to be made between Jews and Greeks.

Romans 3:22 and 10:12: The No-Distinction Texts

Paul, in Rom 3:22 and 10:12, seems to suggest that existing ethnic identities are no longer relevant within the Christ-movement; if that is the case,
it calls into question the continuing social identification idea for 1:16 and
its implications for Jewish covenantal identity. Do not these verses—"The
righteousness of God through faith in Jesus Christ for all who believe.
For there is no distinction" (3:22) and "For there is no distinction between Jew and Greek; the same Lord is Lord of all and is generous to all
who call on him" (10:12)—suggest that ethnic and social identifiers are
quite inappropriate within the Christ-movement?

While these verses could be understood this way, it seems that in
the wider context Paul argues that ethnic differentiation is relevant, and
that communal behavior choices should be made with social identity in
view. Paul wants his readers to understand what some of them apparently did not, that God doesn't "discriminate" based on discernible differences. This understanding builds on Paul's use of διαστολή here, which
the NRSV translates as "distinction." Thus, in relation to the reception
of God's righteousness by those trusting in him or the Lord's acceptance
of all who call on him (i.e., the context in which these verses stand), "no
discrimination is made" despite the distinguishable differences.[58]

These two verses however do differ from one another in their
focus. Romans 10:12 is a more positive statement in comparison with
3:22. Because of this 3:21 should be considered before interpreting 3:22,
since there is some sort of contextual relationship here. Paul begins in
3:21, νυνὶ δέ "but now" or "and now"; this signals either a logical step
or a temporal one. It is difficult to determine but "at the present time" in
3:26 suggests the temporal use is in view, so with the coming of Christ
a new era has begun.[59] Paul continues, χωρὶς νόμου "apart from law" or
"without relation to Torah." This prepositional phrase is often thought to
indicate that the law has been set aside. This is because of the connection
with 3:28, but when that verse is consulted the question arises: is it apart
from the law of Moses that is in view or apart from the works of the law
just mentioned in 3:20 (see also 4:6)?[60] Cranfield reminds interpreters
concerning this phrase that "To appeal to these words as evidence that

---

58. Campbell, "Paul," 340 n. 91; Fitzmyer, *Romans*, 592.

59. Cf. Jewett, *Romans*, 272; Moo, *Romans*, 221; Kruse, *Romans*, 178; BDAG 682.

60. BDAG 1095.

Paul regarded the law as superseded and set aside by the gospel as something now out of date and irrelevant is surely perverse."[61]

The next phrase, δικαιοσύνη θεοῦ "God's righteousness", has been construed in several ways in the history of interpretation; these include: (a) an attribute of God (possessive genitive; "God's own righteousness"), (b) a status given by God (genitive of source; "righteousness from God"), or (c) an activity of God (subjective genitive; "the righteousness that is being shown").[62] Our purpose here is not to resolve this debate, but Middendorf seems helpful: "Some evidence points towards a genitive of source which places more emphasis upon the status received from God by those who believe. . . . [F]ollowing the verbally based noun 'righteousness,' 'of God' functions primarily as a subjective genitive. . . . [T]he Good News is God's righteousness in action."[63] The main verb here, "has been revealed" (πεφανέρωται), controls the discourse. The perfect tense may be construed either as an extensive (consummative), emphasizing the completion of a past action from which the present state emerges (i.e., the cross) or an intensive (resultative), emphasizing the results or present state by a past action (which accounts for the νυνί).[64] Thus, in this first part of 3:21, in an expansive way, Paul is saying: but now apart from [the works of the] law, the righteousness of God (i.e., his righteous activity) has been revealed through the cross in the present time.

Paul continues with an adverbial participle, μαρτυρουμένη "while being testified to." The temporal use is likely here, and the controlling verb is πεφανέρωται "has been revealed." Since the present participle is generally contemporaneous with the action of its verb, "while being testified to" seems appropriate.[65] The participial clause continues, ὑπὸ τοῦ νόμου καὶ τῶν προφητῶν "by the law and the prophets." But this raises a question: to what does this refer? Following 2 Macc 15:9 and Sirach Prologue 1:1, where the same phrase is used, it is evident that Israel's

---

61. Cranfield, *Romans*, 1.201.

62. *GGBB* 81, 109, 113.

63. Middendorf, *Romans*, 1.95. Romans 1:16–17 is crucial here, and δικαιοσύνη, in BDAG 247, offers some help: "all these [Rom 1:17; 3:21f, 25, 26 . . .] refer to *righteousness bestowed by God.*" This presupposes a genitive of source. *NIDNTTE* (1.735) assumes a subjective genitive: "the term δ. Probably means (or at least it must include in its meaning) the manner in which God justifies sinners." For a different approach see Wright, *Paul and the Faithfulness of God*, 928, 996, who sees this as "God's covenant faithfulness." See now Irons, *The Righteousness of God*, 279–89.

64. *GGBB* 572.

65. *GGBB* 623, 625.

scriptural tradition generally is in view. Hultgren picks up on this: "the law and prophets (the scriptural tradition of Israel) anticipated the coming of the Messiah (or messianic age) and the advent of righteousness attending him."[66] For Cranfield, the gospel is continuous with this tradition and witnesses to the righteousness discussed here.[67] Thus, the use of "apart from the law" does not mean that Paul sees no continuing relevance for Israel's scriptural tradition within the Christ-movement. God's righteousness is apart from law, yet at the same time Torah testified to it (3:21). This brings us to 3:22.

Paul continues in 3:22, δικαιοσύνη δὲ θεοῦ "even God's righteousness," emphasizing the centrality of righteousness in the larger context from 1:17 into chapter 4. The δέ here signals that what follows is a new development in the argument while at the same time highlighting a connection with what was just asserted. This suggests that the genitival relationships in the previous verse are likely continued here. The righteousness that is being shown by God is διὰ πίστεως Ἰησοῦ Χριστοῦ "through faith in Jesus Christ" or "through the faithfulness of Jesus Christ." Διά plus the genitive could be understood as means (which would go with the first option since it would be "by means of faith") or agency (which would go better with the second).[68] The perennial debate over the objective genitive (the first) or subjective genitive (second) is almost irresolvable at this point since both sides are firmly entrenched. However, Reasoner helpfully suggests a combined approach: "This would allow one to believe in Christ (objective genitive) and then while doing this to follow in the way in which Christ lived out his faith (subjective genitive) and grow in the virtues."[69] Paul continues, εἰς πάντας τοὺς πιστεύοντας "for all who believe." The εἰς here may be understood as advantage, while the use of πᾶς is likely gnomic. Paul is making a proverbial statement about the way trusting in Christ provides salvific benefits to those trusting.[70]

---

66. Hultgren, *Paul's Letter*, 154.

67. Cranfield, *Romans*, 1.202.

68. *GGBB* 368–69.

69. See Reasoner, *Romans in Full Circle*, 39. This would fall into the category of the plenary genitive, *GGBB* 119–20.

70. *GGBB* 369, 523. Note that εἰς is replaced by ἐπί in some manuscripts. If we take εἰς as advantage, that would hold up grammatically/semantically. There is not an advantage use of ἐπί and its uses with the accusative, spatial and temporal, do not really work in this context (*GGBB* 376). So, εἰς is the more harmonious, congruent reading (as well as earlier, more widely distributed, and shorter).

The substantival participle, "the ones who believe," would be rendered by the phrase "for everyone who believes."[71] So, to summarize Paul's writing here, God's righteousness has been made manifest; it is apart from Torah, testified to by the same law; it is through faith in Jesus Christ, and it is for all who believe in him. This is one way to describe Paul's universalistic gospel discourse in Romans.

This brings us back to the phrase that seems to downplay the continuing relevance of existing identities, οὐ γάρ ἐστιν διαστολή "for there is no difference" (3:22). The question arises, does this go with what was just written or is it more connected with what follows? If the γάρ is taken as explanatory, then it gives additional information about what was just described. If it is construed as an inferential γάρ then it is giving a deduction, conclusion, or summary of the preceding.[72] As mentioned above, the exact same phrase is used in 10:12, so it is likely there is some connection between the two verses. At the lexical level, there is an issue to note. One of the glosses for διαστολή is "distinction,"[73] and it is the word choice of several English translations. However, the entry in BDAG points out the lack of evidence for this sense of the word.[74] It then may be preferable to translate the phrase "for there is no difference," but what does that signify? It explains the inclusive nature of the "all who believe," i.e., there is no difference. Or, if there is a forward movement to the argument, there is no difference since all have sinned. It could be both, but the extensive use of πᾶς in the near context suggests that the focus is more on the "all sinners" idea (3:4, 9, 12, 19, 20, 22, 23). Thus, Paul's argument is that all need God's righteousness, "since there is no difference, for all have sinned and fall short of the glory of God" (3:22c–23). Both Jews and non-Jews need rescuing from sin according to Paul, and the good news of what God has done through Christ is the solution to that problem.

This then brings us to the other part of our research question concerning existing identities generally and Jewish covenantal identity specifically: Does the οὐ γάρ ἐστιν διαστολή phrase mean that distinctions between Jews and gentiles are gone in Christ? Can this verse and 10:12a be used to argue that Israel's distinctive identity has been abrogated? Middendorf begins to move in the right direction: "The

71. See *GGBB* 620–21.

72. *GGBB* 673.

73. BDAG 237.

74. MM 154 also points out a lack of evidence for "distinction" as a gloss for διαστολή.

point is not, of course, that everyone is the same. Numerous differences exist between people who are living apart from the righteousness of God from faith, as well as among those in Christ (see, e.g., 12:3–8; 14:2, 5). There are distinctions in gender, language, culture, station in life, gifts, and so forth."[75] This approach will be extended further in this book since one could acknowledge what Middendorf claims and simply see these as irrelevant, secondary, or an indifferent part of life. However, Paul's thinking about Jewish and non-Jewish identity is load-bearing in Romans; it is not peripheral. Middendorf continues, "The predominant differentiation in Romans is between Jews and Gentiles. Paul only uses 'difference' (διαστολή) two other times, but once is in 10:12, where he more fully expresses the thought: 'for there is not a difference between Jew and Greek.'"[76] Here, however, Middendorf starts to move away from his earlier statement. Paul's argument is based on some level of difference; it is just not clear what that is. Further in this book, it will be suggested that there are different social implications that emerge from the gospel for Jews and gentiles. Finally, Middendorf does pick up on the correct nuance: "Paul's argument is that *God* does not discriminate between people in this respect: all sinners deserve wrath; righteousness is through faith. In 3:22 the clause, 'you see, there is not a difference,' recalls Paul's earlier statement in 2:9–11."[77] The problem is sin. And even though certain sins are more evident among gentiles than Jews, the problem of sin is addressed, as Paul delineates in 3:21–26, through the substitutionary death of Christ on the cross through which God declares sinners righteous. When Paul returns to some of this in Romans 9–11, in the middle of his argument for the way Israel's covenantal identity continues in the messianic era (9:1–5; 11:1, 25–26, 28b–29), he reminds his readers that both Jews and gentiles must call on the same Lord for salvation, "For, everyone who calls on the name of the Lord shall be saved" (10:12–13).[78] Ethnic distinctions are not erased. They are integral to understanding the social implications of Paul's universalistic gospel. Romans 3:22 and 10:12 cannot sustain the idea that Paul thought there were no longer distinctions to be made between Jews and non-Jews. The continuation of existing identities is an important point in the development of a post-supersessionist reading of

---

75. Middendorf, *Romans*, 1.282.

76. Middendorf, *Romans*, 1.282. The other place is 1 Cor 14:7.

77. Middendorf, *Romans*, 1.282.

78. Carraway, *Christ is God over All*, 157.

this letter. While several topics could be highlighted to substantiate this, we will now address the issue of circumcision in relation to Jewish identity, since it seems as though Paul thinks this is now an indifferent matter. If so, it would work against the idea that he expected a continuation of Jewish identity in his gospel. The distinction between Jew and gentile remains for Paul, and that distinction informs the interpretive logic of the hypothetical in-Christ Jewish teacher of gentiles in Rom 2:17–29.

Romans 2:17–29:
The Spiritualizing of Circumcision and Gentile Identity

Circumcision is the sign of Jewish identity for males. This goes back to Gen 17:9–14 where God commanded Abraham to circumcise all the male members of his house.[79] First, circumcision was to be a sign of the covenant. Second, all males needed to be circumcised, including Abraham and his servants. Third, all of Abraham's male descendants would need to be circumcised. Fourth, any male descendant that was not circumcised would be cut off from the covenant. Later in Genesis the covenant was passed down through a particular lineage of Abraham's descendants, from Isaac, to Jacob, and then to his twelve sons who became the tribal leaders in Israel. Abraham's descendants from his other children or grandchildren were not parties to the land and descendant promises (Gen 15:5; 22:17; 26:4). Ishmael was Abraham's son through Hagar and was circumcised; however, he was not a recipient of God's covenant with Abraham. He received blessings of the covenant by being attached to Abraham's house but he was not a transmitter of that covenant. Ishmael had twelve sons who were associated with the Midianites (Gen 25:13–14; 37:28). Abraham also had sons through Keturah his concubine, whom he took after Isaac married Rebekah (Gen 25:1–4; 1 Chr 1:32; Jub. 19:11–12).[80] Yet the covenant, including the seed and land promises, was only passed down through Isaac not Ishmael, and through Jacob not Esau (Gen 25:19–26; Rom 9:6–13).[81] Jacob's descendants became the "children of Israel."[82]

79. Bernat, *Sign*, 27–41.

80. See van Ruiten, *Abraham*, 238.

81. See Longman, *Genesis*, 331–32, on the birth of Jacob and Esau in Gen 25:19–26.

82. The "Children of Israel" are the physical descendants of the patriarch Jacob, whose name was changed to Israel in Gen 32:28 (see 2 Kgs 17:34). In Gen 35:10–11, Jacob's name change is narrated again, but this time it is promised that "a nation and a

All of this goes to show that being a physical descendant of Abraham is not coterminous with being a member of the covenant people. Abraham's family tree had many branches but not all of them were part of the covenant, though their association with Abraham resulted in other blessings. On the other hand, based on Gen 17:14, a Jew who does not circumcise his son cuts him off from the covenant. In Exod 4:24–26, the Lord is described as being on the verge of killing Moses because he had neglected to circumcise his son, apparently not recognizing the covenantal implications. So, Jewish identity is not only genealogical, a matter of physical descent; it is also a choice. It is a willful act on the part of the child's parent to enter him into the covenantal relationship. Thus, circumcision is a sign that one is part of the Jewish people.[83]

Circumcision: Via Galatians or 1 Corinthians?

Circumcision is discussed primarily in Romans 1–4. In chapter 2, there is an argument developed concerning the social implications of circumcision, and in chapter 4 one is developed with regard to Abraham's paternity.[84] Both of these arguments are often heard through the lens of the letter to the Galatians, but that is problematic because there is no crisis in Rome as in Galatia. Paul's perspective on circumcision in Romans is

---

company of nations shall come from you." The phrase "Children of Israel" only occurs six times in the NRSV (1 Kgs 6:13; Isa 17:3, 9; Tob 13:3; Sir 51:12; Rom 9:27); however, this phrase count obscures the fact that the same Hebrew or Greek phrase underlies the translation into other English expressions (e.g., Israelites [Exod 1:12; Heb 11:22], sons of Israel [Exod 1:1], and people of Israel [Jer 39:32; Rev 2:14]). Thus "Children of Israel" is a key self-referential term used by the descendants of Jacob in the Hebrew Bible (but see Sura 17:4). "Children of Israel" is insider language and describes those who have been chosen by God. It indicates a focus on covenantal identity for those who are part of the people of God through Jacob/Israel. Other terms for this group include: "The Hebrews" (Exod 1:22; but see Phil 3:5), and "The Jews," a term that develops later and connects the people to the land of Judea (Ezra 6:14; Neh 1:2; 1 Cor 1:22). See further Tucker, "Children of Israel," 85–86.

83. On the issue of Jewish women not having a parallel covenantal welcoming ceremony, see Cohen, *Why*, 122, 130, 133, who suggests that some Jewish interpreters concluded that their inclusion in the covenant is secure since they were, like the males, recipients of the Sinai revelation (Exod 19:10–11). Cohen also suggests that the lack of male circumcision did not necessarily exclude a male from being consider Jewish, though such a person would have been considered a sinner (210). On the problem that Ishmael creates for Jewish identity, see Foster, *Renaming*, 132–36.

84. The focus here is on Romans 2; Paul's argument in Romans 4 is dealt with beginning on page 62.

more likely informed by 1 Cor 7:18, "Was a man already circumcised when he was called? He should not become uncircumcised. Was a man uncircumcised when he was called? He should not be circumcised." This principle likely guides his instructions in Romans since Paul explicitly mentions that he taught Christ-followers to stay in their existing identity as a "rule . . . in all the congregations" (ἐκκλησίαις; 1 Cor 7:17). So, the discourse in 1 Corinthians should be primary, and the polemical, context-specific assumptions in Galatians should be secondary. Thus, 1 Cor 7:19, "Circumcision is nothing and uncircumcision is nothing. Keeping God's commands is what counts," highlights Paul's primary concern, Torah-informed praxis. There are "commands," but these likely differ for Jews and non-Jews, as hinted at in 1 Cor 9:21. In Romans, Paul's teaching on circumcision reveals one primary area of concern: gentiles need to understand the continuing significance of circumcision for Jewish identity—even within the Christ-movement—and how circumcision for Jews is relevant for them as non-Jews. Tatum notes it this way: Paul "need[s] to acknowledge the worth of circumcision *for Jewish Christians*."[85] He does this in a way that maintains existing identities and construes in-Christ gentile identity at the same time.

The "So-Called Jew" and Gentile Judaizing: A Way Forward?

The identity of the interlocutor in 2:17–29 is a crucial interpretive point. On the surface, Paul seems to be referring to a Jewish person: "But if you call yourself a Jew and rely on the law and boast of your relation to God" (2:17). Middendorf, for example, suggests that "if you call yourself a Jew" should be read "as everywhere else in Romans [where] Ἰουδαῖος refers to a Jewish person."[86] Paul, however, actually says, "But if you *call* yourself a Jew" (2:17a).[87] This wording led William S. Campbell to suggest that this

85. Tatum, "Putting," 64.

86. Middendorf, *Romans*, 191. In regards to Middendorf's claim, it should also be noted that this construction does not directly highlight Paul's perspective on the interlocutor's identity. It reflects the interlocutor's self-ascription. Wright ("Law in Romans 2," 134) thinks Paul applies the group label "Jew" here to both in-Christ Jews and gentiles, an approach that even Barclay (*Paul*, 469) dismisses.

87. Barclay (*Paul*, 469) also sees the referent here as a Jew and not a gentile; this description "directs the attention to the question of what constitutes Jewish identity, which is then answered in 2:28–29." Barclay does not offer a critique of Thorsteinsson, (who is referenced) but dismisses the gentile interlocutor out of hand. Fredriksen, *Paul*, 210.

is not a Jewish person but one who "wants to be called a Jew or simply calls himself a Jew," perhaps a gentile proselyte.[88] Thorsteinsson, Thiessen, and Rodríguez have underlined the idea that Paul continues to interrogate a gentile interlocutor here: "a gentile who has Judaized, perhaps even undergoing circumcision."[89] The type of interlocutor imagined thus reflects the gentile audience of the letter more broadly, and his identity is consistent throughout the letter. Other approaches include Windsor, who thinks the interlocutor is a Jewish teacher within the mainstream synagogue whose vision of the vocational element of Jewish identity is in conflict with Paul's vision, and Nanos, who sees in 2:17–29 a hypothetical/fictive Jewish teacher of non-Jews who does not practice what he preaches.[90] Combining these last two proposals, I suggest that an ideal in-Christ Jewish teacher of gentiles is in view, although I do not fully discount the idea that the interlocutor might have been a proselyte.[91]

The dialog partner seems slightly more likely to be a Jew (Ἰουδαῖος) rather than a non-Jew, in part because Paul consistently uses Ἰουδαῖος to describe ethnic Jews. Even though the rhetorical structure constructs the person as referring to himself as a Ἰουδαῖος, thus omitting any reference to Paul's opinion about his ethnicity, it is more likely that Paul's use of the term, even in the mouth of a rhetorical interlocutor, would reflect his normal usage. The presence of "call" (ἐπονομάζω) in the clause could refer to one who has assumed Jewish identity without being a Jewish person, but it more likely refers to one who is "publicly known" to be a Jew.[92]

The views listed above all agree that 2:17–29 is constructed as a diatribe, "a type of writing that may include rhetorical questions and fictional conversations and partners."[93] This should alert readers to the hypothetical nature of the passage and discourage approaches that see here an actual individual who embodies the pattern of life described. To

---

88. Campbell, *Paul and the Creation*, 108. This at least calls into question the traditional reading of these verses as exemplified in Watson's approach (Watson, *Paul, Judaism*, 212).

89. Thiessen, "Paul's So-Called," 59. Thorsteinsson, Thiessen, and Rodríguez, "Paul's Interlocutor," 1–37.

90. Windsor, *Paul*, 162. See also Campbell, *The Deliverance of God*, 560. Nanos, "Paul's Non-Jews," 41. See also Stowers, *Rereading*, 143–58.

91. See Rodríguez (*If You Call*, 50 n. 12) for a discussion of the way to actually describe this hypothetical character and the confusing nature of these labels.

92. Nanos, "Paul's Non-Jews," 41.

93. Whittle, "Jubilees," 46. Novenson, "The Self-Styled," 139.

understand the rhetorical interlocutor as Jewish, however, does not mean that Paul has turned his attention away from his gentile audience. He is addressing an important point for gentile identity in Christ: the way a continuing valuation of Jewish identity provides an important model for their "obedience of faithfulness."[94] Paul's diatribe relies on a salient rhetorical figure, a Jewish teacher of gentiles, who functions as a model for one vision of embodiment for in-Christ gentiles.

Matthew Thiessen, however, thinks the problem for Paul here is that the "so-called Jew" has transitioned from gentile to Jew. Thus, in his post-supersessionist reading, Thiessen discerns a gentile, rather than a Jewish, interlocutor, an identity performance Paul thinks is impossible. Why? For Thiessen, Paul maintains that for a male to be considered Jewish, eighth-day circumcision is required (Phil 3:5). When read in concert with Jubilees, as Thiessen does, Rom 2:17–29 suggests that the very act of being circumcised later in life breaks the Jewish law.[95] For him, gentiles are not to be circumcised, since the act itself fails to keep the Jewish law of circumcision as regards its timing.[96] However, Thiessen's thesis is problematic because, as noted by Cohen, "not a single ancient Jewish text says that a gentile cannot convert to Judaism because of missing eighth-day circumcision."[97] Also, the individuals in view in the passages cited by Thiessen, including in Jubilees, are Israelites, not gentiles. While Thiessen's approach fits within the post-supersessionist framework, some might suggest that it indirectly undermines Jewish identity by restricting

94. Elliott, *Arrogance*, 45–46.

95. Thiessen, *Contesting*, 71–78. Jubilees can refer to circumcision metaphorically (1:23). The focus of Thiessen is Jub. 15:14, "The male who has not been circumcised— the flesh of whose foreskin has not been circumcised on the eighth day—that person will be uprooted from his people because he has violated my covenant." This is a restatement of Gen 17:14; while there are debates about the textual tradition as it relates to "on the eighth day," it seems likely that the author of Jubilees does not expand on but transmits what was in 17:14 (see also 17:12 and Lev 12:3).

96. Thiessen, *Paul*, 93. This suggests a connection between Gal 5:3 and Rom 2:17–29. Those individuals who undergo circumcision are obligated to keep the entirety of the law (Jub. 15:33). Deuteronomy 24:8–9 similarly references a specific law in a way that stands for the entirety of it. The same idea applies to Gal 6:13, "For even those who receive circumcision do not themselves keep the law." These gentiles who undergo circumcision break the Jewish law, i.e., according to Thiessen (*Paul*, 96), "the timing of the rite, is being broken at the very instant that they undergo circumcision."

97. Cohen, "Review," 380.

it; gentile converts were already being incorporated into the Jewish nation (see the story of King Izates of Adiabene).[98]

Thiessen's discussion of Rom 2:25–27 advances the discussion of the phrase "your circumcision becomes uncircumcision" beyond the traditional reading, but is this new reading convincing? According to Thiessen, the timing of the rite renders the gentile's circumcision a transgression and catches Paul's interlocutor in a trap: he preaches what he himself does not keep.[99] Thiessen's focus on timing, however, takes literally what is meant to be taken figuratively. This phrase does not indicate that gentile converts were not considered Jews. Nor, as in traditional readings, is Paul's point that since no one can keep the commandments perfectly, then we should give them up wholesale, which would imply that circumcision no longer has value for Paul.[100] Thiessen is correct to note that the logic of 2:21–22 focuses on one who preaches against certain actions but then continues to engage in them. Its rhetoric is not designed to discourage law observance. However, Thiessen then goes on to assert that Paul's statement that "Circumcision indeed is of value if you obey the law" (2:25a) also addresses the specific issue of the timing of the circumcision. Thiessen then concludes, "circumcision is of value, if one follows the entirety of the law which pertains to circumcision."[101] He helpfully focuses the discussion of the "circumcision" that has actually become "uncircumcision" on the legislations pertaining to the rite, not to the generic inability of humanity to keep the law perfectly.[102]

While Thiessen is helpful in shifting the focus away from the traditional view of human inability, his genealogical approach to Jewish

---

98. Josephus, *Ant.* 20.17–48, 96. Nanos, "Question," 105–52. Fredriksen, *Paul*, 210. The group of Syrians who began to identify as Jews should also be highlighted here (Josephus, *J.W.* 2.463; 7.45). Nanos, "Paul's Non-Jews," 32–36. For the various approaches to Jewish patterns of gentile inclusion, see Donaldson, *Judaism and the Gentile*, 467–505.

99. Thiessen, *Paul*, 64, 67. While Thiessen's project may be called into question in regards to the genealogical approach, his description of the trap appears on target.

100. Barclay (*Paul*, 470–71) thinks that "[t]he distinctive mark of Jewish difference—male circumcision—is thus strongly relativized."

101. Thiessen, *Paul*, 65. In this way, Paul resonates with Jas 5:1–6, which does not claim that since people sin in one area that they should then stop law observance altogether. He is showing the incongruity between sexual purity and callousness towards the poor.

102. Jub. 15:33 also discusses when circumcision is and is not done in accordance with the entire law, specifically *periah*. Thiessen, *Paul*, 65.

identity would not work practically in the everyday lived experience of antiquity. Collins is also unconvinced that Paul "held a strict genealogical view of Judaism that precluded the circumcision, and thereby the conversion, of Gentiles to Judaism."[103] The texts Thiessen alludes to were not focused on gentile salvation. Thus, Collins concludes: "Paul never suggests that circumcision, and the attendant admission to the covenant people, are privileges that are denied to Gentiles."[104] So, Thiessen's approach, while an improvement on the traditional reading, requires revision as it relates to Paul's genealogical thinking about Jewish identity and the (im)possibility of proselyte conversion. Paul himself could conceive of gentile Judaizing, i.e., a gentile converting to Judaism (Gal 2:11–14).[105]

Instead of gentile salvation, Paul needs to clarify for his gentile audience the importance of the continuation of the Jewish and gentile identity distinctions within the Christ-movement. He does this in 2:25 by highlighting the continuing benefit of circumcision for Jews: "Circumcision indeed is of value if you obey the law; but if you break the law, your circumcision has become uncircumcision." Circumcision and Torah praxis are connected to Jewish identity, and a lack of observance of Torah and uncircumcision are linked to gentile identity. However, as Rudolph notes, "Circumcision is incomplete without the circumcised life."[106] Paul never explicitly teaches that Jews were to cease circumcising their children; rather, he thinks that "circumcision is indeed of value" (2:25a). There do seem to have been allegations that Paul taught against Jews continuing to circumcise in the social orbit of his mission (Acts 21:21).[107] Paul, however, never called for an end to circumcision as an ongoing expression of Jewish covenantal identity. His continued use of

---

103. Collins, *The Invention of Judaism*, 173.

104. Collins, *The Invention of Judaism*, 173.

105. Gal 5:2–3, 11–12; 6:12–13 are passages Nanos ("Paul's Non-Jews," 29) points to for evidence that Paul thought gentiles could become proselytes. "To Judaize," according to Nanos ("Paul's Non-Jews," 33 n. 17), did not refer to the way Jews sought "to persuade non-Jews" but "was used to refer to the actions of non-Jews when they adopt Jewish behavior or become Jews."

106. Rudolph, *A Jew to the Jews*, 74. This is part of the "choice" highlighted above with regard to Jewish identity. This will be seen further in the later discussion of Rom 14:14, 20 beginning on page 212.

107. Romans 3:8 may highlight an accusation leveled against Paul's mission praxis evident in Rome. Garroway (*Paul's Gentile-Jews*, 75, 103) connects this verse with 6:1, 15. He also points to charges of antinomianism hinted at in 3:31 and 7:1. This at least reminds interpreters of the everyday lived experience of those in Rome.

the terms "circumcision" and "uncircumcision" as social identity labels suggests some sort of continuing functionality and salience for social categorization for him.[108] He rejected the forced circumcision of in-Christ gentiles, but not because he rejected the idea that gentile conversion was possible, rather, because it undermined God's oneness and the agency of faith(fullness) (3:30). His rejection of circumcision for gentiles should also not be conflated with the forbidding of this rite or making it a matter of indifference within the Jewish community.[109] As seen above, his instructions were the opposite (1 Cor 7:18). For Paul, circumcision has continuing value. In Rom 2:25 he writes, "Circumcision indeed is of value if you obey the law," and in response to an anticipated query from his audience concerning the ongoing value of Jewish identity and circumcision in Rom 3:1–2, his answer is that there are many advantages for them.[110] As with his discussions of the law, circumcision is never a lone actor in Paul's letters.[111] If there is contextualization going on, it is to bring to the fore the role of "keeping God's commands" (1 Cor 7:19).[112] This, however, is not all that new. Deuteronomy 10:16 says something similar: "Circumcise, then, the foreskin of your heart, and do not be stubborn any longer."[113] Paul does not have in view gentiles being circumcised; that is only for Jews. Rather, he wants the gentiles to see in his example the way

108. This will be discussed further in chapter 9 beginning on page 221.

109. Dunn ("The Jew Paul," 209) remarks concerning Paul: "he never called for Jews to remove the marks of their circumcision, and there is no suggestion that he ever attempted epispasm himself; Paul should never be lumped with the Hellenizers of the Maccabean period."

110. Thorsteinsson (*Paul's Interlocutor*, 236–38) addresses the way the third-person plurals function here in regards to the way Jewish identity is taken away from the gentile interlocutor. Those structural indicators are important, as Thorsteinsson indicates, but they would need to be reread in light of the Jewish interlocutor argued for here. Nanos, "Paul's Non-Jews," 44.

111. Dunn ("The Jew Paul," 209) thinks his concern is "the realization of what the circumcision rite symbolized, the circumcision of the heart (Romans 2:28–29, the Spirit enabling true worship of God)."

112. Thiessen (*Paul*, 9) thinks 1 Cor 7:19 should serve as an organizing hermeneutic for discussions of the continuation of Jewish identity. Circumcision and uncircumcision in this verse relate to social identities, in which case what matters is "only keeping the commandments that God requires of each group of people."

113. Hultgren (*Paul's Letter*, 130 n. 135) lists the following citations: "Philo, *Spec. Leg.* 1.66.305; *Migr.* 16.92; *Jub.* 1:23; 1 QS 5.5; 1QpHab 11.13; 4Q504.4.3.11. Similarly in 1QH 18.20 there is reference to circumcision of the ear, and in 1 QS 5.6–7 the circumcision to be performed is of the evil inclination." See also Jer 4:4; 9:25–26; Ezek 4:4–9.

their bodies should be, according to Nanos, "dedicated to doing God's will in the way that the person with a circumcised body should be."[114]

Jewish Identity and "Real" Circumcision: A Christian Identity?

Romans 2:28–29 does not remove "circumcision" as a marker of covenantal identity for Jews nor does it transfer this identity to in-Christ gentiles. However, this is exactly what Watson argues. He contends that in these verses, "the uncircumcised Gentiles who obey the law are true Jews and truly circumcised, in a spiritual sense."[115] Has Paul really, as traditional interpreters assume, replaced physical circumcision with spiritual circumcision? Paul writes:

> For a person is not a Jew (Ἰουδαῖος) who is one outwardly, nor is true circumcision (περιτομή) something external and physical. Rather, a person is a Jew who is one inwardly, and real circumcision is a matter of the heart (καρδίας)—it is spiritual and not literal (γράμματι). Such a person receives praise not from others but from God.[116]

Here Paul clarifies for his gentile audience aspects of Jewish embodiment of Jewish identity in a manner similar to Israel's prophetic tradition. He commends, according to Watson, the expression of Jewish identity "inwardly," i.e., a "circumcision . . . of the heart," rather than "outwardly," i.e., "circumcision" as it is practiced in general.[117] These two verses, then, have been used to argue that Paul disrupts the meaning of this central marker of Jewish identity and thus enlarges the definition of who may be

---

114. Nanos, "Paul's Non-Jews," 46. A person embodying Jewish identity in a way consistent with Deut 10:16 then served as a model for the way a gentile person embodies the social implications of the good news (Deut 10:16; 30:6; Jer 4:4; 9:25–26; 38:33; Ezek 44:7; 1QS 5.5; Philo, *Spec. Laws* 1.6; QG 3.46–52). Paul's approach to imitation is not one that gentiles follow precisely, since Paul himself remains Torah-observant; it is a pattern of life which in-Christ gentiles follow in the context of different social expectations (1 Cor 4:16; 11:1; 1 Thess 1:6; 2:14).

115. Watson, *Paul, Judaism*, 215.

116. It is important to note that "true" and "real" are added to the NRSV and are not found in the manuscript tradition. Campbell, *Paul and the Creation*, 104–9.

117. Nanos ("Question," 108 n. 5) points out that "[c]ircumcision/foreskinned is also used by Paul and other Jews in an obviously non-literal sense to refer to the state of the heart (Lev. 26:41; Deut. 10:16; Jer. 4:4; Jub. 1:22–24; Rom. 2:29)." Fitzmyer (*Romans*, 323) reminds interpreters that "the real Jew is an Israelite with a circumcised heart."

described as a Jew to include non-Jewish Christ-followers.[118] According to this view, the physical descendants of Abraham, Isaac, and Jacob have been replaced as God's elect people.[119]

The universalistic "Christian" identity reading from Watson is unconvincing, however. First, he assumes a generic "Christian" is in view in 2:26–27, i.e., the uncircumcised law-keeper. Windsor is likely correct to identify this hypothetical person as a "Gentile synagogue adherent," one who is generally following a Jewish pattern of life recognizable within the first-century Jewish community.[120] Second, he argues for a wholesale and radical redefinition of the social identity labels Jew ('Iουδαῖος) and circumcision (περιτομή) that would hardly be likely at this early stage of the Christ-movement and is also foreign to Paul's literary practice elsewhere.[121] Third, the presence of "then" (οὖν) in 3:1 suggests continuity between 3:1–2 and 2:28–29. Thus, a focus on a generic "Christian" identity in verses 28–29 would interrupt the flow of the section which moves forward into 3:2 and provides details concerning the continuing advantage of Jewish identity.[122] Finally, if the "circumcision . . . of the heart" referred to in 2:29 relates to in-Christ gentiles, then Paul would be an unvirtuous reader of Israel's scriptural tradition since those texts connect circumcision, observance of Torah, and the "heart" (Deut 10:16; 30:6).

---

118. Moo (*Romans*, 175), because he sees only a soteriological focus here, thinks that "Paul goes beyond any first-century Jewish viewpoint in suggesting that physical circumcision is no longer required and in implicitly applying the term 'Jew' to those who were not ethnically Jews." See Vlach, *Has the Church*, 129, for a listing of other interpreters whom he thinks hold to the position that gentiles become Jews in some way for Paul. See also Rydelnik, "Relationship," 19.

119. Wright, *Paul and the Faithfulness of God*, 1432.

120. Windsor, *Paul*, 177, 181. Debates about whether gentile synagogue adherents should be circumcised are evident in Philo, *QE* 2.2; *Spec. Laws* 1.51; *Migration* 89–93. Windsor understands the connection here to be between "the physically uncircumcised yet spiritually circumcised state of both kinds of people." Josephus, *Ant.* 20.34–50 also highlights an ongoing debate over whether uncircumcised gentiles may be viewed as observing Torah.

121. Universalistic Christian interpreters often point to Phil 3:3 as counter evidence. See Zoccali, *Reading Philippians*, 88, 134. These interpreters also see contrary evidence in Col 2:11. See Windsor, *Reading Ephesians and Colossians*, 211–14 on that verse. It would seem that the conditions for such a radical redefinition do not emerge until the time of Ignatius; by then Paul could be viewed as one who did not have an appreciation for Judaism. See Campbell, *Paul and the Creation*, 79–83.

122. Windsor, *Paul*, 183.

In-Christ gentiles, since they are still loosely affiliated with the broader synagogue community, need guidance for the way they should view Jewish identity.[123] Paul offers this guidance not to remove them from the synagogue, as Watson argues, but to help them understand the way their affiliation with Jews remains (or should remain) salient within the Christ-movement.[124] In 2:28, Paul draws on the social identity labels Jew (Ἰουδαῖος) and circumcision (περιτομή) to instruct his gentile readers that there are certain public practices that differ for Jews and gentiles within the semi-public synagogue space. He is not disparaging these practices but contextualizing them. Within "the congregations of the nations" (αἱ ἐκκλησίαι τῶν ἐθνῶν), the congregation aligned with the Pauline Christ-movement (Rom 16:4), "public" identity markers are embodied in an others-oriented way (Rom 15:1).

Certain aspects of Jewish identity are defined inwardly or more precisely based on one's motives (2:29). This is not to say that Paul formulates a binary relationship between the outward and the inward here. Nanos points in the correct direction; Paul's focus is on "the motive for undertaking the outward behavior, based upon the conviction that the one who undertakes to teach others" ought to "conduct himself according to that which is taught."[125] The internal motive in view could be the ongoing commitment to Israel's vocation among the nations and the way this vocation is embodied as a unique calling for an individual Jew among non-Jews. The teaching role for this person should reflect their internal dedication to God as one set apart for the sake of the nations, the reality to which the sign of their circumcision points.

This then helps to explain the next phrase concerning circumcision: "it is spiritual and not literal" (2:29).[126] It is difficult to determine if the

---

123. Paul expects that the Roman Christ-followers will continue to relate closely to the Jewish community in Rome, especially if they align themselves with the Pauline Christ-movement (Rom 16:4).

124. Watson, *Paul, Judaism*, 215. Windsor, *Paul*, 184. Nanos, "Paul's Non-Jews," 39–40.

125. Nanos, "Paul's Non-Jews," 49.

126. Nanos ("Paul's Non-Jews," 49) points out that this is a well-known trope that builds on "the difference between legal credentials and the spirit of the ideals to which those credentials should point." Epictetus, *Diatr.* 4.8.17–20. Stowers (*Rereading*, 144–50) lists other philosophers who work with this trope. He recognizes that Paul is not a philosopher but suggests that these ideas still influence him in 2:17–29. Mininger (*Uncovering*, 257–58) concludes that the context of 2 Corinthians 3 is too remote from Rom 2:29 to be of much value.

referent for "spiritual" here is the human spirit or the Spirit of God, or both.[127] If it is the human spirit, then the connection with heart circumcision makes sense. If it relates to the agency of God's Spirit, then Paul connects the two in a way similar to Odes of Solomon 11:1–3. It seems slightly more likely the agency of the Spirit is in view, but, as noted by Stowers, this does not need to presuppose "Christians who have been suddenly and without explanation thrust into the discourse."[128] Stowers continues to reflect on what Jews would have known: the highest value of the circumcised life is the way it points to a life lived in service to God.[129] So, Paul crafts a rhetorical set piece to remind in-Christ gentiles of the importance of dedicated service to God. However, as noted by Nanos, differentiation remains: "these non-Jews should dedicate their bodies and hearts to faithful service to God, even though the circumcision of body— and thus the circumcision of heart—does not apply (literally, and thus figuratively) to themselves."[130] So, in 2:17–29, Paul has helped in-Christ gentiles to understand the continuing significance of circumcision for Jewish covenantal identity and the way the circumcised life can serve as a model for their life of "obedient faithfulness" in Rome (Rom 1:5, 11–12).

The Continuing Worth of Jewish Circumcision in Romans 3:1–2

Sanders long ago thought that Paul relegated two crucial pillars of Judaism into oblivion, i.e., Israel's election and the Mosaic law. However, Romans 3:1–2 suggests the opposite.[131] Here Paul defends Jewish identity and circumcision: "Then what advantage has the Jew? Or what is the value of circumcision? Much in every way. First (πρῶτον), the Jews were

127. A third alternative would be to see the referent here as both the human spirit and God's Spirit since there is ambiguity with regard to the term πνεῦμα; Paul has previously use the term with each of the two referents (cf. Rom 1:4, 9). In this third approach, the promise of the Spirit is linked to a renewal of the human spirit (Ezek 36:36–37). See Middendorf, *Romans*, 212.

128. Stowers, *Rereading*, 155.

129. Stowers, *Rereading*, 155.

130. Nanos, "Paul's Non-Jews," 51.

131. Jewett (*Paul*, 37–38) thinks Sanders's view is problematic: "Paul explicitly affirms Israel's election in Rom. 3:1–2, 9:4–5, and 11:1–11, and defends the legitimacy of the Torah in Rom. 7:7, 9:4, and 13:8–10, and of Torah obedience among Christian believers in Rom. 14:1—15:6. Yet there is overwhelming evidence in support of Sanders's basic contention that Paul criticized Jewish religionists who rejected the gospel of Jesus as the Christ."

entrusted with the oracles of God (τὰ λόγια τοῦ θεοῦ)." This suggests an ongoing expectation for circumcision as a marker of Jewish identity.[132] The starkness of this statement is highlighted when compared to Paul's earlier argument in Gal 5:2, "Look: I, Paul, say to you that if you accept circumcision (περιτέμνησθε), Christ will be of no advantage to you." As highlighted above, Paul's statements in Romans should be read primarily through his rule in all the congregations in 1 Cor 7:17–19 and not through the polemical setting in Galatians. If one allows Gal 5:2 to be the primary lens for understanding Rom 3:1–2, then its meaning in the context of his concerns for congruence between teaching and embodiment is overlooked. Circumcision continues to be an advantage for the Jewish people, and as noted by Nanos, the immediate answer to the question of what ongoing advantage there is for being a Jew is that the "Jews possess the Torah" (Rom 3:2).[133]

The possession of Torah was central to Jewish identity. Is it likely that, for Paul, Torah observance had become optional? Deuteronomy 26:17–19 connects fulfilling the vocation God has set forth for Israel with obeying the commands that he has given to his people. Part of this vocation is to be "a light to the nations" (Isa 49:6). Paul thus seems to refer to this vocational element of Jewish identity. Israel's vocation to draw the nations to God is made explicit through keeping Torah.

So, Paul does not dismiss the continued value of circumcision of Jews in Rom 2:25—3:2. Instead, he writes to gentiles to give them insight into the importance of the alignment between teaching and social practice. His argument also would discourage gentiles from teaching in-Christ Jews that circumcision is redundant. Israel's covenantal identity is still salient, and their vocation as "a light to the nations" has not been superseded. The purpose of this section is not to argue that gentiles can become true Jews through some sort of identity transformation, but that they should seek to live a life of "obedient faithfulness" *as gentiles*, while at the same time to recognize that Jewish identity continues to have value for Jews as they embody their vocation among the nations, just as Paul was doing among them (Rom 1:5).[134]

132. Tatum ("To the Jew," 278) points out that "Paul uses circumcision as a *pars pro toto* for all Jewish privileges."

133. Nanos (*Mystery*, 180) also points out that the rest of the answer for this question will have to wait until Romans 9–11.

134. Nanos ("Paul and Judaism," 138 n. 55) describes it this way: "Only Jews are circumcised in order to indicate in their bodies the dedication to God of their whole

Paul Establishes the Law in Romans 3:31

One point concerning Torah found in the context of Romans 1–4 should be mentioned at this point, since it is one of Paul's more positive statements concerning its continuation. The example of Abraham, as we will see in the next chapter, is crucial for the way Paul views differing identities continuing within the Christ-movement. Paul's argument concerning Abraham in Galatians 3:6–18 is recast in Romans to address issues of boasting. Often, in Galatians 2:18, Paulinist interpreters assume that Paul has torn down Torah; however, the broader context suggests connections with 2:1–10, and the Jerusalem agreement from Acts 15. In that configuration, he is accusing Peter of going back on the agreement, and if he follows Peter's lead, Paul too would become "a transgressor." So, we should not preclude the idea that Paul thinks he upholds Torah in Galatians' (3:21), in which case, what he says in Romans 3:31 agrees with what he writes in Galatians. Tatum is close to the mark when he points out that Paul establishes Torah in Rom 3:31 "by showing that it endures in the eschatological community."[135] This is often missed because interpreters assume that Torah has been rendered redundant now that the Spirit has come. However, the law never functions alone. As Tatum concisely summarizes: "Distinguishing the Torah as received by the pre-justified flesh (ὁ νόμος τῶν ἔργων) from the Torah as received by the justified believers who have received the Spirit (ὁ νόμος πίστεως), Paul defends the Torah itself."[136]

In Rom 3:31, Paul writes: "Do we nullify the law through faith? May it never be! On the contrary, we establish the law." This statement would appear to offer unequivocal support for the continuation of Jewish identity within the Christ-movement.[137] However, in light of Paul's argument begun in Rom 3:21 (especially its formulation in 3:28), what he means by this statement continues to vex interpreters.[138] Barclay's widely discussed essay, "Do We Undermine the Law?" ultimately concludes that Paul does,

---

person, to living according to the precepts God has given for right living, and not merely to teaching them to others. Only they can become in that sense 'true' or 'spiritual' Jews. That identity is particular to Jews, to those of the nation Israel." The closest parallel to this embodied state for in-Christ gentiles is Rom 12:1–2. Windsor, *Paul*, 137–39.

135. Tatum, "To the Jew," 278.

136. Tatum, "To the Jew," 278.

137. See Campbell, *Paul and the Creation*, 168–69.

138. Hultgren, *Paul's Letter*, 173.

though here in 3:31, he thinks that Paul does not.[139] Wagner contends that "For Paul, the Law is rightly pursued only ἐκ πίστεως (through faith 'we establish the Law' [Rom 3:31]); only thus can Israel attain the righteousness they seek."[140] C. Thomas Rhyne argues that Paul's statement is designed to show that it is a "false inference" to conclude that "faith abolishes the law"; rather, faith "actually establishes the law" (3:31a, c). Thus, Romans 4 is not used primarily to argue for justification by faith; instead it is designed to show that Paul's gospel does not obliterate Torah.[141] Moo categorizes Rhyne's view as "especially popular" and notes that it brings to the fore the "witnessing" function of the law.[142] Rosner places 3:31 in the category of prophecy. Thus, based on his earlier arguments, "Paul abolishes the law as law-covenant, but upholds it as prophecy."[143] This function means that the law continues in its capacity to point to the salvific benefits that have accrued through Christ (1:2; 3:21, 31; 4:23–24; 16:25–26).

Rhyne's work is particularly important because he recognizes that the discussion of 3:31 is integral to the way one views the relationship between the Christ-movement and the broader Jewish community.[144] He concludes that there is discontinuity with regard to the two in soteriological inferences and continuity with regard to the way the verse attests to the eschatological appearance of the faith it alludes to. This understanding of 3:31 supports his contention that 10:4 points to Christ as the goal of the law in that "[w]henever someone receives righteousness by faith in Christ, the law's goal of righteousness is realized" and that this "represents the apex of Paul's understanding of the continuity between Judaism and Christianity."[145] Rhyne's work is helpful; however, he assumes an institutional setting at this early stage in the Christ-movement that is properly reserved for a later period. Further, the rhetorical effectiveness of Paul's argument is lost even if the degree of discontinuity highlighted

---

139. Barclay, "Undermine" 37–59; Campbell, *Unity*, 211 n. 26. I discuss Barclay's argument, which is really concerned with Romans 14–15, beginning at page 205.

140. Wagner, *Heralds*, 158.

141. Rhyne, *Faith*, 75. This is discussed beginning at page 85.

142. Moo, "The Law of Christ," 371–72. He ultimately concludes that neither 3:31 nor 8:3 "suggests the continuing relevance of the Mosaic law to believers."

143. Rosner, *Paul and the Law*, 154.

144. Rhyne, *Faith*, 117–21.

145. Rhyne, *Faith*, 120.

by Rhyne stands.[146] Paul, then, is doing what other Jewish writers were doing; he was trying to make sense of God's actions in the context of his continuing faithfulness to Israel and to clarify the social implications for both Jews and these gentiles who are now members of God's family via their union with Christ. Since Paul's primary area of mission was to the nations, his theologizing was directed to this group, but never to the exclusion of Israel.

Conclusion

Romans focuses on the formation of gentile identity in Christ. One key aspect of that social identity is the way these gentiles should view God's earlier choice in history of Israel as his covenant people. Tatum alerts readers to Paul's concern with the nature of continuing Jewish privilege in the letter to Romans. Taking that argument as our point of departure, we suggested that part of the problem Paul sought to address was an early form of what later became Marcionism. This gentile boasting was problematic since the subgroup they were disparaging actually supported them in their spiritual vitality. We then took a brief look at some of the key views of Paul's phrase "to the Jew first" and argued that this phrase might best be understood as a way for him to let these gentiles (and any Jews who might overhear the letter) know that he expected Jewish identity to continue within the Christ-movement as an integral part of gentile identity in Christ. This new social identity is not a stand-alone one for Paul; it is to be entangled with Israel. The two distinction texts in Rom 3:22 and 10:12 were discussed and found not to be arguing for the erasure of existing identities. The way Paul makes this concrete for his audience is by discussing circumcision in a general fashion. Though often Paul is thought to be redefining Jewish identity and handing it over to in-Christ gentiles through circumcision (in 2:28—3:2), it was suggested rather that he was showing his gentile audience that the circumcised life still has relevance as a pattern for the embodiment of faithfulness to the God of Israel. Finally, by showing gentiles that Jewish identity continues to be salient in the eschatological community via circumcision for Jews and that there is also a continued vocational election for Israel, Paul presents an approach that does not disparage but rather upholds Torah (3:31). However, as mentioned earlier, Abraham is central to Jewish identity, and

146. See Nanos, "Question," 150–51.

Paul's inclusion of gentiles among his descendants seems to suggest that he has radically redefined Jewish identity. Therefore, it is to this figure we turn to next. In the next chapter, we will address the question: Has Israel lost Abraham as its founding father?

3

The Fatherhood of Abraham

Introduction

ONE OF THE MORE contested portions of Romans is chapter 4. Almost each subsection has been the focus of key debates between the varying perspectives on Paul.[1] However, for the purposes of this book only one question will be pursued: does Paul's argument in 4:11b–12, 13, 16 indicate that those in Christ who now share in the heritage and promises of Abraham have displaced the Jewish people as Abraham's seed?[2] The increase of gentiles within the Christ-movement precipitated several discursive moments for those leading it.[3] For example, there was a need to address whether this new identity node was distinct from Israel's identity.[4]

---

1. See Schliesser, *Abraham's Faith*, 222–39, for a discussion of some of these as well as his suggestion to organize the primary issues around the ideas of "faith" (4:1–8, 19–25) and "fatherhood" (4:9–18).

2. Isaiah 51:2 assumes Abraham's paternity: "Look to Abraham your father and to Sarah who bore you; for he was but one when I called him, but I blessed him and made him many." Similarly, Josephus contends that Abraham is the father of the Jews (*Ant.* 1.158; 11.169; 14.255) and even sees him as their forefather in a way similar to Rom 4:1 (*J.W.* 5.380). Josephus further connects Abraham with the start of Hebrew ethnicity (*Ant.* 1.122–53, see esp. 1.148–49).

3. Discursive moments or modalities are often compared with coercive ones. These are often implicit in one another, i.e., that which constitutes and that which determines social phenomena interact. See further on the dynamics of power in Paul specifically, Ehrensperger, *Paul and the Dynamics*, 24–33. For more general discussion, see Scobey, "Exterminating," 18–19. It is not the case, however, that reliance on discursive moments results in signifiers that simply float and change meaning from one situation to a new articulation. *Pace* Marttila, *Culture*, 46.

4. Person identity nodes are often used in the field of cognitive psychology as a

In-Christ gentiles were following the Messiah of Israel, worshipping alongside ethnic Jews, and being enculturated into the Jewish symbolic universe by their teachers.[5] It was obvious to some Christ-followers that gentiles were a type of proselyte to Judaism and thus should identify socially as such.[6] However, Paul was not convinced by this argument. For him, the social implications of his gospel were such that gentiles in Christ remained gentiles.[7] This meant that they were not Israel, or Israel redefined, but gentile worshippers of God's Messiah.[8] These in-Christ gentiles would need a cognitive transformation so they could start to view the world through another founding narrative (Rom 4:1; 12:1–2).[9] They would need to understand and embody God's promises to Israel as those promises related uniquely to them, but they would not in this

way to conceive of the processes associated with recognition of the familiar. Paul may be seen as one providing new information concerning Abraham so that he becomes familiar (again) to his audience through the use of his biographical information (Eysenck, *Principles*, 87–90).

5. Cromhout, "Israelite Ethnic Identity," 530–42.

6. Donaldson (*Paul*, 207, 226, 247) rejects the eschatological pilgrimage tradition argued for in this work and favors rather a gentile proselytism model for understanding Paul's mission. Gadenz (*Called*, 304) has critiqued Donaldson's argument: "First, the evidence for a connection between Jewish proselytism of Gentiles and Christian mission to the Gentiles is weak. Secondly, the upshot of seeing Jewish proselytism of Gentiles as the background for Paul's understanding of the Gentile mission is that Gentiles become 'full members of a redefined Israel.'"

7. On the definition of these social implications, see page 82. Gentiles remain gentiles because of the influence of the eschatological pilgrimage tradition and Paul's concern that the One God is seen as the God of *all*, not just of Israel.

8. Donaldson, *Paul*, 247: "Gentiles . . . share in righteousness and salvation by becoming full members of a redefined Israel." Dunn (*Theology*, 507–8) argues that Christian identity understood properly requires the movement to understand itself as "Israel." See further Campbell, "Covenantal Theology," 48–51, for a nuanced discussion in which Israel maintains the covenantal relationship while the gentiles share in the blessings of the covenant. With regard to messianic expectations, see Novenson, *Christ*, 149–60, who shows, with regard to Romans specifically, that Paul does not repudiate the category of Messiah. See further Ehrensperger, "Pauline," 201–9, on the supersessionism of the colored sheep in 1 En. 90:37–38.

9. See on this Kamudzandu, *Abraham Our Father*, 47, who contends that the use of Abraham is in response to social identifications with the *Aeneid*. Wright (*Paul and the Faithfulness of God*, 342, 400) rightly picks up on the worldview construction issues here, though again overstates the discontinuity with regard to Paul's ancestral traditions, but rightly picks up on the discontinuity with regard to the Roman Empire. See Tucker, *You Belong to Christ*, 89–128, on Paul's challenges to key aspects of Roman social identity generally.

process take over the identity of historic Israel (Rom 4:11–13). Paul resists referring to in-Christ gentiles as Israel; rather, they are members of God's empire (Rom 14:17).[10] The kingdom of God, not Israel, is the one organizing rubric for Jews and gentiles in Christ.[11] In this kingdom, ethnic animosity (and ethnicity-based worth) has been overcome, but ethnic distinctions remain salient.[12] This is the difficult rhetorical position Paul finds himself in, and his difficult argument results from trying to maintain both the particular and the universalistic implications of the gospel.[13] Donaldson, however, chooses another path; he is convinced that Paul thinks broadly in the "no distinction" category (Rom 3:22; 10:12; Gal 3:28). Yet, as will become evident, for Paul there is a continuing dif-

10. Scholars often highlight Rom 2:28–29a, 9:6; Gal 6:16b; and Eph 2:12 to argue that Israel's identity has been overtaken by identity in Christ. Longenecker, *Epistle to the Romans*, 490: "all true believers in Jesus, whatever their ethnicity, are 'the Israel of God' (Gal 6:16b)." See Starling, *Not My People*, 175, and Thornhill, *The Chosen People*, 179–84, on Ephesians 2; Abasciano, *Romans 9:1–9*, on 9:6. Wright (*Paul and the Faithfulness of God*, 362) cites 2:28–29a as a "breathtaking" statement that results in a "redefinition of God's people." Outside of Paul, 1 Pet 2:4–10 is often noted; cf. Achtemeier, *1 Peter*, 69; Horrell, *Becoming Christian*, 133–63. While it might seem like some apostolic texts draw on Israel's missional role (e.g., 1 Pet 2:4–10), that does not necessarily imply that the church has replaced Israel without remainder or that the church (Jew and gentile) is the true Israel. For one discussion of the way gentile identity is transformed, but in a nuanced way, see Hunt, "Alien and Degenerate Milk." Part of the issue is that the audience for 1 Peter is assumed to be gentile, but that assumption is being increasingly called into question. See Liebengood, *1 Peter*, forthcoming. The "commonwealth of Israel" in Ephesians 2 is the one place where a closeness of identity may be in view, but the "commonwealth" delimiter creates space where existing identities continue. See Tucker and Koessler, *All Together*, 142–47.

11. Cf. Vlach, "Kingdom," 60; Vickers, "Kingdom," 60–61.

12. Gathercole (*Where*, 226) offers one understanding of the relationship between boasting understood as "confidence in vindication, or justification" (Sir 31:5, 10) and Abraham's example. However, Gathercole assumes that salvific concerns are paramount in Paul's argument. They are not excluded, but the vocational element would temper some of his findings. Furthermore, the participatory category of union with Christ brings to the fore identity issues that seem to be a more acute concern in Romans 4.

13. On the sometimes "convoluted" argument in Romans, see Grieb, *Story*, 16–17. However, Tobin (*Paul's Rhetoric*, 89) suggests the focus should not be on "themes or subject matter" rather "in terms of issues between himself and the Roman Christian audience he was addressing." This then provides more clarity for Paul's argument. Campbell ("Romans III," 261, 64) suggests that argumentative clarity emerges from a focus on Rom 3:21–26 and its resolution in Romans 9–11. His example for the way Abraham fits into this structure is particularly useful in terms of a rationale for Paul's argument.

ference to be seen, though one in which existing identities may be reprioritized contextually.[14]

This understanding of Paul's approach to identity formation and maintenance seems to go against his argument in Romans 4.[15] When addressing the topic of Abraham's universal paternity in this chapter does Paul have anything to say about whether Abraham continues to be the forefather of the Jewish nation? Some supersessionist interpreters think that Israel's relationship to Abraham has changed dramatically in the new covenant and thus contend that he may no longer be claimed as the father of Israel according to the flesh. Thus, despite Jer 31:31, Israel now is made up of Jews and gentiles in Christ. E. P. Sanders exemplifies this approach. For him, Paul's "thought is informed by the conception of 'true Israel.' . . . [T]here is substantial evidence that Paul considered Christians to be 'true Israel.'"[16] In his approach, Israel according to the flesh has lost its covenantal identity and its connection with Abraham: "Paul thought that those who 'turned to the Lord' (2 Cor. 3:16) were the sole inheritors of the promises to Abraham."[17] Michael Cranford (arguing against Cranfield) is another example: "Cranfield states that we must be careful not to conclude from v. 12 that Jews who do not have faith are in any way excluded from the covenant, though that is certainly the implication of the verse, as well as of the section as a whole. Abraham is the forefather of all who have faith and therefore not the forefather of those who do not, even if they are his descendants κατὰ σάρκα."[18] An answer such as Cranford's borders on hard supersessionism and Sanders's on soft supersessionism.[19] For both, the implication of Romans 4 is that

14. Donaldson, "Paul," 298 n. 38. *Pace* Campbell, "Differentiation," 157–68.

15. Esler (*Conflict*, 184–85) rightly picks up this nuance. Contra Boyarin, *A Radical Jew*, 144; Watson, *Paul, Judaism*, 259–68.

16. Sanders, *Paul, the Law*, 173–74. Sanders, *Paul: The Apostle's Life*, 565–66.

17. Sanders, *Paul, the Law*, 175–76. Wright (*Paul and the Faithfulness of God*, 425), in discussing baptism as an identity-definer for those in Christ and the putative setting aside of circumcision, concludes: "Identity 'according to the flesh' is set aside: you and your community are no longer defined by who your parents were." The circumcision/baptism correlation, however, is open to question and thus also his conclusion based on the previous premise. For a critique of a position similar to Wright's see Cottrell, *Romans*, 164–66.

18. Cranford, "Abraham," 85.

19. Novak ("Covenant," 66–67) suggests hard supersessionism indicates that "the old covenant is dead" and that "Jews by their sins, most prominently their sin of rejecting Jesus as the Messiah, have forfeited any covenantal status." This is in contrast to soft

the Jews are excluded from the covenant and have lost the right to claim Abraham as their forefather in any embodied sense. This brings readers to the heart of the debate over supersessionism. As we will see, it seems more likely that the Jewish people continue to be in a covenant relationship with God. The Abraham discourse occurs in an ongoing debate within the Jesus-movement, which itself is still nested within the broader Jewish community, concerning who is more faithful to God. This debate implicitly introduces the remnant idea that Paul will develop in Romans 9. It also points to the larger question: is Jesus really Israel's Messiah?[20] In this chapter, we will focus primarily on three interpretive moves that contribute to a supersessionist reading of Rom 4:11b–12, 13, and 16. We will discuss: (a) whether Israel according to the flesh has lost its founding father, Abraham; (b) if the land promises have been taken up and fulfilled in Christ without remainder; and (c) whether there are differing ways that Abraham informs the identity of Jews and gentiles in Christ.

Has Israel Lost Its Founding Father Abraham?

Does Paul think that only those in Christ have a claim on Abraham's paternity? Is Abraham now properly only the father of those who trust Christ? This question emerges from Rom 4:11–12, where Paul writes, "and he [Abraham] received the sign of circumcision, a seal of the righteousness of the faith which he had while uncircumcised, so that he might be the father of all who believe without being circumcised, that righteousness might be credited to them, and the father of circumcision to those who not only are of the circumcision, but who also follow in the steps of the faith of our father Abraham which he had while uncircumcised." These verses seem to indicate that faith and not human ancestry is determinative. In that case, both Jews and gentiles may be viewed as his children as long as they are characterized by faith. In the traditional reading of Romans 4, Paul makes two other interpretive moves that reinforce a putative replacement reading of Abraham's

---

supersessionism that "does not assert that God terminated the covenant of Exodus-Sinai with the Jewish people." Jews that have not accepted Jesus's messianic claims are "out of step" with what God is doing but have not "forfeited any covenantal status."

20. See Rom 9:5. On the different answers to this question, see Novenson, *Christ*, 150–51; Wright, *Paul and the Faithfulness of God*, 405, 839, on Israel's "representative Messiah;" and Barclay, *Paul*, 522, 529. See Rom 2:28–29 for the intra-Jewish debate idea.

fatherhood for Israel. First, since Abraham existed before the Mosaic Torah, it allows Paul to decouple Torah observance and righteousness. In this configuration, strictly keeping the commandments no longer guides a group's relationship with God. Second, on the more specific level, the one command for circumcision has also been rendered redundant. This is striking in that Abraham and his posterity were required to follow this command, but Paul finds a temporally-oriented answer to this dilemma: Abraham was rendered righteous before his circumcision; therefore there is no necessary correlation between circumcision and righteousness. Thus, it seems that Paul has rendered his ancestral tradition with its focus on Torah and circumcision inoperative and only preparatory. Jon Levenson summarizes this implication:

> The faith of Abraham the Gentile made him righteous in God's eyes even before circumcision made him into Abraham the first Jew. In Paul's theology, the community for which Abraham served as a paradigm was thus a mixed group of Gentiles and Jews, a community created by God and founded upon faith in the gospel of Christ crucified and risen from the dead. It was, in other words, the Church, and so it remains in the minds of most Christians to this day.[21]

One thing should be noted concerning Levenson's claim: these statements concerning Torah and circumcision apply properly to *gentiles, not Jews*. For Paul, gentiles in Christ are to continue to identify socially as gentiles, and the same applies to in-Christ Jews (see 1 Cor 7:17–24).

Gentile and Jewish Paternity

Abraham's role as father of in-Christ gentiles does not remove him from the fatherhood of Israel according to the flesh. Käsemann highlights this by pointing out that the "roughness" of 4:11b is "softened" in 4:12: "As often, Paul hastens to qualify an exaggerated statement. An ongoing relation of the patriarch to Judaism is now acknowledged. In fact, the apostle is concerned to be able to call Abraham also the father of the circumcision, since any other course would take the promise away from Israel and contest its salvation history."[22] Similarly Richard Longenecker: "what Paul is doing here in 4:11b–12 is not attempting to rob Judaism either

---

21. Levenson, *Inheriting*, 7.
22. Käsemann, *Romans*, 116.

of Abraham or of circumcision—that is, neither to discredit Abraham's fatherhood of the Jewish people nor to dismiss circumcision as a valid religious rite—but rather, to insist that without one's possession of the faith of Abraham, his patriarchal status and his circumcision are without meaning for the Jewish people."[23] Or, more concisely Fitzmyer: "Abraham did not cease to be the forefather of circumcised Jews. But Paul insists that they are to be regarded hereafter as his offspring, when they follow in his footsteps and imitate his faith."[24] These three interpreters offer ways to rehabilitate Paul when it comes to an ongoing connection between Abraham and the nation of Israel. However, they all ultimately leave one with a sense that Paul did exactly what they were concerned he was accused of doing: redefined Israel's covenant identity in such a way that it no longer continues or reduced it to an issue of faith. In that configuration, God's faithfulness to Israel's election is properly focused on those Jews who, like Paul, have responded to the gospel in faith. This, either passively or actively, then, would exclude non-Christ-following Jews from any claim on the continued paternity of Abraham and the promises established in that covenant.

If one could establish that Paul did have non-Christ-following Jews in mind, at least notionally, then one could posit a both/and solution here rather than an either/or. This raises the specter of one of the more difficult exegetical issues in Romans 4:11b–12: how many groups does Paul have in mind? And how does one account for the repeated use of τοῖς in 4:12.

In that verse, Paul seems to describe two groups who may claim Abraham as their father. First, he mentions those Jews who are from the circumcision (τοῖς . . . ἐκ περιτομῆς), those who constitute the historic people of God, Israel. This group has not lost their "gifts" or "calling" with the advent of the Christ-event (Rom 9:5; 11:28). Second, he describes further a group that follows in the footsteps of Abraham's faith, which he expressed while still uncircumcised. This group may be properly classified as those who have come to accept the claims of the gospel that Jesus is Israel's Messiah (Rom 9:6). Interpreters, however, as mentioned above, are divided as to whether Paul has one or two groups in view. Moo thinks that only one group is slightly more likely. First, he thinks that the context points to Jewish Christ-followers who have now followed the

---

23. Longenecker, *Epistle to the Romans*, 508.

24. Fitzmyer, *Romans*, 381.

example of Abraham and believed. Second, Abraham's new family then consists of gentiles who believe as well as Jews who believe.[25] Middendorf also accepts the one-group view and offers an argument (presented in the next section) that could account for the presence of the anomalous τοῖς before στοιχοῦσιν.[26] Three arguments seem to be the main ones repeated by these interpreters: (a) the context requires one group; (b) Abraham's fatherhood is properly focused on those who believe; and (c) the presence of the repeated τοῖς, while difficult to explain, does not overrule the otherwise clear meaning, i.e., there is one group in focus.

While it is possible to see one group in 4:12, the discussion below will highlight the weaknesses of this approach: Abraham continues to be the father of Israel generally while also specifically being the father of those who have believed the claims of the gospel. The three lines of argument mentioned above will be combined in the following discussion.

Τοῖς and the Groups

The presence of the extra τοῖς suggests strongly that two groups are in view. Interpreters have long noted the anomaly in this construction and have generally set it aside as a grammatical slip, an idiomatic statement, or a word placed in the wrong location, even if two groups were in view.[27] These types of comments suggest that something is in the text that does not fit squarely into the traditional argument. The presence of τοῖς suggests that Paul does still view Abraham as the father of non-Christ-following Jews even while writing on the centrality of faith for gentiles (and Jews). This is likely another example of Paul trying to maintain the particular covenantal identity for Israel while describing his universalistic gospel (so similarly 1:16; 3:21).[28]

Middendorf rejects the two-groups approach on grammatical grounds: "the position of the first τοῖς *before* οὐκ ... μόνον grammatically rules out the possibility that the two dative plurals refer to separate

---

25. Moo, *Romans*, 270–71.

26. Middendorf, *Romans*, 1.338.

27. Cranfield, *Romans*, 1.237. Middendorf (*Romans*, 1.321 n. 28) suggests we should not see a mistake here.

28. See Livesey, *Circumcision*, 118–19. Livesey takes the second group to be "foreskinned Gentiles."

groups."[29] However, while this could be the case, syntax does not require the one-group approach. Furthermore, Middendorf's approach does not account fully for the presence of the καί in the next clause, nor does he consider that τοῖς could be construed as a dative of advantage, in which case a vocational element may be present.[30] It is more likely that Paul has two groups in view here, and thus Abraham continues to be the "father of the circumcision," understood as non-Christ-following Jews, and of those who have followed in the footsteps of Abraham's faith, a group that is not ethnically defuse but maintains their distinctness (see further below on this).[31]

The suggestion here is that there is a continuing vocational element for Jewish identity that is alluded to in 4:11b–12, an element often missed because of the assumption that only soteriology is in view in Romans 4.[32] Paying attention to the seeming superfluous τοῖς provides a grammatical basis for seeing two differentiated groups. What interpretive value accrues? Windsor offers an expansive translation based on this understanding: Abraham is "the father of circumcision—for the benefit (τοῖς), not of the circumcision only, but also for the benefit of those (τοῖς) who walk in the footsteps of the faith of our Father Abraham that he had while uncircumcised."[33] This Jewish-only vocational element of Abraham's fatherhood is not directly relevant to in-Christ gentiles, and they are not expected to embody this identity nor think that they needed to become Jewish to secure salvation (Rom 4:9–10). The circumcision of Abraham and his "according-to-the-flesh" descendants was to have salvific signifi-

---

29. Middendorf, *Romans*, 1.321. Cf. Moxnes, *Theology*, 41–45, on the presence of a polemic that accounts for the structure. Moxnes thinks that non-Christ-following Jews are in view as is being argued here; see *Theology*, 112 n. 18.

30. Windsor, *Paul*, 69; *GGBB* 142–44.

31. Livesey (*Circumcision*, 119) suggests we are dealing with gentiles here and not Jews.

32. Barclay (*Paul*, 481) sees both views: "Our task is to integrate Paul's dual portrayal of Abraham, as both *believer* in God and *father* of a multinational family." Barclay seems to be primarily interested in the way this happens while Wright (*Paul and the Faithfulness of God*, 422–24) pursues the why question. More generally on this issue, see Visscher, *Romans 4*, 231–32. Jipp ("Rereading," 218) differs from Visscher and sees more complexity with regard to the topics discussed. Zoccali, "Children," 254: "[T]he matter of how persons are brought into a proper relationship with God is inextricable from the matter of who, i.e., what group(s), is or can be in a proper relationship with God, and it is these interconnected notions that Paul is pursuing in this section of the letter."

33. Windsor, *Paul*, 83.

cance for the nations (Gen 17:11; Isa 49:6; 59:21; Rom 11:27).[34] There is an integrative salvific/vocational "seed of Abraham" relationship evident here, one that is obscured by the lack of explicit recognition of the τοῖς. This vocational element, from Paul's perspective reserved for the Jews, is seen in his embodiment of their mission to the nations. When Paul asks if God has set aside historic Israel, he describes several identity nodes related to the remnant discourse: "I ask, then, has God rejected his people? By no means! I myself am an Israelite, a descendant of Abraham (ἐκ σπέρματος Ἀβραάμ), a member of the tribe of Benjamin" (Rom 11:1; see also 2 Cor 11:22). Windsor, rightly I think, connects this with Isa 41:8, "But you, Israel, my servant (παῖς), Jacob, whom I have chosen, the offspring of Abraham (σπέρμα Αβρααμ), my friend" (see also Acts 3:25–26). The context in Isaiah connects the service of the nation Israel with the nations. They are God's servant and his representative; they show his strength through their obedience and trust in him. Isaiah describes this vocation with the group label "seed of Abraham."[35] Thus, it is plausible that Paul still sees an ongoing missional necessity for Abraham's Jewish descendants, even in a passage that highlights a new identity node for gentiles in Christ, i.e., members of the seed of Abraham.[36] This is another example of the way that Jewish particularism continues in Paul's universalistic gospel discourse and suggests, further, that historic Israel has not lost its founding father Abraham. Paul, in Rom 4:11b–12, argues that in-Christ gentiles have not taken over the vocational identity of historic Israel. Thus, Abraham continues to be the nation's father in Paul's mind. However, another significant reason that Israel's identity is thought to have been eclipsed in Romans 4 is because Paul appears to spiritualize their historical claim to the land by his universal statement that Abraham's descendants now inherit the world. Thus, the next section addresses this broader contextual argument and also alludes to some of the faith-based questions reserved for the full discussion of Rom 4:16 later in the chapter.

34. See further on the integrated nature of Israel's suffering and the reconciliation of the nations (Rom 11:15), Kinzer, *Postmissionary*, 135.

35. Windsor, *Paul*, 69. See, e.g., Isa 61:9; Ps 105:1, 6; 1 Chr 16:13–22.

36. Thus, this section is not just about gentile inclusion, although it is sometimes presented as such. Siker (*Disinheriting*, 75), e.g., after highlighting Rom 4:11–12, 17–18, concludes that for Paul the "emphasis on Gentile inclusion provides *the* constant feature in Paul's use of Abraham." I am not discounting this fully, but as will be seen on page 139 on Rom 9:24–26, gentile inclusion is better described as a secondary concern.

Has Israel Lost Its Land Promise?

In Rom 4:13 Paul writes, "For the promise to Abraham or his seed that he would be heir to the world did not come through Torah (νόμου) but through the righteousness of faith." This verse continues to receive significant attention and is crucial to the way earlier promises to historic Israel survive Paul's universalistic gospel.[37] W. D. Davies recognized the potential that reflection on the role of the land played in the parting of the ways.[38] He concluded that the Christ-movement paid little to no attention to the land in relation to God and Israel.[39] Further, he thought that "spiritualization" of the land-discourse was evident as well as a general transcendence, inherited from Judaism, of these concerns.[40] Munther Isaac prefers the term "universalized" when speaking of the land promises in contrast to Davies's "spiritualization" discourse.[41] The Abrahamic promise has been fulfilled in Christ, and this "would necessarily have important ramifications for both the people and the land."[42] Thus, for Isaac, Paul rejects territorial- and nationalistic-oriented readings of Abraham and aligns himself more closely with certain strands of diaspora Judaism that had already started to universalize the original land focus.[43] Gary Burge builds on Davies's approach and notes that 4:13 "is the only place where the apostle refers explicitly to the promises for the land given to Abraham and in this case Paul fails to refer to Judea."[44] He points out that in Genesis Abraham's inheritance was a parcel of land; however, in Romans it has been expanded to include the "world."[45] Thus, Paul's argument in the hands of Burge is that "the formula that linked Abraham

---

37. For Barclay (*Paul*, 488) the promises could not come through the law since it "leads only via transgression to wrath (4:15; cf. 3:10–20); it cannot provide the glorious future envisioned by the promise." Wright (*Paul and the Faithfulness of God*, 1002–7) recognizes the original land nexus and the early expansion of the understanding of this promise. He also, rightly, picks up on the empire-critical significance of this discourse. See further Wright, "Romans," 522. Cf. Wright. *Paul and the Faithfulness of God*, 1305–19; Barclay, *Paul*, 456 n. 15, who rejects Wright's empire-critical approach.

38. Davies, *Gospel*, 5.

39. Davies, *Gospel*, 365.

40. Davies, *Gospel*, 367. See further Isaac, *From Land to Lands*, 5.

41. Isaac, *From Land to Lands*, 240.

42. Isaac, *From Land to Lands*, 239.

43. Isaac, *From Land to Lands*, 239.

44. Burge, *Jesus*, 85.

45. Burge, *Jesus*, 85.

to Jewish ethnic lineage and the right to possess the land has now been overturned in Christ."[46] While many other scholars could be highlighted here, these three represent an approach to Rom 4:13 that results in key aspects of Israel's covenantal identity being relativized by the coming of Christ.[47]

However, some interpreters point out that for some first-century diaspora Jews, like Paul, the idea that Israel no longer has a right to the land seems unthinkable.[48] Walter Brueggemann explains: "While the image undoubtedly is transformed, it is inconceivable that it should have been emptied of its reference to land. The Abraham imagery apart from the land promise is an empty form. No matter how spiritualized, transcendentalized, or existentialized, it has its primary focus undeniably on land."[49] Mark Forman furthers Brueggemann by arguing that the "application of the promise is not only spiritual but physical as well."[50] He sees a "promise-fulfillment trajectory" that is based on the Abrahamic tradition itself and ultimately results in "God's universal socio-physical-spiritual blessing of the world and the associated ideas of Israel's permanent possession of land and Israel's constant interplay and engagement with 'the nation.'"[51]

David Rudolph and the Both/And Approach to the Problem

David Rudolph provides a set of arguments that offer clarity on this issue.[52] This section will discuss his work and build upon it. He is convinced that interpreters like Davies, Isaac, and Burge are mistaken in their rejection of the continued salience of the land promises in Christ. First, the argument put forth by these scholars is formally one from silence since Rom 4:13 does not say that the land promise has been abolished. Such promises were made originally in Gen 12:7; 13:15, 17; 15:7, 18–21; 17:8. Genesis 12:7 reads: "Then the Lord appeared to Abram, and said, 'To

46. Burge, *Jesus*, 86.

47. Burge, *Jesus*, 86. Burge would demur from this claim and argue that his approach to Rom 4:13 represents "a unique return to Israel's highest calling for the world."

48. Burge, *Jesus*, 86, 15–24. Burge offers evidence for the way some diaspora Jews could envision a landless existence.

49. Brueggemann, *Land*, 170. Cited in Forman, *Politics*, 63–64.

50. Forman, *Politics*, 71.

51. Forman, *Politics*, 71–72.

52. Rudolph, "Zionism," 167–94.

your offspring I will give this land (τὴν γῆν).' So he built there an altar to the Lord, who had appeared to him." The other texts listed provide subsequent restatings. However, the land promise was reinterpreted by other Jewish writers to include significantly more than the original land of Canaan. Sirach 44:21 is one example: "Therefore he established by means of an oath with him that nations would be blessed by his seed (σπέρματι), that he would multiply him as the dust of the earth and like the stars to exalt his seed (τὸ σπέρμα) and to give them an inheritance (κατακληρονομῆσαι) from sea to sea and from the river to the end of the earth (τῆς γῆς)" (NETS). So, even if one were to grant that Paul had universalized the land promise, he is still in accord with other Second Temple writers. Thus, his usage does not reflect a rejection of Israel's hope for a political kingdom (or his having left Judaism).[53] One of the reasons for the potential expansion of referent is that the same Greek word (γῆ) can function for both land and world. For example, while Gen 12:3 uses האדמה and 12:7 has הארץ, the LXX version of 12:3, like 12:7 cited above, still reads, "in you all the families of the earth (τῆς γῆς) shall be blessed."[54] Even if one were to allow for a universalization of the referent from the parcel of land to the world, it does not exclude the original referent still being the particular focus for the promise in a special way. This could be a both/and proposition.

Second, many interpreters operate with an underlying assumption that the movement from the particular to the universal is Paul's ideological perspective. Rudolph points to this as a place where the influence of F. C. Baur continues to be felt. One brief quote should highlight the issue: "The particularism of Judaism must disappear."[55] Yet Paul is not necessarily a binary thinker when it comes to the issue of universalism and

---

53. See Kamudzandu, *Abraham as Spiritual Ancestor*, 118; Rock, *Paul's Letter*, 283; Lewis, *Paul's "Spirit,"* 108–10.

54. See van Kooten, "Philosophical Criticism," 382.

55. Baur, *Church History*, 1.59. See further Lincicum, "Baur's Place," 153–55. Wright (*Paul and the Faithfulness of God*, 387 n. 125) contends that "Paul did insist on a clean break with Jewish identity markers, and he did not adopt gentile ones in their place, not because of a belief in 'universality' as opposed to 'particularity,' but because he believed that the crucified and risen Messiah was now the identity marker of the renewed people, whose unity and holiness had to provide the symbolic strength to sustain the new worldview." The second part of this statement may be accurate but the first part would leave these Christ-followers in an unsustainable embodied existence. It is more likely that existing identities are reprioritized in Christ rather than obliterated as suggested by Wright. Rudolph, "Zionism," 171 n. 10.

particularism; he can maintain both of these in tension.[56] It should not be assumed that "inherit the world" indicates an erasure of Jewish particularism in relation to the land. Jewish particularism was not a problem to be overcome. In fact, streams of Jewish particularism were quite universal in their orientation.

> For the sake of my servant Jacob.
>
> And for Israel my chosen one
>
> So that they may know from east to west
>
> That there is none but me:
>
> I am YHWH and there is no other (Isa 45:4, 6)

The particularism of Jewish identity serves a purpose in the wider world. The vision here is not one of withdrawal and sectarianism; rather, it is a vision in which God's people Israel serve the rest of humanity.[57] Paul's eschatological perspective includes Jews and the nations worshipping together (Rom 15:10).[58] It would seem antithetical to this vision to view the phrase "inherit the world" as a universal claim that lacks the particularism of the vision found in 15:10.[59]

Third, the promise-fulfillment scheme is often the default interpretive framework when it comes to Paul's use of Israel's scriptural tradition.[60] In this approach, the type is absorbed in the anti-type, especially as it relates to the way Christ is seen as the true Israelite.[61] This is not Paul's primary way of understanding this relationship. He is most clear in Rom 15:8 where he says that Christ came to "confirm (βεβαιῶσαι) the promises

---

56. Ehrensperger (*Mutually Encouraged*, 94, 100) picks up on this tendency among mainstream interpreters.

57. See further Levenson, "Universal Horizon," 155.

58. Fredriksen, "Judaism," 547; Zoccali, "Children," 267–68; this is rejected by Donaldson, "Paul," 282.

59. This passage will be discussed on page 237. The eschatological particularism evident in Romans 15 is earlier described in 11:11–32.

60. Conway, *Promises*, 146: "For Paul, the gospel is the fulfillment, or at least the inauguration of the fulfillment, of the promises of God made to Abraham."

61. Beale and Gladd, *Hidden*, 172–73. Jesus Messiah as the faithful Israelite is vital to Wright's project. Wright, "Romans," 470: "His faithfulness completed the role marked out for Israel and did so for the benefit of all, Jew and Gentile alike." Cf. Wright, *Paul and the Faithfulness of God*, 839, 1050. Barclay (*Paul*, 476) rejects the idea that a faithful Israelite was required for salvation to occur. Vlach ("What Does Christ," 54) offers several critiques of the position suggested by Beale, Gladd, and Wright.

given to the patriarchs."[62] That slight shift suggests there is more in view than a straightforward fulfillment. Rudolph picks up on this: "Romans 4:13 indicates that the Abrahamic promise ultimately points to Christ and the Church, but this does not necessarily imply that the particular territorial dimension of the Abrahamic promise has been 'overturned.'"[63] One classic example of the promise-and-fulfillment scheme is worth considering since this is such a crucial issue. Supersessionist interpreters often emphasize Paul's statements that those in Christ are now the temples of the Holy Spirit. They conclude that these new creation temples are a replacement for the temple in Jerusalem (1 Cor 3:16; 6:19; 2 Cor 6:16).[64] However, Paul seems to work with this discourse in a different fashion. In Rom 9:4 ("the glory" . . . "the worship"), he considers the temple to be an ongoing focal point for Jewish worship. Further, Luke describes Paul, in Acts 21:17–26, entering into the temple and participating in offerings. Finally, the ongoing ritual life of the temple is expected in that in 2 Thess 2:3–4, the "man of lawlessness . . . takes his seat in the temple of God."[65] The universalistic imagery of those in Christ as temples of the Holy Spirit does not render the Jerusalem temple redundant.[66] Paul can think in other than binary categories.

Fourth, Rudolph addresses the argument that an absence of a specific reference to Judea in Rom 4:13 strongly suggests that land is not in view for Paul.[67] This position carries a bit of weight; it may be the case that the land is not in view here, and the focus is rather on people. In that perspective, "inherit the world" refers to the portion of the promise that addresses the inheritance of the many nations.[68] The focus would then be on Gen 12:2–3 instead of 12:7, which is possible given the ambiguity of the Greek, as noted above. If this argument is granted, then Rom 4:13 says nothing about the continuation or fulfillment of the land promise. Nelson Hsieh has recently put this view forward, contending that 4:13 does not expand the land promise to encompass the world. He argues,

62. This is discussed further beginning on page 231.

63. Rudolph, "Zionism," 172.

64. Ehrensperger, "To Eat," 124.

65. See Harrison, *Paul*, 71–95, for discussion of this text and Caligula. Harrison combines the historical and parousia perspectives on this text.

66. On the temple see Macaskill, *Union*, 147–71; Heinsch "What Does Hagar," 1–14.

67. Burge, *Jesus*, 85; cited by Rudolph, "Zionism," 172.

68. See Christiansen, *Covenant*, 285 n. 48.

from the context of the passage, that Rom 4:17–18 clearly highlights the "many nations" part of the original promise.[69] Finally, he provides good evidence that the putative expansions (such as Sir 44:21 mentioned above) require more nuancing in order to be probative.[70]

Fifth, keeping in mind the concerns raised by Hsieh with regard to the Second Temple textual comparisons, there is a sense in which some of these interpreters expect the continuation of Jewish identity in the midst of universalistic inheritance of all things. Rudolph, rightly I think, based on Romans 2–3 and 9–11, suggests that since Paul does not envisage the obliteration of Israel's election, gifts, and calling with the inauguration of the messianic age, interpreters should allow him to speak in concert with these Second Temple voices.[71] In Jub. 22:14, Abraham makes the following pronouncement on Jacob:

> And may he cleanse you from all unrighteousness and impurity,
> That you may be forgiven all the transgressions; which you have committed ignorantly.
> And may he strengthen you,
> And bless you.
> And may you inherit the whole earth.[72]

So, inheriting the earth was part of Israel's eschatological expectation. This goes back to Ezek 36:8–12, where nature will burst forth in fruitfulness and Israel will receive their due inheritance. So similarly, 1 En. 5:7ab: "But for the elect there shall be light and joy and peace, and they shall inherit the earth." This inheritance becomes a reality as God forgives their transgressions and reestablishes his covenant with Israel. This covenant renewal is seen in Jub. 22:15:

> And may he renew his covenant with you.
> That you may be to him a nation for his inheritance for all the ages,

---

69. Hsieh ("Abraham," 108) points out that many interpreters overlook the lexical data showing that κόσμος can refer to either the "physical earth" or "humanity in general."

70. Hsieh, "Abraham," 110. See also Kamell, "Sirach," 66–72, who brings to the fore the antithetical ways in which Paul and Sirach understand Abraham; Gregory, "Abraham," 66–81.

71. Rudolph, "Zionism," 173–74. See further, Visscher, *Romans 4*, 198–99. On the significance of Jubilees, see Forman, *Politics*, 80–84. On Ezekiel the Tragedian, see Horbury, "Gifts," 91–109.

72. See Morales, *Spirit*, 165; Mermelstein, *Creation*, 88–132.

> And that he may be to you and to your seed a God in truth and righteousness throughout all the days of the earth.

Thus, Paul's discourse in Rom 4:13 sounds quite similar to that of other Jewish writers. One difference is that these writers expected obedience to Torah as the condition for the inheritance of the land.[73] For Paul, the accent falls on the faith/faithfulness of Abraham, not on the law since it had not yet been given (Rom 4:10).[74] However, his statement "not through the law" should not be construed to mean that he sought to obliterate Torah.[75] In Rom 4:14, 16, Paul says that "those from the law" who express "faith" are also "heirs," and the "promise" is made sure to both "those who are of the law" and "those who are of the faith of Abraham." Thus, Abraham is the exemplar for both groups.[76] His fatherhood for in-Christ gentiles does not negate this same paternity for "those from the law." This phrase differs from the earlier phrase: "those from the works of the law" or a "works-of-the-law type person."[77] Supersessionist interpreters often conflate these two ideas, but for Paul being "from the law" is not a problem to be overcome. His concern is elsewhere on "a works-of-the-law type person." This sounds like a minor shift but it is crucial, and will be discussed further.[78]

Sixth, as mentioned above, it is plausible that either Gen 12:3 or 12:7 are in view in Rom 4:13. Rudolph, however, concludes that it is slightly more likely that Gen 22:17–18 is a/the focal point, especially as it relates to the idea of "possessing" the gates:

---

73. Lev 26:2–13; Deut 30:15–20; Ezek 36:22–38; 37:24–28; Pss. Sol. 14:1–2, 9–10. It may be worth reflecting on the implications of Paul's argument if one separates out his instruction to gentiles from his thoughts on this issue with regard to continued Torah obedience for Jews especially in light of 1 Cor 7:19 (see also Rom 3:1–2).

74. Nanos, *Mystery*, 139–43.

75. Abraham observed the law even though it was not revealed until later to Moses (Jub. 16:28; Sir 44:20; 2 Bar. 57:2; Philo, *Abraham* 5–6, 60–61, 275; b. Yoma 286; m. Qidd. 4:14; cf. Gen 26:5; Longenecker, *Triumph*, 32 n. 14). See also 1 Macc 2:51–53; Jub. 23:10.

76. This is the key finding of Esler (*Conflict*, 184–88). He prefers the more precise term "prototype." For a similar approach, see Zoccali ("Children," 256), who focuses more on the role of the development of a superordinate identity. *Pace* Campbell (*Unity*, 77) who, while not downplaying fully the exemplar role, focuses primarily on ancestor and the way gentiles in Christ relate to the God of Israel through Abraham as promise-bearer.

77. See p. 102 for further discussion of these phrases in relation to the law.

78. See further on this p. 95.

> I will indeed bless you, and I will make your offspring (זַרְעֲךָ) as numerous as the stars of heaven and as the sand that is on the seashore. And your offspring (זַרְעֲךָ) shall possess (וַיִּרַשׁ) the gate of their enemies, and by your offspring (בְזַרְעֲךָ) shall all the nations of the earth gain blessing for themselves, because you have obeyed my voice.[79]

The subjugation of those in the promised land is implied in the phrase "possess the gates of their enemies." Wenham notes that this provides a more concrete delineation of the content of the promises than the earlier presentations.[80] There is also a connection with the promise of descendants and of blessing the nations of the earth. These ideas are restated by Isaiah: "your descendants (וְזַרְעֲךָ) will possess (יִירַשׁ) the nations and will settle the desolate towns" (Isa 54:3). Oswalt sees a connection between Isa 54:3 and Gen 12:7 based on the presence of descendants; concomitantly, he also highlights, based on the combination of "descendants," "seed," and "possess" that "God's promise to give Israel the land of Canaan" is in view (Deut 9:1; 11:23; 12:2; 31:3).[81] Paul was aware of this aspect of Israel's hoped-for restoration since he quotes Isa 54:1 in Gal 4:27.[82] The LXX translates ירשׁ with κληρονομέω, and Paul uses a closely related term in Rom 4:13, κληρονόμος.[83] These texts and their connections suggest that the particular focus on the land does not include a universalistic impulse. Abraham and his descendants, in Rom 4:13, are described as "heir of the world," but this does not include the idea that Abraham's promise to his physical descendants has been occluded. Those who argue such a case, like Davies, Isaac, and Burge, have likely overstated their position.

So, with regard to Abraham, Paul can see a both/and in terms of discrete groups represented: Israel according to the flesh, and in-Christ Jews and gentiles. Further, in highlighting Abraham's seed as those who inherit the world, the particular promise for the land has not been swallowed

79. There is an issue here with regard to whether the nations find this on their own or by the agency of Abraham. See Noort, "Abraham," 3–32; Halpern-Amaru, *Rewriting*, 25–54.

80. Gen 12:1, 7; 13:15–17; 15:7–8; 17:8; Wenham, *Genesis*, 112.

81. Oswalt, *Isaiah*, 417.

82. See further Willitts, "Isa 54,1," 201, for the way 4:27 bears on the earlier verses. Cf. Thiessen, *Paul*, 132; Starling, *Not My People*, 23–60, who argues that gentiles take this promise over from historic Israel; Bachmann, *Anti-Judaism*, 98; 192 n. 82.

83. See further on this connection Gen 26:1–5; 35:11–12; so also Rudolph, "Zionism," 176.

up by the universalistic impulse. For Paul, existing identities continue to matter, and one of the ways this works out will be seen in the next section.

Abraham and Existing Identities in Romans 4:16

In 4:16, Paul writes, "For this reason it is by faith, in order that it may be in accordance with grace, so that the promise will be guaranteed to all the descendants, not only to those who are of the law, but also to those who are of the faith of Abraham, who is the father of us all."

Abraham is the bearer of "the promise" (ἡ ἐπαγγελία), and that is why he is crucial for the formation of Christ-movement identity for both Jews and gentiles. Romans 4:16 thus focuses Paul's rhetoric from 4:11b–12.[84] One particular way in which Abraham is the bearer of the promise relates to him being the "father of many nations" (Rom 4:17). In the context of Abraham's paternity of Israel, Paul places in-Christ gentiles within the symbolic universe of the Jews. They do not become Israel; they remain the "from-the-nations-other-than-Israel seed of Abraham." However, this does allow Paul to make the claim that Abraham has become "the father of us all" (4:16). William S. Campbell summarizes: "Abraham is the father of both the descendants by his blood and also those by adoption through incorporation into Abraham's blood descendant, Christ."[85] Thus, Abraham is more than an example of one who has faith; he is the founder of a renewed family that connects Jews and gentiles in Christ together as well as with the "rest" of Israel (Rom 11:7–10). This "seed" of Abraham is a plurality of several groups who are inheritors of the promise in asymmetrical ways. Abraham's universal fatherhood does not negate his particular fatherhood for the people of Israel.[86]

---

84. The promise(s) are detailed in Fitzmyer, *Romans*, 384: "in the Genesis story God makes several promises to Abraham: the promise that Abraham's name would be great (Gen 12:2), the promise of inheritance of the land of Canaan (Gen 12:7), the promise of an heir to be born of Sarah (Gen 15:4; 17:16, 19), the promise of a numberless posterity to be descended from him (Gen 12:12; 13:14–17; 17:8; 18:18; 22:16–18). Cf. Sir 44:21." As regards the distinction between quantitative and qualitative referents for this final promise, see recently Burnett, "So," 234.

85. Campbell, *Paul and the Creation*, 63; Rom 1:3–4.

86. Cranfield, *Romans*, 1.238: "But, while recognizing that Paul is here concerned with a kinship with Abraham which depends on the sharing of his faith, we must be careful to avoid the mistake of concluding from what is said here that Paul intended to deny the reality of the kinship κατὰ σάρκα (cf. v. 1) with Abraham of those Jews who did not share his faith or that he believed that such Jews were altogether excluded

Paul's primary argument, however, in Romans 4 seeks to address the way in-Christ Jews and gentiles relate to Abraham as his "seed," though again this does not remove this identity from historical Israel. Paul uses "seed" (σπέρμα) differently in Gal 3:16 as compared to Rom 4:13, 16, and 18 (see also 9:6–7), yet all too often these passages are conflated.[87] In Galatians, "seed" (σπέρμα) is understood as the one seed that is Christ, while in the Romans setting, as argued above, it refers to two different groups of people. The first group is described as "those who adhere to the law" (τῷ ἐκ τοῦ νόμου) while the second group is labeled "those who share the faith of Abraham" (τῷ ἐκ πίστεως Ἀβραάμ).[88] The inclusive nature of these labels is supported by the "not . . . only but also" (οὐ . . . μόνον ἀλλὰ καί) structure for the clause.[89] The beginning of 4:16 makes it clear that "faith" (πίστις) is a requirement for these groups to exist, and that it is given without regard to one's worth, but rather as a "gift" (χάριν).[90] This then suggests that Paul maintains a distinction between Jewish Christ-followers and non-Jewish ones.[91] Campbell describes it

from the promises (cf. what was said of 2.28f)." With regard to Rom 2:28, Windsor (*Paul*, 61) offers a more nuanced view; he thinks Paul sees Jewish identity embodied most correctly by Jews within the Christ-movement. In this reading, Christ-following gentiles are not "spiritual" Jews.

87. See for example, Wright, *Climax*, 150, 167. In the latter reference, he explicitly argues that Galatians 3 and Rom 4:13–17 are mutually "reinforced." However, see Wright, "Paul and the Patriarch," 554, for a more recent corrective. Johnson-Hodge (*If Sons*, 103–6) conflates the referent of the "seed" in Galatians and Romans. Cf. Campbell, "Covenantal Theology," 50.

88. Moo, *Romans*, 278: "'Those who are of the law only' could, especially in light of the contrast with 'those who are of the faith of Abraham,' refer to unbelieving Jews. In this case, Paul would be asserting that Jews continue to be part of the 'seed of Abraham,' in a different way, however, from that in which Christians are the seed of Abraham. Such a point would not, if properly nuanced, be incompatible with Paul's thought (see Rom 11:11–30)." After considering this view, Moo does not think it is persuasive and concludes that "[t]he meaning, then, is that the promise is for the Jew who is part of the seed through faith" (279).

89. Barclay (*Paul*, 488) recognizes that "from the law" is a title "describing some who *are* included among the offspring."

90. Barclay, *Paul*, 488–89. Barclay notes further: "Because God acts in incongruous grace, and thus without regard to worth, there is no possible limit on the membership of this people, no ethnic frontier that would keep some nations out." One might query: what is it about Israel's ethnicity that appears to keep out God's new people by faith?

91. Cf. Käsemann, "Faith," 86: "The promise to Abraham then really only applies to the group of the circumcised who have become Christians." Longenecker (*Epistle to the Romans*, 491) concludes that "while Paul's emphasis is on the spiritual factor of

this way: "the two groups listed here must signify the Jewish Christian and gentile Christian 'branches' on 'the tree of Abraham.'"[92] The maintenance of existing identities is not simply a matter of social comportment; rather for Paul, both of these branches need to exist so that Abraham may properly be understood as "the father of us all" (4:16) and also so that the promise from Gen 17:5 that Abraham would become the "father of many nations" would be fulfilled.[93]

Paul's use of Abraham was not simply to offer a proof text for justification by faith, though it does show the way Abraham was justified.[94] Nor was it simply designed to reveal his multi-ethnic paternity, though his dependence upon God's grace results in him becoming an inclusive figure for these disparate groups.[95] Interpreters often assume that Paul's use of Abraham was determined by outside exigencies, potential resistance, or polemical situations.[96] These assumptions contribute to the view that Paul's use of Abraham does not fit comfortably into his gospel, or that he was forced to use Abraham.[97] Offering a middle path, Campbell thinks that in Rome there was an ongoing debate over the social implications of the gospel as it relates to walking in the footsteps of Abraham. This would then be a proxy war for the broader halakhic discussions concerning one's relationship to the Torah.[98] Paul's disparate comments concerning

---

Abraham as 'the father of all who believe,' whether circumcised or uncircumcised, he also acknowledges that Abraham was the 'forefather' or 'father' of the Jewish nation—which dialectic between 'spiritual' and 'physical' features will reverberate extensively in all his later discussions of 'national Israel' and 'the remnant of Israel' in 9:1—11:36."

92. Campbell, *Unity*, 60.

93. See also Lincicum, "Genesis," 112. Moo, *Romans*, 278: "As is the case throughout Romans, and certainly in chap. 4, Paul's 'universalism' is a 'qualified' universalism that gives the Gentiles the same opportunity as Jews to respond to the gospel and to become part of the people whom God is calling out of the world in the last days." Zoccali ("Children," 257) picks up on the mission and theological significance here.

94. In Rom 4:1–12, Paul offers two examples of individuals who were justified by faith: Abraham (4:1–4, 9–12) and David (4:5–8). This raises the question, what is Paul's primary purpose here? It is to show that justification does not come from anything that a person can or cannot do. So similarly Jewett, *Romans*, 309: "Paul's question is whether Abraham's heroism can properly be said to have derived from his fleshly achievement." Barclay (*Paul*, 486) would say no, since Paul perfects grace that is incongruous and since "God acts in the absence of human worth."

95. Cf. Hays, *Conversion*, 83; Barclay, *Paul*, 488 n. 105.

96. Neutel, *Cosmopolitan*, 104–11. Foster, *Renaming*, 74–75.

97. See Thiessen, *Paul*, 74–75, for a critique of these interpreters' view of Paul's use of Abraham.

98. Davies, *Faith*, 169: "Paul does not assert that those who obey the law, or who

the law in Romans and his teaching in Romans 14–15 makes this quite likely.[99] If so, then Abraham serves as a good example for Paul's rhetorical goal of uniting "all God's beloved in Rome" (1:7).[100] In 4:16–17, he provides a common ancestry for them.[101] However, as was seen in the group descriptors, "those who adhere to the law" and "those who share the faith of Abraham," Paul expects different social identifications to continue in Christ (14:5, 23). So, he likely seeks to carve out relational space among the Christ-followers for different patterns of life, one more Jewish in its orientation and the other inclusive of various aspects of existing cultural identities in Rome.[102] Therefore, those who argue that "those who adhere to the law" is a negative descriptor have likely overstated their case. Paul's purpose is not to disparage those who continue to identify with Torah but as Campbell remarks: "This description of Jewish Christians demonstrates that in Paul's theology there was no absolute opposition between Christ and the law."[103] The crucial and irreplaceable characteristic is that the pattern of life or social identification must be "from faith" (4:16; ἐκ

---

are 'of law,' will not inherit the promises, but that they do not inherit them *by* the law. Rather, it is those of the law who do not exercise faith who will be disinherited (cf. 3.1–4)." See also McFarland, "Whose Abraham," 107–29.

99. Nanos (*Mystery*, 142) contends that Abraham is a model of one who "grew strong in faith." This, then, shows a connection between Romans 4 and 14–15.

100. Nanos, *Mystery*, 141–42. Nanos shows the various ways Abraham's faith is depicted by Paul.

101. Cranfield (*Romans*, 1.227), in remarking about 4:1, concludes: "The implicit thought is that, while we (i.e., the Jews) are Abraham's children κατὰ σάρκα, Abraham has other children who are his in a different way (cf. vv. 11, 16ff); not that we have another forefather who is our forefather otherwise than κατὰ σάρκα." Johnson-Hodge, "The Question," 159–64.

102. This may offer some hint as to the teaching in Rom 13:1–7. Krauter (*Studien zu Röm*, 249) makes several connections with existing civic expectations and the way Paul's rhetoric might have been heard.

103. Campbell, *Unity*, 60. How this would work in practice would be a challenge. For example, Barclay (*Paul*, 488) highlights several issues associated with the continued intermingling of the categories of "grace" and "law." He does not argue that they are antithetical *per se*, only that one would have had to be careful not to "introduce a criterion of positive worth" since "Abrahamic faith [had] none." Moo, *Romans*, 279: "'Out of the law' must mean something different from what it does in v. 11, and designate Jews as such, 'those who had the advantage of being under the Mosaic economy.' In light of the contrast indicated by 'not only . . . but also,' 'those out of the faith of Abraham' are Gentile believers. It is in this sense that Abraham is the 'father of us all'—the spiritual forefather of all of 'us' who are believers."

πίστεως).[104] For Paul, Abraham proves to be an inclusive figure that can accommodate just such diverse patterns of living.

Conclusion

While this chapter could not address all the weighty issues in Romans 4 in regards to Abraham, it did uncover an interpretation for several verses that does not presuppose supersessionism. It was found that in Rom 4:11–12 Paul did not think Israel had lost its founding father, and that the inclusion of gentiles into Abraham's paternity does not result in its removal from the Jews. This understanding built on the anomalous τοῖς in 4:11b–12 which pointed to two differing groups. In this configuration, gentiles in Christ have not taken over the vocational identity of the nation of Israel. Abraham is the continuing father of the nation. Next, the vexing problem of the land promises made to Abraham were discussed, and I concluded that Paul did not think these were set aside or diffused in light of gentile inclusion. David Rudolph's work was reinforced, and a both/and approach to the land was found to be the most compelling. This then supported the earlier two-group approach to Romans 4 in which the groups represented were Israel according to the flesh and in-Christ Jews and gentiles. The continued salience of existing identities was then discussed in the context of Abraham. He was found to be crucial for Paul since he was the initial bearer of the promise. This had differing social implications for Israel and the nations, which should not be fused nor flattened out. Building on the work of William S. Campbell, Abraham was found to be the key figure for uniting the diverse patterns of life among the Christ-groups, patterns of life that were to be approached with mission in view. These diverse patterns of life existed because Jewish identity was not just a theological one but a fully embodied pattern of living. Thus, if Paul, as is generally thought, saw no continuing validity of Torah, this would result in the erasure of Jewish identity in the Christ-movement and an eventual assimilation of Israel into the nations. It seems highly unlikely that Paul's theologizing concerning Torah would lead to the erasure of Jewish flesh in the body of Christ. Thus, we turn next to consider the continuing validity of Torah in Romans.

---

104. The phrase ἐκ πίστεως is used throughout Romans: 1:17 two times; 3:26, 30; 4:16 two times; 5:1; 9:30, 32; 10:6; 14:23 two times. The final two are probative since there Torah-informed praxis is connected to a life "from faith."

4

The Validity of the Law

Introduction

Does Jewish identity continue in any meaningful way in Christ if Torah, the law of Moses, has no continuing validity? That is the narrow question I raise in this chapter.[1] Earlier in this book, the stipulated understanding of Jewish identity was put forth by building on Nanos's nuanced approach: ethnic identity along with behaviors associated with the way Jews live in light of Israel's scriptural tradition.[2] So, a person embodies a Jewish identity to the degree they practice the ancestral customs of the Jews in ways recognizable in a specific context. Casey, as mentioned earlier, in a somewhat different approach, offers eight indicators: "ethnicity, scripture, monotheism, circumcision, Sabbath observance, dietary laws, purity laws and major festivals."[3] The presence of these would indicate the degree to which a person would be considered Jewish or, in the absence of them, non-Jewish. Clearly all of these issues are discussed in Romans, and though there is some significant theologizing occurring surrounding these issues, it is also clear that Jewish identity has not been obliterated in the gospel of God to which Paul has been set apart (Rom 1:1).

However, many NT scholars are not convinced by such a claim. First, for example, Peter Richardson and Paul Gooch contend that Paul no longer saw himself as a Jew. Even though he does call himself that in

---

1. Other aspects of this question are discussed in other portions of this book; for example, see page 58 for a discussion of 3:31 and page 153 for a discussion of 10:4.

2. See page 4 n. 12. Nanos, "Paul's Non-Jews," 27–28.

3. Casey, *From Jewish*, 12. Casey's approach is a bit more restrictive than Nanos's but helps to make concrete some of the abstractions in Nanos's understanding.

Gal 2:15, they point out that it was in debate with Peter where he was arguing that "although they are Jews by birth they ought not to continue to live like Jews now that they are Christians."[4] Second, E. P. Sanders, remarking on Rom 14:1–6, concludes that "the factors which separated Jews from Greeks . . . must be given up by the Jews."[5] Third, D. A. Carson notes regarding 1 Cor 9:20 that Paul's relationship to Torah places him in a *"third ground"* between Jews and non-Jews, since "his understanding of God's redemptive purposes in history left Torah *qua* covenant superseded."[6] More could be added to this list but these are sufficient to highlight the contours of the erasure approaches to Jewish identity and Torah-informed praxis in Christ.[7]

William S. Campbell, on the other hand, doubts the veracity of these claims and contends that "for Paul Jewish identity is not obsolete for those in Christ, but constitutes a viable and recognized sub-group identity pattern."[8] This chapter takes Campbell's position as its point of departure, builds on the work of Windsor, Ruzer, and Snodgrass, and offers an argument that suggests that Paul sees the law of Moses as having continuing validity in the constitution and formation of Jewish identity in Christ. It did, however, have differing social implications for non-Jews whom Paul thought needed to recognize it as a part of Christ-following gentile identity.[9]

There is no way to address the entire topic of Paul and the law in this chapter; my hope is only to suggest a way forward when considering the continuation of Jewish identity in relation to Torah and why this should

4. Richardson and Gooch, "Accommodation Ethics," 96, 111.

5. Sanders, *Paul, the Law*, 177–78.

6. Carson, "Pauline Inconsistency," 37; Carson, "Mystery," 403.

7. Tatum ("To the Jew," 286) thinks the problem in Rome is that some non-Jews are "verbally abusing Jews for their observance of the Torah." Hedner Zetterholm ("Question," 80, 91) contends that the nature of Torah observance continues to be a problem among interpreters. She points out that what is needed on both sides of this debate is "a more nuanced" understanding of "what it meant to be a Torah observant Jew in the first century." Halakhic debates were an integral part of first-century Jewish life since the general nature of biblical commandments required situationally specific interpretations and applications (see, e.g., the debates concerning work on the Sabbath in Exod 20:8–11; m. Shabb. 7:2). She further asserts that we actually know very little about the nature of "halakic observance in the first century." Thus, it is difficult to determine what was considered a violation and what was acceptable.

8. Campbell, *Paul and the Creation*, 96.

9. Windsor, *Paul*, 44–95; Ruzer, "Paul's Stance," 75–97; and Snodgrass, "Spheres," 93–113.

matter in the formation of gentile identity in Christ.[10] Indeed, Paul's audience in Romans was gentile (Rom 1:13–15; 11:13), so the negative material concerning Torah in Rom 6:14–15 and 7:4, 6 is directed to them.[11] "Torah-observance is not for you," Paul says, "or at least not in the same way it is for Jews."[12] However, even though he is addressing gentiles, he assumes a certain amount of continuity of thought with regard to Jews in light of the gospel. He occasionally brings to the fore issues of Jewish identity and the law of Moses, and these will be our concern here. In the constraints of this chapter, I will focus first on the continuing significance of the law of Moses for Jewish identity in Christ; then I will narrow the focus to the enduring implications of being ἐν νόμῳ or ἐκ νόμου for Jewish identity in Christ, and then I will finally briefly suggest a way forward more broadly, reading Paul and Torah in the light of post-supersessionism following the work of Klyne Snodgrass.

The Continuing Significance of the Law of Moses for Jewish Identity in Christ

For Paul, the law of Moses is a salient node for Jewish identity. In 2 Cor 3:15, Paul writes: "But to this day whenever Moses is read (ἀναγινώσκηται), a veil lies over their heart." In the context, "their" refers to the Jewish people, who as a group, read Moses. This reading occurs in the synagogue, and thus this public reading is a crucial way to reinforce Jewish identity. Furthermore, since Moses is seen as the human author of the law, he becomes an exemplar of Jewish identity. Josephus begins his *Antiquities* by writing: "But because almost all our constitution (τοῦ

---

10. With regard to the broader debates on Paul and the law one should consult the following monographs and collections of essays: Rosner, *Paul and the Law*; Hübner, *Law*; Räisänen, *Paul and the Law*; Sanders, *Paul, the Law*; Dunn, *Paul*; Adeyemi, *New Covenant*; Schreiner, *The Law*; Westerholm, *Israel's Law*; Rhyne, *Faith*; Thielman, *Paul*; Meyer, "Romans 10:4"; Davies, *Faith*; Das, *Paul, the Law*; Bockmuehl, *Jewish Law*; Boccaccini and Ibba, *Enoch*; Tait and Oakes, *Torah*; Rapa, *Meaning*; Koperski, *What Are They Saying*; Watson, *Paul and the Hermeneutics*; Kruse, *Paul*; Tomson, *Paul*; Badenas, *Christ*. Also, see the following articles or essays: Snodgrass, "Spheres"; Wilson, "Supersession"; Watson, "Law"; Hedner Zetterholm, "Question."

11. See below beginning on page 104 for an excursus that discusses these verses and the addressee issue. While my argument stands regardless of the resolution of these verses, if the suggestions in the excursus are found probative, it would strengthen the case being made for the continuing validity of Torah in this chapter.

12. Ruzer, "Paul's Stance," 83–84.

νομοθέτου) depends on the wisdom of Moses, our legislator, I cannot avoid saying something concerning him beforehand, though I shall do it briefly" (1.18). He then describes the pattern of life and worldview that Moses laid out for the Israelites (1.21, 26, 29, 33–34). The weekly reading of Moses in the synagogues reinforces this pattern of life, and the holiness of Israel in contrast to the nations. All too often in discussions of the continuing validity of the law of Moses, "the law" is presented in a dehistoricized manner, removed from the embodied and communal experience of first-century Jews. For Paul, in Rom 3:19, the law continues to speak: "Now we know that whatever the law says (λέγει), it speaks (λαλεῖ) to those who are in the law (ἐν τῷ νόμῳ), that every mouth may be closed, and all the world may become accountable to God" (Rom 3:19). This ongoing communication may even bring penetrating insights from Israel's scriptural tradition: "But I ask, did Israel (Ἰσραήλ) not understand? First Moses says, 'I will make you jealous of those who are not a nation; with a foolish nation I will make you angry'" (Rom 10:19). This already highlights that Paul sees some sort of ongoing validity for Moses—the text. Paul's problem may not properly be with Moses but with the way his coreligionists are interpreting Moses. In the broader Pauline corpus, Moses attests to the meaning of Christ's death, the inclusion of the nations, and is a model of social identification (1 Cor 10:1–11; 15:3–4; Gal 4:21–31). He is not impugned when the text is understood correctly. Moses may still function as a salient node for in-Christ Jewish identity. Paul is concerned for this generally, and more specifically in relation to gentiles who may, according to Tatum, have been causing a problem in Rome by "verbally abusing Jews for their observance of the Torah."[13]

Jewish identity is further indexed through the possession of the law of Moses. In contrast, the non-Jews are outside of it. In Rom 2:13, Jews are described as those who are "hearers (ἀκροαταί) of the law." They are also labeled in 2:20 as those "having . . . the law" which he further describes as the "embodiment of knowledge and truth." Paul sounds similar to Philo in this regard, who describes the followers of Moses as those who find "knowledge . . . happiness . . . and true everlasting life" (*Spec. Laws* 1.345). The gentiles, on the other hand, are those not properly understood as members of the Jewish community. Paul describes them (ἔθνη) as "those who do not have the law" or similarly "without the law (ἀνόμως)" (Rom 2:14, 12). This is more than a simple behavioral issue, since in Rom 2:14,

13. Tatum, "To the Jew," 286.

the gentiles are described as those who "by nature (φύσει)" are without it. When Paul discusses nature or natural, he is highlighting a specific index of identity related to what appears to be self-evident in antiquity. The specter of essentialism is close at hand. A similar notion of "natural" gentile identity is evident in the use of φύσις in Rom 2:27: "And he who is physically (ἐκ φύσεως) uncircumcised." Jewish identity is described using the same term in Rom 11:21: "For if God did not spare the natural (κατὰ φύσιν) branches." Thus, even though with regard to the availability of righteousness God makes no distinction between Jew and gentile (Rom 3:22; 10:12), Paul's use of φύσις suggests that this does not extend to the level of the obliteration of existing identities: in-Christ Jews remain Jews (by nature) and gentiles remain gentiles. While contemporary notions of physicality may obscure identity discourse, Paul indexes identity based on a people group's possession of the law. In this, Paul is similar to Philo, but Philo describes Moses's followers positively and the nations, those without the law, more negatively as: "atheists and dead as to their souls" (*Spec. Laws* 1.345). Similar to Paul's use of ἀνόμως in Rom 2:12, Josephus, in *Against Apion* 2.151, refers to those who live "without possessing the law (τῶν ἀνόμως)" as those being from the nations other than Israel (2.150). Paul, Philo, and Josephus all agree that the possession of the law is integral to the embodiment of a specific Jewish social identity.

The law of Moses is divine revelation given to the Jewish community. Philo describes Moses as "the most admirable of all lawgivers (νομοθετῶν)" and asserts that the laws he gave are "truly divine" (ἀληθῶς θεῖοι) (*Moses* 2.12). Similarly, Josephus contends that the laws given to Moses "were taught to him by God" (διδαχῇ τοῦ θεοῦ).[14] Aristeas likewise claims, "the law is sacred and of divine origin" (τὴν νομοθεσίαν καὶ διὰ θεοῦ γεγονέναι) (Let. Aris. 313). Sirach 24:23 reminds us that this divine revelation was the unique possession of Jews: "All this is the book of the covenant (βίβλος διαθήκης) of the Most High God, the law (νόμον) that Moses commanded us as an inheritance for the congregations of Jacob (κληρονομίαν συναγωγαῖς Ιακωβ)." Paul does not divert from his Jewish heritage on this point; he also thinks that the law was given to the Jewish people. In Rom 3:1–2, he writes, "Then what advantage has the Jew? . . . Much in every way. To begin with, the Jews were entrusted with the oracles of God (τὰ λόγια τοῦ θεοῦ)." Furthermore, he states in Rom 9:4, "They are Israelites (Ισραηλῖται), and to them belong . . . the giving of the

___

14. Josephus, *Ant.* 17.159

law (ἡ νομοθεσία)." Paul thinks that this state of affairs was integral to God's purposes in the world, purposes that were accomplished by means of Israel through Abraham, who becomes a paternal exemplar of one who is counted/declared/regarded (λογίζομαι) righteous by faith and not by circumcision/works (ἐργάζομαι) (Rom 4:4–5; Gen 15:6).

According to Paul, Jewish identity is not exactly like any other social identity; it is closely aligned with the law as divine revelation and thus has significant epistemic advantages, though these advantages are not (and never were) salvific in a direct fashion. In Rom 2:12, Paul writes: "All who have sinned without the law (ἀνόμως ἥμαρτον) will also perish without the law, and all who have sinned in the law (ἐν νόμῳ ἥμαρτον) will be judged by the law." And in Rom 7:9–10, he writes: "I was once alive apart from the law (χωρὶς νόμου); but when the commandment (τῆς ἐντολῆς) came, sin became alive and I died; and this commandment, which was to result in life, proved to result in death for me." Even though it is beyond the narrow purposes of this chapter, I see in Rom 7:7–25 the law functioning as a continuing witness of the need for the gospel of Christ, since again Paul does not think possession of the law is salvific in a direct way.

Even here, however, Paul is not unique. He is entering an ancient and ongoing debate that reaches back as far as Jer 31:31–34, where proper following of the law requires an internal transformation. This is also found in Ezek 36:24–29, where the agency of the Spirit is required for the acceptable observance of God's ordinances (36:27). Closer to the time of Paul, the Rule of the Congregation (1QS 11:7–19) highlights a similar need for God's transforming work to occur for righteousness to be achieved, even in a community that clearly follows a Jewish pattern of life: "To those whom God has selected he has given them as everlasting possession; until they inherit them in the lot of the holy ones . . . and from his hand is the perfection of the path . . . he will free my soul from the pit and make my steps steady on the path . . . in his justice he will cleanse me from the uncleanness of the human being and from the sin of the sons of man . . . so I can extol God for his justice." Further, in 1QS 4:20, those "refined by God" are described as a group that has been given a new interpretation of Torah: "Meanwhile, God will refine, with his truth, all man's deeds . . . and cleansing him with the spirit of holiness from every irreverent deed. He will sprinkle over him the spirit of truth. . . . In this way the upright will understand knowledge of the Most High." In the Thanksgiving Hymns (1QH 4:17–26), the agency of the Spirit is highlighted as a necessity for achieving righteousness: "[I give you thanks, Lord,] for the spirits you have placed in me . . . to confess my former sins, to bow low and beg favor for . . . of my deeds and the depravity of my heart . . . you have spread your holy spirit upon your servant." Thus, a Jewish people of the Spirit emerges as a salient social identity node for those connected to the documents found at Qumran.[15] In light of these texts, Paul was not unique in pointing out that possession of the divine law does not ensure direct salvific benefits. Furthermore, some of the Qumran documents and the earlier passages in Jeremiah and Ezekiel show that Paul's emphasis on the agency of the Spirit in fulfilling the law can be seen as part of an intra-Jewish debate concerning the law and the Spirit and their implications for a salient Jewish identity, a debate that had relevance for in-Christ gentiles.

Paul's contribution is found in Rom 7:14—8:11, but only a couple of phrases can be highlighted here: "We know that the law is spiritual; but I am carnal, sold under sin" (7:14); "For the law of the Spirit of life has set you free in Christ Jesus from the law of sin and death. For God has done what the law, weakened by the flesh, could not do: sending his own Son . . . in order that the just requirement of the law might be fulfilled (πληρόω) in us, who walk not according to the flesh but according to the Spirit (8:2–4)." Some of the binary thinking, as in the Qumran documents, is evident in 7:14 (as well as 8:9), and 8:3–4 highlights the way Paul sees the law transformed through the "death-accomplishing-righteousness-work" of Jesus. For Paul, that work is then applied through the Spirit so that the veil is removed (2 Cor 3:16), and, when the law is encountered via the Spirit, it brings righteousness and new life (Rom 7:6).

Paul's understanding of this dynamic of the Spirit and the way it transforms the law of Moses in the messianic age is evident in Rom 13:8–10, a passage Michael Bird refers to as a "headache" for those who see no continuing relevance for the law of Moses within the Christ-movement.[16] Rosner concludes that Rom 13:8–10 teaches that "[t]he fulfillment of the law through love is effectively the law's replacement."[17] This is based on his understanding of πληρόω here and in 8:4. On the other hand, Keck thinks that Rom 13:8–10 does not "replace the law with love."[18] For Keck, πληρόω does not point to a contrast with the law but to its actualiza-

---

15. See further, Ruzer, "Paul's Stance," 92.

16. Bird, *Romans*, 453.

17. Rosner, *Paul and the Law*, 124.

18. Keck, *Romans*, 329.

tion. It is no wonder that Kruse concludes that "[t]his text has important implications for our understanding of the relationship of Paul's gospel to the Mosaic law."[19] In Rom 13:8, Paul writes: "Owe no one anything, except to love one another; for the one who loves another has fulfilled (πεπλήρωκεν) the law." He then quotes four of the Ten Commandments and offers a summary statement after which he concludes in 13:10: "Love does no wrong to a neighbor; therefore, love is the fulfilling (πλήρωμα) of the law." Rosner's argument builds on the idea that Christ-followers are called to "fulfill" the law, not to "do" it.[20] Jewett does not see a distinction between the two: "'fulfill' is an equivalent expression for 'doing,' 'performing,' or 'keeping' Torah."[21] There is significant debate as to what gave rise to the use of πληρόω here, but Rosner, to his credit, highlights an important piece of evidence, Testament of Naphtali 8:7–9, a passage that shows πληρόω in the context of obedience discourse: "For the commandments of the law are twofold, and through prudence they must be fulfilled. For there is a time for a man to embrace his wife, and a time to abstain from that for his prayer. So there are two commandments; and, unless they be done in their order, they cause sin." Rosner acknowledges this text but thinks "it is an isolated instance."[22] While, granted, there is slender evidence to make such a connection, one could at least consider that this text may have influenced Paul in 1 Cor 7:5 where he teaches similarly with regard to the temporary cessation of sexual activity in a marriage for reasons of piety.[23] So, the "doing" of commandments and the "fulfilling" of these may not be binary options for Paul. This is not to deny the agency of Christ here; it just highlights that Rosner's case may not be as strong as it appears at first glance. Hultgren may offer insight by concluding: "one does not dispense with the commandments, but one's focus is now on the love commandment."[24] Though again, it does not follow that the law of Moses has been reduced to this commandment.[25]

In Rom 13:9, Paul cites four commandments from the second table of the Decalogue: "'You shall not commit adultery; You shall not murder;

19. Kruse, *Romans*, 502.

20. Rosner, *Paul and the Law*, 121.

21. Jewett, *Romans*, 808 n. 39.

22. Rosner, *Paul and the Law*, 122.

23. One could at least suggest there is a common tradition both authors draw from; so Deming, *Paul*, 121–22.

24. Hultgren, *Paul's Letter*, 485.

25. So similarly Hafemann, *Paul*, 179 n. 249.

You shall not steal; You shall not covet'; and any other commandment, are summed up in this word, 'Love your neighbor as yourself.'" Rosner does not think Paul quotes these "to bind Christians as those who are under the moral law"; rather, "love brings the law to completion and effectively replaces it as law with something better."[26] The tension in his position is evident as he acknowledges that the quotation of Lev 19:18, "Love your neighbor as yourself," highlights the continued importance of the law for "holy living" and its place in Paul's ethics.[27] However, this is precisely the point that is being debated, and so it seems that, at this juncture, Rosner's hermeneutical solution for Paul's use of the law weakens. Is it the case that Paul can simultaneously hold that the law has been repudiated as law-code, replaced by Christ's law, and then re-appropriated as prophecy and wisdom for living? This approach would not seem to work within the everyday lived experience of these Roman Christ-followers.[28]

The continued presence of the law of Moses as a unique possession of the Jewish people, as divine revelation, as constitutive of life in the Spirit and as relevant for ethical instruction suggests that erasure-oriented scholars like those mentioned in the introduction may have gone too far. For Paul, Jewish social identity is made salient within the orbit of the law of Moses, and if some of the gentiles in Rome were thinking in erasure categories, Paul responds that this is problematic. His response, however, raises another question concerning Romans: Does Paul think that those in Christ are still "under" the law? It is to that question we now turn in light of his use of the phrases "in" the law and "from" the law.

The Continuing Significance of Being ἐν νόμῳ or ἐκ νόμου for Jewish Identity in Christ

Sometimes scholars read νόμος discourse by fronting theological concerns in a way that obscures Paul's identity-forming discourse. There are social uses of νόμος that are often downplayed or overlooked. Issues of identity often precede theology, and the theological statements that

26. Rosner, *Paul and the Law*, 195.

27. Rosner, *Paul and the Law*, 195.

28. Fredriksen ("Question," 187–88, 193, 194, 198) places these references to the four commandments within ongoing critical questions of worship and the conceptions of ritual life that differed between Jews and non-Jews. So similarly, Nanos, *Mystery*, 324: "13:8–10 is a call to the Judaic norms of righteous behavior, not to earn salvation but because of it."

are studied were written to address previous identity questions rather than our later (and often anachronistic) theological concerns. To start with, the use of νόμος can be nuanced from a syntactic point of view. The prepositions ἐν and ἐκ may not, by themselves, imply a salvific deficiency in the way ὑπό does when it is construed with νόμος. If a person is ὑπὸ νόμον "under the law," Paul sees this as a problematic state of affairs (Rom 6:14–15; 1 Cor 9:20; Gal 3:23; 4:4–5, 21; 5:18).[29] However, when he uses ἐν νόμῳ "in the law" or ἐκ νόμου "from the law," he sees these as potentially neutral social identifications not incommensurate with his gospel discourse. In other words, a person who socially identifies as ἐν νόμῳ or ἐκ νόμου would not be required to set that aside as an identity that does not continue in Christ.

For example, two classes of sinners are described in Rom 2:12, "Those who have sinned without the law (ὅσοι . . . ἀνόμως ἥμαρτον)" and "Those who sin in the law (ὅσοι ἐν νόμῳ ἥμαρτον)." Both of these groups are judged justly even in their different social situations. In Rom 2:13, "the hearers of the law (οἱ ἀκροαταὶ νόμου)," i.e., the Jews, are not automatically righteous, but, on the other hand, it does not follow that being a "hearer of the law" excludes one from being declared righteous as a Jew (see Rom 2:9–10). Rather, Paul's claim seems to be that being a Jew "is not strictly coterminous with the set of righteous people."[30] In this case, being *"in* the law" or a *"hearer of* the law" is not the problem; being in the sphere of sin is.[31] Paul's theology of "spheres of influence" indicates that participation with Christ transfers the law out of the sphere of sin, death, and condemnation and into the sphere in which it was intended (Christ, Spirit, and faith), which then results in seeing the law as "the expression of the will of God" which "is for life (Rom. 8.7; 7.10)."[32]

A similar point can be made in Rom 4:14 where Paul describes a group as "[t]hose from the law (οἱ ἐκ νόμου)" who, if they were the "heirs," then "faith is made void and the promise is nullified." This would seem to suggest that Jewish identity is incommensurate with the gospel.

29. See the excursus below on 6:14–15; the "under the law" problem in view here is only the problem of being "under the *curse* of the law." This is a separate issue from the prepositional phrase being used to describe the Jewish people, though it seems that Paul uses different prepositions for that general description. It may be the case that in Romans he focuses on one set of prepositional descriptions for contextual reasons.

30. Windsor, *Paul*, 69.

31. See below the discussion of Snodgrass, "Spheres," 99, beginning on page 101.

32. Snodgrass, "Spheres," 99.

However, in Rom 4:16, Paul writes, "so that the promise will be guaranteed to all the descendants, not only to those who are of the law (οὐ τῷ ἐκ τοῦ νόμου μόνον) but also to those who are of the faith of Abraham." Thus, when the social identity labels in Rom 4:14 and 4:16 are seen in context we can at least claim along with Campbell that the phrases are used here "in a neutral rather than a pejorative sense" and that "Paul specifically stresses the national or ethnic sense—the inclusion of Jews *per se* and not simply Christ-following gentiles or nondescript individuals."[33] So, this further suggests that the Jew-and-gentile binary categories are not theologically mutually exclusive groups, but now the heirs of promise have been expanded to include more than those ἐν νόμῳ or ἐκ νόμου.

One final phrase should be mentioned. In Rom 3:19, Paul writes, "Now we know that whatever the law says, it speaks to those who are in the law (τοῖς ἐν τῷ νόμῳ)." This highlights the continuing significance of Jewish identity, i.e., a vocational election in God's wider purpose with regard to the nations (Gen 12:2–3; 22:18; Isa 41:8–9; 49:3, 6b). Yet a universalistic impulse emerges in the second half of the verse: "so that every mouth may be closed and all the world may become accountable to God." Jewish identity, according to Paul, relates directly to the proclamation of the gospel to the nations: "And he said to me, 'You are my servant, Israel, in whom I will be glorified. . . . I will make you as a light for the nations, that my salvation may reach to the end of the earth'" (Isa 49:3, 6b; Acts 13:49). So, Paul's use of ἐν νόμῳ and ἐκ νόμου in Romans suggest that the law of Moses still has significance, though neither phrase "determine[s] a person's standing in relation to divine judgment or salvation."[34] This is often missed by erasure interpreters since they read νόμος discourse only through a salvific lens and miss the vocational/social/missional dimension.

Paul's identity-forming antithesis is often configured as between faith and law, but the passages just highlighted suggest that the antithesis is more nuanced. It might therefore be better described as a contrast between faith and works of the law/doing the law. The law of Moses rightly interpreted is not out of line with faith: "Do we then overthrow the law by this faith? By no means! On the contrary, we uphold/maintain the validity of the law" (Rom 3:31).[35] As mentioned above, ὑπὸ νόμον has a nega-

---

33. Campbell, *Paul and the Creation*, 127. For my discussion of Romans 4 see the section beginning on page 62.

34. Windsor, *Paul*, 70.

35. See the earlier discussion of Rom 3:31 beginning on page 58.

tive sense to it and when speaking of the law of Moses, doing (ποιεῖν) works (ἔργα) or doing (ποιεῖν) righteousness/justification (δικαι-) seems to have a similar negative orientation to it (though not unproblematically so as mentioned with the reference to the Testament of Naphtali 8:7–9). So, as in Rom 4:16, a "from-the-law" (ἐκ τοῦ νόμου) person may receive the promise of Abraham while a "from-the-works-of-the-law" (ἐξ ἔργων νόμου) type person receives condemnation. In Rom 9:31, too, "Israel, who did strive for the righteousness that is based on the law (εἰς νόμον), did not succeed in fulfilling that law."[36] The law again is not the problem: "The law is holy, and the commandment is holy and righteous and good" (7:12). Jewish covenantal identity and identifying socially with νόμος is also not the problem. More information is needed in order to determine whether the situation is positive or negative. For example, if a person views him- or herself (and others in Christ) as "under the law" (ὑπὸ νόμον) or requires the re-coupling of righteousness/justification with the law, then Paul would say there is a problem. There is no *Sonderweg* for Jews—all who are saved are saved through faith in Messiah Jesus.

Paul is often seen as an anomalous Jew when it comes to his view of the law of Moses.[37] However, his view that Jewish identity is inter-related with the law, and that, further, it is divine revelation, places him firmly within the ongoing debates about the significance of both Jewish identity and divine revelation. These ongoing debates occurred in the weekly synagogue gatherings. Acts 15:21 demonstrates that Moses was probably read (ἀναγινωσκόμενος) in the synagogue each week. Further-more, Josephus, in *Against Apion* 2.175, discusses the practices of Israel with regard to the weekly gathering to hear and learn from the law: those from Israel "assemble together for the hearing of the law, and learning it exactly, and this not once or twice, or oftener, but every week." Similarly, Philo notes that these gatherings are where Jews assembled in "syna-gogues (προσευχάς) . . . most especially on the sacred sabbath days, when they publicly cultivate their national philosophy (φιλοσοφίαν)" (*Embassy* 1:156). Philo further describes these synagogue (συναγωγίοις) gatherings as places where "the law/the sacred Books" (τὰς ἱερὰς βίβλους) would be "read" (ἀναγινώσκοντες) and then an exposition (i.e., explaining what is "not clear" [μὴ τρανές]) would be offered, followed by public discus-sion over the implications of the "philosophy of the ancestors" (τῇ πατρίῳ

---

36. See further on this the discussion beginning on page 162.

37. Barclay, *Jews*, 381. See Bird, *An Anomalous Jew*, 25–27, for his recent qualifi-cation and nuance in relation to Barclay's original claim.

φιλοσοφίᾳ) (*Dreams* 2.127). This provides a plausible institutional context for the ongoing debates over the way the law of Moses contributes to the formation and maintenance of a unique Jewish identity. Thus, Paul's discussion is in concert with the broader Jewish community.

In Acts 18:4, Luke records concerning Paul in Corinth: "And he reasoned in the synagogue (συναγωγῇ) every sabbath, and persuaded the Jews (Ἰουδαίους) and the Greeks (Ἕλληνας)." Note that in Acts 18:2, Aquila and Priscilla are described as recently arriving from "Italy . . . because Claudius had ordered all Jews (Ἰουδαίους) to leave Rome." By the time Paul writes Romans, these two have become Paul's co-workers, so he greets them in Rom 16:3. Thus, while there is evidence that Paul and those who were part of the Pauline mission continued to engage in an intramural debate over whether Jesus was Israel's promised Messiah, it does not follow that there were not other significant tensions as well (Acts 18:5–6). Specifically, Paul disagrees with a significant number of his fellow Jews as regards the extent to which the law of Moses continues to constitute/inform Jewish identity in the messianic age. For example, in Rom 3:19–21, the law of Moses (*qua* Pentateuch) is qualified by the phrase the "Law and the Prophets" (τοῦ νόμου καὶ τῶν προφητῶν). In other words, as argued by Francis Watson, the law of Moses remains authoritative for Paul, "but it must be read through the Prophets as a witness to the gospel."[38] This results in the formation of a Jewish identity that is defined by Christ (the Davidic Messiah), one that is continuous with some interpretations of Israel's ancestral traditions and at the same time discontinuous with it.[39] However, it is evident that Paul has not left his ancestral tradition altogether (e.g., 2 Cor 11:24 detailing his discipline within the synagogue community), though others may have considered him to have done so (Acts 21:29 and the accusation concerning taking Trophimus the Ephesian into the temple). For Paul, being ἐν νόμῳ or ἐκ νόμου continues to be a valid pattern of life in Christ for Jews, and he wants to ensure that gentile Christ-movement members made space

38. Watson, *Paul and the Hermeneutics*, 71–77.

39. Novenson ("Messiah," 99) reminds interpreters that there is nothing like "the Davidic interpretation"; rather, "there is a cluster of texts and traditions associated with the house of David, but from this cluster Paul picks and chooses at will in ways that suit his other theological beliefs." In this, Paul is quite like other Jewish interpreters of the tradition: "Paul has a Davidic messiah who dies and rises from the dead (Rom 1:3–4). 4 Ezra has a Davidic messiah who dies but does not rise from the dead (4 Ezra 7:28–29). The Qumran Community Rule has a Davidic messiah who is himself a priestly messiah (1 QS IX, 11)." See also Heb 7:11–17.

for that. This may also shed light on Paul's arguments in Romans 14–15, the key there being a pattern of life rooted in "faith" (Rom 14:22–23).[40] Torah-informed praxis is a valid pattern of life in the messianic age, if it springs from faith (Rom 14:23) and is empowered by the Spirit (Rom 8:4–5). However, the same is not the case for a pattern of life that is ὑπὸ νόμον (Rom 6:14). Now that Christ has come, Torah-informed praxis as a pattern of life (social identification), when coupled with righteousness/ justification-discourse, leads to condemnation (Rom 6:14; 7:1). The determinant for the continuing validity of the law is the sphere into which it is placed.[41] The law is never a rhetorical actor on its own.

Torah for the messianic age is a viable way to describe Paul's approach to the law of Moses. The key verse in Romans that connects these two ideas is Rom 10:4: "For the Messiah (Χριστός) is the end-goal (τέλος) of the law so that there may be righteousness for everyone who believes." It is beyond the scope of this chapter to address whether this verse indicates (a) end as in termination; (b) goal as in fulfillment; or (c) some sort of combination end-goal/fulfillment view, but that question will be discussed in relation to Paul's argument in Romans 9–11 since it is one of the crucial interpretive moves that contributes to a supersessionist reading of that section of the letter.[42] However, based on my translation it is clear that I take it as end-goal/fulfillment. Paul understood that now that Messiah Jesus had come, the focal point had shifted to him since he was the law's τέλος (10:4). This does not result in the abrogation of the law; rather, it results in the law being placed into the sphere of Christ, the Spirit, and faith, in which it may function as it was originally intended before it was co-opted by S/sin, death, and the flesh (as in Rom 14:22–23).

Paul is convinced that the messianic age has begun in Christ. In Rom 9:5, in the context of his listing the ongoing privileges of Israelite covenantal identity (Christ-following and otherwise), Paul writes: "Theirs are the patriarchs, and from them is traced the human ancestry of the Messiah (ὁ Χριστός), who is God (θεός) over all, forever praised! Amen."[43] This messianic figure was earlier introduced as a Davidic one.[44] In Rom 1:3, Paul had written: "regarding his Son, who as to his earthly

---

40. This passage is discussed beginning on page 208.

41. Snodgrass, "Spheres," 99. For an extended discussion of Rom 6:14, see the excursus beginning on page 104.

42. This discussion begins on page 153.

43. The messianic implications concerning 9:5 are discussed on page 130.

44. This will be discussed further beginning on page 236.

life was a descendant of David," and later in Rom 15:8, Christ is described as "a servant to the circumcision," one who "confirms the promises made to the patriarchs." Jesus's Davidic messianic identity ("the root of Jesse") is then further described in Rom 15:12 by the citation of Isa 11:10: "The Root of Jesse will spring up, one who will arise to rule over the nations; in him the non-Jews will hope."

Paul's belief that Jesus is the Davidic Messiah forces him to deal with the law of Moses because of the earthly and political nature of the promised kingdom (Pss. Sol. 17:4). In some ways, the Davidic Messiah simply rules in righteousness and carries out the judgments of the law. This is the focus of 2 Baruch 51:1–16. However, Psalms of Solomon 17–18 see a more expansive role for the Messiah. The nations serve under his "yoke" and see his "glory," both descriptions of the law of Moses (Pss. Sol. 17:30–31). However, it is not a static law; 17:32 says, "he shall be a righteous king *taught by God*." While this could simply refer to something similar to 2 Baruch 51, Psalms of Solomon 17:42 suggests there is more: "This is the majesty of the king of Israel of which God has knowledge, so as to raise him up over the house of Israel to educate them." This wisdom context of the Davidic Messiah in Psalms of Solomon suggests an eschatological vision for the way the law of Moses would be transformed during the messianic era. It also, parenthetically, ameliorates some of the militaristic references often cited to dismiss the relevance of Psalms of Solomon 17–18 for Paul's messianism.[45] A continuing wisdom tradition, the mosaic Torah taken up in the hands of Christ, may also account for Paul's use of four of the Ten Commandments in Rom 13:8–10 along with a summary of the Levitical command to love and other allusions to the sixth commandment in Rom 2:21–22; 7:1–4; and 1:26–27.[46] Paul's perspective on the nature of the law of Moses in the messianic age may account for the places in which his discourse oscillates between direct citation and summary statements designed to distill the wisdom from his inherited tradition taken up in the hands of the Davidic Messiah (Gal 6:2; 1 Cor 9:20).

The law of Moses in the messianic age does not completely overwrite the law of Moses as it stood before. Romans 3:31 is crucial to the claim that Paul's gospel does not abolish but continues to uphold the law. The organizing principle of the law of Moses was the *Shema*, "Hear, O Israel,

---

45. Jipp, *Christ*, 4–16.

46. See D'Angelo, "Roman," 538.

the LORD is our God, the LORD is One" (Duet 6:4). Nanos comments: "The *Shema* reminds Israel not only of God's loyalty and promises but also of the love of God that is central to Jewish identity."[47] For Paul, the existing identities of Jews and the nations remain salient in his eschatological/apocalyptic thinking. Here is an expanded translation of Rom 3:29–30: "Or is God the God of Jews only? Not the God of members of the other nations also? Yes, of members of the other nations also, since God is one." For Paul, God's oneness would be undermined if gentiles were required to become proselytes by being circumcised since Jesus came to redeem both Israel and the nations. Greg Magee adds two more reasons for the *Shema* quotation: "[it] reorients the reader's focus back to the purpose of the law—to foster wholehearted devotion to God . . . [and] increases the overall credibility of Paul's advocacy for faith by linking faith to the central command of the law."[48] Thus, by showing his gospel aligns with the *Shema*, "the heart of the Mosaic law" and of "Jewish identity," Paul can then reject the argument that it undermines the law.

The *Shema* also was understood to have a future orientation to it. Sifre on Deut 6:4 (Piska 31) expands God's role in teaching and reigning over Israel to also teaching and reigning over "this world" and "in the world to come." It ends with a quote from Zech 14:9 "[T]he Lord shall be king over all the earth. In that day shall the Lord be one and His name one."[49] Paul, though with obviously a differing referent for the messianic agent, describes a similar future scenario in Rom 15:5–13 where he highlights Israel and the nations together worshipping the God and Father of our Lord Jesus Christ. This passage connects the Davidic Messiah, the restoration of Israel, and the continuation of both Jewish and gentile social identities as vital parts of Paul's eschatological vision. This suggests that those, such as N. T. Wright, who argue that the unique identity of Israel has been subsumed/displaced into the church of Jews and non-Jews have gone too far with regard to the way Paul reconfigured Israel's traditions.[50] As Hafemann remarks, "The 'climax of the covenant' remains Israel's future restoration for the sake of the nations."[51] For Paul, the *Shema* clarifies the way existing identities continue to matter. The law

47. Nanos, "Paul and the Jewish Tradition," 63.

48. Magee, "Paul's Gospel," 345.

49. Cited in Nanos, "Paul and the Jewish Tradition," 69.

50. Wright, "Romans," 746–47.

51. Hafemann, "Redemption," 212–13.

of Moses properly interpreted supports Paul's gospel rather than opposes it. For gentiles, this is important since they are non-Jewish actors on a Jewish stage. God's faithfulness to Israel is thus a crucial apologetic for the formation of a salient in-Christ social identity for non-Jews (Rom 11:25–32). Before this chapter ends, it would be appropriate to offer some thoughts on the way Torah might function more broadly in the Christ-movement. This was alluded to earlier in the chapter as the sphere in which Torah was functioning. It is to that we now turn.

Snodgrass's Spheres of Influence: A Way Forward

The continuing validity of Torah in Romans seems rather unproblematic when the following verses are highlighted: "We uphold the law" (Rom 3:31); "The law is holy and the commandment is holy, just, and good" (Rom 7:12); and ". . . in order that the righteous requirement of the law might be fully met in us" (Rom 8:4). With these three verses, Lauri Thurén begins the third chapter of his monograph *Derhetorizing Paul*. His derhetorizing program, however, ends up reinforcing the traditional understanding that Paul abrogates the continuing validity of the law: "As participant in the death of Christ, the Christian is wholly exempt from obedience to the law and should not even try to comply with its ordinances."[52] Klyne Snodgrass, on the contrary, thinks that Paul's theology of the "spheres of influence" indicates that participation with Christ transfers the law into the sphere in which it was intended (Christ, Spirit, and faith), which results in seeing the law as "the expression of the will of God" which "is for life (Rom. 8.7; 7.10)."[53] Snodgrass's approach provides a more satisfactory solution to the problem of the relationship between

52. Thurén, *Derhetorizing Paul*, 130, but see his qualifications concerning Romans (110). There is no possible way to address the massive amounts of literature associated with this much-discussed topic. My intent in this chapter is not to overturn the idea that something has changed with regard to the law now that Christ has come; rather, it is to argue for a more robust understanding of the way Torah as instruction continues especially as it relates to Jewish covenantal identity (but also with a concern for the differing social implications for in-Christ gentiles). This should become more explicit in this section of the chapter.

53. Snodgrass, "Spheres," 99. I would suggest that Thornton ("Sin," 148–49) has missed the trajectory of Snodgrass's argument in that the transferal from one realm to the other allows the Mosaic law to continue in a transformed manner.

Paul and Torah within the Pauline Christ-movement: "*The determinant for the law is the sphere in which it is placed.*"[54]

The participatory nature of Paul's theologizing and the transfer terminology brought up by these two scholars remain crucial in this debate. However, the continuing legitimacy of the law in Romans is challenged when the following verses are brought to the fore: "no one is justified by works of the law" (3:20); "But law came in, with the result that the trespass multiplied" (Rom 5:20); "You have died to the law" (Rom 7:4); "We are discharged from the law" (Rom 7:6); "Christ is the end of the law" (Rom 10:4); and "We are not under law but under grace" (6:14). Frank Thielman concludes that these and other similar statements "do not stand in tension with the positive statements but describe the law from the perspective of the unbeliever."[55] Thielman's larger concern is E. P. Sanders's solution-plight framework.[56] Sanders, on the other hand, contends that "these negative statements arise from the discussion of membership requirements, first of all for Gentiles and then also for Jews."[57] Thus, the negative statements concerning the law form the crux of the debate concerning the referent for "works of the law," since what one determines concerning this phrase reveals whether Paul is narrowly concerned about indexes of identity or more broadly with the inability to do all that the law requires.[58]

54. Snodgrass, "Spheres," 99.

55. Thielman, *Plight*, 91. He concludes that "[f]rom his or her perspective, says Paul, the law cannot be kept (1:18—3:20; 9:30—10:8), brings wrath (4:15), and multiplies sin (5:20; 7:1–13)."

56. Thielman, *Plight*, 93. Thielman continues: "All of this demonstrates, we are told, that Paul thought backwards from solution to plight. He was less concerned with the form that the plight took than that it corresponded to the solution which he was convinced was correct: salvation is found in Christ." Cf. Sanders, *Paul, the Law*, 123–32; Visscher, *Romans 4*, 44–47; Nanos, *Mystery*, 150–51.

57. Sanders, *Paul, the Law*, 84.

58. Resolving this debate is beyond the scope of this chapter and this book. I follow closely Snodgrass, "Justification," 83–84. See the recent rejoinder by Wright, "Justification," 95. Dunn (*Romans*, 1.158) points out that works of the law refer "particularly [to] circumcision" but expands it as "those actions which were performed at the behest of the law, in service of the Torah; that is, those actions which marked out those involved as the people of the law, those acts prescribed by the law by which a member of the covenant people identified himself as a Jew and maintained his status within the covenant." He continues, as is well known, to bring to the fore "the function of the law as an identity factor, the social function of the law as marking out the people of the law in their distinctiveness (circumcision, food laws, etc.)." Cf. Moo, *Romans*, 213–17, "We conclude, then, that Paul criticizes Jews for thinking that the Mosaic covenant is

Snodgrass again seeks to steer a middle path with regard to these negative statements by noting that the law is never alone in Paul's discussions; there is always another entity or qualifier near that needs attention. The law functions in a specific sphere, and paying attention to that sphere brings clarity to Paul's statements: "The law characterized by faith does not merely refer to the witness function of the law, although that may be included. It means the law brought into the sphere of faith where it was intended to function."[59] With regard to "works of the law," Snodgrass does not downplay the issue of boasting in the context of Romans 1–5, but concludes: "ἔργα νόμου then reflect identity markers, but they are a particular 'sub-set' of ἔργα in general, by which people seek to present themselves to God."[60] The usefulness of Snodgrass's approach is evident when the theology of the spheres of influence is incorporated: "ἔργα νόμου [works of law], γράμμα [written code], σάρξ [flesh], and ἁμαρτία [sin] belong together on one side and that ἔργον [works], πνεῦμα [Spirit] and such phrases as δικαιώματα τοῦ νόμου φυλάσσειν [one who observes the regulations of the law, 2:26] belong together on the other side."[61] In this configuration, the sphere in which the term or phrase in question resides determines whether Paul suggests a negative nuance. So, the distinction being made relates to the sphere of the activity not the presence or absence of the activity itself, e.g., "observing the regulations of the law" within the sphere of the Spirit would be seen by Paul as an admirable endeavor. The purpose here is not to dismiss the negative nuance from the verses highlighted above; rather, it is to point out that these statements should be read in their correct contexts. Differing functions or aspects of the law may be Paul's focuses.[62]

Snodgrass's contention is that interpreters too quickly assume that the law is something bad that needs to be removed from within the

---

adequate without that perfection in 'works' without which any system of law must fail to bring one into relationship with God." Nanos (*Mystery*, 9) thinks that "works of the law" properly delineates circumcision. He also rejects the negative estimation attached to this phrase in both Dunn and Moo.

59. Snodgrass, "Spheres," 101.

60. Snodgrass, "Spheres," 102. See further on boasting, Gathercole, *Where*, 216–51.

61. Snodgrass, "Justification," 85.

62. For example, with regard to Gal 3:23–25, interpreters assume that law as a παιδαγωγός indicates that the law has been superseded; however, it is more precisely stated that *this function* of the law has been suspended and that the broader question of Torah *qua* Torah is left open. See Wilson, "Supersession," 236–37.

Christ-movement. While the law could have a negative side (the verses highlighted above point in that direction), its initial purpose was separating holy people from impure ones. Paul understood that the law was from God and thus holy (7:12). He also understood that now that Messiah Jesus had come, the focal point had shifted to him since he was the law's end-goal/fulfillment (10:4).[63] This does not result in the abrogation of the law; rather, it results in the law being placed into the sphere of Christ, the Spirit, and faith. There it functions as it was originally intended before it was co-opted by sin, death, and the flesh.[64] Thus, the law is understood in light of the Jesus tradition, i.e., "the law *of Christ*" (13:8–10; Gal 6:2; 1 Cor 9:21).[65] This way of thinking about Paul's statements on Torah in Romans suggests that one may claim ongoing validity for it within the Christ-movement.

Excursus: Romans 6:14–15 and 7:4, 6— The No Longer under Law Texts

It strikes me that Rom 6:14–15 and 7:4, 6 are so apparently supersessionist that one might set aside the arguments in this chapter if a post-supersessionist reading of these verses is not offered. Thus, this excursus presents one potential way forward. It does so by engaging Rosner's excellent work on Paul and the law, with some nuancing of my own.

One way to resolve the dilemma of the negative statements concerning the law in Romans is to argue that they are addressed to gentiles and thus irrelevant to Jews. Romans 6:14–15 serves as a good case study. According to Rosner, Rom 6:14–15 indicates that believers in Christ are not under the law as law code: "For sin will have no dominion over you, since you are not under law but under grace. What then? Should we sin because we are not under law but under grace? By no means!"[66] Rosner goes to great lengths to argue that gentiles were never under the law, although

63. This verse will be discussed further in the context of Romans 9–11, beginning on page 160, since its contextual associations with 10:5–6 require significant engagement.

64. The function of the law in the sphere of faith is crucial to Paul's argument in Rom 14:22–23, discussed further beginning on page 208.

65. Tucker, *Remain in Your Calling*, 110; there I describe Christ's law "as a lenient halakhah," one in which "the Mosaic law is interpreted by Christ."

66. Rosner, *Paul and the Law*, 54.

Jews historically were. However, he concludes that believers in Christ are not under the law regardless of their ethnic identity.[67]

This raises a crucial question for this book: what about Christ-following Jews? Are they no longer under the law once they are in Christ? This is the significant tension point in the universalistic approach to Christ-movement identity: it presupposes that existing identities are theologically irrelevant in Christ. Several points require further clarification. First, Rosner claims that "Paul is addressing a mixed audience of Jewish and Gentile believers."[68] However, Rosner has already argued that gentiles are not under the law. So, if that is Paul's existing ideological stance, then why would he now need to state afresh that these gentiles are not under the law? Further, Rosner seems convinced that Paul's discourse is focused primarily on Jews, yet he has already argued that they were "under the law."[69] Thus, the implication of these two strands of his argument is that Rom 6:14–15 addresses in-Christ Jews, and that, therefore, Paul abrogates the law in such a way that Christ-following Jews are, in reality, no longer Jews.[70] Rosner comes to this conclusion based on the presence of the phrase "under grace": "Romans 6:14–15 describes the new age inaugurated by the death and resurrection of Christ in which the distinction between Jew and Gentile is redundant."[71] How can Paul be addressing a mixed audience while at the same time think Jewish and gentiles identities have been made redundant? This is one of the major challenges in dealing with Paul's Torah discourse: later de-historicized theological debates are read back into the everyday, lived experience of the mid-first century CE.[72] The abiding distinction between Jews and

67. Schreiner (*Christians*, 77–80) thinks that "Gentiles are included in those who are in the realm of the law" (78).

68. Rosner, *Paul and the Law*, 54.

69. Rosner, *Paul and the Law*, 55. Rosner seems to see chapter 6 and 7 as confronting "Jewish objections." However, this presupposes a problem with Judaism that only emerges at a later period in church history.

70. This implication is made explicit when Rosner (*Paul and the Law*, 49) argues that Paul sees himself as an Israelite but not as a Jew. The argument that Paul makes a distinction between a Jew and an Israelite was discussed on page 45 n. 82.

71. Rosner, *Paul and the Law*, 56.

72. Rosner, *Paul and the Law*, 54. Rosner seeks to resolve this tension by concluding: "for Jewish believers, 'not under the law but under grace' is a reference to their transference from one realm to another, but for Gentile believers it is simply a preferring of one realm (under grace/in Christ) over the main alternative (under the law)." This, however, does not actually solve the problem since this is not the comparative

non-Jews is crucial for maintaining interpretive clarity in verses dealing with Torah. Gentiles seeking identity transformation is not the same issue as Torah's continuing role as a demarcator of the Jewish people.

Second, Rosner assumes Paul's gospel is "law-free" and that Jews are the ones who have a problem with law-free living.[73] It is clear the text could be understood that way, but is it required? Should Rom 6:14–15 be understood as an explicit repudiation of the law? That is Rosner's position, and he concludes that what Paul rejects in these verses is the law as law-covenant.[74] However, Rom 3:19–20 indicates an ongoing role for the law as a testimony to the gospel.[75] While Rosner places this text in his "law as prophecy" section in that it provides a witness to the gospel,[76] Windsor notes that these verses highlight a "dual aspect" to the law in that "[w]hen the world witnesses this failure, it gains recognition of sin."[77] In this view, the continuation of Jewish Torah-observance serves the ongoing purposes of the gospel in the world. This is somewhat of the inverse of Christ-following gentiles living in a manner so as to make Jews jealous (Rom 11:11).

Rosner also assumes that law and grace must be set in an antithetical relationship. These verses instead highlight the way a Christ-follower, once freed from the punishment of the law through the reception of grace, is then able to obey (cf. Rom 8:2).[78] Finally, Cranfield highlights that the contrast between "under law" and "under grace" likely indicates "that Paul is here thinking not of the law generally but of the law as condemning sinners; for, since χάρις denotes God's undeserved favour, the natural opposite to ὑπὸ χάριν is 'under God's disfavor or condemnation.'"[79] Thus,

---

language Paul uses. This is one of the reasons why Snodgrass's ("Spheres," 98–100) approach is preferred. Cf. Rodríguez, *If You Call*, 116, on the "Christian-theological context."

73. Rosner, *Paul and the Law*, 55. Circumcision-free gospel may be a more precise way to describe it. See Rodríguez, *If You Call*, 75 n. 3 and Garroway, *Paul's Gentile-Jews*, 125, who contends that Christ circumcises non-Jews (Rom 15:8; Col 2:11–13); Rom 15:8 is discussed on page 224.

74. Rosner, *Paul and the Law*, 45.

75. The presence of ἵνα in 3:19, "so that (ἵνα) every mouth may be silenced," suggests accountability is the continuing purpose of the law (cf. Rom 5:20–21). See further Windsor, *Paul*, 242.

76. Rosner, *Paul and the Law*, 151–55.

77. Windsor, *Paul*, 215 n. 95.

78. See Shulam and Le Cornu, *Romans*, 223.

79. Cranfield, *Romans*, 1.320. For another perspective see Schreiner, *Christians*,

these verses suggest that the Christ-follower is no longer under the *curse* of the law (cf. Rom 8:1). Therefore, these verses should not be used to support the idea that Paul's addressees are no longer under the law; rather, they are no longer under Torah's condemnation as it had been expressed through the dominion of sin.[80]

This raises again the highly contested issue alluded to above: who are the addressees in view here? Rosner, reflecting on the connections between Romans 6 and 7, points to the addressees being Jews: "he is not addressing all believers but rather 'brothers and sisters . . . who know the law' (Rom 7:1), that is, Jewish believers" and so "[t]his information is not directly applicable to Gentile believers."[81] On the other hand, Mark Nanos thinks the issues addressed in these chapters "were framed for gentiles accepted by faith into the people of God without becoming Jews."[82] The position that the addressees are Christ-following gentiles seems on target. This is the audience that Paul has encoded (Rom 1:5–7, 13–14; 11:1; 15:16), and the diatribal elements that re-emerge at the beginning of chapter 6 suggest that the gentile interlocutor is in view once more.[83] Paul is not establishing a law and grace dichotomy; rather, he is instructing gentiles on the way in which their relationship to God should be structured, i.e., through the gospel.[84] Paul does not have a problem with Torah that needs repudiating.[85] His concern is much narrower: gentiles

---

73–76.

80. For an argument that understands "under the law" as "under the curse of the law" in Galatians, see Wilson, *Curse*, 44.

81. Rosner, *Paul and the Law*, 55.

82. Nanos, *Mystery*, 230.

83. Rodríguez, *If You Call*, 116.

84. Rodríguez, *If You Call*, 116–17. Rodríguez continues, "rather than Torah, the Mosaic covenant that structured *Israel's* relationship with YHWH."

85. If Paul did not think that the law was something that needed to be removed from the Christ-movement, but that, rather, it was to continue to be a standard for life, then what does this say about Paul's expectation with regard to Torah observance? Watson ("Law," 106) questions the premise of the preceding statement and argues that Torah observance, if it did exist, served only a "subsidiary" function to the "gospel" within the Christ-movement. My concern with Watson is whether there is a binary relationship between the two, or if it may be described in another fashion. Similarly, Barclay (*Paul*, 170, 557) in discussing the sociological and hermeneutical context of grace asserts, "Paul detects within the Scriptures a contrast between faith (as human acknowledgement of divine initiative) and Torah observance (the product of human agency), a contrast evident in Galatians 3:11–12 and Romans 10:5–8." However, in his discussion of Romans 9–11, he points out that "unbelief" is that which "disqualifies

seeking to become Jews by means of circumcision and Torah-observance (cf. Rom 3:19). This is the "you" encoded in ἐστε in 6:14; this group overcomes their passions and attains self-mastery not by becoming Jews but through their union with Christ.[86]

However, it does not follow that these gentiles are to live law-free. These in-Christ gentiles are not "under Torah" in the way that non-Christ-following Jews are, but they are becoming part of the broader synagogue community (or at least Jewish-like subgroups) and are living next to those who continue to orient their lives "in Torah" since it continues to guide the life of Israel.[87] The challenge of living in such proximity is massive. As described by Nanos, these non-Jews are "learning to live according to Torah-based norms in order to understand how to live faithfully to the righteousness expected of all humanity ('under grace . . . slaves . . . of obedience to righteousness,' Rom. 6:16)."[88] The interpretive challenge is to distinguish between Paul's rejections of the practice of gentiles transitioning to Jewish identity while maintaining group norms that align quite closely with prevailing halakhic practices.[89] Thus, what might appear at first to suggest an explicit repudiation of the law may in fact prove to be otherwise: a statement that in-Christ gentiles are no longer under the curse of the law.[90] This interpretive possibility immediately

---

the value of Torah-observance." This at least raises the possibility that in the context of belief the value of Torah observance would be confirmed. But Torah observance itself requires definition. See further Watson, *Paul, Judaism*, 129–30; Watson, *Paul and the Hermeneutics*, 314–53. Barclay (*Paul*, 556) uses the term "Torah-praxis" in discussing Rom 9:30—10:4. A portion of this passage is discussed beginning on page 154; see also Hedner Zetterholm, "Question," 80–91, for more on trying to define Torah observance.

86. See Stowers, *Rereading*, 44. Rodríguez (*If You Call*, 120) also highlights the way in which Philo (*Spec. Laws* 1.172–76) argues that Torah provides a better path to self-mastery. Cf. Philo, *Spec. Laws* 1.190–93; 2.195.

87. Rosner (*Paul and the Law*, 50) does acknowledge that "[f]or Paul there is nothing inappropriate about keeping the law as a matter of tradition or preference." The question is: are we talking only about social identity or is there a continuing covenantal identity ascribed to Jewish identity by Paul? Rosner seems to think this option is primarily in the cultural heritage category.

88. Nanos, "Introduction," 27.

89. Rosner (*Paul and the Law*, 86–88) rejects the idea that halakhah had significant impact in Paul's congregations.

90. See Wilson, *Curse*, 44; Schreiner, *Christians*, 74–75. So, also Jews in Christ are no longer under this curse either. This is just not Paul's particular concern here.

raises the question: what about Paul's statements that seem to go further than saying Christ-followers are no longer under the curse of the law?

Two of Paul's starkest statements about the relationship between the law and Christ-followers occur in Rom 7:4a and 7:6ab, where he writes: "Therefore, my brothers and sisters, you were made to die (ἐθανατώθητε) to the law (τῷ νόμῳ)" and "But now we have been released (κατηργήθημεν) from the law (ἀπὸ τοῦ νόμου), having died (ἀποθανόντες) to that by which we were bound (κατειχόμεθα)." This raises a few questions. First, what does it mean to "die to the law"? Second, what does it mean to be "released from the law"? In light of Paul's earlier statement in 3:31 and later ones in 7:7 and 13:8–10, he is likely not saying that the law has been superseded in total. These statements more likely have a narrower focus; they point to a particular function or feature of the law to which Christ-followers are now "dead" and have been "released," i.e., aspects of the law that have been suspended in the "now" time (7:6).

One of these functions is the law's capacity to facilitate righteousness, which has now been relegated to one's identification with Christ (3:21–31). Another is its curse that has been overturned through the Spirit (8:1–4).[91] Both of these features are evident in Rom 7:1–6, the context of the two verses cited above. In 7:4a, the dying to the law was "through the body of Christ" with the result that one is now "joined" to him by his resurrection. In 7:6c, the liberation that occurs allows Christ-followers to "serve in newness of the Spirit." While these conclusions raise further questions with regard to the function of the law of Moses within the Christ-movement along the "Jew-gentile axis," they at least highlight the problems interpreters face when arguing, in the words of Todd Wilson, for its "supersession and superfluity."[92]

---

91. So similarly Wilson, "Supersession," 242. Campbell (*Paul and the Creation*, 110) in discussing Paul, Jewish identity, and Torah in Romans 7, reminds interpreters: "Even the weaknesses of the law so clearly set out in Rom. 7.7–23 are accompanied by what may fairly be described as an apologia on behalf of the law, so that although in the new era in Christ the law by itself is inadequate for salvation, it is diagnosed as weak not because it is not God-given and holy and just and good but because of the sinful context it addresses (7.13–20)." *Pace* Middendorf (*Romans*, 1.200), who concludes that "[t]he entire Law, the Torah, was certainly a gift to Israel. This is even true of the commands, the laws within the Torah. The problem is that the Law itself, apart from faith in God's salvation, was never intended to be the defining basis for Israel's identity." It is not clear how Middendorf can claim that the fulfilling/doing of Torah is somehow separate from the identity that was part of God's revelation to Israel as a nation.

92. Wilson, "Supersession," 242–43. On its function see below, page 111.

Wayne Coppins has recently called into question aspects of the reading offered here. He asks, in what sense "have we been released (or are we free) from the (Jewish) law?"[93] First, since the issue is whether one is considered an adulteress, the point of 7:3 is that Christ-followers are released "from the law's condemnation."[94] I think this is clearly on target; 7:1, 2, and 6 highlight the idea that one has been "released from its sphere of power or jurisdiction," especially as it relates to its curse.[95] Second, Coppins thinks that suggesting Christ-followers are only freed from the law in relation to sin does not say enough; rather, he argues that Paul's claim is about the law's "jurisdiction."[96] While 7:3 could be understood this way, it still seems that the proper subject is sin and "its unavoidable consequence, everlasting death."[97] Third, Coppins points out that even if one were to grant that Paul is not concerned about being free from the law, he still "never explicitly speaks of being 'free for (obedience to) the law.'"[98] This again raises the question of whether Paul thinks those in Christ "fulfill" the law but do not "do" it.[99] Coppins, in a properly

93. Coppins, *Interpretation*, 132. The issue here is whether one may question whether Torah is even in view. In 7:2, Paul highlights the idea that "the law concerning the husband" is the likely referent. So, in this reading, he indicates that once the husband dies the surviving spouse is "discharged" legally from the marriage; however, it does make sense that the point of the illustration is to address some aspect of Christ-followers' relationship to Jewish law. Moo (*Romans*, 411–14) suggests the details of the marriage illustration should not be pressed too far.

94. Coppins, *Interpretation*, 132.

95. Coppins, *Interpretation*, 132. See further Gal 1:8–9; 3:10, 13. Wilson, "Supersession," 242. The difference here may ultimately be one of degree.

96. Coppins, *Interpretation*, 132.

97. Schnelle, *Apostle Paul*, 437. Sloan ("Paul," 54–55) concludes that "Paul's affirmation of the law's inability to save . . . does lie near the center of Pauline thought, . . . *not* because Paul has rejected Judaism (as if he were a proto-Marcionite; Marcion may have been a Paulinist, but Paul would not have been proud of his offspring)."

98. Coppins, *Interpretation*, 169.

99. One example of the problems associated with the term "doing" versus "fulfilling" relates to the Jewish way in which Paul argues in 7:1–6. As Tomson (*Paul*, 120, 123) asserts, the statement in 7:2, which is also present in 1 Cor 7:39, attests to the presence of halakhah in Paul. He points to a reference from the end of the Mishna: "the woman acquires herself by divorce and the death of her husband" (m. Qidd. 1:1). This rule is referenced in two distinct letters, which suggests that this is part of Paul's body of instructions, one that also aligns with the Jesus tradition (Deut 24:1; Matt 19:3–9). The presence of halakhah concerning marriage should at least suggest that the wholesale rejection of Torah here in Rom 7:1–6 may not be primarily in view, especially in that the pericope is addressed to those "who know Torah" (7:1). If Paul

reserved manner, recognizes the potential for Rom 8:4 and 13:8–10 as counter examples to his claim; however, while one may grant the thrust of Coppins's third point, he slightly overlooks a way forward, one that he alludes to in his first argument mentioned above.

Coppins's first argument concerns the condemning function of the law. This function deserves further discussion as it relates to that from which Christ-followers have been liberated. Romans 7:1–6 actually focuses on the function of the law as a tyrant in the context of facilitating righteousness and imposing the curse of death (7:5). Snodgrass points this out: "Christians are transferred from a sphere where law is a tyrant to another sphere where all is determined by Christ" (7:4, 6).[100] The sphere of the flesh in 7:5 is the realm in which the "sinful passions" result in "death." It is likely that the transference out of this power-field into Christ results in the ability to bear fruit and serve in the Spirit (8:1–4, 7). So, while the specific phrase "do the law" is not used in 8:4, as Coppins correctly notes, Snodgrass reminds interpreters that "the law's legitimate requirements are lived out in the sphere of Christ by the work of the Spirit."[101] The law of Moses is not superfluous in the age of the Spirit; rather, it serves as "an abiding standard of behavior."[102] Paul was able to discern what aspects of the law of Moses had continuing validity in the messianic age, including those that resulted in differing social implications for Jews and non-Jews in Christ (Romans 14–15).[103] So, the negative statements about Torah often noted in conjunction with Romans 7 may in fact allude to "the usurped law in the sphere of sin, flesh, and death," while the positive statements elsewhere in Romans "describe the law in its proper sphere where God intended it, the sphere of faith, Spirit, and Christ."[104] Thus,

---

were rejecting Torah, his example would seem to weaken his argument. See further Hedner Zetterholm (*Jewish Interpretation*, 141) who contends, rightly I think, that during the tannaitic period "do Torah" and "fulfill the commandments" are synonymous concepts; see further on this page 166.

100. Snodgrass, "Spheres," 104.

101. Snodgrass, "Spheres," 107. See further below on Rom 13:8–10 with regard to doing the law, page 91.

102. Wilson, "Supersession," 242.

103. See Thielman, "Coherence," 252. Cf. Wilson, *Curse*, 7. On this see further the chapter beginning on page 197.

104. Snodgrass, "Spheres," 107–8. While this does not fully address Coppins's concern about resolving the "question of the relationship between Paul's negative and positive statements concerning the law," it does at least offer a way forward (Coppins, *Interpretation*, 169).

Paul's concern is not with the law *per se* but with specific features and functions of it within the Christ-movement. If the law functions in the sphere of Christ, Spirit, and faith there is no *a priori* reason to preclude its continuing validity within the Christ-movement.

The centrality of the day-to-day experience of the agency of the Spirit for the argument being developed here requires comment concerning another phrase found in 7:6: "so that we are slaves not under the old written code (γράμματος) but in the new life of the Spirit."[105] Rosner concludes that "Paul uses *gramma* as a technical term for the law as an obsolete Jewish legal code, from which Christians are exempt."[106] Scott Hafemann recognizes the letter/Spirit binary as referring to the law without the Spirit as experienced by Israelites under Sinai, and the law with the Spirit as experienced by those in Christ. So, the addressees in 7:6 are freed from the former in order to experience the latter (but not such that the law is disposed of or made redundant). Thus, as Hafemann contends, "this ought not be taken to mean that the Spirit works independent of or as a replacement for the law itself" since "this same law, when encountered by the changed heart in the Spirit, brings righteousness to fruition."[107] In this way of reading the text, the problem is not the law but the sphere in which it functions. This understanding counters the all-too-often expressed contention that what Paul does here is replace the letter with the Spirit.[108] So, scholars who claim 7:4, 6 as evidence that Paul thinks the law of Moses has been superseded or been made superfluous *in toto* have likely overstated their case.[109] To die and be released from the

---

105. With regard to the idea that Christ-followers are "slaves of the Spirit," see Goodrich, "Sold," 495, who points out the broader exile motif and Paul's warning concerning the relationship between the Spirit and the law in "moral transformation." Further, Goodrich ("From Slaves," 530) provides a significant argument with regard to the cross-cultural nature of the slave discourse in Romans. In critiquing Horsley, Byron, and Holland, Goodrich asserts: "Paul's slavery metaphors, therefore, are Jewish—insofar as they build on a familiar scriptural concept—*as well as* Greco-Roman—insofar as they draw on aspects of contemporary slave practice" (520).

106. Rosner, *Paul and the Law*, 100.

107. Hafemann, *Paul*, 180 n. 250.

108. So, e.g., Seifrid, *Christ*, 98, though he recognizes that an "absolute rejection" is not in view.

109. Hagner, "Paul as a Jewish Believer," 106. In the context of Rom 7:1–6, the death that has occurred relates to sin and not to Torah (7:5–6). This also aligns with the broader contextual discussions in Romans 5–6. Paul writes in 7:6b that his addressees are now "dead to that which held us captive." Often the assumption is that it is Torah that held them captive; however, 7:5 indicates that one's "sinful passions" is the

law means to be free from its condemning effects, now that righteousness is facilitated through Christ. The curse, including the difficulties of our day-to-day lived existence, is overturned through the Spirit, but not in a way in which life in the Spirit makes the law unnecessary or results in a law-free existence (1 Cor 7:19b).[110]

Conclusion

I began this chapter by trying map out how, if Jewish identity continues in any meaningful way in Christ, the concomitant necessary continuing validity of the law of Moses even in the inauguration of the messianic era might be understood. I have shown that if one removes the law of Moses completely then Jewish identity is effectively eviscerated of its core marker. In contrast to much of the dominant scholarship, Paul was found to support the idea that Jewish identity continues for Jews in Christ (and impacts gentile in-Christ identity as well). There is a vocational calling on Israel with regard to the possession of divine revelation. Although there are debates concerning the pattern of Jewish life in Christ, Paul was found not to be as anomalous as some think. Rather, he saw a positive role for the law of Moses in the messianic era and did not view Jewish identity as incompatible with life in Christ—as long as it emerged from and functioned within the sphere of faith. So, maybe one did not have to choose between Paul and Moses—the texts are more in concert than the dominant form of Paulinism allows and Paul can be seen as one who could pray as the Psalmist does in Ps 119:18: "Open my eyes, so that I may behold wondrous things out of your law."

---

referent. So, the "sinful passions" are what Christ-followers have died to rather than Torah *qua* Torah.

110. Tucker, *Remain in Your Calling*, 79: "Paul interjects [in 1 Cor 7:19] what is central for both Jews and gentiles, 'keeping the commandments of God.' This step in his discourse repositions the ingroup by redefining what action is acceptable within the community and what is unnecessary. Paul's teaching here contains a distinctly Jewish element. Ehrensperger notes that Paul's teaching presupposes a vital role for Torah in the maturity of the gentile Christ-followers in that 'guidance given in Torah and the Prophets' is to be 'applied to gentiles who now live in the realm of God through Christ.' Did Paul actually expect gentiles to follow Torah? Campbell notes a comparison to Gal 6:15 and then concludes, 'Whatever Paul meant by "the commandments of God," at a minimum, even for those in Christ, this must include keeping at least some of the commandments of Judaism. The commandments do count for something since they still have a paraenetic function for Christ-followers'" (Ehrensperger, *Paul and the Dynamics*, 168; Campbell, *Paul and the Creation*, 93).

While there are a few more details to discuss with regard to the law and righteousness, the idea of gentile inclusion in the identity of Israel and the putative reworking of Israel's scriptural tradition are two crucial issues in Paul's otherwise positive argument for Israel's continuing covenantal identity in Romans 9–11. The next chapter will not be a formal exegesis of all of chapter 9 but will address three challenges to the thesis of this book that Jewish identity continues in Paul's universalistic gospel discourse.

5

Israel's Present Covenantal Identity

Introduction

ONE OF THE STRONGEST arguments against Jewish covenantal identity continuing in Paul's universalistic gospel is that in-Christ gentiles have taken over the identity of and inherited the promises made to Israel according to the flesh. Some of this was addressed in the earlier chapter dealing with Abraham, but Romans 9 raises several key issues with regard to this putative identity transfer. Robert Foster, in *Renaming Abraham's Children*, sees just such an identity transfer and thus calls into question the idea that Israel's present covenantal identity continues unabated in the era of Messiah Jesus since now the "people of God" are determined by faith and not works of the law. Foster thinks Paul has expanded Jewish identity so that it includes righteous in-Christ gentiles and at the same time excludes ethnic Jews "from Abrahamic descent apart from faith in Christ."[1] A key part of Foster's argument is the way he views Paul's reading of Genesis. He thinks Paul "refuses to read Genesis as an unambiguous charter of Jewish ethnic solidarity."[2] Paul's reading of Jewish identity through Genesis results, rather, in its disaggregation; this reading only makes sense through Foster's understanding of Paul's Christo-centric perception (1 Cor 10:11).

Foster's project is an improvement on previous attempts to wrestle with Paul's theologizing concerning Israel in Romans 9. However, some

1. Foster, *Renaming*, 83.
2. Foster, *Renaming*, 83.

specific concerns require attention. First, Foster is convinced that "Israel's covenantal adoption has been not dissolved but redirected exclusively towards the Messiah."[3] The non-dissolution language might be helpful, but the conclusion drawn from his redirection claim is still problematic. He seems to bifurcate that which Paul does not, or so it will be suggested below. Second, Foster, while recognizing that "*New Israel* language" is not present in Paul's letters, thinks that Paul's "dialectical reconfiguration" of "Israel's traditions" calls for just such an organizing framework.[4] It is not clear, however, that Paul incorporates in-Christ gentiles into Israel, or does so in a way that requires the forfeiture of covenantal identity for "Jewish unbelievers."[5] Third, Foster's case relies on various examples of reversals of election throughout Romans 9; the incorporation of the gentiles/nations in 9:24–26 with its reinterpretation of Hosea provides him with significant justification for his view.[6] However, Foster's claim for a reinterpretation needs further attention. Gentile inclusion may not be the point of 9:24–26, and a promise given to historic Israel may not have been appropriated by in-Christ gentiles. In this chapter, we will only focus on three interpretive moves that result in a supersessionist reading of Romans 9 as a way to address some of Foster's arguments. I will (a) offer a positive construction of the continuing covenantal identity for Jews in 9:1–5; (b) address the renewal within Israel in 9:6–9; and (c) present the insertion of gentiles into a promise reserved for historic Israel in 9:24–26 as a model for the way Paul reads Israel's scriptural tradition in light of gentile inclusion into God's family.

Before moving further into the chapter, a nuance in Foster's argument should be noted. This rejection of unbelieving Israel, according to Foster, seems to be Paul's position in all of his writings, except Romans. Foster thinks Paul's view changed concerning Israel.[7] Paul was a supersessionist when he wrote 1 Thess 2:14–17; Gal 6:16; 2 Cor 3:7–9, 14–16; and 1 Cor 9:19–21. However, he came to realize that his earlier teaching was wrong and that the distinction between Jew and non-Jews continues in Messiah.[8] This allows Foster to say that Paul in Romans develops in

---

3. Foster, *Renaming*, 56.

4. Foster, *Renaming*, 72 n. 73.

5. Foster, *Renaming*, 73.

6. Foster, *Renaming*, 186–90, 237.

7. Foster, *Renaming*, 84.

8. Foster, *Renaming*, 101.

such a way that his earlier supersessionism is exactly as it seems and his later rejection of supersessionism is exactly as it seems.[9] Why would Paul change? It is his mission and literary exigence: "Romans is an apologetic defense of the apostle written to counteract the defamation against him and establish the credentials necessary for a partnership with the Roman Christians for the future of his missionary endeavors."[10] This solution is quite simple and appealing; however, as mentioned above, Foster still sees much of Paul's earlier supersessionist rhetoric in Romans 9, though nuanced for his purposes in this letter. This suggests that Foster's work is somewhat helpful in arguing against supersessionism in Romans 9–11, but not so his understanding of Paul in his other letters. I find more continuity between all of Paul's letters in regards to his rejection of supersessionism than does Foster, and even though he qualifies his statements, he seems to not break Paul fully out of supersessionist thinking, especially in Romans 9, which is the focus of this chapter.[11]

The Continuation of Israel's Covenantal Identity (9:1–5)

Jewish Covenantal Identity Described (9:1–3)

Jewish covenantal identity is marked by the ongoing privileges seen in Romans 9:4–5, but this identity is also the cause of anguish for Paul because of the rejection of his message by many within the nation. In Rom 9:1, Paul writes, "I speak the truth in Christ, I am not lying" (Ἀλήθειαν λέγω ἐν Χριστῷ, οὐ ψεύδομαι). Notice that he does not include a connective; the asyndetic construction highlights the emotional nature of Paul's rhetoric. The placement of "truth" (ἀλήθεια) at the front of the clause gives it prominence, and the addition of his rejection of the claim that he is "lying" (ψεύδομαι) reinforces the veracity of the argument that he develops. Its truthfulness is further supported by a claim that what he is about to argue is true "in Christ" (ἐν Χριστῷ). Paul is speaking as a Christ-follower, although not to the exclusion of his continuing identity

---

9. Foster, *Renaming*, 102–3.

10. Foster, *Renaming*, 104.

11. Most of our differences relate to Paul's writing in 1 Corinthians, which is beyond the scope of this present book. I am grateful to Robert for his kind engagement and personal communications that allowed me to hear clearly his arguments. See Foster, *Renaming*, VI.

as an Israelite (11:1).[12] This simultaneous social identification rightly describes the nested social dilemma that Paul seeks to address in Romans 9–11, i.e., what does one's in-Christ identity mean for one's existing identity? In this specific case, is an Israelite identity compatible with an in-Christ one?[13]

Paul further substantiates his claim to truthfulness by writing, "because my conscience bears witness to me in the Holy Spirit" (συμμαρτυρούσης μοι τῆς συνειδήσεώς μου ἐν πνεύματι ἁγίῳ). This genitive absolute construction, with its circumstantial participle of cause, highlights the reason that Paul should be seen as truthful: because his conscience, through the agency of the Spirit, bears witness to it. This phrase parallels the previous one and reveals Paul as one who thinks that both the ongoing experience of being in Christ and in the Holy Spirit combine to support his argument.[14] Why has Paul gone to such lengths to establish his veracity? It is likely that he had been accused of rejecting his own people Israel.[15]

Having established the genuineness of his claim, Paul describes, in Rom 9:2, the degree of emotion associated with his argument: "that my sorrow is great" (ὅτι λύπη μοί ἐστιν μεγάλη). This raises the question, what has caused this sorrow? As Wright notes, the audience does not yet know.[16] Further, he says "and" (καί) there is an "unceasing pain in my heart" (ἀδιάλειπτος ὀδύνη τῇ καρδίᾳ μου). This heightened rhetoric suggests connections with prophetic lament over Israel's present situation (11:20, 23; 3:3). Paul becomes Moses in this section. Michel Quesnel has highlighted Paul's rhetorical construction of Moses in Romans 9–11 more generally, while Wallace has made a similar but more substantial, genre-based claims with regard to Moses, lament, and midrash in these chapters.[17]

12. So correctly Barclay, "Unnerving Grace," 91.

13. On nested social dilemmas, see Tucker, "Paul's Particular Problem," 407 n. 1. It seems that some of the gentiles in the Roman Christ-groups thought that a Jewish identity was incompatible with an in-Christ one.

14. Naselli and Crowley, *Conscience*, 34.

15. Cosgrove, "Did Paul" 281. Longenecker (*Epistle to the Romans*, 782) suggests that Paul may have heard this from some of those he greets in Rom 16:3–16.

16. Wright, "Romans," 628.

17. Quesnel ("La figure," 321–24) points out that in 9:15 Moses appears as the hero of the exodus story, that then in 10:5 he is connected with the justice that comes from the law, and finally that in 10:19 he functions as a prophet seeking change from Israel. This last persona aligns closely with Paul's rhetoric in these chapters. Wallace

Paul continues to see non-Christ-following Jews as his kin even as he intercedes like Moses for Israel.[18] In 9:3, he writes, "For I could wish that I myself were accursed and cut off from Christ for the sake of my brothers (τῶν ἀδελφῶν), my relations according to the flesh." Toews contends that "The implication is that the Jewish people are accursed, and Paul wishes to take their place."[19] While Toews's view is adopted by a significant number of scholars, a more nuanced approach may be in order. For example, one should at least consider the function of this kinship discourse. Cranfield, commenting on Paul's use of "brothers," concludes: "unbelieving Israel is within the elect community, not outside of it."[20] The difficulty here is that interpreters focus only on the salvific use of calling discourse. When the English gloss "election" is used, it triggers a soteriological encyclopedia that overwhelms other interpretive possibilities.[21] The vast majority of the times that Paul uses kinship terms, the referents are others within the Christ-movement. Further, in 11:1–2, Paul makes it clear that God has not rejected his people Israel.[22] These two pieces of evidence suggest that Paul still views even "unbelieving Israel," to use Cranfield's phrase, within the community of those called according to God's purpose.[23] As has been noted in other places in this book, it does not follow that there are direct salvific benefits that accrue to this calling, though it would not exclude those. The focus is likely vocational. Toews's

---

(*Election*, 11–14, 33–35, 38–40) describes the lament-midrash structure and its bookends (9:1–5; 11:33–36). He builds on the idea that Paul functions as Moses especially as it relates to his desire to be accursed for other Israelites.

18. Crisler (*Reading*, 152) reminds readers that the phrase "great grief and unceasing pain in my heart" points to the lament genre, and the "accursed from Christ" phrase echoes Gen 32:32 specifically and Genesis 32–34 generally. The idea of prophetic critique helps to recenter Paul as one who still functions within the Jewish symbolic universe.

19. Toews, *Romans*, 241.

20. Cranfield, *Romans*, 2.459. Middendorf (*Romans*, 2.837–38) strongly rejects this view. See Moo, *Romans*, 559, for an evenhanded discussion of these possibilities. Also, Barth, *CD* II/2, on election of the community and the individual. See also Sonderegger, *The Doctrine of God*, 407; Givens, *We the People*, 234.

21. For more on encyclopedias, see Eco, *Semiotics*, 83–84; Alkier, "New Testament Studies," 233–37; Hunt, "Jesus Caesar," 42–47.

22. These verses will be discussed below starting on page 172.

23. On the issue of referring to non-Christ-following Jews as "unbelievers," see Kinzer, *Postmissionary*, 140–42.

has likely claimed too much; the disbelief of certain or even many Israelites does not result in God's rejection of the Jewish people.[24]

Kinship discourse continues as the next noun in apposition describes the group further as Paul's "relations according to the flesh" (τῶν συγγενῶν μου κατὰ σάρκα). Moo, rightly I think, points out that Paul uses this descriptor of "his fellow Jews to demonstrate the degree of his continuing identification with, loyalty to, and concern for them. 'Apostle to the Gentiles' he may be; but a Jew he remained."[25] The use of συγγενής here indicates that they "belong to the same people group."[26] The invoking of "people group" however raises the specter of essentialism with regard to identity, a false interpretive move that Givens's work seeks to correct.[27] With regard to "according to the flesh" (κατὰ σάρκα) he comments: "in the present context is the gracious continuity—everywhere contingent and subject to decay—by which the living relatives of Paul in view have emerged as such from the long past of Israel, by which the Christ himself is Israelite (cf. Rom. 1:3; 8:3)."[28] Givens's work is helpful in regards to recognizing the presence of ethnic discourse and the way some contemporary people-group theories may result in non-embodied interpretive moves.[29] However, Givens's solution ultimately results in the obliteration of Jewish flesh and identity for Paul.

I would contend that "relations according to the flesh" (τῶν συγγενῶν . . . κατὰ σάρκα) is a neutral and not a derogatory way to refer to an "Israelite according to physical birth," a group he further describes by noting "in as much as they are Israelites" (οἵτινές εἰσιν Ἰσραηλῖται).[30]

---

24. Windsor (*Paul*, 202–10), however, highlights another issue, i.e., that here one sees the conflict between Israel's vocation and Paul's vocation as light to the nations.

25. Moo, *Romans*, 559.

26. BDAG 950, with others being described this way in Rom 16:7, 11, 21.

27. Givens, *We the People*, 346–50.

28. Givens, *We the People*, 347.

29. This is his primary critique of Wright's work. He thinks Wright has bought into the "modern myth of ethnicity," and it has led him to see a literary "foil" in Israelite ethnicity focused on "merely physical descent." In this construction, the inevitable result is some form of supersessionism. See Givens, *We the People*, 347 n. 5; Wright, "Romans," 636. On supersessionism specifically see Givens, *We the People*, 172.

30. Kinzer (*Searching*, 24) refers to this group as "Genealogical-Israel." This has some advantages, and Kinzer notes the following: "(1) the phrase has biblical resonance, since genealogies are a central component in the way the biblical narrative establishes membership in familial groupings; (2) the phrase emphasizes physical descent, as is also the case in Paul's use of *kata sarka*; (3) at the same time, the phrase allows for the inclusion of individuals who enter the family from outside the genealogical grouping

This is a somewhat similar construction to 1 Cor 10:18, "Consider Israel according to the flesh (βλέπετε τὸν Ἰσραὴλ κατὰ σάρκα)." The honorific title Israel is used in both places, though 1 Cor 10:18 uses Ἰσραήλ while Rom 9:4 uses Ἰσραηλίτης. This raises the question, are Ἰσραήλ and Ἰσραηλίτης overlapping terms? Dale Martin contends that these two terms are differentiated for Paul. He notes that 1 Cor 10:18 is the only place where "Israel" (Ἰσραήλ) is used to describe those who do not believe in Christ (though I am not convinced that this is the inference from the use of the phrase κατὰ σάρκα).[31] While this is a possible interpretation on the lexical level, Paul gives those two terms overlapping semantic construals. Although in Rom 9:3–4, Paul uses Ἰσραηλίτης rather than Ἰσραήλ to identify Jews who are "outsiders" with regard to Christ-faith, in 2 Cor 11:22 Paul uses Ἰσραηλίτης to describe himself as an "insider" with regard to Christ-faith. But in Phil 3:5, he also uses Ἰσραήλ to describe himself.[32] Thus, Paul can use these terms in different, overlapping contexts, which then limits the force of Martin's contention. Paul does not use one term positively and the other negatively. For him both are descriptors of the covenant people, and they function as sliding, multilevel, intra-group discourse.[33]

Interpreters generally construe κατὰ σάρκα in a negative way. However, it cannot be completely so since the delimiter κατὰ σάρκα is used in a positive (or at least a neutral) manner in Rom 9:5, which reads: "To them belong the patriarchs, and from whom (ἐξ ὧν), according to the flesh (κατὰ σάρκα), is the Christ." Jewett, however, thinks that this usage is somewhat "polemical" because of the way it introduces the argument in 9:6–13, but a positive use is more likely in light of an earlier use in the letter.[34] Romans 1:3 employs κατὰ σάρκα in a positive manner: "concerning his Son, who was descended from David according to the flesh (κατὰ σάρκα)." These two similar uses of κατὰ σάρκα (Rom 1:3 and 9:5) support

(as with Tamar, Ruth, and Bathsheba in Matthew's genealogy of Jesus—see Matt 1:3, 5, 6); and (4) the phrase also permits the inference that membership in the family is socially as well as biologically constructed, since not every biological descendant is mentioned in a biblical genealogy (e.g., only as an exception are women included)."

31. Martin, "Teleology," 99.

32. Zoccali, *Reading Philippians*, 72, 88, 118.

33. Tajfel and Turner, "An Integrative Theory," 33–47. Intra-group discourse, in the context of self-categorization, emphasizes ingroup similarities and de-emphasizes difference. I see Paul's use of a term such as "Israel according to the flesh" as just such intra-group discourse.

34. Jewett, *Romans*, 566.

the contention that Paul could use this phrase to describe those who are Israelites by physical birth—those who are ethnic descendants.[35]

So, one should not assume that when Paul uses κατὰ σάρκα he is trying to emphasize something negative, though obviously he can use it that way in other contexts (and this is undoubtedly his predominant use of κατὰ σάρκα, e.g., Rom 8:13).[36] Furthermore, interpreters should be cautious to determine which way the comparison occurs (if we are going to claim an implicit metaphor). Paul's comparison could also be positive, as in Ezek 11:19 and 36:26, where "flesh" (בשׂר) is used to describe "spiritual receptivity" and "Israel's renewed allegiance to the Lord in the eschaton."[37] Based on the similar usage in Romans 9, it is just as likely that "Israel according to the flesh" in 1 Corinthians could be understood as a positive group identifier, since the comparison in 10:18 is the ritual life of Israel, a ritual life in which Paul still participates (see Acts 21:24; 1 Cor 9:20; 7:17–18, 20), as compared to the fellowship with demons that occurs in the worship of the nations with their native gods. The suggestion being made here is that this is a positive group identifier describing members of the public synagogue community. This would then include non-Christ-following Jews as well as Jewish Christ-followers in their priestly representation of Israel to the nations, as seen in Rom 11:16: "If the dough offered as firstfruits is holy, so is the whole lump, and if the root is holy, so are the branches."[38]

This raises a further issue: if no negative inference is suggested by κατὰ σάρκα why employ it? Many scholarly conceptions of Paul's use of κατὰ σάρκα specifically and σάρξ more generally have difficulties with this phrase because of their implicit Platonism. Romans 2:28–29 serves as the hermeneutical basis for understanding Paul's "fleshly" and "spiritual" references as binary thinking. Daniel Boyarin is a good example of one who, as noted by Love Sechrest, "reads Paul through the lens of dualistic Platonism, in which the phenomenal world represents the higher 'inner' spiritual realm that is opposed to the lower 'outer material plane.'"[39]

---

35. Nanos, "Romans," 271. In this instance, Wright's translation of 1 Cor 10:18 appears on target: "Consider ethnic Israel" (*Paul and the Faithfulness of God*, 1345), but then see 1242 where he pulls back from the ethnic reference and opts for the phrase as a trans-ethnic label for *ekklēsia* members.

36. Dunn, *Theology*, 65–66.

37. *NIDOTTE* 778.

38. Kinzer, *Postmissionary*, 124–25; see further discussion on this in chapter 7.

39. Sechrest, *Former*, 211, citing Boyarin, *A Radical Jew*, 93–95.

Ehrensperger has discerned a similar reading of Paul through the lens of Platonic dualism in the work of Elizabeth Castelli. She notes the centrality of a supposed "dualistic opposition between spirit and flesh" in her reading that results in a downplaying of ethnic connections for Paul.[40] This is part of the larger problem, that reading Paul through the lens of Platonic dualism results in "a general devaluation of the concrete, material world in Christianity, with its devastating impacts, not exclusively but particularly on women and Jews, who as such were associated with this concrete, material, and 'fallen' world."[41] Paul's way of thinking had its basis in Israel's scriptures, in which, if one were able to discern abstractions, they are focused on the concrete details of the everyday lived-out experience. Paul's thinking is more apocalyptic than dualistic, and in apocalyptic discourse, "visions and revelations serve as a means for understanding contemporary events in the light of Scripture."[42] If the assumption of Platonic dualism is removed, then a more concrete, embodied understanding of κατὰ σάρκα seems more likely, an understanding that is not inherently negative with regard to Israelite flesh.

Israel's Present Covenantal Identity (9:4–5)

The continuation of Israel's covenantal identity in Rom 9:1–3 directs us to the focus of this section, which picks up the question Paul started to answer in Rom 3:1–2a: "Then what advantage has the Jew? Or what is the value of circumcision? Much, in every way." Here in 9:4, he writes: "They who are and remain Israelites (οἵτινές εἰσιν Ἰσραηλῖται), to whom belong the adoption as sons, and the glory and the covenant and the giving of the law and the temple service and the promises." As we have just seen, a negative inference does not need to be assumed simply from the use of Ἰσραηλίτης. However, the presence of the οἵτινές has led interpreters to suggest that Paul distances himself from some of his ethnic group.[43] Leander Keck notes that Paul "does not say 'we are Israelites,' but refers to them in third person (hoitines, 'they are the ones who'), as he does

40. Ehrensperger, *Mutually Encouraged*, 168, citing Castelli, "Romans," 292.

41. Ehrensperger, *Mutually Encouraged*, 56–57.

42. Ehrensperger, *Mutually Encouraged*, 83.

43. See recently on this Gaventa, "Thinking," 242–47. One way forward on this issue may be Ticciati, "Nondivisive," 265: "The danger is that Gentile believers in Christ will construe themselves competitively in relation to Israel as those who have displaced Israel."

throughout chapters 9–11; despite his ethnic solidarity with them, 'we' has become 'they.'"[44] If Paul's Jewish identity continues to be salient, why refer to the Israelites as "they"?[45]

In 9:4, Paul uses the present tense verb εἰσιν "they are," suggesting that all of those from historic Israel continue to embody the label "Israelite." Keck does pick up on this and notes that the εἰσιν was unnecessary, which in turn suggests that Paul was "pointing out that despite their current unbelief they *are and remain* Israelites."[46] In a similar fashion, Kendall Soulen sees the present tense in 9:4 and the implied present tense in 11:28 as bookends for Paul's argument for the continuing covenantal identity for Paul's relatives "according to the flesh" (9:3). Soulen refers to this belief as Paul's "*credendum*, [i.e.,] the 'present tense' election of Paul [*sic*] kinsmen 'according to the flesh.'"[47] He is correct to point out that Paul thoroughly deconstructs their continuing election but then ultimately emerges with his original *credendum* intact, which then propels him forward in adoration and worship (11:33–36). Soulen's argument may be strengthened by recognizing that the present tense εἰσιν may be further classified as a customary present. Wallace describes the customary present as a tense usage designed "to signal . . . an ongoing state." In discussing the differences between the iterative and customary present tense usage, he notes that "the customary present is an iterative present with the temporal ends 'kicked out.'"[48] This suggests that the social identity label "Israelite" continues to be salient for Paul in describing his "relations according to the flesh." If the customary present category is applied to εἰσιν, then the phrase οἵτινές εἰσιν Ἰσραηλῖται could be translated: "They who are continually Israelites" or "They are and remain Israelites." Thus, Keck and Soulen both have alerted us to the importance of the

---

44. Keck, *Romans*, 227.

45. Along with the arguments just given, one should also note that Paul does self-identify as an Israelite in Rom 11:1. This, I would argue, blunts some of the force of the division within Israel noted by Keck.

46. Keck, *Romans*, 227.

47. Soulen, "They Are Israelites," 499.

48. *GGBB* 521. Campbell (*Verbal Aspect*, 64) would take a different approach: "Present tense-forms often end up depicting a state. This is also a natural implicature of imperfective aspect. Imperfective aspect combines with a stative lexeme to create a stative *Aktionsart*, if this is not overturned by context. A stative lexeme is a word that describes a state of being rather than a process or transitive action." Thus, although Campbell's analysis differs, the force of his conclusion is the same.

present tense in determining the ongoing nature of Jewish covenantal identity.[49]

The ongoing nature of this identity is made more explicit by the listing of several of the continuing gifts given to Israel (see further 11:28–29 which seem to point back to 9:4–5). The gifts are arranged in a chiastic fashion with "the adoption" (ἡ υἱοθεσία) being first, likely picking up on the earlier references to it in 8:15, 23.[50] Paul writes, "to whom belongs the adoption as sons (ὧν ἡ υἱοθεσία)." While it is correct that υἱοθεσία does not occur in the LXX, Burke misses the mark when he downplays the conceptual links to Exod 4:22–23: "This is what the Lord says [to Pharaoh]: Israel is my firstborn son (υἱὸς πρωτότοκός μου Ισραηλ) . . . 'Let my son (τὸν λαόν μου) go, so that he may worship (λατρεύσῃ) me'" (CSB).[51] This is further suggested by the restatement of this sonship in Hos 11:1: "When Israel was a child, I loved him, and out of Egypt I called my son." The presence of "the giving of the law (ἡ νομοθεσία)" in Rom 9:4 suggests that the Exodus narrative is in Paul's discursive framework. Adoption discourse is also mentioned in verse 4 (see further 11:17–24, which references adoption using the image of engrafting). It is likely that throughout this section Paul is responding to ideas similarly found in Jubilees, e.g., "and I will be their Father and they shall be my children. And they shall be called children of the living God, and every angel and every spirit shall know, yea, they shall know that these are my children, and that I am their Father in uprightness and righteousness" (Jub. 1:25).[52]

The ongoing covenantal identity of Israel is affirmed by the acknowledgment of "the glory (ἡ δόξα)." The referent here is likely God's presence. One example of this use of the word is found in Exod 16:7, which reads: "and in the morning you will see the glory of the Lord,

49. See further Rudolph, "Zionism," 182–94.

50. Rightly so Scott, *Adoption*, 148, who also sees adoption as the most significant gift. However, if one follows Christiansen's chiastic structure then the focus would be on covenant and the giving of the law. Christiansen, *Covenant*, 219:

A: the adoption,
   B: the visible presence,
      C: the covenant,
      C[1]: the giving of the law,
   B[1]: the temple service,
A[1]: the promise

51. Burke, *Adopted*, 48–49, but see 170, where he does recognize that adoption discourse is relevant to Israelites in some sense.

52. Dunn, *Romans*, 2.526.

because he has heard your grumbling against him." Moses then goes on to describe the way the Israelites will be cognizant of the Lord's presence. The entire community is summoned, and 16:10 states: "While Aaron was speaking to the whole Israelite community, they looked toward the desert, and there was the glory of the Lord appearing in the cloud." The glory referred to in that instance, then, is God's presence. It includes various manifestations of God's preeminence throughout the universe and his miraculous works towards the nation (Ps 19:1; Exod 14:19–20, 24; 33:18).[53] Jubilees, in a significant rewriting of Exod 24:12–18, begins by highlighting God's glory. Moses is told to go up to Sinai where "the glory of the Lord abode." Then after seven days, out of a "cloud," the "glory of the Lord" appeared "like a flaming fire" (Jub. 1:1–3).[54] For Paul, though he relies on Exodus 19, rather than 24 like Jubilees, the glory of the Lord still rests upon Israel.[55]

Paul continues by describing another of the ongoing privileges of the Jews: "the covenant (διαθήκη)."[56] This is echoed in the composite citation from Isa 59:20–21 and 27:9 in Rom 11:27: "and this will be my covenant (διαθήκη) with them when I take away their sins." For Paul there is one covenant with Israel. It is the one mentioned in Exod 19:5, "Now if you obey me fully and keep my covenant (τὴν διαθήκην μου), then out of all nations you will be my treasured possession." The covenant in Exod 19:5 establishes Israel's identity in a unique manner.[57]

There is a text-critical question about the number of διαθήκη, but the singular reading is followed here. Why is the singular reading preferred? First, as is often acknowledged, the external evidence for the singular variant is quite strong. However, it is often set aside because the plural is the harder reading.[58] While this general text-critical rule may be granted, the singular reading would actually be more difficult in the

53. See Ross, *Recalling*, 46–49.

54. See further on this Doering, "Reception," 487.

55. Longenecker (*Epistle to the Romans*, 784) picks up on some of the same insights but then expands this prerogative to include "Israelites, as the remnant of Israel, or as believers in Jesus of whatever ethnicity." This raises the question: is Paul's purpose here to expand these benefits or are they properly focused on Israel? For Paul's continued Israel-centric reading of glory, see 2 Cor 3:13.

56. This takes the singular marginal reading rather than the plural καὶ αἱ διαθῆκαι.

57. Christiansen, *Covenant*, 222.

58. So Middendorf, *Romans*, 2.831–32, even though he opts for the plural reading. The vast majority of the uses of διαθήκη in the NT are singular (Rom 11:27; 1 Cor 11:25; 2 Cor 3:6, 14; Gal 3:15, 17).

context since the referent would be the Sinai covenant as the preeminent one. This reading, however, would in some ways amount to a tautological expression and thus is set aside by commentators. Commentators usually interpret the plural as a listing of all the covenant restatements, which has the effect of blurring Paul's focus in this verse.[59] Christiansen summarizes the issue: "the heart of the matter is whether Paul refers to plural covenants from an overall perspective of historical succession and replacement."[60] It is more likely that Paul sees an overarching covenant with Israel, and not several as is often thought today. Second, the singular reading is preferred since Israel's scriptural tradition describes the covenant that way (1 Chr 16:15–17).[61] Thus, Paul could simply state it in this list without further explanation. If he had chosen the plural then this distinctive usage would have required additional comment. Christiansen picks up on the reason most interpreters prefer the plural reading: "the choice of *plural takes the sting out of Paul's argument*."[62] The referent to Sinai and a more limited understanding for covenant would have been particularly jarring in light of his earlier use of Abraham in Romans 4. As has been evident, each item in Paul's listing so far connects to Exodus as well as to Jubilees's rewriting of that tradition.[63]

The ongoing centrality of Torah for Jewish identity is summed up by Paul in the next item on the list: "and the giving of the law (καὶ ἡ νομοθεσία)." This may point back to the earlier answer to the question of what advantage there is to being a Jew (Rom 3:1–2). The last part of the answer there was: "the Jews were entrusted with the oracles of God (τὰ λόγια τοῦ θεοῦ)." The phrase, "oracles of God," encapsulates what occurs in Exodus 20. The giving of the law opens up Jubilees as well, "God spoke to Moses, saying: 'Come up to me on the mount, and I will give you two tables of stone of the law and of the commandment, which I have written, that you may teach them'" (Jub. 1:1).

---

59. E.g., Longenecker, *Epistle to the Romans*, 785: "God's covenants with Abraham (Gen 15:18; 17:2, 7, 9); with Isaac (Gen 26:3–5; Exod 2:24); with all three of the patriarchs, Abraham, Isaac, and Jacob (Exod 6:4–5; Lev 26:42); with Moses (Exod 24:7–8); and with David (2 Sam 23:5)."

60. Christiansen (*Covenant*, 221) continues "whether he, as in Galatians, sees covenants in tension, or prefers a singular covenant for *theological* reasons."

61. Christiansen, *Covenant*, 4–11.

62. Christiansen, *Covenant*, 222, emphasis original.

63. See Halpern-Amaru, *Rewriting*, 25–55.

The list of Israel's privileges continues with "the temple service (καὶ ἡ λατρεία)." Sarah Whittle thinks this "is the worship or sacrificial service which is God-ordained for the people of God to carry out."[64] Its focus is on cultic service, and it includes those activities associated with Passover as it is practiced in the land (Exod 12:25) and with the renewal of the covenant (Josh 22:27). So far, this analysis is not particularly controversial. However, whether this service is shared with in-Christ gentiles as the newly redefined people of God is another question. Whittle, building on Wright, summarizes the position: "This is one more place where Israel's privileges are shared with the Gentiles. It is a redefinition and reappropriation which can 'hardly be overemphasized.'"[65] This raises again the concern that has emerged throughout this book: has gentile inclusion redefined Israel's covenantal identity to the point where the presence of the Spirit in the new covenant has rendered Israel's cultic service redundant? As shown in Acts 21:24, the earliest in-Christ Jews continued to participate. Thus, in Romans, it seems rather that this list has Israel's continued covenantal identity in view and not gentile inclusion. Rather than the spiritualized worship that emerges from a reading that attempts to incorporate gentiles into the performance of this gift from God, the focal point for λατρεία is more likely on Exodus 25–31 and the details associated with the cultic worship. For Israel, the gift of worship culminates with 31:18, "And he gave to Moses, when he had finished speaking with him on Mount Sinai, the two tablets of the testimony, tablets of stone, written with the finger of God."

The sixth and final privilege for Israel includes "the promises" (αἱ ἐπαγγελίαι). This word presents another text-critical question, whether one should read the singular ἐπαγγελία or the plural. In this case, however, the external evidence supports the plural reading. With regard to internal evidence, the earlier discussion of "promise" in 4:13, 14, 16, and 20 suggests the singular should be preferred; however, in 15:8 the confirmation of "the promises" made to the patriarchs is highlighted. Further, as noted by Longenecker, "the 'remnant' of Israel" are described "as 'children of promise' (9:8)" while "both Sarah and Rebecca" are "recipients of God's promises (9:9–13)."[66] The singular or plural, then, is difficult to determine. If it is the singular, then God's promise in Exod 19:5–6

---

64. Whittle, *Covenant Renewal*, 82.

65. Whittle, *Covenant Renewal*, 82. Whittle also references Wright, "Romans," 704. Longenecker, *Epistle to the Romans*, 786, also focuses on a redefinition of worship.

66. Longenecker, *Epistle to the Romans*, 787.

that Israel will be a "holy nation" (ἔθνος ἅγιον) in whom God's presence will remain may be in view. This is especially probative in light of Paul's argument in Rom 11:26–27. Jubilees 1:17, too, picks up on this connection: "And I will not forsake them nor fail them; for I am the Lord their God."[67] However, it may be the case that the promises of land and people discussed in Romans 4 are not fully out of Paul's field of reference. Either way, this list supports the idea that, for Paul, Israel's covenantal identity remains salient. However, the more crucial question now becomes: was this one covenant made with all of Israel or only with a part of Israel?[68] Before Paul turns to that question in his discussion of the remnant, he highlights central figures for the formation of Jewish covenantal identity: the patriarchs and the Messiah.

Jewish covenantal identity in intertwined with the patriarchs and Israel's Messiah. Paul writes in Rom 9:5, "whose are the fathers, and from whom is the Messiah according to the flesh, who is over all as God blessed forever! Amen."[69] The first term suggests that for Paul Israel still has "the fathers (οἱ πατέρες)." It may also suggest, as was argued in chapter 4 concerning Abraham's paternity for Israel, that Paul still views the patriarchal lineage as relevant for them; it is not only the possession of those who have the faith of Abraham. The chiastic structure (see footnote 50) is interrupted by the presence of ὧν, though it does connect it back to the beginning of the list where an earlier ὧν was present in ὧν ἡ υἱοθεσία. The reason "the fathers" are not listed in the chiastic structure may relate to the way in which those from the nations are included as gentile worshippers of the God of Israel. This seems to be a point where a both/and emerges for Paul. Abraham, Isaac, Jacob, and his twelve descendants are properly understood as the founders of ethnic Israelites. This then is the

---

67. So similarly Christiansen, *Covenant*, 222–23.

68. This will be one of Paul's concerns starting in Rom 9:6.

69. The last phrase above follows Longenecker, *Epistle to the Romans*, 779. The extensive debate over Christ's identity in relation to the God of Israel is beyond the focus of the present argument. Those interested should consult particularly the following: Jewett, *Romans*, 567–69; Dunn, *Romans*, 535–36. See also Schreiner, *Romans*, 487–89, for a succinct argument for a positive reference to Christ as God here. See now Longenecker, *Epistle to the Romans*, 788–91, who likewise affirms that Paul refers to Jesus as God here; however, he also provides an even-handed consideration of the difficult syntax. Note also that the approach of this book is properly described as an evangelical post-supersessionist one. It thus affirms that Jesus shares in the unique identity of the God of Israel. See briefly also Jipp, *Christ*, 171–72.

way in which Israel's blessings are passed down.[70] However, Paul uses the phrase in two other places that hint at a potential identity transformation among their descendants. In Rom 11:28 he writes, "As regards the gospel, they are enemies for your sake. But as regards election, they are beloved for the sake of their forefathers (τοὺς πατέρας)." This suggests a division within Israel, but the referent remains Israel-centric so even then the phrase is not problematic for a post-supersessionist reading. The other usage of the term is in 1 Cor 10:1, "For I do not want you to be unaware, brothers (ἀδελφοί), that our fathers (οἱ πατέρες) were all under the cloud, and all passed through the sea." Martin thinks this verse indicates that in-Christ gentiles have now been written into Israel.[71] I have addressed this more fully elsewhere, but here I would simply mention: (a) Paul views in-Christ gentiles as worshipping the God of historic Israel so some of this kinship discourse would be expected, but (b) they do this as gentiles who have been grafted into God's family while remaining distinct from the natural branches.[72] For Paul, the patriarchs still belong to the Israelites even as the blessings of the covenant are now being realized by gentiles in Christ.[73]

Paul had become convinced that Jesus was the Messiah, and so he completes his description of Israelite advantage by writing: "and from whom is the Messiah according to the flesh" (καὶ ἐξ ὧν ὁ Χριστὸς τὸ κατὰ σάρκα). Jesus's identity as a Jew, a descendant of David, is vital to Paul's gospel. He began his letter in Rom 1:3 with a similar affirmation: "concerning his Son, who was descended from David according to the flesh" (κατὰ σάρκα). He then brought the letter to an end in Rom 15:12 citing Isa 11:10: "The root of Jesse will come, even he who arises to rule the gentiles; in him will the gentiles hope." Jesus's Jewish flesh is integral to his identity as Messiah (cf. 2 Tim 2:8; Rev 22:16).[74] The titular use of ὁ Χριστός here in 9:5 as well as in 15:3 and 15:7 strongly suggests his messianic status. With his continued service to Israel, "Christ became a

---

70. Exod 3:13–16; Num 20:15; 26:55; Deut 1:8; 8:3, 16, 18; 9:5 are references given by Middendorf, *Romans*, 2.841. See further Tucker, *Remain in Your Calling*, 131 n. 70.

71. Martin, "Teleology," 99.

72. See further Tucker, *Remain in Your Calling*, 131–32; Tucker, *Reading 1 Corinthians*, 98–102.

73. For example, in Gal 3:8, Paul refers to the promise concerning the inclusion of gentiles and quotes Gen 12:3, which, referring to Abraham, reads, "in you all the nations will be blessed." See further Tucker, *Remain in Your Calling*, 129–30.

74. See Rudolph, *A Jew to the Jews*, 177–78, especially n. 13.

servant to the circumcision" (15:8). This suggests that for Paul, "God has not rejected his people whom he foreknew" (11:2). Paul's universalistic gospel never loses its focus on Israel.[75]

Paul's listing of Jewish covenantal identity in Rom 9:4–5 is stated, however, in the context of his prophetic anguish and lament in 9:2. Paul is not simply committed to his ethnic heritage but views Israel as a continuing covenant partner. As noted by Kinzer, "Israel may be in crisis, but she is still Israel."[76] So, somewhat unexpectedly, Paul's argument takes a turn to address the issue of the spiritual insensitivity among the nation. Kinzer's solution is to point to Rom 11:5 where Paul uses "the biblical term 'the remnant'" to describe "an Israel *within* Israel, an elect core *within* the elect nation."[77]

Israel within Israel Divides Historic Covenantal Identity (9:6–9)?

Division within Israel (9:6)

Paul has just written a strong argument for the continuing covenantal identity for Israel. Now he addresses the way it has also been renewed in the messianic age. Paul writes in Rom 9:6, "It is not as though the word of God had failed. For not all Israelites truly belong to Israel." This is one of the key places where Israel's covenantal identity is thought to have been transferred to another group.[78] This raises the question: Does Rom 9:6 include Christ-following gentiles in the social identity group, Israel? C. H. Dodd considers this possibility, "If He chooses to reject the Jews and to elect Gentiles, then the true 'Israel' is composed of those whom He

---

75. Rudolph, *A Jew to the Jews*, 169.

76. Kinzer, *Postmissionary*, 124.

77. Kinzer, *Postmissionary*, 124–25.

78. This verse along with Rom 2:28 are often presented together. See the earlier discussion on 2:28 starting on page 53. Nanos (*Romans*, 215–16) reminds interpreters that there is no underlying Greek word for "truly," and so this supposed "qualification" is not textually determined. He also notes that the statement here could be that of Paul's interlocutor, one he seeks to undermine (11:11). Finally, he mentions 9:6 could be punctuated differently resulting in: "But are not all these Israel, who are from Israel?" This would make sense in light of 9:2–5 and would suggest Paul wants the gentiles to social identify primarily with "the Jewish communal subgroup of Christ-followers" (Nanos, *Romans*, 116).

elects."[79] Similarly, C. K. Barrett suggests that "'Israel' cannot be defined in terms of physical descent, or understood simply 'on the human side' (v. 5); it is created not by blood and soil, but by the promise of God."[80] Dunn nuances the discussion but still concludes that "believing Gentiles are being incorporated" into "[t]he Israel of God."[81] These three interpreters highlight the general tendency among scholars to conclude that Rom 9:6 creates a new social category, i.e., in-Christ gentiles as Israel, in which Jewish ethnicity has been transcended. In this view, Paul makes a distinction between Israel according to the flesh and believing Israel, which now includes members from the nations other than historical Israel. However, 9:6 more likely does not teach that in-Christ gentiles have taken over the identity of historic Israel. Instead, it describes a division within this historical group: Jews who believe in Jesus as Israel's Messiah and those who do not or will not. Thus J. A. Fitzmyer concludes "that 'Israel' in the second instance refers to Jewish Christians, to those of ethnic Israel who have put their faith in Christ."[82] C. E. B. Cranfield concludes similarly,

79. Dodd, *Romans*, 155. The inference from this is that the historic nation of Israel has forfeited its covenantal identity and blessing. Cf. Givens, *We the People*, 349.

80. Barrett, *Romans*, 180. Wright ("Romans," 636) recognizes a division within Israel here, one that implicitly sets Israel according to the flesh at odds with God's purposes: "Paul has put down a marker that from this point on the word 'Israel' has two referents, just as with the word 'Jew' in 2:28–29." The multiple referent approach is central for many contemporary interpreters. See e.g., Zoccali, *Whom God*, 131. Givens (*We the People*, 347) sees this modern understanding of ethnicity to be a problem: "the foil to descent by election for Wright (as for many others) is 'merely physical descent': 'reckoned as seed' . . . means being part of the elect group, *as opposed to merely physical descendants* (636, my emphasis). But the Bible, including Paul, knows nothing of 'merely physical descendants.' There is in fact no such thing, for there is always more to bodily descent than the abstraction 'mere physicality.'"

81. Dunn, *Romans*, 2.540. Abasciano (*Romans 9:1–9*, 189) after discussions of individual and corporate election in Rom 9:6 concludes: "Paul has made the point that not all who are from ethnic Israel are part of the true, spiritual Israel, which is heir to the covenant promises of God." He represents the view that there is a division within Israel and thus only those who have not rejected Christ are properly understood to have a continuing covenantal identity. Nanos (*Romans*, 216) points out that such a view concerning chapter 9 goes against what Paul writes in chapter 11; however, it is more likely that chapter 11 "confirms[s]" chapter 9 rather than "contradict(s)" it.

82. Fitzmyer, *Romans*, 560. It must be acknowledged that the statement here is perplexing with regard to the nature of Israel's identity; however, it seems best to maintain that Paul is not redrawing the boundaries around Israel such that it now includes in-Christ gentiles. Further, it does not seem that highlighting a group of Israelites within Israel who have been uniquely called by God removes the covenant relationship from the other Israelites. This is another example where vocational and soteriological

that "the point Paul is making is that not all who are included in the comprehensive Israel are included also in the selective, special Israel. But this does not mean what it has so often been taken to mean—that only part of the Jewish people is the elect people of God. Paul is not contriving to disinherit the majority of his fellow-Jews."[83] Finally, as Sanday and Headlam long ago asserted, "Paul does not mean here to distinguish a spiritual Israel (i.e., the Christian Church) from the fleshly Israel."[84]

The case of those who think that Rom 9:6 includes Christ-following gentiles in the identity of Israel suffers for the following reasons. First, there seems to be a tendency to read the "Israel of God" from Gal 6:16 into Rom 9:6. However, the referent in the Galatians verse is debatable and need not be understood to refer to the *ekklēsia*.[85] Second, and similar to the first point, there is a presupposition that 1 Cor 10:18 with its referent to "Israel according to the flesh" implies an Israel according to the Spirit (read as Jews-and-gentiles-in-Christ) and Rom 9:6 seems to suggest something similar. However, the group referred to in 1 Cor 10:18 is not necessarily negative for Paul. It is more likely that in that instance

---

concerns must be recognized and not conflated. See Windsor, *Paul*, 50–51. Nanos (*Romans*, 116) downplays the division within Israel here. He thinks the "distinction" is between Israelites who "properly represent Israel presently" through their announcement of good news, and those who "presently" do not but will "in the end." This shifts the focus from soteriology to vocation.

83. Cranfield, *Romans*, 2.473. *Pace* Justin, *Dial.* 135; and the critique in Skarsaune, *In the Shadow*, 267–68.

84. Sanday and Headlam, *Romans*, 240. Bird (*Romans*, 325–26) suggests thinking about this division within Israel not as "true" or "spiritual" Israel but as "promissory Israel." This is an embedded Israel within ethnic Israel. This group is aligned more precisely with those who are "Abraham's children" in a way that the larger group is not. In Bird's configuration, "hereditary connection to Abraham is not the basis for belonging to Abraham's chosen 'seed.'" This is an improvement over Wright's approach since Bird maintains that the referent here is ethnic Israelites. If this group is expanded to include in-Christ gentiles then it becomes problematic since Jewish covenant identity would be diffused into a new entity composed of those in Christ. See Horner, *Future Israel*, 93.

85. Campbell (*Paul and the Creation*, 49, 52, 129–33) is particularly convincing. Paul does not designate gentiles in Christ as Israel; the "Israel of God" refers to historical Israel. Ehrensperger ("Pauline," 199–200) rightly sees in Gal 6:16 a blessing on "the nations and for Israel"; rather than "a blessing for a new Israel or a new humanity." Eastman ("Israel," 367–95) offers a view in concert with Campbell and Ehrensperger, building a particularly strong exegetical case for idea that Paul does not make those in Christ into "the Israel of God" in Gal 6:16 (cf. Nanos, *Romans*, 225–33; Windsor, *Paul*, 55–61; Zoccali, *Reading Philippians*, 63 n. 30; and Tucker, *Remain in Your Calling*, 133 n. 83, for slightly different post-supersessionist nuances).

Paul used the term in a neutral way. Third, the context of Rom 9:1–5 works against the transcending or incorporative reading. Paul makes it clear in these verses that even unbelieving Israelites are still the recipients of Israel's covenantal privileges; all Jews continue to be God's people—period.[86] Fourth, Paul's rhetorical intent in 9:6–9 is to show that God's word has not failed even if there is a division within historic Israel with regard to the apprehension of some of the promises.[87] Thus, it is more likely that the "Israel of God" of Rom 9:6 should be understood not as in-Christ gentiles but as Jews.

Paul's division within Israel is not one that would set him outside the bounds of Judaism. The Damascus Rule describes just such a distinction: "But with the remnant which held fast to the commandments of God, he made his covenant with Israel forever, revealing to them the hidden things in which all Israel had gone astray" (3:13–14). There is a sense in which the covenant is properly for those who are following the commandments. The writer then envisions a distinction between those keeping the covenant and those who do not. Aageson, rightly I think, envisages a covenant-faithful group within the "physical entity" of the nation of Israel.[88] While the sectarian nature of the Qumran community differs from Paul's vision of socially integrated missional communities, it does suggest that this imagery does not require the transference of identity suggested by Moo.[89] Most would not suggest the Qumran com-

---

86. Barrett, *Romans*, 474. Nanos (*Romans*, 227) also reminds interpreters that the message of 9:7–16 is "explaining that God chose a particular line of genealogical descendants to undertake a special task as 'the seed.'" Some are not discharging this vocation, but they have not lost their identity as descendants because of this. They are still "protected" or "safed." Nanos's conclusion, "'all Israel will be *protected*,'" highlights the idea that these Israelites are being and will continue to be *preserved safely* in their already *preexisting* covenantal standing in spite of present circumstances that Paul's addressees might be tempted to interpret differently, such as in the direction of later Christian replacement theology" (218). This is a helpful nuance, though there is also a future orientation to this, one that will be developed further beginning on page 184.

87. Sanday and Headlam, *Romans*, 240. Nanos (*Romans*, 229) alternatively suggests that "Paul is referring metaphorically to whether the word of God has *fallen* in the sense that many of the Israelites have not joined Paul and other Christ-followers as messengers bringing the gospel—the news of good awaited—to the nations." It has not "fallen" because Paul and other Israelites are confirming Israel's vocation as a "light to the nations" (Isa 49:6).

88. Aageson, *Written*, 92, though on page 93 Aageson adds "those who believe in Christ are Israel."

89. Moo, *Romans*, 574.

munity had left Judaism but do not extend the same possibility to Paul. Yet that possibility should not be excluded. So, even if he makes a division within Israel it does not follow that those who are yet to be (or may not be) convinced by his gospel have forfeited their membership in Israel.[90]

Σπέρμα as Covenant or Kinship Identity (9:7)

Paul, in 9:7, explains this division within Israel further by picking up on the covenantal (and not just kinship) implications of σπέρμα "children" as compared to τέκνα "offspring": "and not all are children of Abraham (σπέρμα Ἀβραάμ) because they are his offspring (τέκνα), but '[t]hrough Isaac shall your children (σπέρμα) be named.'" Not all who might claim Abraham as their father are properly his σπέρμα; only those who are his descendants through Isaac, and by extension Jacob/Israel. The σπέρμα are described in a covenantal context, so the word is not functioning as a generic kinship term as does τέκνα here. The more narrow and covenantal understanding of this term is evident in the original Abrahamic usage in Genesis. Not all of Abraham's children are children of promise.

90. Qumran and supersessionism has been a crucial point of discussion as it relates to Wright's supersessionist project. He demurs at the use of the term for his work and thinks that Qumran's theology would be seen as supersessionist if it were judged the way Wright's has been judged (*Paul and the Faithfulness of God*, 810). It may appear then that my argument does not differ from Wright's and is itself supersessionist—what is the difference? Wright thinks Israel's vocation has been fulfilled in Christ and that Jews may be part of the new community, the *ekklēsia* (*Paul and the Faithfulness of God*, 367, 806–10, 1206). On the other hand, my view is that Israel's vocation continues, and while Jews participate in union with Messiah, they do not leave their membership in the historic people of God, Israel, in the process. If they fit the category of the remnant, then they serve as a bridge, a sanctifying part, between the *ekklēsia* and the larger part of the nation (though Paul's ultimate vision is for something grander than a remnant, 11:25–27). Wright's fulfillment discourse ultimately is totalizing, Qumran's was not, nor is the argument in this book. Wright also resists the "hard" or "sweeping" supersessionist label associated with the letter of Barnabas and again opts for a Qumranite "Jewish supersessionism" focused on fulfillment rather than replacement (*Paul and the Faithfulness of God*, 807 n. 106, 809). But this will not do. Wright's fulfillment reworking leaves nothing of Israel's covenantal identity in its wake—it may be described as a double-fulfillment schema. So similarly McGowan, "Ecclesiology," 589. Wright's claim in regards to Qumran also omits attention to the restoration in the land. For Qumran, restoration to the land is still expected once the temple has been cleansed. Thus, the land promise is only in a holding pattern. For Wright, the promise for restoration in the land has been swept away with the arrival of Jesus. While Wright thinks his approach does not amount to supersessionism since it is similar to Qumran's, it is not actually as similar as he maintains.

It is only through Isaac and Jacob/Israel that the promise goes forward. In Gen 17:19 we read that "God said, 'No, but Sarah your wife shall bear you a son, and you shall call his name Isaac. I will establish my covenant with him as an everlasting covenant for his offspring after him.'" This is restated a few verses later in 17:21: "But I will establish my covenant with Isaac, whom Sarah shall bear to you at this time next year." Then it is repeated again in 21:12, but with the distinction between the descendants clarified: "But God said to Abraham, 'Be not displeased because of the boy and because of your slave woman. Whatever Sarah says to you, do as she tells you, for through Isaac shall your offspring (σπέρμα) be named (κληθήσεται).'" From this verse it becomes even more evident that only those who descend through Isaac may properly be understood as σπέρμα. There is an implicit connection here between promise and covenant. The promises of the covenant are restated for Jacob in Gen 28:14, "Your offspring (σπέρμα) shall be like the dust of the earth, and you shall spread abroad to the west and to the east and to the north and to the south, and in you and your offspring shall all the families of the earth be blessed."

Ishmael is also a descendant of Abraham but is not considered σπέρμα. However, he still receives blessings. The covenant promises are restricted to Abraham's σπέρμα (land, numerous descendants, and blessings to the world), but his other children are blessed and given gifts. Regarding Ishmael, Gen 17:20 states, "As for Ishmael, I have heard you; behold, I have blessed him and will make him fruitful and multiply him greatly. He shall father twelve princes, and I will make him into a great nation." The same applies to the children of Keturah (Gen 25:1–4); the text describes this in 25:6: "But to the sons of his concubines Abraham gave gifts, and while he was still living he sent them away from his son Isaac, eastward to the east country." Thus, all of Abraham's children were blessed but were not properly party to the covenant tied to Isaac. This would suggest that σπέρμα is not functioning as a normal kinship term but as a descriptor of those who inherit the promise and the covenant relationship. The blessings are not limited, but the subgroup identity of the bearers of the promise is restricted to those associated with Israel. The blessings do go beyond Israel and thus have a universal orientation to them but the Israel-centric focus is never lost. Jubilees 15:30–32 picks up on this particular-universalism:

> For he did not draw near to himself either Ishmael, his sons,
> or Esau. He did not choose them (simply) because they were
> among Abraham's children. But he chose Israel to be his people:

> He sanctified them and gathered them from all humankind.
> For there are many nations and many peoples and all belong to
> him. He made spirits over all in order to lead them astray from
> following him. But over Israel he made no angel or spirit rule.
> Because he alone is their ruler.

Ehrensperger rightly picks up on the way these verses align with
Paul's concern in Rom 9:7; there continues to be diversity among people
groups from God's point of view. Yet amidst this diversity, God's dealings with the world still emerge with a continued Israel-centricity. God
has an interest in the nations, but this interest does not decenter Israel's
nationhood.[91]

Romans 9:8—A Description of Jewish Christ-followers

Romans 9:8, then, is a description of Jewish Christ-followers specifically
and not a label for Christ-followers generally.[92] One significant implication of the traditional reading of "Israel according to the flesh" from
1 Cor 10:18 as implying an "Israel according to the Spirit" is that it is a
small step from there to gentiles in Christ replacing Israel or becoming
the "real" Israel.[93] Schmidt, for example, in his discussion of "Israel according to the flesh," implies the existence of an "Israel according to the
Spirit."[94] However, this is a phrase that Paul never uses. Schmidt provides
it by reading Rom 9:8 and Gal 6:16 into 1 Cor 10:18. Romans 9:8 reads:
"This means that it is not the children of the flesh (τὰ τέκνα τῆς σαρκός)
who are the children of God, but the 'children of the promise' (τὰ τέκνα
τῆς ἐπαγγελίας) are counted as offspring (σπέρμα)." Campbell has persuasively argued that Rom 9:8, should be translated, "For it is not those
of fleshly descent alone, but those of fleshly descent and of promise who
are Abraham's seed." He continues:

> In Paul's terms, the children of promise is here a subgroup
> within those of fleshly descent from Abraham, and at this point

---

91. Ehrensperger, "Narratives," 385–86.

92. *Pace* Esler, *Conflict*, 279, though he rightly I think does provide a nuance often
missed by interpreters: "Paul does not identify the Christ-movement with Israel. He
comes perilously close, but avoids taking that final step." This is the problem I see with
Sechrest and Schmidt.

93. So, similarly Ehrensperger, *Mutually Encouraged*, 168.

94. Schmidt, "ἔθνος," 371. See, similarly, Sechrest, *Former*, 142–45.

in Chapter 9, he does not yet (prior to 9.24) include any (e.g., gentiles) beyond this group. It is not warranted to simply generalize this sub-group to refer to gentiles who at this stage in Paul's argument are not directly in focus.[95]

Romans 9:9—Promise-bearer Identity Restated

Paul continues in 9:9, "For this is what the promise (ἐπαγγελίας) said, 'About this time I will return and Sarah shall have a son (υἱός).'" Promise is given a position of prominence by its location in the syntactical structure. Paul's argument in this section has been that promise identity is what is ultimately preeminent. Isaac comes through promise. Paul's reference here is a conflation of Gen 18:10 and 18:14, but it communicates the general sense of the original context.[96] God is faithful to his promise. He has not turned away from historical Israel. Paul uses this reference to specify a particular identity node: a promised child of Abraham.[97]

Kevin Conway recognizes the problematic aspects of the traditional interpretation of Paul's gospel that require an explanation: "Have God's promises to Israel really been fulfilled, and, if not, can believers trust God to fulfill his promises to the church (See Rom 8)?"[98] Conway's larger project is concerned with the connection between the gospel and the promises. His focus is to account for the use of the plural "promises" (ἐπαγγελίαι) in 9:4 and the singular "promise" (ἐπαγγελίας) in 9:8, 9. While his argument, which ties the number of the noun to a reference to either soteriology or vocation, is difficult to sustain, he rightly, I think, sees in Paul's use of the various descriptors, "children of promise," "seed of Abraham," and "children of God," an implicit comparison with "children" and "children of flesh" (9:7–9). He concludes then that "The fact that

95. Campbell, *Paul and the Creation*, 124. See further on this in the section dealing with Rom 9:24–26 beginning on page 139. *Pace* Esler, *Conflict*, 279, who contends that more than Israelites are in view here. This is based on the connections with Romans 4: "There Paul had made crystal clear that the descendants who would fulfill the promise God made to Abraham would do so through faith and would include Israelites and non-Israelites (4:11–17)." This is a good example of a focus on soteriology that excludes vocation and thus creates interpretive challenges. Cf. Windsor, *Paul*, 82–84; Bell, *Provoked*, 185–86.

96. See Fitzmyer, *Romans*, 561; Dunn, *Romans*, 541–52, who sees an eschatological reason for the conflation.

97. Mounce, *Romans*, 198, though the notion of "true" slips into his conclusion.

98. Conway, *Promises*, 188.

there is already a remnant of Israel that has received saving righteous-ness in Paul's day demonstrates the validity of 9:6's contention that the word of God (i.e., the promises) has not failed."[99] Whether one accepts Conway's soteriological reading, his general approach has highlighted a central concern: "Paul see[s] the εὐαγγέλιον fulfilling God's ἐπαγγελίαι in Scripture."[100] Paul's gospel discourse contributes to the formation of a promise-bearer social identity, a subgroup identity for Jewish Christ-follows amid "the rest" (Rom 11:7).[101]

Paul has started his argument in Rom 9:1–29 to show that God's word to Israel has not failed. He began by highlighting the continuing covenantal identity of Israel in 9:1–5, and then in 9:6–9 he made a dis-tinction within the group between promise-Israel and ethnic Israel. This distinction provided descriptions of the multiple identities for Christ-following Jews rather than that of a new group of gentile Christ-followers who putatively took over the identity of Israel as a new or true Israel.

Gentiles Taking over Israel's Promises (9:24–26)

It may seem counterintuitive, but the way Paul construes gentile identity is crucial to the broader argument concerning the way Jewish identity continues in Christ. In this section, I have chosen to limit my focus to Romans 9:24–26 since it is one of the key places where gentiles seem to have taken over historic Israel's identity.[102] What will be seen, however, is that gentile identity does not become Jewish but maintains its salience for social and eschatological reasons.

99. Conway, *Promises*, 192.

100. Conway, *Promises*, 193.

101. For a post-supersessionist understanding of the "remnant," see Campbell, "Remnant," 79–101.

102. As I mentioned in the introduction of this chapter, I have been selective in the sections I engage. I have tried to pay attention to those verses referenced most often in the debates over Paul's alleged supersessionism. Obviously 9:10–23 are important to Paul's conception of Israel but these verses do not add significantly new information to the broader argument. The proof from Isaac, e.g., is supported by the proof from Ja-cob (9:10–13). The broader debates here concerning vocational election or individual salvation are crucial but space does not allow proper engagement with those issues. I would highlight Thornhill (*The Chosen People*, 229–53) as one author who comes quite close to getting this section correct with regard to corporate election but not so much with regard to the "people of God" discourse; see especially 252–53.

Gentiles as Eschatologically Restored Israelites (9:24)

In Romans, Paul seeks to transform gentile identity such that former associations with idolatry and immorality are no longer defining for in-Christ gentiles. However, this does not obliterate other key aspects of their existing social identity. In one sense, this subgroup within the Christ-movement in Rome could be described as former gentiles but still gentiles, or as Paula Fredriksen refers to them, "ex-pagan, pagans."[103] This in-between-ness to their ascribed identity raises a question: Can we be more precise with regard to the resulting social identity of gentile Christ-followers? One of the primary social identities that is often mentioned in this regard is that once a gentile becomes a Christ-follower, he or she ceases to be a gentile. For example, G. K. Beale, based on Rom 9:24, sees a reference to "gentiles as eschatologically restored Israelites."[104] Is Beale's claim on target? Does the phrase "but also from the gentiles" introducing the citations from Hos 1:10 and 2:23, with their promises of renewal for Israel, indicate that, for Paul, gentiles in Christ have become Israel, Israel-redefined, or eschatological Israel?

Chris Zoccali is representative of the dominant reading of Rom 9:24–26, though without the traditional supersessionist impulse. He understands Paul's use of Hos 2:23 and 1:10 as pointing "to the creation of God's new covenant people that includes both Jews and gentiles in Christ."[105] I, on the other hand, contend that the referent in Rom 9:25–26 continues to be historic Israel, as in the original prophecy, and only secondarily references gentiles. Thus, the verses support Paul's argument concerning Israel's restoration and the role the nations/gentiles play in that restoration. Furthermore, any connection with gentile calling is then only at the correspondence level (as discussed below) but not in a manner that removes or dilutes the covenantal identity of historic Israel.[106] So, which viewpoint is to be preferred? Is Paul's focus here on the inclusion of the gentiles and the formation of the new covenant people (i.e., the *ekklēsia*), or is it on the restoration of Israel and the role the nations/gentiles play in Israel's restoration? To answer this question, I will offer a brief survey of the Hosea citations and note differences in the text that may indicate Paul's rhetorical purpose. This section also reflects what a

---

103. Fredriksen, *Augustine*, 34–35.

104. Beale, *Biblical Theology*, 708.

105. Zoccali, *Whom God*, 109 n. 45. See Zoccali, *Reading Philippians*, 52.

106. Campbell, *Paul and the Creation*, 130.

post-supersessionist methodology might entail with regard to the way Paul draws from Israel's scriptural tradition.

The Citations of Hosea 2:23 and 1:10 in Romans 9:25–26

As is often noted, Paul's use of Hosea includes changes from its original context. This suggests that he has taken over his source and provided new insights based on the messianic times in which he found himself. N. T. Wright points out that the retelling of Israel's story in Rom 9:6–29 is rather uncontroversial with the exception of the addition of "but also from the gentiles" in introducing the Hosea quotations.[107] Concerning Rom 9:25 and its citation of Hos 2:23, Paul's emphasis can be seen in a few changes he makes to the actual text. First, καλέσω τὸν οὐ λαόν μου λαόν μου "Those who were not my people I will call 'my people'" comes before τὴν οὐκ ἠγαπημένην ἠγαπημένην "her who was not beloved I will call 'beloved.'" This results in the phrase τὸν οὐ λαόν μου "those who are not my people" being emphasized. Paul's focus is thus more on the identity of this group, the "not my people." Second, Hos 2:23 (v. 25 IN LXX) has ἐρῶ "I will say" while Rom 9:25 uses καλέσω "I will call." The verb ἐλεήσω "I will have pity" in Hosea has been omitted in Rom 9:25, and an implied καλέσω "I will call" must be supplied to complete the sense of the participle ἠγαπημένην "my beloved." The change from ἐρῶ "I will say" to καλέσω "I will call" connects the citation to Rom 9:24, which also uses a form of καλέω (ἐκάλεσεν) and emphasizes the centrality of calling (cf. Rom 9:7, "not all of Abraham's descendants are his children"; v. 12 "the older will serve the younger, Jacob/Esau"). Furthermore, the forms of ἐλεέω "to pity" have been replaced by forms of ἀγαπάω "to love." The rationale for this latter change is somewhat underdetermined, though it is possible that the discussion of Jacob and Esau in Rom 9:10–13 may have influenced Paul, especially if the connection with Esau as a type of excluded gentile is considered.[108] Paul's use of Hos 2:23, therefore, likely has its basis in his reflection on the transformation of gentile identity since he is now focused on those who were previously not his people and since God's love and calling has now been extended to the gentiles.

Romans 9:26, in UBS5, follows perfectly the text of Rahlf's LXX Hos 2:1 (with the exception that Paul does not cite the first part of the verse).

---

107. Wright, *Paul and the Faithfulness of God*, 1194.
108. Wagner, *Heralds*, 82.

However, if P46 is considered, two further pieces of evidence arise. First, if P46 is what Paul wrote, then he changes ἐρρέθη "it was said" to κληθήσονται "they will be called," a similar change as was found in 9:25 (i.e., from ἐρῶ "say" to καλέσω "call"). This reinforces the centrality of calling discourse in Romans 9. Second, if P46 is what Paul wrote, then the particle ἐάν "ever" has been added after οὗ "where," resulting in the English gloss "wherever" and producing the following translation: "And it shall be in the place wherever they are called." In this case, there is a textual basis for expanding the original referent "them" (i.e., northern kingdom of Israel) to "wherever they" (Israelites and gentiles). Thus, the P46 reading provides a strong case that an expansion to include gentiles is warranted as well as a potential "de-territorializing" of this promise.

However, this expansion should not be read only as a replacement for the original promise for the restoration of the land. It seems to be the case that the Romans passage does address Israel as a nation especially in 9:26 with its description of "in that very place" and "there," likely alluding to Jerusalem in the context of Israel's restoration.[109] The promise referenced in this verse is expanded based on Paul's awareness of the restoration of Israel that has begun and of the role that the nations play in this restoration.[110] The nations, those who were "not my people," now have the opportunity to be part of God's family, i.e., "children of the living God." So, both citations reinforce the idea of gentile identity, not as a stand-alone identity but as one that finds its salience in the continued story of Israel. This is one crucial area of disagreement with Wright. For him Christ has fulfilled Israel's story whereas I would suggest that the story continues.[111]

109. Here I am suggesting that the eschatological pilgrimage tradition may be in view, contra Donaldson (*Paul*, 76, 78), who opts for the gentile proselytism model: "the Gentiles' share in salvation was dependent on their becoming full members of Israel ('the true circumcision'; cf. Phil 3:3) on equal terms with Jews ('there is no distinction'; Rom 10:12). But the substance of his conviction was reconfigured: the equal terms are to be found not in the Torah, but in Christ." Zoccali (*Whom God*, 46 n. 13) offers substantive critiques of Donaldson with regard to the presence of the eschatological pilgrimage tradition in Paul's argument.

110. Note here the earlier argument beginning on page 72 that the so-called expansion to the world does not remove the promise for the land. It will be argued below that Rom 11:25-27 presupposes this political dimension. See further, Reasoner, "Salvation," 269-72.

111. Thus, he and I have different eschatological accents on our reading of Romans 9-11.

The Function of the Citations in Rom 9:22–29

Romans 9:24–26 is found within a telling of Israel's story, a narrative that extends over Rom 9:6–29 and in many ways parallels the "rest of the story" found in Rom 11:1–32.[112] Focusing for the moment on Romans 9:22–23, we note that it contains a number of rhetorical questions designed to point out the sovereign nature of God's works in the past. Some of these actions are linked to "objects of wrath," those whom God has endured with much patience, and to "objects of mercy," those to whom God desires to make known his glory. The rhetorical function of Rom 9:24 is to make explicit the identity of the "vessels of mercy." While it is possible that 9:24 addresses the rhetorical question from 9:22 (concerning the "objects of wrath"), it is more likely that it clarifies the identity of the "vessels of mercy" in 9:23 and leaves the identity of the other group undetermined. Understood in this way, the citations found in the broader passage, Rom 9:25–29, further clarify the identity of the "vessels of mercy." It is in this context that we find Paul's assertion that this group of called ones includes both Jews and the nations.

The citations are introduced in 9:25 by ὡς καὶ ἐν τῷ Ὡσηὲ λέγει "as also he says in Hosea." There is significant debate concerning how to understand ὡς καί "as also," whether it connects back to 9:22,[113] develops the claim of 9:24,[114] or sets up the thesis to be defended by the citations.[115] Without space to deal with this debate here, the following may be briefly noted. It seems likely that ὡς καί connects the citations in 9:25–26 with those "called" (ἐκάλεσεν) in 9:24 (B and B¹ in my chiastic structure below). This verse is itself a relative clause embedded in a larger sentence that began back in 9:22. "Endured" (ἤνεγκεν) (i.e., what God has endured) is its controlling verb. Thus, the Hosea citation is central to the broader retelling of Israel's story found in 9:6–29 (which may account for its awkward location in 9:25, since it has a larger discourse function). In this understanding, the calling of the gentiles is only a secondary concern, at least until the next discourse unit that begins in 9:30.

Thus, I would suggest the following rhetorical structure to Rom 9:22–29:

---

112. Wright, *Paul and the Faithfulness of God*, 1195.

113. Cranfield, *Romans*, 2.498.

114. Dunn, *Romans*, 2.571.

115. Schreiner, *Romans*, 525.

A Rom 9:22–23: God's purposes among both objects of wrath and objects of mercy

   B Rom 9:24: God's inclusive calling of Jews and gentiles

   B¹ Rom 9:25–26: the restoration of Israel and the inclusion of the nations

A¹ Rom 9:27–29: the saving remnant as part of God's ongoing purpose for Israel

In this structure, Paul's argument is that previously rejected Israel as well as the other nations of the world (i.e., the not-my-people) will be restored, and in the process the "members of the nations other than Israel" (an expansive definition of τὰ ἔθνη) will likewise be blessed. Thus, the Hosea citations still primarily support the idea of Israel's restoration, a restoration that sweeps up the nations in its wake.[116] Thus, the function of the citations in Rom 9:25–26, within the context of Rom 9:22–29, is to express Paul's claim that the restoration of Israel had begun and likewise the reconciliation of the nations as promised in the scriptures (and not that in-Christ gentiles have replaced Israel as God's people).

The Hermeneutical Problem of Paul's Use of Hosea in Romans 9:25–26

Another critique can be launched against the traditional interpretation of Rom 9:25–26 that Paul has appropriated promises for Israel's restoration and applied them to gentiles. Douglas Moo, for example, concludes that "this text reflects a hermeneutical supposition for which we find evidence elsewhere in Paul and in the NT: that OT predictions of a renewed Israel find their fulfillment in the church."[117] I would call Moo's conclusion into question: it is not clear that Paul sees the promise of Israel's renewal as being fulfilled in the "church," a somewhat anachronistic term in any case, and missing from most of Romans (see below). However, he has rightly pointed out the interpretive tension point. Below is a summary of the way scholars have attempted to resolve the hermeneutical dilemma, followed by my proposed approach: paradigm-rendition.

116. Ehrensperger, *Paul and the Dynamics*, 138.

117. Moo, *Romans*, 613.

First, Thomas McComiskey does not see a problem here since he thinks that gentiles were included in the original referent in Hosea, particularly the vast numbers of people loyal to God language.[118] The "sand of the sea" reference offers particularly strong support for McComiskey's argument, especially as it relates to the promise to Abraham (Gen 12:3; 22:17–18; Isa 54:1). Ultimately, however, there is not enough evidence to sustain McComiskey's claim, because the Hosean context has Israel too acutely in view. John Battle also does not see a problem in the Romans quotation of Hosea since he thinks the referent in Rom 9:25–26 continues to be Israel, but with a focus on explaining Israel's continued unbelief (rather than the inclusion of the gentiles).[119] The problem with his approach is that Paul appears to justify the calling of both Jews and gentiles in 9:24 on the basis of the citations of Hosea in 9:25–26. Further, his approach does not account fully for the explicit and thus redundant reference to Israel in 9:27.[120]

The majority approach to this problem is that Rom 9:25–26 refers to gentiles who were once alienated from God but now have been included in God's plan. This is supported in three different ways: (a) the original referent has changed in light of Messiah's coming; (b) Israel's covenant identity has been fulfilled (displaced or cast away) in Christ and is now connected with those in a third entity, the church, the new-covenant community; and (c) a hermeneutics of mystery is being used based on Paul's mission experience.[121] This group builds on the key phrase "but also from the gentiles" in 9:24. While this tri-partite view is clearly possible, there are several claims to consider. First, it is not clear why the citations would only (or primarily) refer to "those from the gentiles." The preceding reference to "the Jews" should not be excluded from the discussion. Second, it seems that the argument that Paul began in 9:1 would have led his audience, when hearing 9:22–23, to conclude that he is still talking about God's dealings with the Jews (see Rom 9:1–6). Third, while early in the letter, gentiles are central to Paul's arguments, they have not been explicitly referenced since the Abraham discourse in Romans 4.[122]

---

118. McComiskey, *Hosea*, 29.

119. Battle, "Paul's Use," 127.

120. Das, *Paul and the Jews*, 113.

121. Glenny, "The 'People of God,'" 51; Tanner, "The New Covenant," 101, 105; Wright, *Paul and the Faithfulness of God*, 1194.

122. This doesn't mean that Paul is addressing Jews; rather, he is addressing the way in-Christ gentiles need a transformation in the way they should view Israel's

Fourth, the centrality of "calling" words in Rom 9:24–26 suggests that the passage refers equally to Jews and gentiles.[123]

The problems with the majority approach open the door for considering the correspondence view. This view claims an analogical relationship between the Hosean context and Rom 9:25–26 that led Paul to draw from this tradition a correspondence between the identity of the gentiles and those described as "not my people." Thus, a transformation of identity has occurred, and in-Christ gentiles are now part of God's people. But does this not suggest that these in-Christ gentiles have taken over the identity of Israel? For example, James Dunn argues that Paul can apply a prophecy that originally was directed to the northern kingdom of Israel to gentiles in Christ because now that the gospel of Jesus has come, there is no longer a distinction to be made between Jews and gentiles (Rom 10:12; 3:23).[124] It is more likely, however, that these identities have been reprioritized. Campbell has recently argued further that the issue in Rom 10:12 and 3:23 is not so much "distinction" as "discrimination."[125] In his reading, Paul's argument is that now that Christ has come there is to be no discrimination based on ethnic identities, not that such identities have been obliterated now that Christ has come.

I think some sort of storied typological view is warranted, but not one that leads to a supersessionist understanding of the text.[126] This allows the triumphalist "promise-fulfillment" scheme to be replaced with a "paradigm-rendition" approach, in which "the new performance is clarified and authenticated precisely insofar as it corresponds to the old, exalted original."[127] Thus, the use of a passage from Israel's scriptures in later apostolic writings does not suggest replacement; rather it builds on the first text as a continuation and unfolding of a narrative. This differs from N. T. Wright's or Richard Hays's approaches, which emphasize the fulfillment/completion of Israel's story in the church.[128] The new approach is post-supersessionist, but not two-covenant or *Sonderweg*. It eliminates the traditional bifurcation between the OT and NT as well as the "un-

---

covenantal identity. Gentile identity in Christ is not a stand-alone identity.

123. So similarly Stanley, *Arguing with Scripture*, 159 n. 51.

124. Dunn, *Romans*, 1.149.

125. Campbell, "Differentiation," 161–62.

126. See e.g., Seifrid, "Romans," 648.

127. Boulton, "Supersession" 18.

128. Wright, *Climax*, 18–136, 265; Hays, *Echoes*, 90.

intentional Marcionism" inherent in such constructions.[129] The Hebrew Bible was not merely preparatory but is an integral, irreplaceable, and continuing part of God's story. The literary-critical approach helps in this pursuit by allowing for a reading of the text that does not propose any subordination or inferiority of the old in comparison to the new.[130] The earlier narratives reflect the hope that the biblical writers now believe has been realized; Israel's Messiah has come. Their hope continues in the unfolding of Israel's restoration.

The Continuation of Gentile Social Identity in Romans

I have argued that it seems problematic that in-Christ gentiles would have taken over the identity of Israel; rather, they remain distinct. It may be useful at this juncture to note a few places in Romans that support the idea that gentile identity continues in Christ.[131] Romans 11:13–14 and 16:3–4 are two places where gentile social identity continues to be a live option for Paul.

First, Paul describes his addressees as gentile, providing a basis for this social identity continuing. In Rom 11:13–14, he writes, "Now I am speaking to you gentiles (τοῖς ἔθνεσιν). Inasmuch then as I am an apostle to the gentiles (ἐθνῶν), I magnify my ministry in order to make my fellow Jews (μου τὴν σάρκα) jealous, and thus save some (τινάς)." Here Paul addresses those whom he identifies as gentiles (apparently they would have been distinct enough to know to whom he was referring). In so doing, he emphasizes his ministry among this subgroup of Christ-followers.

Second, Paul used the term "gentile" as a continuing way to describe some of the Christ-movement congregations. In Rom 16:3–5a, he writes, "Greet Prisca and Aquila, my fellow workers in Christ Jesus, who risked their necks for my life, to whom not only I but also all the congregations of the gentiles (αἱ ἐκκλησίαι τῶν ἐθνῶν) give thanks; greet also the congregation (ἐκκλησίαν) in their house." The description here brings to the fore the importance of another Jewish couple who are part of this Jewish mission to the nations (and specifically in Rome). The precise referent

---

129. Gard, "Functional Marcionism," 217–21.

130. Tolmie, *Narratology*, 1–5.

131. As compared to e.g., 1 Cor 12:2, where it appears to be something in the past. See Concannon, *When*, 16, who picks up on the "malleability" of "ethnic identity." See further on this Tucker, *Reading 1 Corinthians*, 83–85; 115–17.

for the phrase αἱ ἐκκλησίαι τῶν ἐθνῶν would be various congregations within the Pauline Christ-movement throughout the Mediterranean basin (or at least those in Corinth and Ephesus). Prisca and Aquila, said to have risked their lives for Paul, are thus among a group of others who are connected to him; they form regional assemblies that socially identify as gentile ἐκκλησίαι. The subgroup that meets in the house of Prisca and Aquila are the only ones described as an ἐκκλησία in Rome (Rom 16:3–5). So, it is at least plausible that from Paul's point of view, gentiles in Christ continued to be gentiles, and that he described the congregations aligned with his movement as gentile assemblies.

This raises an important question: does this not argue that Paul's assemblies were already separated from the larger Jewish community? Do we not see in this term evidence of first-century Gentile Christianity? Ralph Korner has provided arguments that would answer these questions in the negative: these groups are still part of the Jewish community and the big-"G" Gentile Christianity has yet to emerge.[132] As Korner sees it, first, ἐκκλησία was not necessarily used the same way across the earliest Christ-movement. Instead, it could be used as a label for a continuing social identity (which it appears to be for the Pauline Christ-movement) and as a temporary descriptor for semi-private gatherings within the larger Jewish community (e.g., in Jerusalem). Second, it is often assumed that Paul used this term to create a separate identity for his congregations vis-à-vis Israel. However, one should not preclude the idea that he used it in order to connect his predominantly gentile assemblies with historic Israel (e.g., the olive tree metaphor in Rom 11:17). Also, Paul may not use ἐκκλησία similarly to its use in the civic context. Civic assemblies did not continue to be described as ἐκκλησίαι once the group had dispersed. The only context from which Paul would have developed ἐκκλησία as a permanent subgroup identifier would be the LXX, where it was used to describe the nation of Israel. It should also be noted that Philo, Josephus, and Ben Sira could use ἐκκλησία to describe both local assemblies of Jews and also as a temporary group identifier of its members. In this context, the phrase αἱ ἐκκλησίαι τῶν ἐθνῶν might be fruitfully compared with ταῖς ἐκκλησίαις τῶν ἁγίων "the congregation of the holy ones" in 1 Cor 14:33b–35, which likely described those groups identifying closely with James. The argument that is being put forth here is that ἐκκλησία should not be understood to distance Paul's Christ-movement from the

---

132. Korner, "The *Ekklēsia*," 455–99.

larger Jewish community; rather, it describes a synagogal-type assembly related to the larger Jewish community, but also open to gentiles (whom Runesson describes as "Christ-fearers").[133] Thus, αἱ ἐκκλησίαι τῶν ἐθνῶν describes a local/regional assembly that socially identified with the Pauline Christ-movement and its Jewish mission to the nations.

This brings us back to the question we started with: how do we account for Paul's use of καὶ ἐξ ἐθνῶν in Rom 9:24 to introduce a promise originally designed for Israel? It is evident that the gentiles are key actors on the stage of Israel's story. The "fullness of their numbers" and "all Israel" (Rom 11:25–26) are related recipients of God's mercy and call. So, in Rom 9:24–26, Paul expanded an implicit echo with regard to Abraham. Although his primary concern was still with Israel's story, he recognized that something had changed as God acted in Christ. So a paradigm-rendition typological relationship describes the way that promises made to Israel correspond to the calling of the gentiles, but such that the promise to Israel remains. Wagner summarizes it this way: "In the end, the entire weight of Paul's argument in Rom 9–11 comes to rest on just this point: that God alone determines the identity and destiny of Israel and the Gentiles alike."[134] I agree, but it was left for Paul, as an entrepreneur of identity, to help Jewish and gentile Christ-followers to understand the social implications of their transformed and continuing social identities.

Gentile Identity Sourced in Israel's Covenant History in Romans 11:1–36

The claims that gentile identity remains salient within the Pauline Christ-movement and that it finds it orientation from Israel's covenant history raise the question that is at the core of this book: is Israel out? First I would point to the work of Ross Wagner and Richard Hays, who both remind us that the original context of Paul's citations is important for understanding the full implications of Paul's argument.[135] A brief survey of Hosea 1–2 brings to the fore God's faithfulness to Israel. God's judgment against Israel as it had been earlier described in Hosea 1–2 is reversed.

133. Runesson, "Inventing," 73.

134. Wagner, "Not from the Jews," 429.

135. Wagner, *Heralds*, 10; Hays, *Echoes*, 155; Stanley, *Arguing with Scripture*, 157–58; here also is where Christopher Stanley's informed audience may prove useful, though he demurs with regard to the original context.

Hosea 2:23 indicates that God will now have mercy on those who had not previously been recipients of it. Furthermore, those who had been identified as "not my people" are now transformed again into God's people, in spite of their failures. Two key issues in Hosea's context that are particularly germane to the argument of Romans 9 include the extension of mercy and the resulting transformation of identity. Paul's combination of Hos 2:23 and 1:10 resonates with many of the themes evident in the original context, especially as it relates to the restoration of Israel. However, Paul's interpretation of this promise now includes gentiles in his field of reference without excluding Jews. This is a broadening of the promise rather than a diminishment of it.

One way to see how Israel's restoration sweeps up the nations in its wake is to highlight the end of the story as found in Rom 11:1–36.[136] Paul's earlier reference in 9:3 to his "own people, my kindred according to the flesh," socially categorizes him in relation to his Jewish identity and thus creates a temporary outgroup identity for those who do not identify socially as Jews. (However, Paul does not seek to create extensive distance from these gentiles either, since he also refers to them with the inclusive "we" in 9:24 and the kinship term "brothers" in 10:1.) In Rom 11:1, Israelites are referred to as God's people, and Paul identifies himself with several Israel-centric identity nodes: "an Israelite, a descendant of Abraham, a member of the tribe of Benjamin." He then clarifies that "God has not rejected his people" (Rom 11:2). So, in this discursive context, where has Paul emplotted gentiles? To answer this first in the negative, they are certainly not included in the identity of the subgroup Israel in a proper sense. Instead, Paul includes himself within "the remnant" (11:5) while he categorizes some Israelites as "the rest," those who "were hardened" (11:7). In this context, as in Romans 9, that which legitimizes Jewish covenantal identity is calling discourse (cf. 9:24; 11:1, 5, 7). If "the rest" are identified with Jewish covenantal identity as in Hosea 1–2, Paul has a link between his thoughts in Romans and the Hosea text.

To address the question positively, we note that Paul clearly names the group "gentiles" (Rom 11:13). Though they are not Israel, he, despite his list of Jewish descriptors, identifies closely with them, even as their "apostle" (11:14). In other words, gentile identity and Israelite identity intersect. They are not absorbed into one another; each maintains their

---

136. A passage N. T. Wright sets in parallel with Rom 9:6–29 (technically he only sets 11:1–32 in parallel); Wright, *Paul and the Faithfulness of God*, 1195.

distinctiveness as a result of God's mercy and call.[137] Wagner brings to the fore the future orientation of this gentile identity: "their own future is inextricably bound up with Israel's unfinished story."[138] Paul alludes to something similar in 15:27, where gentiles (τὰ ἔθνη) in Christ have received "spiritual blessings" (τοῖς πνευματικοῖς) because of their "participation" (ἐκοινώνησαν) with Jewish Christ-followers in Jerusalem and, in 11:7, because of the hardening, or better, callusing of "the rest" (οἱ λοιποί) of Israel.[139] Thus, gentile identity is more transformed than is often thought. It is "participation" with the "remnant" *and* a sharing in the covenant history with "the rest" of Israel. This dual-identity connection likely accounts for the use of the phrase καὶ ἐξ ἐθνῶν in 9:24.

Israel's stumbling has brought riches to the gentiles. However, this does not mean that Israel has been cast aside. Rather, there is an expectation of their "full inclusion" (11:12) and "acceptance" (11:15), a situation that will be effected by God and is described as "life from the dead!" In Rom 11:11–36, Paul describes two aspects of God's mercy and call: (a) the salvation of gentiles (11:11–24) and (b) the restoration of Israel (11:25–36). Continuing with the imagery of "gentile actors on a Jewish stage," these gentiles have received God's mercy (11:30) that Paul's "fellow Jews" (μου τὴν σάρκα) might be made "jealous" (παραζηλώσω) (11:14; see 10:19 and its quotation of Deut 32:21).

The analogy of the grafting of gentiles onto the olive tree in 11:17–24 provides an apt description of the way new life in Christ, i.e., "new creation," does not displace existing identities, i.e., "creation." The tree is not a description of Israel; rather it is a description of the various members of God's family. The distinct identities of the branches remain intact. Those mentioned in 11:17 that have been "bent" or "broken" (ἐξεκλάσθησαν) seem to align with "the rest" from 11:13; those "grafted in" (ἐνεκεντρίσθης) seem to describe gentile Christ-followers (11:17). If the gentiles, the ones who have been "grafted in," become "arrogant" (κατακαυχῶ) (11:18) and think they have no need for the "natural branches," Paul reminds them that they could also be "cut" (ἐκκοπήσῃ) (11:21–24). The "mystery" (τὸ μυστήριον) of God's salvation is distributed to both "the full number of gentiles" and "all Israel" (11:25). In the context of the calling of "the

---

137. See Ehrensperger, *Paul at the Crossroads*, 29–36, on the rejection of hybridity or fusion of identities in Paul.

138. Wagner, "Not from the Jews," 425.

139. Nanos points out "If Paul meant 'callus,' this need not carry the negative valence that 'harden' does" ("Callused," 63).

nations" and "Israel," drawing from Israel's scriptures in Isa 59:20–21 (and 27:9), Paul declares "Out of Zion will come the Deliverer; he will banish ungodliness from Jacob." Paul's hope for "hardened Israel" is, as per Soulen, "God-in-Christ's direct intervention on Israel's behalf at the end of the age."[140] Paul does not argue here that the "grafted in" become Israelites; rather, they remain distinct branches in God's family. However, gentile identity is not an autonomous one. It finds its source in God's mercy revealed in the context of Israel's covenant history (11:30), a story in which God's mercy triumphs over Jewish and gentile "disobedience" (ἀπείθειαν) (11:31–32).

Conclusion

Romans 9:1–29 forms a long argument that shows that God has been faithful to Israel and continues as such. The section began with Paul's anguish concerning his relations since many have rejected the gospel. He sought to remind gentiles of Israel's ongoing covenantal privileges while at the same time highlighting that a division within the nation is nothing new. What is new is the development of gentile identity on the stage of Israel's story. The presence of those without a covenantal relationship required explanation, and Paul drew from Israel's story to show his readers the way gentile identity fits into God's ongoing and future purposes. However, the current stumbling of Israel needed further rationale, so Paul turned to that question in 9:30—10:21. Clearly, Israel had stumbled over Christ. However, this raised questions concerning the continuation of Israel's covenant identity within Paul's gospel. Generally speaking, traditional interpreters understand two contrasting principles of righteousness: Christ and Torah. So, the argument becomes that Israel rejected Christ because his gospel resulted in the termination of the Torah and the removal of, or an almost complete redefinition of, Jewish covenantal identity. Thus, the next chapter addresses another plank in the supersessionist argument: Has Christ rendered Torah redundant?[141]

140. Soulen, "They Are Israelites," 501.

141. There are obviously several debated points within Romans 10 with regard to supersessionism. However, the reader is reminded that the argument of this book is not questioning the salvific efficacy of the gospel. It is addressing a narrower issue: whether there is justification for claiming that Israel's covenantal identity continues in this gospel. With that said, I will address the connection between 10:4 and 10:5–6 since it is so highly contested. The primary reason is that I seek to establish more continuity than is often seen between the gospel and Torah, when the latter functions in the sphere of Christ.

6

Christ Fulfills Torah

Introduction

PAUL OFFERS A CONTEXTUALIZATION to Torah in Rom 10:4 in light of the Messiah's coming, but what is the nature of that contextualization? Is Torah now rendered redundant? Has its goal been realized? Is there a fulfillment nuance suggesting some sort of continuation? These questions highlight the general contours of the debate concerning what Paul writes in 10:4, "For Christ is the end (τέλος) of the law so that there may be righteousness for everyone who believes" (NRSV). Obviously, the translators of the NRSV have made their determination on this matter. If the "end" nuance is there, then Israel's covenantal identity is eviscerated of much of what first-century Jews would have understood it to be.

Some see the three traditional argumentative approaches to 10:4, as highlighted in the questions above, as wrongheaded. Beverly Gaventa finds the three approaches unhelpful but ultimately concludes that "God's creation and maintenance of Israel, even God's unchanging call of Israel, [is] without reference to an ongoing role for the Mosaic law."[1] N. T. Wright, though building on Gal 3:15–18, thinks that Torah creates two families for Abraham, but "God intended to give Abraham a single family. . . . The Torah must therefore not be absolutized in such a way as

---

1. Gaventa, "Questions," 134. This suggests that she would fall within the "end" category, though her nuance would not be the same as those mentioned below, especially as it relates to the apocalyptic context of Paul's writing.

would create two families, a Jewish one and a Gentile one."[2] Tatum, on the other hand, rejects this approach: "The eschatological people of God is *binary* by nature: Israel as such and the Nations as such worshipping the one God of Israel together in the unity of the κοινωνία of Christ (Rom 15:8–13)."[3] While Paul argues against circumcision and thus identity-transformation for gentiles, it is another thing to conclude that he sought to suppress Torah-observance for Jews, especially in light of his rule in all the congregations in 1 Cor 7:17–24. That passage suggests that Paul expected Jewish Christ-followers to maintain the observation of Torah. If this is the case, what sort of contextualization is in view in Rom 10:4?

This chapter revisits the three approaches to Torah in 10:4 and then addresses the debate in 10:5–6 regarding two ways of righteousness (one failed, the other not). Wright sees Paul's exegesis of Deuteronomy 30 guiding his thoughts here. Specifically, he sees Israel's story brought to its climax with the coming of the Messiah, so now there is "a new kind of 'doing of Torah' available through the Messiah and the spirit, and all who 'do Torah' in this way will be saved."[4] The link between 10:5–6 and 10:4 is determinative for the way interpreters see these verses. Some see a contrast and others a complementary nuance. This debate will be the focus of the second half of this chapter.

Christ is the End, Goal, or End-Goal of the Law in Romans 10:4

Brian Rosner, who was discussed earlier in chapter 5 dealing with the continuing validity of Torah, thinks that Rom 10:4 should be construed to mean that Christ is the "end" of the law. Romans 9:30—10:13 contrasts "two different paths to righteousness. One comes from faith, the other from obedience to the law and is based on doing. One prevails; the other will fail, 'for Christ is the end of the law so that there may be righteousness for everyone who believes.'"[5] However, is such an antithetical stance required by the text? Is there a binary opposition in Paul's discourse or has that been assumed based on other hermeneutical considerations?

---

2. Wright, *Paul and the Faithfulness of God*, 868. In relation to Rom 10:4, he seems to go with a combination of "end" and "goal" but with different implications than those that are developed in this chapter. See Wright, *Paul and the Faithfulness of God*, 1035.

3. Tatum, "Law," 318. I develop this out further in chapter 9 below.

4. Wright, *Paul and the Faithfulness of God*, 704.

5. Rosner, *Paul and the Law*, 72.

The translation of τέλος in Rom 10:4 continues to be a significant point of debate and serves as an important entry point into the larger discussion concerning the continuing covenant identity for Israelites. The three major approaches to this debate are (a) Christ is the end of the law as a set of regulations that order communal life and righteousness; (b) Christ is the fulfillment of the law as regards that to which it pointed, yet its role is not terminated with the advent of the Messiah; and (c) Christ is both the end of the law with regard to righteousness while simultaneously being an ongoing set of ordering principles for communal life and identity. While there are nuances within these various positions, these are the general contours of the debate. If Christ is found to be the end of the law, then Jewish identity with its close connection to the law would not continue in any meaningful way.[6] If Christ, on the other hand, is seen as the goal of the law, that could open up the possibility that its salvific role abides. Finally, in some sort of combination view, one is left with a level of ambiguity that may not be fully satisfying or a conclusion that simply does not recognize the significance of the debate between the two traditional options. While those two points are noted, it still seems that a nuanced combination view aligns most closely with Paul's theologizing here in light of what he writes in other portions of this letter.

Christ is the End of the Law

Interpreters who understand Paul to be describing an end to the law in these verses bring to the fore discontinuity between the law and righteousness. Francis Watson concludes concerning 10:4: "Since the regime represented by the Leviticus text [Lev 18:5] has been terminated by the righteousness of faith, the contested term *telos* should be translated 'end,' not 'goal.'"[7] Watson contends that there is a clear boundary between a righteousness that is secured by the "law" and the one by "faith" (10:5–6), and between "works" and "faith" (9:32).[8] Thus, for Watson, Paul's use of Lev 18:5 points to the idea that there is significant discontinuity between these two approaches to righteousness. Thomas Schreiner, as one who also supports the gloss "end" for this verse, thinks the strongest argument

---

6. Rosner, *Paul and the Law*, 48, 51; Westerholm, *Perspectives*, 300; Rudolph, *A Jew to the Jews*, 153–59; Windsor, *Paul*, 67.

7. Watson, *Paul and the Hermeneutics*, 332.

8. Watson, *Paul and the Hermeneutics*, 332.

is at the lexical level: "The word τέλος often contains a temporal meaning, while only one New Testament passage (1 Tim. 1:5) uses τέλος in the indisputable sense of 'goal.'"[9] To be fair, Schreiner thinks this verse is misused by most in this debate since the close connection with 10:3 indicates that Paul is not making "some overarching theological statement on the relationship between gospel and law."[10] Marvin Pate offers a third argument for understanding τέλος as termination: "If indeed 10:5 portrays the law negatively, consistency dictates a similar rendering in 10:4. Indeed, the connecting word between 10:4 and 10:5, *gar* ('for, since'), seems to link the negative statement in 10:4 with a similar remark in 10:5."[11] This grammatical analysis supports Pate's broader argument concerning the "replacing of nomism with fideism (law with faith) and particularism with universalism (salvation for the Jews with salvation for all who believe)." This interpretive position can only be maintained, according to Pate, if there is a severing "of wisdom (Christ) and the Torah."[12] Since these three arguments are often put forth in support of the termination perspective, it would be worthwhile to briefly offer responses to their claims.

First, does Paul's use of Lev 18:5 point to a radical discontinuity? Watson's comments have been developed significantly in the work of Preston Sprinkle, who concludes that for Paul, "Lev 18:5 means that the law is antithetical to righteousness by faith (esp. Gal 3:11–12)."[13] More recently, Rosner has built on Sprinkle and concludes that what the use of Lev 18:5 highlights is "that law is a failed path to righteousness."[14] What Watson, Sprinkle, and Rosner agree on is that Paul uses Lev 18:5 in order to contrast two paths to righteousness and that Paul understands the text differently than in the original Leviticus context and in concert with later Jewish texts.[15] One of the difficulties that the interpreter comes to in Rom 10:5 is the tendency to use Gal 3:11–12 as a "hermeneutical lens." Gregory Tatum, on the other hand, suggests reading the quotation as a

---

9. Schreiner, *The Law*, 134.

10. Schreiner, *The Law*, 135.

11. Pate, *Romans*, 203.

12. Pate, *Romans*, 198.

13. Sprinkle, *Law and Life*, 1.

14. Rosner, *Paul and the Law*, 72.

15. On this see page 162.

"point of contrast."[16] This subtle shift allows one to hear Paul's argument in the context of Romans.

Second, does τέλος carry its temporal nuance in contrast to its sense of goal? The work by Robert Badenas is particularly probative here. He highlights the selective use of evidence by some scholars for the temporal nuance of τέλος and concludes that "just three to five instances out of thirteen of Paul's total usages" may indicate the temporal nuance. Additionally, those usages also "appear in eschatological contexts," which is not the case here.[17] Plutarch uses τέλος in a non-temporal phrase that aligns closely to Rom 10:4. In *Amatorius* 750 E, he writes: τέλος γὰρ ἐπιθυμίας ἡδονή "for the goal of desire is pleasure" which follows the same structure as τέλος γὰρ νόμου Χριστὸς "for the goal of the law is Christ." Badenas concludes that "[t]he grammatical and philological burden of proof is therefore upon those who translate Rom 10.4 [with] a temporal-terminal sense."[18]

Third, how should the γάρ between 10:4 and 10:5 be construed? The γάρ in 10:5 provides the last reason from a sequence of reasons found in 10:2–4, all of which contain γάρ.[19] Dunn sees the tendency to take 10:4 out of context as the primary reason that interpreters downplay τέλος as end: "What Paul has in view therefore is the zeal for the law which fights to preserve Israel's distinctiveness (10:2) and righteousness

---

16. Tatum, "To the Jew," 275. Rosner, *Paul and the Law*, seems to pick up on this tension when he notes that the discontinuity approach is only "implicit" in Romans, though he highlights 1:18–3:20 as pointing to discontinuity in a more explicit fashion. See Hagner, "Paul's Quarrel," 136–37. He adds the negative statements about the law from Gal 2:16, 21; 3:11, 21, 23–25; 5:4. One of the difficulties with Hagner's approach, and with the scholarly approach to this issue more generally, is the interpenetration of the rhetorical exigencies of Galatians and Romans in a canonical context. For example, in Gal 2:19, Paul is clear: "I through the law died to the law," and then he is equally clear in 5:15, "For all the law has been fulfilled in the one statement 'You will love your neighbor as yourself.'" Paul surely expects the Galatian Christ-followers to "love your neighbor," but then in 5:18 he restates his earlier claim: "But if you are led by the Spirit, you are not subject to the law." Finally, as Snodgrass, "Spheres," 93, notes, Paul's statements are "often enigmatic" on this issue. He asks the question that highlights the difficulties of dealing with Paul and the law in the canonical dialogue of Romans and Galatians: "How is it that the same law can be both γραφή (Gal. 3.22) and γράμμα (Rom. 7.6)?"

17. Badenas, *Christ*, 79.

18. Badenas, *Christ*, 47.

19. Dunn, *Romans*, 2.600–601.

defined in terms of the law as Israel's (10:3)."[20] Dunn is correct to alert interpreters to the importance of γάρ in these verses, though the implications of their presence that he presents is not wholly convincing. In 10:5, the γάρ is functioning to explain the previous verse further, but it is referring to more than those aspects of Torah that provide Israel with its distinctive identity. There is at least some sort of semantic connection with 10:1. Windsor has highlighted the linguistic connections between Rom 3:20–22a and Rom 10:2–4: "But the Law's purpose is not ultimately to establish Jewish righteousness. Rather, the Law's purpose is to provide 'recognition' of sin to all the world (Rom 10:2. 3:20; cf. 7:7) and thus to testify to the 'righteousness of God' (Rom 10:3, 3:21; cf. 7:24—8:1)."[21] These connections suggest that at least part of the problem relates to Israel's vocation. It is not being embodied by the majority of Israel in the way Paul thinks that it should, and their role as a light to the nations has been obscured.[22]

Christ is the Goal of the Law

Interpreters who argue that Christ is the goal of the law emphasize continuity between the Christ and Torah and downplay the nuance of termination or obliteration of the law. First, the overall teaching of Romans suggests that Christ as the end of the Torah would be an inappropriate assertion. Paul begins the letter by pointing out that his gospel was "promised beforehand through his prophets in the holy scriptures" (Rom 1:2). Similarly, in 3:21, his gospel is "attested to by the law and the prophets." Paul is convinced that his teaching does not "overthrow the law"; rather it "uphold[s] the law" (3:31). Matera connects the statement in 3:31 with the use of Abraham in chapter 4, since it testifies to righteousness by faith.[23] Also, against Christ as the end of Torah, in 7:12 Paul contends that "the law is holy" while in 7:14 "the law is spiritual." Combined, these verses suggest that those who gloss τέλος as "end" in Rom 10:4 have gone beyond the evidence. Second, the idea that Christ is the goal of the law is preferred, as argued by Cranfield, since Paul's point is "to show that Israel has misunderstood the law, because it failed to recognize what it was all

---

20. Dunn, *Romans*, 2.590.

21. Windsor, *Paul*, 215.

22. Cf. Stowers, *Rereading*, 307–8; Windsor, *Paul*, 216; Vanlaningham (*Christ*, 125) sees soteriological implications here as well.

23. Matera, *Romans*, 245. He also highlights these scriptures.

about."[24] What was it all about? The goal was Christ "so that there may be righteousness for everyone who believes" (10:4; see 1:16; 9:32–33). Third, Christ as the goal of the law accounts for the racing imagery from 9:30–33 more fully since, as noted by Keck, "τέλος was used to refer to the goal line."[25] Further, Badenas's lexical study concludes that "termination is not the basic connotation for τέλος."[26] Now that these three points have been summarized, we can unpack them more fully one by one.

First, Paul undoubtedly makes several positive statements concerning Torah in Romans; however, that is not the full story. In Rom 5:20, Paul writes, "But law came in, with the result that the trespass multiplied," and in 7:5, he writes, "While we were living in the flesh, our sinful passions, aroused by the law, were at work in our members to bear fruit for death." Dunn points out that these imply significant criticism of the law. Further, the alignment with sin and death adds to the sharpness of the critique ultimately concluding with the question in 7:7, "Is the law sin?"[27] Of course, 7:7—8:4 offers a defense of the law such that Paul would disagree with the conclusion some have deduced from his argument.

Second, is it clear that the goal of the law was always Christ? The difficulty in responding to this argument is that interpreters mean different things by the idea that the law was always pointing to Christ. Kruse focuses the issue and asserts that the debate is really about the fact that Christ is "bringing to an end the era of the law's jurisdiction." This then acknowledges aspects of the claim of Christ as goal but relies on inferences from Gal 3:23—4:7 and 2 Cor 3:7–11, which assert the temporary nature of the law's jurisdiction and the transitory nature of Moses's ministry.[28] Furthermore, it leaves open the question about the propriety of drawing significant interpretive inferences outside of the text in question. With regard to the specific point raised above, one may grant a positive testimonial relationship between Christ and Torah (Rom 3:21) but as Kruse notes "it is quite another matter to say that, because the law

24. Cranfield, *Romans*, 2.519.

25. Keck, *Romans*, 249.

26. Badenas, *Christ*, 145–47.

27. Dunn, *Theology*, 155–56.

28. Kruse, *Romans*, 403. For post-supersessionist alternative readings to that put forth by Kruse see Hardin, "Equality," 224–29; Campbell, *The Nations*, 135–36, 311–13, on Gal 3:23—4:7 and Duff, *Moses*, 137–71; Campbell, *The Nations*, 153–92; Tucker, "The Role of Moses," on 2 Cor 3:7–11. NB: Campbell, *The Nations*, was published too late to engage it further in this book, though it clearly is an important post-supersessionist work on Paul's hermeneutics.

testifies to Christ in this way, he did not bring the era of the law to an end so that righteousness may be made available to everyone who believes."[29]

Third, with regard to the lexical argument, the evidence is somewhat inconclusive and ambiguous so the understanding of τέλος as either end or goal must be solved on contextual grounds.[30] Philip Esler contends that the context requires "termination and definitive replacement."[31] He understands Paul to claim that righteousness pursued by means of the law is "opposed to God's righteousness, which comes via faith in Christ" which gives rise to "two clearly differentiated collectivities—the Christ-movement and Israel, ingroup and outgroup."[32] Thus, the broader context of 9:30—10:4 suggests Christ is the end of the jurisdiction of the law not just the goal of it. Of course, one could also assert that the "law of righteousness" is employed because Christ is the goal of the law. Also, as noted by Matera, Paul's primary concern was not the practice of the law *per se* but the lack of understanding that its righteousness was available to all through faith.[33]

Christ is the End-Goal/Fulfillment of the Law

The lack of conclusive arguments for either of the first two approaches has led some scholars to suggest there is some sort of overlap between the points, so one should see in the use of τέλος a combined end-goal understanding for Paul's contextualization of the law. Paul, in 3:21, may provide a basis for understanding 10:4 as end-goal: "But now, apart from law, the righteousness of God has been disclosed, and is attested by the law and the prophets" (Rom 3:21). This verse seems to suggest that there is both discontinuity "apart from law" and continuity "attested by the law and the prophets" in Paul's theologizing on Christ and Torah. C. K. Barrett asserted something similar, "Paul's word (τέλος) may mean not only 'termination' but also 'purpose,' or 'intention,' or 'goal'; and there is no reason why two, or even all, of these should not be combined."[34] While

29. Kruse, *Romans*, 404.

30. Davis, *Antithesis*, 145; Kruse, *Romans*, 403. However, Moo, *Romans*, provides significant lexical data suggesting that there is a lack of clear support for the goal/teleological understanding of τέλος, 639 n. 41.

31. Esler, *Conflict*, 285.

32. Esler, *Conflict*, 284.

33. Matera, *Romans*, 245.

34. Barrett, *Romans*, 184.

Barrett does pick up on this interpretive possibility, some rather unfortunate language—e.g., suggesting the law may be "discarded" once it has served its "purpose"—renders his position untenable.[35] Moo's articulation of this both/and option is certainly probative: "Paul is implying that Christ is the 'end' of the law (he brings its era to a close) and its 'goal' (he is what the law anticipated and pointed toward)."[36] Badenas, on the other hand, avers and thinks that there is not sufficient "semantic substantiation" or "contextual evidence" for "such a *double entendre*."[37] However, the contextual justification for Moo's approach is substantial, and the lexical information is such that neither "end" nor "goal" can be excluded.[38] While it is difficult to tell which of the approaches is preferable, end-goal seems to have the most nuance, especially if it is understood (as, e.g., in Matt 5:17) in the sense of embracing the idea of "fulfillment" and rejecting the concept of "obliteration."[39] This is one way to describe Paul's contextualization of the law in Romans.

One point of contention that requires brief discussion is whether Moo's salvation-historical framework is sufficient for Paul's argument. Windsor also follows the both/and approach but recognizes the difficulties associated with Israel's identity and vocation as they are entangled with the law. In this configuration, the value of the law (which, thus, is not terminated) continues in a redefined manner in that it is a witness to the gospel rather than a set of regulations that would lead to life (however that is understood—see below). Further, even if one were to grant some level of discontinuity for the law in the sense that its role as a law code *leading to life* has ended, it still functions as a law code with regard to

35. Barrett, *Romans*, 184.

36. Moo, *Romans*, 641.

37. Badenas, *Christ*, 147.

38. BDAG 998–99; LSJ 1772–74; see Hultgren, *Paul's Letter*, 383.

39. See further on this Tucker, "Matthew's Missional Particularism," 19. In that paper I engaged with the argument of David Sim and suggested that gentiles following Christ would need to follow the community's halakhic standards as they pertained to righteous gentiles (those from the nations residing within Israel). It seems historically that is what is going on with regard to the continuation of Torah within the earliest Christ-movement. This view builds on Nanos's earlier work in Romans (*Mystery*, 35–40), especially as it relates to the Jerusalem edict in Acts 15. While often interpreters reject the use of the gospels since they were written after Paul's letters, Ehrensperger, "Paul and the Authority," 291–319, has offered a useful methodological approach that suggests seeing Paul's writings as influencing the writing of the Gospels.

Israel's vocation.[40] This is one area where Rosner, who sees a repudiation of the law as a law code, and Windsor, who sees it as an expression of Israel's enduring calling (though without direct soteriological agency), differ.[41] The distinction between soteriology and vocation is crucial for understanding Paul's law discourse within a post-supersessionist framework. Israel still has a distinct identity and calling in the world in the context of the messianic era inaugurated by Christ.

Leviticus 18:5 in Romans 10:5–6: Antithesis or Complementarity

In Rom 10:5–6, Paul references Moses, who "writes concerning the righteousness that comes from the law, that 'the person who does these things will live by them.'" He continues, "But the righteousness that comes from faith says, 'Do not say in your heart, "Who will ascend into heaven?"'" (that is, to bring Christ down)." There continues to be significant debate over these verses. Here we will focus on (a) what does Paul mean by "the righteousness that comes from the law" and (b) what significance does he attach to the citation of Lev 18:5. These two questions will help clarify our overarching concern in this chapter as regards the continuation of Israel's covenantal identity within the Christ-movement generally and specifically, in this subsection, with the way Torah continues to inform that identity.

Righteousness Based on Torah

Brian Rosner thinks that Paul establishes a stark contrast here with regard to a righteousness based on Torah and one that comes by faith (Rom 10:6).[42] This antithetical understanding of the relationship between 10:5 and 10:6 is the dominant reading of this passage. It also aligns quite nicely with the earlier interpretive conclusion that Christ is the end of the law in 10:4. Sprinkle's arguments for the antithetical approach are adopted by Rosner and worth highlighting. First, Sprinkle contends that the antithetical reading is required because this relationship is evident in Gal 3:12 where Paul sets Lev 18:5 and Hab 2:4 in the same opposition.

---

40. See Windsor, *Paul*, 215.

41. Rosner, *Paul and the Law*, 59–73; Windsor, *Paul*, 212–16.

42. Rosner, *Paul and the Law*, 71.

Second, the grammatical construction itself is highly suggestive of an antithetical reading. The presence of δέ in 10:6 and of righteousness ἐκ πίστεως in close proximity to ἐκ [τοῦ] νόμου reduces the likelihood of a correlative understanding between these verses. Third, the broader context of Romans suggests the contrastive meaning since there are several places where law and works are set in an antithetical relationship to faith (3:21–22, 28; 4:13, 14, 16). Romans 4:13, especially, aligns law and faith in an antithetical relationship, thus providing precedence for the contrastive understanding between 10:5 and 10:6. Fourth, the idea of "doing" the law is part of a larger domain of ideas that Paul resists in Romans 9–11, especially as it relates to concepts associated with God's initiative versus human effort. Finally, Paul's lack of inclusion of the phrase "doing the commandment" from Deut 30:12–14 supports a contrastive understanding.[43] These arguments are substantial, and Sprinkle has clearly shown that the text can be understood this way. However, is it the most likely understanding of the relationship between Lev 18:5 and Deut 30:12–14 in Rom 10:5–8?

While it is clear that the majority of interpreters understand an antithetical relationship between faith and works in Gal 3:10–12 and see the proximity of righteousness ἐκ πίστεως to that ἐκ [τοῦ] νόμου as supporting such a contention, these conclusions are not universal. Willitts, for example, contends that the reason interpreters understand the Galatians text in such a manner is because of a prior commitment to a law/gospel antithesis.[44] He suggests, rather, a redemptive historical approach that sees in the language of law and faith "an *epochal delineation.*"[45] Willitts anticipates Sprinkle's work by drawing on the later use of Lev 18:5 in Ezek 20:11, 13, 21; Neh 9:29 and CD III, 16. He also highlights the original covenantal blessings introduced in the covenant formula in Lev 8:1–5. Ezekiel and Nehemiah argue that the potential for these blessings is not realized because of Israel's actions, i.e., "the nation remains under the covenantal curse awaiting redemption."[46] The Damascus Document, however, highlights the Qumran community as the remnant who have realized the covenant potential found in Leviticus 5. Willitts concludes that the almost exclusive focus on the Pentateuchal context

---

43. Sprinkle, *Law and Life*, 31–34.

44. Willitts, "Context Matters," 106.

45. Willitts, "Context Matters," 108, emphasis original

46. Willitts, "Context Matters," 114.

has hindered interpreters from seeing this "eschatological development in the interpretive tradition."[47] This leads Willitts to reject the contrast between "faith" and "law" in Gal 3:11b–12, since it is not discussing "two mutually exclusive bases for righteousness (law/gospel)"; rather, it is contrasting "*historical periods* in salvation history: the period of *unrealised* covenant potential (3:12) and the period of *realised* covenant potential (3:11b)."[48] Paul's point then is that now that Christ has come and sins have been atoned for, the Deuteronomic curses, which remained in the earlier period, have been set aside, and participation in the eschatological age by faith brings justification and also "brings about the realisation of covenantal blessing."[49]

The presence of δέ in 10:6 could be understood as adversative; however, there is no specific reason to assume that it has to be. If the adversative nuance was specifically desired one might expect ἀλλά. The connective use of δέ is just as likely here, in which case what follows adds an additional element without the contrastive inference. In this case, 10:6, like 10:20, uses δέ "to signal a change of speakers" for the citation.[50] Finally, Glenn Davies broadens the discussion by looking at the γάρ . . . δέ construction from 10:5 and 10:6 and concludes that in Romans the majority of these constructions do not imply "contrast or negation; they simply introduce, in the final clause, a supplementary, parallel or explanatory statement."[51] While it is true that this connective use of δέ cannot decide the issue by itself, it at least suggests that interpreters should not preclude the complementary reading here. Keck, who also follows the complementary reading, reminds us what is on debate: "whether what faith-derived righteousness says is a christological *alternative* to what Moses says or a christological *appropriation* of it."[52]

The broader text of Romans and its putative law and works antithesis is a wide ranging argument that can only be addressed in a suggestive fashion here.[53] William S. Campbell highlights one of the major problems with this approach. It reveals Paul to be an inconsistent reader of Torah

---

47. Willitts, "Context Matters," 117.

48. Willitts, "Context Matters," 119.

49. Willitts, "Context Matters," 121.

50. Wagner, *Heralds*, 161 n. 132.

51. Davies, *Faith*, 190.

52. Keck, *Romans*, 254.

53. Several of these texts have been addressed in other parts of the book. See page 40 for 3:21–22, 28 and pages 72, 78, 80, 94–95 for 4:13, 14, 16.

for he reads Lev 18:5 as an instance of "the wrong kind of righteousness—law-righteousness" but then understands Deut 30:12–14 to "support faith-righteousness."[54] So, the idea that there is a contrast is more in
keeping with a presupposition with regard to the nature of Paul's view
of the law as opposed to what he actually says. Campbell concludes
concerning 10:5 and 10:6: "Paul intends both quotations to support his
claim that the righteousness now realised in Christ is that to which Moses also pointed."[55] So, rather than seeing a contrast one might posit a
corresponding nuance in which the ἐκ [τοῦ] νόμου of 10:5 correlates to
the ἐκ πίστεως of 10:6. With regard to Rom 3:21–22, 28, Windsor has
shown that the vocational element is also in view, especially when these
verses are compared with 10:2–4.[56] What this means for a critique of the
antithetical approach is that while one may grant a contextualization for
the role of the law with regard to eschatological life, "the ultimate 'goal'
of Israel's Law is to testify paradoxically, through Israel's failure, to the
universal gospel of righteousness through faith in Christ."[57] Thus, the soteriological component is present, but there is also a vocational element
that cannot easily be disentangled from Paul's dual view of the law and
righteousness in 3:20–22. With regard to 4:13, 14, 16, interpreters often
assume a derogatory nuance for ἐκ τοῦ νόμου while Campbell argues
that it is rather being used in a neutral manner.[58] Paul offers an inclusive
salvation in the context of existing social identities, not to their exclusion. One of the ways he accomplishes this is by contextualizing the law.[59]

54. Campbell, *Paul's Gospel*, 64–65.

55. Campbell, *Paul's Gospel*, 65.

56. Windsor, *Paul*, 215–16. For example, the acknowledgement of sin is evident
in both passages as well as the testimony of God's righteousness that comes through
faith in Christ for those who trust in him. In this way, Christ becomes the τέλος of the
law. Windsor then makes an important interpretive move: "Paul understands Jewish
identity to be fundamentally defined by the possession of and communal engagement
with the Law of Moses." The focus on τέλος here relates both to the law and to Israel.
Windsor then concludes, "As Paul now goes on to demonstrate, this contrast between
two different ways of reading the Law has profound implications, not only for Israel's
present soteriological status, but also for Israel's divine vocation in relation to the rest
of the world." Thus, Paul sees in his preaching the proper embodiment of Jewish identity (Rom 10:5–8). This ultimately leads Windsor to make the connection highlighted
above: Rom 10:2b–4 expounds on the earlier teaching in 3:20–22. See further, Windsor, *Paul*, 217–18.

57. Windsor, *Paul*, 215 n. 95.

58. Campbell, *Paul and the Creation*, 127.

59. See further Zoccali, "Children," 265–67.

This is not to deny that there are no identity-forming antitheses in Rom 3:21–31; it is just that their starkness is often overplayed.[60]

Rosner builds a significant portion of his argument on the idea that Christ-followers may be described as fulfilling the law, but not as doing the law (Rom 8:3–4; 13:8–9).[61] The focal point for both Rosner and Sprinkle is whether Paul would view ὁ ποιήσας αὐτά in 10:5 as a description of appropriate human effort, in light of the broader argument in Romans 9–11 that sets in a binary relationship God's initiative and human endeavor.[62] The challenge here is trying to frame this discussion within the context of existing Jewish teachings on this topic. First, Karin Hedner Zetterholm has shown that the expressions "do Torah" and "fulfill the commandments" are synonymous.[63] Thus, the distinction put forth by Rosner and Sprinkle may not be as probative as it first appears. Second, as pointed out by Wilson, the assumption being made by these interpret-

---

60. Watson, *Paul, Judaism,* 218, 229–34.

61. This issue will be discussed below in the section dealing with Rom 13:8–10, beginning on page 91; the earlier statements by Hafemann concerning the Spirit can be referenced on page 112.

62. Watson, "Constructing," 102. Of course, Watson does agree that "the Pauline antithesis between faith and law is a Pauline *construct.*" He has shown by his reading of 4QMMT, 4 Maccabees, and Paul that there was a diversity of viewpoints concerning divine and human agency, and these are attributed to the diversity among the hermeneutical approaches of the authors. So, the Pauline antithesis between grace and works did not develop in an analogous way with that of 4QMMT and 4 Maccabees but was, in fact, a construct of Paul. Watson argues that one cannot know the extent to which Paul's antithesis corroborates or differs from other viewpoints held within Second Temple Judaism in that Paul's construct is more clearly defining his gospel, not summarizing views of others contemporary to Paul. Thus, the distinction that is being made here may not be as probative as it first appears because of the differing hermeneutical perspective of texts that might be brought to bear on this debate. The interaction between divine and human agency is evident in Barclay, "By the Grace," 156–57. He provides a comparative reading of Philo and Paul concerning divine grace and human agency. Both Philo and Paul emphasize the priority of grace but differ about its place in their theological frameworks: Philo associates it with creation while Paul connects it with the Christ-event, and for Philo a "resting sage" is the ideal person while for Paul the ideal person is an obedient person. Barclay concludes that "Paul's central theology of participation requires that human agency is reconceived without being abandoned, the self not merely relocated but reconstituted by its absorption within the *non-coercive power of grace.*" While both Watson and Barclay are quite close to Rosner and Sprinkle, they both highlight the challenges associated with the difficult topic of God's initiative and human response to God's action. Thus, while I am not in full disagreement with Rosner and Sprinkle on this issue, my concern is more a matter of degree, and to what extent one can distinguish between doing and fulfilling the law.

63. Hedner Zetterholm, *Jewish Interpretation,* 141.

ers is that with the advent of the Spirit "there is no need for the guiding, restraining influence of the law."[64] Yet law and Spirit are not opposites in the same manner as sin and righteousness or death and life but, as noted by Meyer, "as powerlessness [law] and life-giving power [Spirit] (8:2–4)."[65]

Finally, there is significant debate concerning the way in which Paul understands Deuteronomy 30 in relation to its original context. Sprinkle is right to point out that Paul leaves out "doing the commandment" that occurs three times in Deut 30:12–14.[66] Roy Ciampa takes this a step further, noting that Paul removes the phrases expressing the need to obey the Torah and in their place "introduce[s] references to Christ and the gospel message."[67] Thus, both Sprinkle and Ciampa think that Paul has severed Deuteronomy 30 from its original meaning. The apparent antithesis here is based on the idea that there are two types of righteousness in Rom 10:5 and 10:6, but Kaiser demurs, suggesting that these contrasting ideas disappear if both "have their final aim in Christ. Christ witnesses to the fact that the inward principle was the focal point for both passages."[68] Further, Deut 30:6 refers to the circumcision of the heart which suggests that the antithetical elements have been overemphasized. Paul's reading of the end of Deuteronomy has been a central part of the work of N. T. Wright. Concerning Deut 30:12–14, he thinks that Paul "discerns within it a pattern which he recognizes: it is the pattern of the Messiah, seen as God's revelation of his own 'word,' coming from God to Israel and enabling Israel to be God's people in a new way."[69] I have highlighted specific concerns with regard to Wright's claim for a reconstituted Israel and

---

64. Wilson, "Supersession," 238.

65. Meyer, "Romans 10:4," 71–73. He sees Paul in Rom 9:30—10:4 as a "Jewish Christian whose new religious identity depends on continuity with his old; who must, for his own sake and the sake of those who have made the move with him, as well as for the sake of the right understanding of his gospel on the part of the Gentile Christians (11:13), undertake such a review." Similarly, Jewett, "Law," 354. He concludes that "Paul's argument in 9:30—10:4 is that the ultimate purpose of the law was that all persons, Jews and Gentiles alike, might find righteousness. If Christ is the 'goal of the law,' the path of faith can be pursued without repudiating the Torah. The crucial point is the avoidance of zealotism, the assumption that conforming to a particular standard guarantees superiority over those who do not conform. Such zealotism is a perversion possible to Jews as well as Christians." See further Ortlund, *Zeal*, 118–36.

66. Sprinkle, *Law and Life*, 172.

67. Ciampa, "Deuteronomy," 108.

68. Kaiser, "Leviticus," 27.

69. Wright, *Paul and the Faithfulness of God*, 1173.

the implications this has for a post-supersessionist reading of Romans.[70] However, I think here he picks up on something important that calls into question the contrasting approach to Rom 10:5–6. He suggests that in the Deuteronomy 30 passage there is an "implicit theology of grace at work."[71]

Complementarity: Obedience that Springs from Faith

Rather than interpreting 10:5 and 10:6 as antithetical, it seems that Paul views these two citations as complementary and as offering further substantiation for his claim in 10:4 that Christ is the end-goal/fulfillment of the law.[72] Several scholars have noted this possibility, so I will highlight the arguments that may be put forth in support of this position below. By doing this, I am not suggesting that Sprinkle's work has been defeated; rather, I am asserting that the antithetical approach is not as strong as is oftentimes thought. As a reminder, Schreiner thinks that the two strongest arguments for the antithetical reading include the idea that the desire to establish one's own righteousness in Rom 10:3 aligns closely with the doing of the commandments of the law in 10:5. Further, he brings in the antithetical discourse in 9:30—10:13 to provide justification for seeing a contrasting nuance between 10:5 and 10:6.[73] The argument put forth here, however, is that it is more likely that Paul is interested in highlighting the obedience that springs from faith.[74]

Beyond the critique of the contrasting readings set forth above, another reason to view 10:5 and 10:6 in a complementary fashion is that the antithetical reading results in one scripture, Lev 18:5, maintaining a position that differs from another, Deut 30:11–14. In this configuration, Leviticus teaches about a righteousness that comes from the law while Deuteronomy teaches about one that comes from faith. One way forward is to discern more precisely Paul's concern here by paying attention to the connective and what differs from the original citation. First, the γάρ in

---

70. See p. 128.

71. Wright, *Paul and the Faithfulness of God*, 1173. For the discussion of a reconstituted Israel see 194.

72. See Zoccali, *Whom God*, 169. He thinks that "vv. 5–6 do not set Lev. 18.5 and Deut. 30 in opposition with one another, as if the latter negates the former . . . but rather Paul interprets Lev. 18.5 in light of Deut. 30."

73. Schreiner, *The Law*, 104–12. See Moo, *Romans*, 646. He briefly offers further reasons for rejecting the complementary approach.

74. See on this Davies, *Faith*, 177–204; Badenas, *Christ*, 112–33.

10:5 offers further amplification with regard to the use of τέλος in 10:4, i.e., why Christ is the goal-end/fulfillment of Torah based on what Moses says. Second, the phrase in 10:5, τὴν δικαιοσύνην τὴν ἐκ [τοῦ] νόμου "the righteousness that comes from Torah," is not in Lev 18:5, and this addition indicates that this is Paul's primary concern in Rom 10:5.[75] So, as Toews points out, "The concern in Romans 10:5 is doing the righteousness of the law, not doing the law as in Galatians."[76] This minor distinction is crucial since Gal 3:12 is often used to understand Paul's argument in Rom 10:5 more precisely. Toews's position is made more plausible by the reminder that Paul maintains ἄνθρωπος as the subject in Romans, a move he does not make in Gal 3:12. Further, the textual variants in 10:5 substantiate Toews's reading in that αὐτά is omitted after ὁ ποιήσας and ἐν is followed by αὐτῇ rather than αὐτοῖς. This results in his interpretive rending: *"the person who does it [the righteousness of the law] will live by it [the righteousness of the law]."*[77] So, the retention of ἄνθρωπος as the subject and the variant that replaces αὐτοῖς with αὐτῇ suggest that Paul's focus here is primarily on the righteousness of the law rather than on the regulations as in Gal 3:12. At least, this argument is a reminder to allow these disparate contexts to stand and to not be used to mutually interpret one another.[78] So far, the understanding presented here calls into question an interpretation of 10:5–6 that sees Paul setting aside a putative Jewish way of seeking righteousness in contrast to his own new understanding. He is clearly setting aside something in the context, but it is more likely that his concern is with the manner in which the law had been read, as a discourse focused on works as compared to faith. In this way of reading the text, the problem is not doing, but *doing without faith.*

While more could be said, the understanding of 10:4 as end-goal/fulfillment is further supported by the complementary interpretation of 10:5 and 10:6. Thus, the obedience described by Moses is the obedience of faith. In that case, both citations affirm the same thing. They bring to

75. See Moo, *Romans*, 645–47, for the possible interpretations of this phrase. He concludes it has a negative inference.

76. Toews, *Romans*, 263.

77. Toews, *Romans*, 263. Though this is helpful, the argument does not depend on accepting this reading, which is based on early manuscripts and is also the harder reading. Also, the variant that moves the ὅτι after γράφει would suggest this is more of an expansive paraphrase. That is to say, it diverts from the LXX text that we have; however, this alternative reading is syntactically more correct since now the antecedent for δικαιοσύνην is properly αὐτῇ. See further Badenas, *Christ*, 118–19.

78. See further, Badenas, *Christ*, 119.

the fore the centrality of Christ as the object of faith. So, the righteousness that Moses spoke of and that which is central to Paul's gospel discourse are the same.[79] The allusion to Deut 30:12–14 begins with μὴ εἴπῃς which hearkens back to a similar construction in Deut 8:17 and 9:4 where presumption was a problem for Israel. This leads Davies to conclude that "[i]n the same vein, Paul has indicted Israel for pursuing the law of righteousness, as if it were by works (9.32)."[80] Thus, the criticism by Schreiner above has some force. However, it is not altogether clear whether Paul is devaluing these same works if they are done by faith since the context of Deuteronomy 30 keeps both works and faith together. This raises an issue with regard to the lack of ποιέω in 10:6–8, as mentioned above (used in Deut 30:12, 13, 14). While the weight of that observation is granted, Paul does use ποιέω in 10:5 so it is not clear that he would need to restate it in order to communicate effectively. Further, those opposing Paul's argument could simply point out his omission of ποιέω and weaken his case. The assumption by those holding to the contrasting perspective is that Paul is developing a works versus faith discourse; however, Davies reminds interpreters that his argument is not against "doing" *per se*, but "doing without trusting."[81] This also seems to be Paul's concern in 9:32 and in 10:3 in that what could not be accomplished previously has been revealed: "For Christ is the end-goal/fulfillment of the law, that everyone who has faith may be justified" (10:4). Thus, 9:31 is not an illegitimate goal and, as noted by Klyne Snodgrass, "The law still has its proper role in the sphere of Christ, the Spirit, and faith."[82] Paul will explain the way this works in Romans 14–15.

Conclusion

The previous chapter offered a positive conception of Israel's continuing covenantal identity in Romans 9. Israel's identity has been somewhat transformed in line with those born of the promise. This transformation extends to the inclusion of the nations; however Paul still maintains Israel as a concrete historical group. The role of the crucial phrase, "Christ is the τέλος of the Law," includes some kind of continuing nuance; the

79. See Davies, *Faith*, 200.

80. Davies, *Faith*, 201.

81. Davies, *Faith*, 201 n. 1.

82. Snodgrass, "Spheres," 107.

righteousness/law antithesis that is so crucial to traditional Paulinism has likely been overplayed.

The findings of these past two chapters contribute to a cumulative case that God's promises to Israel have not been abrogated. What has been implicit in this episodic reading of Romans 9–10 requires further elaboration: Paul thinks that Israel's covenantal identity survives the Christ-event, and therefore there is a future component to it that will become clear in the consummation of all things. This claim requires a brief engagement with two opposing views that result in the reduction of Israel's continued covenantal identity in Romans 11, and a discussion of some of the details that make a post-supersessionist reading difficult. It is to that we now turn.

7

Israel's Future Covenantal Identity

Introduction

WHEN DETERMINING WHETHER ISRAEL'S covenantal identity continues in Paul's universalistic gospel, Romans 11 could almost be offered as a proof text for an affirmative answer, especially 11:1, which reads: "I ask, then, has God rejected his people? By no means! I myself am an Israelite, a descendant of Abraham, a member of the tribe of Benjamin." Additionally, 11:28b–29 states clearly, "as regards election they are beloved, for the sake of their ancestors; for the gifts and the calling of God are irrevocable." Most interpreters grant that God has not fully cast aside his original people Israel, but they construe the implications of this in markedly different ways.

One example is Francis Watson. He recognizes that his interpretation of Romans may be understood as supersessionist; however, he is not particularly concerned for the following three reasons: "(1) [the supersessionist result] expresses an alienation from the parent religious community integral to the sect model employed in this work; (2) religious professionals are constantly seeking to supersede views held within interpretative communities other than their own; (3) nothing that Paul says on any topic should be taken as a *direct* mandate for contemporary theology or practice."[1] Watson is correct that some of the ingroup and outgroup language he discerns is there because of the disparate Jewish and gentile group identities. However, if one doesn't assume an institutional

---

1. Watson, *Paul, Judaism*, 321–22 n. 36.

separation at this early stage, then more work needs to be done.[2] Furthermore, the contemporary mandate part of his quote raises questions; interpreters are, in fact, ethically responsible for their interpretations. It is not enough to simply state that we don't have to follow the implications of a supersessionist first-century text.[3]

This chapter, due to self-imposed constraints, will focus on the second half of Romans 11, but vv. 1–10 are important to mention because of the way they challenge post-supersessionist readings.[4] Francis Watson, for example, concludes: "In 11:5–6 Paul explicitly says that the remnant (among whom the Roman Jewish Christians would number themselves) is chosen by grace, and that 'works' are irrelevant to this. In other words, continued observance of the law and membership of the Jewish community are inessential to the identity of Jewish Christians, who should rather regard themselves as chosen by grace just as the Gentiles are."[5] These arguments have been addressed in other parts of this book and will not be restated here; however, it should be noted that Watson continues the exegetical move used by other supersessionist interpreters, who over-emphasize and atomize Rom 11:1–10 in their arguments. Hill remarks, "Imagine that chs. 9–11 had ended at 11:10: 'let their eyes be darkened so that they cannot see, and keep their backs forever bent.' In that case, Paul might with good reason be regarded as a thoroughgoing Christian supersessionist. 'Israel failed to obtain what it was seeking' (v. 7), and so Israel has been set aside in favour of the church. The fact that Paul has been read this way for centuries amply demonstrates that Rom 11:11–36 has not been given its due weight."[6] This chapter will take Hill's concern as its point of departure.

---

2. Korner, "*Ekklēsia* as a Jewish Synagogue Term," 72–73; Korner, *Origin*, 81–149; 213–57. He contends that *ekklēsia* language suggests that the Christ-movement was still institutionally within the broader synagogue community and further that its use by Paul should not be seen supersessionistically.

3. Patte, *Ethics*, 125–29.

4. I earlier addressed some of these verses beginning on page 149 at the end of chapter 5.

5. Watson, *Paul, Judaism*, 342. See Nanos, *Mystery*, 276: "Paul does make a distinction among Jews between the 'remnant' and the 'part hardened' so that he can say 'they are not all Israel who are descended from Israel.'" Kinzer, *Postmissionary*, 131: "Israel's remnant—the Jewish Yeshua-believers—is now seen as the 'elect' (Romans 9:11; 11:5, 7). However, their election does not replace the election of the people as whole, but instead anchors it. They are the elect within the elect."

6. Hill, "Romans," 1102.

Diatribe and the Stumbling Allegory in Rom 11:11–16

After the opening of chapter 11 just mentioned, Paul continues his argument in 11:11 with the transition, "So I ask (Λέγω οὖν), have they stumbled so as to fall?" The presence of the first person singular indicates Paul's use of the diatribe, a rhetorical device he used frequently in Romans.[7] The literary character asks, "have they stumbled so as to fall?" The pronoun "they" in this verse refers to the Israelites, but it cannot refer to all Israelites since Paul, despite calling himself an Israelite (11:1), has not stumbled. Instead, it refers to a particular subgroup of Israelites that have not, as of yet, become convinced by the gospel.[8] Many contemporary interpreters might suggest, "yes, they have stumbled so as to fall." But Paul continues with a diatribe marker declaring the opposite: "By no means! (μὴ γένοιτο)."

Note that when Paul refers to Israel's current situation as a "stumble" rather than a "fall" in 11:11, he minimizes it and also demonstrates that it is not final. Furthermore, this current situation has provided a way for the gentiles to be counted among God's family. Paul offers four elements of this current condition. First, some among the nation of Israel embodied a "false step," which may simply be another way of referring to their current "stumble." This opened a way for gentiles to come in, which he describes in 11:12 as "riches for the world." Then, in 11:15, Israel's temporary stumble also brought reconciliation to the world. Paul hoped that the new availability of these riches for gentiles would rouse a sense of fervor among his kin so that they too would become convinced by the gospel. He seems to think that is likely since in 11:12 he highlights "their fulfillment," which suggests a covenantal identity for Israel that continues into the future (11:15, 26).

The phrase "For if their rejection" in 11:15, could be understood supersessionistically, but is Paul referring to God's rejection of Israel or Israel's rejection of God or of the gospel? The objective genitive reading, supported by Schreiner, would suggest the Jews were the object of God's rejection, but that seems to work against the flow of the argument. The subjective genitive makes more sense, in that they, some in Israel, have

---

7. Thorsteinsson, Thiessen, and Rodríguez, "Paul's Interlocutor," 19.

8. Wright, *Climax*, 249. He contends that his approach is not supersessionistic since physical Jews are not barred from salvation. While this is accurate, it is not generally the way debates concerning supersessionism proceed.

rejected the gospel.[9] While the subjective genitive reading is a minority one, and the idea that God has temporarily rejected Israel is standard fare among interpreters, as Fitzmyer concludes, it "is something read into the text that is not there."[10] Furthermore, it is often appealed to in order to make sense of Romans 9–11, but rather than providing clarification, it introduces an unwarranted supersessionist motif into those chapters.

This is seen further in the last half of 11:15, where Paul's use of "acceptance" is thought to mean "acceptance by God." But again, if the subjective genitive reading is accepted, that opens the possibility that "acceptance of the gospel" is in view. So, the temporary rejection by some first-century Jews opened up a door for "reconciliation" for those from the nations, and if/when these same individuals accept the gospel, their new creation existence will be "life from the dead."[11] Paul maintains a hope for Israel's restoration. He does not think that God has temporarily rejected the nation, though he does think many within it have rejected the gospel.

In 11:16, Paul highlights two more details concerning Israel's disobedience. The first builds on Num 15:17–21, "If the dough offered as first fruits is holy, so is the whole lump." And the second detail is that "if the root is holy, so are the branches." Clearly the "whole lump" and "branches" refer to all of historic Israel as an entirety. But to what does "dough offered as first fruits" and the "root" refer? The "root" is best understood as referring to the patriarchs and the "first fruits" as referring to Jewish Christ-followers, i.e., the remnant (see further below). Earlier, in relation to Rom 9:6, Kinzer was highlighted as one who sees an elect core within the elect nation, an Israel within Israel.[12] In Rom 11:5, we discussed the way Paul describes this group as the "remnant": "So too at the present time there is a remnant, chosen by grace." Nanos rightly picks up on this and notes, "Paul does make a distinction among Jews between the 'remnant' and the 'part hardened' so that he can say 'they are

---

9. Schreiner, *Romans*, 597–98. Fitzmyer, rightly I think, says the genitive phrase "is better taken as a subjective gen., i.e., the Jews' rejection (of the gospel), in view of what Paul has exclaimed in 11:1, where he rejects the idea that God has rejected his own people" (*Romans*, 612).

10. Schreiner, *Romans*, 612.

11. Schreiner, *Romans*, 613. Fitzmyer also cites John 5:24 as a parallel to what Paul may have in view here.

12. Kinzer, *Postmissionary*, 124.

not all Israel who are descended from Israel.'"[13] This remnant, however, does not replace Israel. Instead, in 11:16, as noted by Kinzer, Paul uses "holiness discourse" concerning the "first fruits" and "whole batch" to refer to a remnant that "represents and sanctifies Israel."[14] Jewish Messiah-followers then serve as a bridge between the nation Israel and gentiles in Christ. Furthermore, 11:16 suggests that "in Paul's view the remnant does not replace Israel but instead represents and sanctifies Israel. It serves a priestly function on behalf of the entire nation."[15] Kinzer goes even a step further. He compares Romans 8 with 9–11, and provocatively asks: "is it possible . . . that Israel's temporary unbelief in Yeshua is itself, paradoxically, a participation in Yeshua's vicarious, redemptive suffering?"[16] This is an important insight that responds to N. T. Wright who, in contrast, sees Jesus as Israel such that Israel's identity is taken over by Christ.[17] The salience of Israel's covenantal identity, and not its temporary rejection, is crucial for a proper understanding of Romans 11. The continuation of existing identity continues in Paul's olive tree imagery.[18]

Olive Tree Imagery and the Transformation of Identities in Romans 11:17–24

The grafting imagery highlights primarily the hazardous position in which boasting gentiles may find themselves. This perspective differs from interpreters who see the focal point here as Israel. While some within Israel are in an injured state, they have not been completely

---

13. Nanos, *Mystery*, 125 cited in Kinzer, *Postmissionary*, 125 n. 36.

14. Kinzer, *Postmissionary*, 125.

15. Kinzer, *Postmissionary*, 125. See also Harink, *Paul*, 174.

16. Kinzer, *Postmissionary*, 133. On Israel-Christology see Kinzer, *Searching*, 21–23.

17. Wright, *Climax*, 250: "throughout the letter as well as elsewhere . . . [Paul] systematically transferred the privileges and attributes of 'Israel' to the Messiah and his people." See Vlach, "What Does Christ," 43–54.

18. Runesson, "Paul's Rule," 219: "Being Jewish or non-Jewish means nothing—*in relation to the keeping of the commandments and salvation* (1 Cor 7:19; cf. Gal 5:19–23; Rom 1:32; 13:13; 1 Cor 6:9–11). All that matters is faith, which opens up for the Spirit's salvific outpouring of love, enabling all to fulfill the law. For Paul this does not, however, change the fact that the world still consists of two basic categories: the Jewish people (according to the irrevocable promise; Rom 11:29) and the rest of the world. Paul permitted no conversion between these worlds, since conversion would negate God's acceptance of all regardless of ethnic identity. The unifying elements between the worlds are faith and the outpouring of the Spirit on both."

removed. This suggests that interpreters who bring to the fore the idea that Israel has been broken off from their covenantal identity may have over-interpreted the rhetoric of these verses. Romans 11:17–24, rather, offers a renewed vision of God's family, one that includes branches from Israel and the nations. This reading works against those such as Watson who thinks the reading offered below is unsustainable since it seeks "to stress Paul's continuity with Judaism at the expense of discontinuity."[19] However, as will be shown below, Paul's metaphor does maintain continuity with his ancestral tradition even as the nations are now included in the family of God.[20]

Gentile Christ-followers and the Remnant

Jewish covenantal identity continues, but it is also transformed in Christ. This is seen in Paul's directive to accept in-Christ gentiles into God's family without requiring them to become proselytes to Judaism (1 Cor 7:19). Jewish Christ-followers, in a mirror of that directive, are not required to abandon their own existing identities in order to follow Christ. Israel's scriptural tradition and the resulting social identifications continue to inform their communal existence, though with some adjustments in light of the revelation and inauguration of the messianic era. The idea of unity within diversity becomes the underlying framework for Paul's theologizing on in-Christ identities. The olive tree imagery becomes the focal point for this framework. As Campbell notes:

> A process of self-definition was doubtless ongoing in the Christ-movement at Rome but the image of the olive tree which Paul sets forth in Rom. 11.17–24 as a model takes full account both of the nature of the commonality and diversity that then existed in the Christ communities at Rome. The groups may differ but they are branches of a common tree and should not boast over their differences from one another.[21]

Gentiles in Christ and the remnant do not combine to make up Israel. The remnant is a prolepsis of the future faithfulness of God to Israel and not a substitute for it. Paul envisions gentile Jesus-believers socially identifying with, while remaining distinct from, historic Israel

19. Watson, *Paul, Judaism*, 340.

20. See Windsor, *Paul*, 52–53; Nanos, "Romans," 276.

21. Campbell, *Paul and the Creation*, 79.

in anticipation of Israel's future restoration.[22] Campbell shifts the focus specifically to the identity of Jewish followers of Christ and concludes that "to apply to gentile Christ-followers the promises of God to Israel need not in and of itself signify that these believers were the true Israel in such a fashion as to deny any validity to the way of life or status of Jewish Christ-followers. . . . What Paul is insisting is that these gentile Christ-followers are truly God's people—true people of God, distinct but not unique!"[23]

Paul does not argue that in-Christ Jews are to abandon the law or the synagogue. The ongoing witness of their covenantal faithfulness is crucial for Paul. Francis Watson contends that one of Paul's primary aims was to generate a desire for the in-Christ Jews to end a life of Torah praxis and to establish an institutional identity separate from the broader Jewish community. Watson thinks there needs to be a clear distinction between these two asymmetrical identities, in-Christ and Jewish ethnicity.[24] However, his argument does not seem compatible with Paul's argument in Rom 11:11–32 with regard to the engrafting of the gentiles onto the olive tree and the way this results in a continuing social identification with Israel as a social implication of Paul's gospel.[25] How then, with these different approaches in mind, does reflecting on the olive tree imagery help readers discern the way Jewish covenantal identity continues? Drawing on the work of Mark Nanos, I would like to offer an alternative reading of some of the debated points of Rom 11:17–24 that supports the claim that Israel's covenantal identity remains salient even with the coming of Christ. In 11:17–19, Paul offers the following: (a) Israelite branches are "bent," not "broken off"; (b) the gentile nations are grafted in *among* Israel, not in Israel's place; (c) the gentile nations are not to boast over the branches; and (d) the Israel-forgetting group are warned.

Dislocated, Not Broken Off (11:17)

In 11:17, Paul writes: "But if some of the branches were broken off (ἐξεκλάσθησαν), and you, a wild olive shoot, were grafted in their place

22. Campbell, *Paul and the Creation*, 100.

23. Campbell, *Paul and the Creation*, 72.

24. Watson, *Paul, Judaism*, 22, 106, cited by Das, *Solving*, 50–51.

25. Dunn, *Romans*, 1.lvii; Longenecker, *Introducing Romans*, 119. See further critiques of Watson in Jewett, *Romans*, 85–86.

(ἐν αὐτοῖς) to share the richness of the olive tree" (NRSV). There is a confusing point here if "broken off" (ἐκκλάω) is read with "stumbled" *but not "fallen"* earlier in 11:11. These two words seem to suggest two different states. The rhetorical tension may be resolved by noting that ἐκκλάω does not require "broken off" as its English gloss, though this is the pattern followed by the overwhelming majority of English translations.[26] Pausanias, *Description of Greece* 8.40.2, describes a situation in which a wrestler's toe was "dislocated" (ἐκκλᾷ) during a match. The injury was quite severe but the toe was not "broken off." While there are contextual differences that should be kept in mind here, "dislocated," "broken," or as suggested by Nanos, "bent," are plausible glosses, ones that would propose that Paul's rhetorical image is not of branches completely removed from a tree; rather, they are still attached, but in an injurious situation.[27] If one were to view the branches as "bent," then the inconsistency with the earlier "stumbled" but not "fallen" is lessened. The imagery of "bent" and not "broken off" also aligns more closely with the harvesting imagery of the olive tree where one would expect branches to be "bent" in the process but not intentionally "broken off."[28]

"In Their Place" or "Among Them" (11:17)

Paul continues in 11:17 with the singular, "you, a wild olive shoot." Nanos perceptively picks up on the number of ἀγριέλαιος, showing that Paul's imagery includes among the cultivated branches only one wild one: the gentiles (11:13).[29] The NRSV translates Paul's next thought, "you … were grafted *in their place*" (ἐν αὐτοῖς). This last prepositional phrase sounds clearly like replacement theologizing, but is "in their place" an appropriate translation of ἐν αὐτοῖς? A more straightforward rendering of ἐν αὐτοῖς would be "among them" or "in them." If the earlier image of "broken off" were to continue, then the branches among which the gentile shoot is grafted would be on the ground. But in the image Paul is creating, the gentiles are grafted in "among them," i.e., on to the olive

26. Nanos ("Images," 12) points to the fourteenth-century Wycliffe translation that goes with "broken" without the subsequent "off." "What if ony of the braunchis ben brokun."

27. Nanos, "Images," 12.

28. Esler, *Conflict*, 298–300.

29. Nanos ("Broken Branches," 348–50) also sees here a supporting argument that a small gentile minority was meeting among the larger synagogue community.

tree of God's family. Thus, translating ἐκκλάω as "bent" or "dislocated" receives some contextual support in that it would keep the existing but stressed branches attached to the tree, among which these engrafted in-Christ gentiles are also now attached "to share the rich root of the olive tree" (Rom 11:17). The vast majority of English translations go with "in among them" with the NRSV being an outlier here. Paul's point is that these in-Christ gentiles are sharing the same root as the other branches, which would not be the case if those branches had already been "broken off" and removed from the olive tree.

No Boasting over the Branches (11:18)

Paul then gets to his concern, the tendency of gentiles to boast. In 11:18 he writes, "do not boast over (μὴ κατακαυχῶ) the branches." The imagery here stresses the ideas from the previous verse; the existing branches are still part of the tree and not out of it. Since this is Paul's view of the situation, he instructs the gentiles to not look down on those bent branches, i.e., "do not boast over" them (11:18).[30] This instruction makes sense, especially if some of the in-Christ gentiles were boasting that they had replaced the Jews as God's people. This boasting would be especially acute if they are a subgroup within the larger synagogue community. Paul continues, "If (εἰ) you do boast, remember that it is not you that support the root, but the root that supports you." There is some debate about whether these gentiles have actually begun boasting or are simply inclined towards that action. Paul's primary concern is for the gentiles to recognize that they are being carried along by the "root" (ῥίζα). The promises made to Israel's patriarchs are likely in view, though the referent is difficult to discern.[31] Campbell concludes, "the gentiles are reminded not to boast over the branches since they are not the stem but are borne (βαστάζειν) on the stem of Abraham."[32]

30. I have argued in other places that cultural boasting is one of those areas in which gentile identity does not continue in Christ. Tucker, *You Belong to Christ*, 14; Tucker, *Remain in Your Calling*, 115 n. 3.

31. Contra Barclay, *Paul*, 550, emphasis original. It is not likely Israel or the patriarchs *per se* but, "*the calling or election of God* that constituted them as patriarchs, and thereby constituted Israel as a whole. The root is the unconditional favor of God on which Israel's existence depends." Middendorf, *Romans*, 2.1122, sees the root as the patriarchs.

32. Campbell, *Paul and the Creation*, 38.

Warning and Grafting Benefits (11:19)

Paul, then, in 11:19, tries to anticipate what this Israel-forgetting group of gentiles might say via the continued use of a hypothetical interlocutor: "You will say, 'Branches were broken off (ἐξεκλάσθησαν) so that I might be grafted in (ἐγκεντρισθῶ).'" Note here again the NRSV uses "broken off" to describe the "branches" i.e., non-Christ-following Jews. However, even in the imaginary interlocutor's voice, Paul does not think in terms of complete separation from the tree. He saves that imagery for another group later in the passage (11:22; ἐκκόπτω).

Another argument that supports the claim that the branches were only dislocated and not removed is found in the actual manner in which ancient olive tree grafting was practiced. It was not practiced by breaking off a branch and adding a new branch in its place; rather, it was accomplished by segmenting the existing branch and setting the new one into it. Thus, Philip Esler has shown how an overreliance on Columella's description of grafting and an underuse of Theophrastus has led to a misunderstanding of the nature of the imagery here. Paul's inclusion of the gentiles will result in more fruit, but it does not serve as a critique of the lack of fruit-bearing by Israel.[33]

Interlocutor Is Correct But Only to an Extent (11:20–21)

Beginning in 11:20, Paul addresses the unstable status of gentiles in Christ. He does this first by acknowledging the accuracy of one aspect of the interlocutor's claim by writing: "That is true (καλῶς)." The Greek word here could be understood as "indeed" indicating an "exclamation of assent," but it is often used, as noted by Porter, "as an adjunctive adverb" in which case it would be an even more neutral "well."[34] This way of understanding the καλῶς would distance Paul from the interlocutor's "supersessionist view whereby Gentile Christians have replaced Israel *in toto*."[35] Paul's claim is much more restrained. Only a portion of Israel are in view: "They were broken off (ἐξεκλάσθησαν) because of their unbelief (τῇ ἀπιστίᾳ)" (NRSV). As mentioned earlier, the NRSV continues to overinterpret ἐκκλάω here as "broken off" when "bent" or simply "broken" is still appropriate. The reason for this state is described as "unbelief"

33. Esler, *Conflict*, 301–5.

34. Porter, *Romans*, 213–14.

35. Bird, *Romans*, 388.

(τῇ ἀπιστίᾳ). This translation could easily be misconstrued as a focus on cognition, but "unbelief" would better be translated as "unfaithfulness" and thus emphasize something more embodied.[36]

For Nanos, the issue is whether these Israelites are announcing the good news to the nations or not.[37] So, the "broken" or "bent" group has been "unfaithful" with regard to their vocation of being a light to the nations. Whether this is the extent of the "unfaithfulness" of this group is an open question, but what is more explicit is that this "bent" status for some Israelites and the "grafting in" status of a gentile remnant does not provide a basis, as noted by Bird, "for some kind of replacement theology, with the Gentile church supposedly replacing Israel once and for all."[38] Paul next reminds these in-Christ gentiles (11:13) that they are in this new position by "faith," and thus they should not become "proud." Rather, they should "stand in awe." Paul suggests awe instead of arrogance for these gentiles since pride will not be rewarded but faithfulness will be. If they are not properly circumspect they might find themselves in a position similar to some of the Israelites (11:21).[39]

Wild Shoots Could Be Cut Off (11:22)

Paul continues in 11:22, "Note then the kindness and the severity of God: severity toward those who have fallen (τοὺς πεσόντας), but God's kindness toward you, provided you continue in his kindness; otherwise you also will be cut off (ἐκκοπήσῃ)." Paul cannot be using "those who have fallen" to refer to Israel since back in 11:11 he made it clear that the Israelites, as a group, have not actually fallen. They have stumbled, but they have *not* fallen. We may receive some help by noting a change of word at the end of the verse. Here in 11:22 Paul uses "cut off" (ἐκκόπτω), but that is not the same Greek word that was used earlier in 11:17, 19,

---

36. Kinzer (*Postmissionary*, 141) notes that unbeliever is not a term Paul uses for non-Christ-following Jews: "The nonremnant Jewish community may be caught in unbelief, but this condition is not so fundamental to its identity that its members should be called unbelievers."

37. Nanos, "Gifts," 6–7.

38. Bird, *Romans*, 389. On the idea of the gentile remnant, see Longenecker, *Epistle to the Romans*, 893–94.

39. Porter (*Romans*, 214) notes the presence of the explanatory γάρ indicating that since "God did not 'spare' the 'natural branches,' Paul makes clear, neither could he be expected to spare 'you,' the wild branches, who were later arrivals on the scene."

and 20, "bent" (ἐκκλάω). But unlike ἐκκλάω, ἐκκόπτω is appropriately understood as "cut off." It is particularly interesting to consider who he is talking to in 11:22: the "wild olive shoot" (11:17). He is not discussing Israel, i.e., the other branches. Rather he is addressing gentiles specifically. Their status as cut off or only bent, however, could cause confusion for them so Paul changes the verb to ἐκκόπτω.

An analysis that takes into account the use of ἐκκόπτω seems productive; however, as Nanos notes, the word "also" (καί) in 11:22 seems to suggest the same negative situation for both Jews and gentiles. If so, then why did Paul not use the same verb? Nanos suggests that the "wild olive shoot" came from another tree, and it was from that tree that it had been "cut off" (ἐκκόπτω). Paul appears to be developing a type of *a minori ad maius* (all the more) argument: if God was willing to "dislocate" those branches that were native to the tree how much more will he "cut off" those who were engrafted in from a foreign tree. Based on this, you gentiles better not be arrogant![40]

God Can Heal the Dislocated (11:23–24)

In 11:23–24, Paul offers one last warning to the gentiles: even those Jews who are presently "bent" can be set straight since that is well within God's power. These two verses often provide the basis for the "broken-off" view found in 11:17, 19, and 20. Doesn't Paul seem to imply here that non-Christ-following Jews are no longer part of the family of God? There are two reasons that this is not the case. First, the two verses are still designed for some of the in-Christ gentiles who think they are in no need of the natural branches, to remind them that they are in a precarious place. Second, the earlier arguments concerning "bent" not "broken off" should be used to understand these verses rather than using these verses to override Paul's lexical choices in the earlier section.

If Paul thinks that some of Israel is in a dislocated state, the grafting language might simply be understood as the process by which the dislocation is healed.[41] Campbell is correct to note, "the solidarity of

40. Nanos, "Gifts," 6–7, 16.

41. Nanos ("Callused," 62–67) suggests that rather than "hardened" the underlying Greek word πώρωσις should be translated as "callused." This brings to the fore the "protective" nuance to Paul's argument in 11:25. The "part of" (ἀπὸ μέρους) here, in the phrase "a hardening has come upon *part* of Israel," Nanos (*Romans*, 195) takes as "for a while" in line with the temporal element for the same phrase in 15:24. This

the people of Israel is not sacrificed despite the wedge Paul appears to drive within his own people."[42] This is especially evident in the "all Israel" language that emerges 11:26. The dislocated state, as I argued earlier in chapter 4, suggests that Israel is not limited only to those who share Abraham's faith. Paul, throughout Romans 9–11, has been wrestling with the fact that many Israelites have not become as convinced as he had about the necessity of the Christ-event or the dawning of the new age. So, as noted by Ehrensperger, "However critical he might be of his own people, he would never perceive Israel as rejected by God (Rom 11:1). Not only would Paul demolish any assertion that God has cast off his people; he also stresses, especially in Romans, that there is nothing the Gentiles could ever boast of over against the Jews, since the Jews are the root supporting the ingrafted Gentile branches (Rom 11:18)."[43]

This brings us back to the rhetorical purpose of these verses specifically and of the larger pericope generally: gentile boasting over the Jews is unacceptable—period. It is likely then, as Nanos noted long ago, that Paul is addressing an early form of supersessionism among the Roman Christ groups.[44] The point here is that Paul is not really depicting Israel. Some argue for that conclusion, but Nanos thinks that the tree is the people of God, the branches are Israel (the historic family of God), and another group, the "wild shoot," represents those from the nations who have been added to this family through embodying the faith of Abraham. So, the Christ-followers from the nations have been grafted in among Israel into the family of God.[45] Thus, those who claim that 11:23–24 support the removal of Israel's covenantal relationship have very likely gone too far.

Israel's Future Covenantal Identity in Romans 11:25–27

This section of the chapter will argue that Jewish covenantal identity continues in Paul's universalistic gospel. We know this because in Rom

---

highlights the temporary nature of Israel's experience, one that protects them until the time of Israel's full restoration: "a callus temporarily has formed for [the protection] of Israel" (195).

42. Campbell, *Paul and the Creation*, 124. He points to both Rom 9:6 and 11:23.

43. Ehrensperger, *Mutually Encouraged*, 151; Nanos, *Mystery*, 21.

44. Nanos, *Mystery*, 16.

45. Nanos works with the people of God imagery here; it seems family of God is more appropriate since peoplehood remains unchanged with the coming of Christ, both for Jews and non-Jews.

11:26 he holds out a hope for the salvation of "all Israel." This phrase cannot refer to a multi-ethnic community of Christ-followers as argued for by N. T. Wright.[46] Nor is it simply another way to restate the identity of the Jewish remnant, those who respond in faith to the gospel. We will see that this latter view, which is not itself supersessionist, has been argued for recently by Chris Zoccali, but still needs further comment.[47] The traditional view (the Jewish eschatological approach), that Rom 11:26 describes a large-scale turning of the Jewish people to the Messiah Jesus close to or at the time of the parousia, has been put forth recently by John Goodrich.[48] We will see that this approach provides a basis for the continuation of Jewish covenantal identity, especially when combined with Rom 15:7–13.[49] Wright's view does not explicitly allow for such a continuation since even though he allows for Jews being saved in the future, Jewish patterns of life as expressions of ongoing covenantal identity are deemed inappropriate. Zoccali's view makes space for Jewish patterns of life but lacks the forward thrust argued for here.[50] In light of this, the Jewish eschatological approach is slightly more convincing; however, this should not be understood to mean that Jewish covenantal identity is only future; it continues throughout salvation history.[51]

Ecclesiology: Multi-ethnic Community in Christ View

In Rom 11:25–27, Paul writes:

> Lest you be wise in your own sight, I do not want you to be unaware of this mystery (τὸ μυστήριον τοῦτο), brothers: a partial hardening has come upon Israel (τῷ Ἰσραήλ), until (ἄχρι οὗ) the fullness of the gentiles has come in. And in this way (καὶ οὕτως) all Israel (πᾶς Ἰσραήλ) will be saved (σωθήσεται), as it is written, "The Deliverer will come from Zion, he will banish ungodliness

---

46. Wright, *Paul and the Faithfulness of God*, 1243–46.

47. Zoccali, *Whom God*, 106–7.

48. Goodrich, "Until," 5–32.

49. This passage will be discussed in chapter 9 as part of a future-identity configuration for Israel and the nations worshipping the Messiah together.

50. See on that Merkle, "Romans 11," 709–21.

51. If that is an implication to be drawn from the argument here, then Zoccali's approach becomes slightly more preferable since it explicitly maintains Jewish identity throughout salvation history.

from Jacob"; "and this will be my covenant (ἐμοῦ διαθήκη) with them when I take away their sins."

Paul starts by making it clear that he wants his audience to understand the "mystery" (μυστήριον). Wright rejects the idea that there is a "*new* 'mystery,' a secret piece of wisdom or doctrine which he is about to reveal."[52] In other words, he sees, in the next couple of verses, a restatement of the earlier arguments beginning in 9:6. Wright warns interpreters not to use the presence of μυστήριον to fill in content based on broader apocalyptic discourse.[53] Bockmuehl avers and thinks that "what Paul is meting out must belong to the category of the eschatological mysteries of God."[54] This comes into focus in the οὕτως of the much debated phrase καὶ οὕτως in 11:26. So, for Bockmuehl, what is new is "the idea that according to the plan of God Israel was first to be hardened and the Gentiles converted, before 'all Israel' could be saved."[55] Finally, Goodrich, rightly I think, points out that the disclosure formula in the clause prior to μυστήριον suggests strongly that what follows is new information and not simply a restatement of the previous argument.[56]

Wright thinks that Israel's hardening is permanent.[57] Thus, he rejects the idea that there will be a mass removal of the "hardening" in line with gentile responsiveness to the gospel, an interpretive move made by the traditional Jewish eschatological approach. His main concern seems to be whether this text indicates a mass conversion of every Israelite at some future point or not. First, Wright over-interprets "has come" (γέγονεν); in the context of chapter 11, Paul makes it clear the hardening is not final: "So I ask, have they stumbled so as to fall? By no means!" (11:11). He makes this statement at the beginning of the section and then right before the hardening comment, he contemplates "natural branches be[ing] grafted into their own olive tree" (11:24). The hardening is not permanent. Second, Wright's claim that the "hardening" is perpetual is

---

52. Wright, *Paul and the Faithfulness of God*, 1232, emphasis original.

53. On apocalyptic discourse here is Gaventa, "Thinking," 253–54.

54. Bockmuehl, *Revelation*, 173.

55. Bockmuehl, *Revelation*, 173.

56. Goodrich, "Until," 8.

57. Wright, *Paul and the Faithfulness of God*, 1239. What is difficult in this section is to pin down precisely Wright's view. Earlier he wrote: "To repeat: Paul is not saying that all those presently 'hardened' are bound to remain in that condition," 1237. The debate appears to be over the nature of the "until" clause, "until the fullness of the nations comes in."

misplaced since he misconstrues the significance of the perfect tense of the verb. Wallace reminds interpreters that the perfect tense does not indicate what Wright suggests there: "Even more misleading is the notion, frequently found in commentaries, that the perfect tense denotes *permanent* or *eternal* results."[58] Third, Paul's ministry focuses on the idea that his physical relations will become "jealous" and become "sav[ed]" (11:14), or will turn from their "unbelief" (11:23). From Paul's point of view, the future point is "until (ἄχρι οὖ) the full number of gentiles has come in" (11:25). The temporal sense for "until" makes contextual, if not strict grammatical sense and suggests that Wright's case is not as strong as it first appears.[59]

Wright's concern about "every Israelite" raises the question that vexes interpreters, the identity of the "all Israel" group. James Scott has shown that individual Israelites are likely not in view since that is not the way "all Israel" was used; thus, one of Wright's concerns is overstated.[60] Scott suggests rather that "all Israel" "probably refers either to the presently hardened majority of Israel which will be saved at the parousia or to the sum total of the nation which will have been saved as of or through the parousia, including both the previously saved minority (the remnant) and the presently hardened majority of Israel."[61] The second option is more likely correct because of the reference to "Jacob" in 11:26 with its citation of Isa 59:20–21. The earlier reference to "full inclusion" of the Jewish nation in 11:12 (taken with the "all Israel" of 11:26) and, as

---

58. *GGBB* 574.

59. Middendorf, *Romans*, 1136. He also points out that the subjunctive "has come in" need not refer to "uncertainty" but "an indefinite period of time until the occurrence."

60. Scott, "All Israel," 507, concludes that "all Israel" relates to the tribal structure and can be used in a representative fashion but "is never used to refer specifically to all *individuals* within the nation." See for all twelve tribes: Exod 18:5; 1 Sam 3:20; 2 Sam 8:15; 1 Kgs 4:7; Mal 3:24; and Dan 9:11. See for a representative segment from the tribes: 1 Sam 4:5; 2 Sam 10:17; 2 Kgs 3:6. And for the northern tribes see: 1 Sam 18:6; 2 Sam 5:5; 1 Kgs 12:1; Dan 9:7; and Ezra 2:70. In other Jewish literature, it does not appear too often, but does refer to an idealized group either present or future. It also in these texts does not refer to every individual Israelite (Scott, "All Israel," 515). The twelve tribes label is found in T. Jos. 20:5; Jub. 50:9; CD 3:8–16; m. Sanh. 10:1–3; Tob 1:3–6; and 1 Macc 5:63. The representative use is found in LAB 22:1; 1 Macc 5:45; CD 15.5; 4Q164; and 11Q19.

61. Scott, "All Israel," 518: "the presently hardened majority of the nation will be saved along with 'all Israel' at the parousia, which almost certainly includes the northern tribes, along with the rest of the worldwide Diaspora of Israel."

noted by Scott, the parallel "full number of the gentiles" in 11:25 combine to suggest that Paul envisions a national or political entity.[62] It is likely that the group "all Israel" refers to those who are members of the nation of Israel at the time of the consummation (the northern tribes and the diaspora).[63] This conclusion takes the "and thus" (καὶ οὕτως) temporally, an admittedly weakly attested use.[64] This forward movement along with the reversal of sequence in regards to the Jews and the gentiles seems to be the sequence Paul details in these verses.[65] However, Wright's conclusion is that if such an abrupt reversal is in view, then Paul's argument is a "fantasy," and he "ought really to have told Tertius, his scribe, to throw away these three chapters and start again."[66] Why? It seems that Wright sees in this reversal reading another way of salvation for the group in question and thus a confounding of Paul's rhetorical aim. However, such is not required: Goodrich points out that such a reversal is not incompatible with the nature of Romans 9–11 as lament since this genre moves from sorrow to rejoicing with no indication of a lack of integrity on the part of the writer.[67] Wright also overlooks an ongoing vocational role for Israel in history that would account for such a reversal. Rudolph describes it this way: "The relationship between Jews and Gentiles is one of interdependence and mutual blessing. The salvation of Israel cannot happen without the faithful witness of Jesus-believing Gentiles to the Jewish people (Rom 11:11–14, 25–26, 30–31), and world revival cannot take place until Israel becomes a messianic Jewish nation (Rom 11:12, 15)."[68] Paul maintains a future orientation for Israel's covenantal identity; it is at the same time one that the nations draw strength from (Rom 11:17) and one to which the nations continue to be indebted (Rom 15:27).[69]

62. Scott, "All Israel," 518–19.

63. See Scott, "All Israel," 519; Longenecker, *Epistle to the Romans*, 897–98; *pace* Middendorf, *Romans*, 1160–62.

64. Wright, "Romans," 691 n. 459.

65. Keener, *Romans*, 136–37.

66. Wright, *Paul and the Faithfulness of God*, 1238.

67. Goodrich, "Until," 11.

68. Rudolph, "Zionism," 186.

69. Rudolph, "Zionism" 186. On the possibilities for the "all Israel," see Zoccali, "And All Israel," 289–318. This indebtedness also includes the historical faithfulness of the Jews to Torah, which made the God of Israel visible to them, along with scriptures that attested to a coming Messiah.

Wright's view ultimately relies on an understanding of Israel between 11:25 and 11:26 that is unpersuasive. Originally, his contention was that the referent changed for Israel between these verses. This has been rightly critiqued by interpreters, and now Wright contends that the referent in both verses for Israel is the multi-ethnic church, i.e., Jews and gentiles in Christ.[70] It is, however, unlikely that Paul would use this referent for anyone other than ethnic Israel.[71] Also, the olive tree analogy would argue against such a fusion of identities. Goodrich points out that if the ethnically inclusive view of Wright is applied, then when one arrives at 11:28 and its description of "enemies," interpretive clarity is lost.[72] Such a destabilized referent to Israel continues to be a significant weakness is Wright's overall argument.

Finally, Wright rejects the idea that the citations of Isa 59:20–21 and 27:9 have the parousia in view; rather, Paul "is *describing* the same event as in 11.14 (the possibility that presently unbelieving Jews will be made jealous and will come to faith and so to salvation) . . . and the fulfillment of the Deuteronomic 'new covenant,' as interpreted further in Isaiah and, by echoing implication, Jeremiah."[73] Wright has correctly alerted interpreters not to overplay the parousia position, which has its own challenges. However, as pointed out by Goodrich, ultimately Wright's alternative is no more probative than the traditional parousia view.[74] For Wright there is no future for ethnic Israel because its covenantal identity has been fulfilled in Christ; they have lost their "favoured nation clause."[75]

As this section has shown, the ecclesiological approach of Wright is not successful in overturning the idea of a future social identity for Israel

---

70. Wright, *Paul and the Faithfulness of God*, 1244: "Israel in verse 25 consists of the whole people of God, within which many Jews are presently 'hardened' but into which many Gentiles are being incorporated, so 'all Israel' in verse 26 must reflect that double existence." One of the major challenges for Wright's "double existence" approach is accounting for the hardening of the elect; see Grindheim, "Election," 333.

71. Vanlaningham (*Christ*, 215) points out the "polemical redefinition" is "problematic" since the "immediate context suggests that 'Israel' be understood as a reference to *ethnic* Israel. Ethnic Israel is referred to in 11.23 . . . and 11.30–32 in the contrast between Gentiles and Jews," emphasis original.

72. Goodrich, "Until," 14.

73. Wright, *Paul and the Faithfulness of God*, 1246.

74. Goodrich, "Until," 15.

75. Wright, *Paul and the Faithfulness of God*, 1253–54. See the discussion of the timing of the parousia for further arguments that might be applied against Wright's perspective more generally.

that is salvifically determined through Jesus Messiah. This future orientation potentially adds to the broader contention of this book that Jewish
identity is intrinsic to Paul's universalistic gospel. However, another approach has been put forth that challenges my claim that Jewish identity is
integral to Paul's universalistic gospel. That approach is amenable to the
continuation of Jewish identity and thus is not supersessionist; however,
it raises other concerns that ultimately suggest that it may be less helpful
than sometimes thought.

Jewish Remnant View

Chris Zoccali rejects the view that there will be a future large-scale salvation for ethnic Jews. He contends that this approach would rob Romans 9–11 of its coherence, especially as it relates to 9:6 and 10:12. He
thinks, rather, that the referent for "all Israel" includes the elect Jews, the
remnant, during this era. Further, since there is now only one means of
salvation (10:13), Zoccali thinks it unlikely that Paul would now propose "an alternative means by which 'all Israel' is saved."[76] This ultimately
leads him to reject any sort of future extraordinary salvific event only
for Israel and thus also to reject a *Sonderweg*. As we will see below, Paul's
argument does not require such a solution.[77] God could still work within
the normal means at a specific future point, from Paul's point of view, to
accomplish his salvific purposes.[78]

Zoccali thinks Paul's concerns relate to the views, contemporary to
him, that God had rejected his people Israel (11:1, 11). He is correct to
note that gentile replacement theologizing is the focus of the context. It
seems that some gentiles in Rome thought they had replaced Israel as
God's people. Thus, for Zoccali, a future mass salvation of Israel intrudes

76. Zoccali, *Whom God*, 104–5.

77. Vanlaningham (*Christ*, 219) avoids the *Sonderweg* approach as well. He does
this by noting that "the citations of Isa 59.20–21 and 27.9" indicate "that Israel is not
saved at the time of the second coming, but prior to it." Whether he is correct is an
open question; what is clear is that a *Sonderweg* is not necessitated by the Jewish eschatological miracle view.

78. Windsor (*Paul*, 245 n. 186) seems to follow Zoccali that the "all Israel" describes "the complete number of elect from the historical/empirical nation." He recognizes however that there is a general process being described here and that this does
not require "all Israel" to include "every individual Jew or that it will occur all at once
at the Parousia."

into the context too much and misses Paul's main focus.[79] He is correct that the passage could be understood without these future eschatological concerns, but as noted by Vanlaningham, it seems unlikely that present replacement concerns should preclude other considerations. Donaldson has long since pointed out that the existence of the remnant was not only a benefit for themselves but also served as a signpost for God's future faithfulness to Israel.[80]

Zoccali thinks that the future orientation of the Jewish eschatological view works against the focus of the passage: The remnant is a present reality (11:5). Paul's ongoing mission work anticipates that some Jews will become faithful to Christ (11:14), and the multiple occurrences of "now" suggests that the "mercy" shown is not a future idea (11:31).[81] Paul's ongoing mission work and the way he embodied the vocation of Israel as a light to the nations is a strong argument. It is not exactly clear, however, that Paul thought his efforts alone would be the impetus for Israel's salvation. Paul clearly had an ongoing expectation for salvation among the Jews, but this should not preclude the possibility that a future hope on a larger scale was also part of his understanding. As regards the multiple "now"s in 11:31, the mutuality between Jews and gentiles should be considered; Goodrich points to at least some implicit future orientation to this verse.[82]

Zoccali's final argument builds on his understanding of the "mystery" in 11:25b–26. First, he questions the stress placed on ἄχρι οὗ "until" in 11:25b and opts for "while." Thus, the duration of the hardening in his view differs from the eschatological Jewish view, i.e., he suggests it does not come to an end once the fullness of the gentiles occurs.[83] Thus, the hardening of non-elect Israel and the fullness of the gentiles occur simultaneously throughout history with the remnant then functioning as the "all Israel." However, according to Moo, the majority of usages of ἄχρι οὗ suggest the temporal nuance, and the context does not suggest the use of the English gloss "while."[84] Second, Zoccali rejects the idea that there

---

79. Zoccali, *Whom God*, 106.

80. Vanlaningham, *Christ*, 219–20; Donaldson, "Jewish Christianity," 50–52, cited by Vanlaningham.

81. Zoccali, *Whom God*, 106.

82. Goodrich, "Until," 26.

83. Zoccali, *Whom God*, 109.

84. Moo, *Romans*, 717 n. 30. See Middendorf, *Romans*, 2.1136, 1149. Particularly, Zoccali's appeal to the Lord's Supper is not persuasive (*Whom God*, 107). Vanlaningham

is a temporal nuance to καὶ οὕτως "and then" in the context of 11:26.[85] He favors a modal sense "and so" for καὶ οὕτως. He is likely correct about the grammar, but, as pointed out by Goodrich, "the interdependence between Israel and the Gentiles in 11:11–24 and 11:30–32 requires a temporal sequence."[86] Third, one of the inferences from the earlier discussion concerning ἄχρι οὖ as "while" is that Zoccali correctly notes that a point in time at which the hardening will be removed or "reversed" is not in the text.[87] However, there does seem to be a "temporal shift from Paul's present in 11.1–24 to the future in 11.25ff," as noted by Vanlaningham. Paul may be an example of one whose hardening was proleptically softened, and this resulted in his being "set apart for the gospel of God" (Rom 1:1).[88] Zoccali has offered a plausible reading of the text but one that does not account for a future orientation for Israel's covenant identity. The Jewish eschatological view, on the other hand, maintains a unique role for Israelite flesh in God's work in the world.

Israel and Judah Restored to the Land

Within a future eschatological miracle understanding of "all Israel will be saved" is an often overlooked idea that this also means that Israel will need to be restored to the land.[89] As just argued, Paul has a stable referent for Israel in Rom 11:26. He still thinks of Jerusalem as the center of God's work in the world. He writes: "I appeal to you, brothers and sisters, by our Lord Jesus Christ and by the love of the Spirit, to join me in earnest prayer to God on my behalf, that I may be rescued from the unbelievers in Judea, and that my ministry to Jerusalem may be acceptable to the saints, so that by God's will I may come to you with joy and be refreshed in your company" (Rom 15:30–32).[90] Paul's concern for the predicament

---

(*Christ*, 188–89) argues that the use of ἄχρι οὖ with regard to communion points out that its "kerygmatic implement *will cease* when Christ returns," emphasis original.

85. Zoccali, *Whom God*, 111. For further discussion of the temporal and modal debates, see Rock, *Paul's Letter*, 294 n. 27.

86. Goodrich, "Until," 28.

87. Zoccali, *Whom God*, 107.

88. Vanlaningham, *Christ*, 194.

89. Reasoner, "Salvation," 257.

90. Paul's collection from the gentiles for the poor in Jerusalem can be seen as a fulfillment of Isaiah 66 and Zechariah 8. See Zoccali, *Reading Philippians*, 35–38, on the eschatological pilgrimage tradition.

in which some in Israel find themselves is similar to that found in Israel's prophets. Thus, Israel's salvation must include a political dimension overlooked among too many interpreters.[91]

The challenge for interpreters is to see here a both/and not an either/ or. In other words, they need to keep Israel and those who are members of the Christ-movement in view as they read these texts. This interpretive approach is demanded by Rom 11:20–23; thus, post-supersessionist readings maintain simultaneous space for historic Israel and the Christ-movement in their exegetical decisions. This has already been suggested in the reading of Rom 9:24–26 offered earlier in this book. But now a further insight can be added. Reasoner, rightly I think, has picked up on that which ties together the chain of citations beginning in Rom 9:13: "all of Paul's scriptural quotations relate to the political situation of the physical heirs of Abraham, Isaac, and Jacob."[92] Salvation for Paul is holistic; it is not just a promise of otherworldly existence.[93] The original context of the citations, the concern for Israel's continued existence amid the threat of the Assyrians, whom, nevertheless, God is using to judge the nation, may offer insights into what Paul is doing here. He is trying to understand the way Israel's covenantal identity continues despite potential destruction of the nation (9:20–33).

In Rom 11:27, Paul writes, "And this is my covenant with them, when I take away their sins." This citation from Jeremiah 31 highlights the prophetic hope for the restoration of the houses of Judah and Israel (Jer 31:31, 33–34). The context of Jeremiah predicts a return from exile to the land for God's people. Romans 11:27 may shed light on Paul's "partial hardening" language in 11:25 since it precedes the Jer 31:33 quotation: some of God's people, Israel, are still in exile. The connection between hard-heartedness and exile is seen throughout Israel's scriptural tradition (2 Chr 36:13; Ezek 2:3–4; Deut 31:27–29).[94] N. T. Wright has been particularly helpful in uncovering exile narrative structures throughout

---

91. Scott, ("All Israel," 520) reminds interpreters that "salvation" frequently included "the gathering and bringing home of the dispersed from the whole world." See Jer 38(31):7–8; 26(46):27; Zeph 3:19; 8:7–8; 10:6 and Ps 105:47, "Save us, O LORD our God, and gather us from the nations."

92. Reasoner, "Salvation," 267.

93. This is one of the complaints of Wright about traditional readings of the gospel.

94. Staples, "Gentiles," 371–90. For a critique of Staples's approach see Goodrich, "Until," 15–22.

Paul's writings. He also helps interpreters by reminding them that salvation in the first-century setting was about rescue from Israel's enemies and restoration in the land. It was not about otherworldly eternal bliss.[95] However, as also noted by Reasoner, Wright doesn't apply this insight to his own exegesis of Romans 9–11, where he sees Israel redefined.

It is more likely that Paul has been moving towards the conclusion that begins at 9:13: "his concern for Israel includes her exile and . . . his hope for Israel's salvation includes the restoration of Israel and Judah."[96] The reference to Jer 31:33 in Rom 11:27 suggests that since restoration in the land was part of the prediction in Jeremiah, part of the "mystery" that Paul is revealing includes Israel's restoration. This is particularly probable given the subjugation of Israel at the hands of the Romans in Paul's day.

Israel's Covenantal Identity Irrevocable in Romans 11:28–29

In 11:28–29 Paul writes, "As regards the gospel (τὸ εὐαγγέλιον) they are enemies (ἐχθροί) of God for your sake; but as regards election they are beloved, for the sake of their ancestors; for the gifts and the calling of God are irrevocable" (NRSV). First, it should be noted that the delimiter "of God" is not in the Greek, which only has "enemies" (ἐχθροί). None of the standard English translations repeat the NRSV's "of God" delimiter here. It is an unnecessary intrusion into the context and contributes to a supersessionist understanding of this chapter. The adjective ἐχθρός "enemies" might better be understood as "alienated." This coheres with the adjectival use of "beloved" (ἀγαπητοί) in the next clause as well as with the larger context where Israel is described as being "bent" or "stumbling." Israel is suffering for the sake of the nations, but they are beloved for the sake of the fathers to whom promises have been made, promises that Christ confirms.[97]

---

95. Wright, *New Testament*, 300. In his Romans commentary, he writes: "The phrase 'all Israel,' then, is best taken as a polemical redefinition, in line with Paul's redefinition of 'Jew' in 2:29, of circumcision in 2:29 and Phil 3:3, and of 'seed of Abraham' in Rom 4, Gal 3, and Rom 9:6–9. It belongs with what seems indubitably the correct reading of 'Israel of God' in Gal 6:16" ("Romans," 690).

96. Reasoner, "Salvation," 270.

97. Nanos ("Gifts," 5) notes, "Yes, Paul's view does express a criticism of those other Jews based upon his convictions about Jesus; however, this alternative highlights that Paul regards this temporary state to represent vicarious suffering on behalf of the

Why is such a seeming irreconcilable situation possible in Paul's argument? In 11:29, he answers that question: "for the gifts and the calling of God are irrevocable (ἀμεταμέλητα)." God cannot go back on the promises he has made to the nation of Israel. While the NRSV has "irrevocable" at the end of the sentence, in Greek it is the first word, giving it prominence. Rudolph notes that "Paul's point is that Israel's general state of unbelief does not compromise its election, gifts or calling. ... God remains faithful to Israel despite Israel's unfaithfulness."[98] Paul had made this clear earlier in Rom 3:3–4 where the unfaithfulness of some does not "nullify the faithfulness of God." Here that principle is applied to Israel's election. Furthermore, the phrase, "the gifts and the calling of God," likely points back to the ongoing covenantal identity described in Rom 9:4–5. The parallel descriptors, "the adoption" (ἡ υἱοθεσία) and "the giving of the law" (ἡ νομοθεσία), along with the present tense, suggest strongly that if Jewish Christ-followers are among the "Israelites" (Ἰσραηλῖται), then the giving and receiving of Torah continues to belong to them. It is a sign of the kinship between Israel and God, one that continues in the messianic era.[99] Romans 11:28b–29 then restates what Paul wrote earlier in the form of a rhetorical question: "Has God has not rejected his people? By no means!" (11:1). Rudolph concludes, "Paul could not have been more loud and clear in affirming the irrevocability of Israel's election."[100]

Conclusion

Romans 9–11 is Paul's most sustained reflection on Israel in the messianic age. The focus in this chapter has been on the continuation and renewal of Israel's covenantal identity. It found that Rom 11:11–24 provides a strong basis for a post-supersessionist understanding since Paul does not remove the distinct identity of Israel in the midst of his theologizing over gentile identity in Christ. Israel's covenantal identity also has a future orientation to it in 11:25–27. Such a future consummation identity for Israel has been expressed in two primary opposing views: the community in

---

addressees without also suggesting that they are *enemies* of the addressees or, just as importantly, that they are "enemies *of God*" (an addition the NRSV makes without any manuscript evidence)."

98. Rudolph, "Zionism," 193.

99. Kinzer, *Postmissionary*, 124, and in private communication.

100. Rudolph, "Zionism," 194.

Christ and the Jewish remnant view. These were critiqued in a way that supports the traditional reading that Paul saw a future for Israel and that its covenantal identity and promises had not be abrogated. This chapter also suggested that the salvation of Israel envisioned by Paul included the restoration of the nation to the land. Finally, Israel's continued covenantal identity was clearly supported in Rom 11:28–29, since Israel's election is irrevocable.

Contemporary views of Jews and Judaism should be more positive than is often thought. Whereas Romans 11 is often cited to support a critique of Judaism, this chapter has offered alternative renderings that argue that the Jewish people are part of a covenant that has never been revoked. These alternatives find their basis in good exegetical and historical work; they are not, despite what is sometimes contended, simply the result of our current post-Shoah environment (or of some ideological imposition into the text).[101] The reading proposed in this chapter rejects zero sum thinking and opens up the interpreter to the idea that Israel's covenantal identity continues in Paul's universalistic gospel.[102]

William S. Campbell provides an apt summary of these discussions and points us to the content of the next chapter of this book: "A distinction remains in Paul's thought between Israel, whether or not it is faithful Israel or 'the rest,' and those gentile Christ-followers who though not being Abraham's physical descendants become his lineage by virtue of Christ. It is not surprising then that later in Romans, Paul emerges as a defender of those who retained their Jewish sympathies and way of life."[103] It is to the way Paul creates space for Jewish expressions of life and identity that we now turn.

---

101. Wright, "Paul in Current Anglophone Scholarship," 368. In referring to William S. Campbell and Douglas Harink, Wright suggests that their commitment to the post-Shoah setting "has generated its own distorting and moralizing rhetoric." Wright's statement here is wide of the mark and doesn't do justice to the work of these two scholars.

102. Nanos, "Callused," 57.

103. Campbell, *Paul and the Creation*, 125.

8

The Weak and the Strong

Introduction

THE TRADITIONAL UNDERSTANDING OF Paul's guidance in relation to the food laws in Rom 14:14 and 14:20 results in the erasure of Jewish covenantal identity within the Christ-movement. This understanding reinforces the Paul of Paulinism and establishes him as the champion of a law-free gospel that allows the Pauline Christ-movement to burst the boundaries of late Second Temple Judaism.[1] Francis Watson is an example of this view. He sees Rom 14:1—15:13 as crucial for his understanding of the entire letter: "Paul's purpose in writing Romans was to defend and explain his view of freedom from the law (i.e., separation from the Jewish community and its way of life), with the aim of converting Jewish Christians to his point of view so as to create a single 'Pauline' congregation in Rome."[2] Richard Longenecker, on the other hand, is more con-

---

1. Nanos (*Reading Paul*, 50) provocatively concludes: "Whether one judges *Paul's Judaism*—or Pauline Judaism, if you will—to be right about these claims, or in its criticisms of other Jews and Jewish points of view, is another matter entirely. But in my view, what Paul would find wrong in Paulinism is this: *it is not Judaism*." Nanos ("A Jewish View," 160) describes Paulinism as a "Comparative denunciation of Judaism's supposed ideals [that] is built into the very language used to describe Paul's unique contribution to the foundations of Christianity. Paulinism is a traditional construction of these Christian ideals supposedly championed by Paul and then faithfully reiterated and adapted in later generations by his disciples." Such a traditional Paulinism ultimately rests only on each generation of scholars citing and quoting the conclusions of the previous generation for its correctness. As it relates to Paul's view of Judaism, much if not all associated with it is then called into question. Many thanks to Nanos for pointing these references out to me.

2. Watson, "Two Roman Congregations," 207. The rhetorical unit goes from 14:1

ciliatory and concludes that "Paul expresses no direct rebuke of those believers in Jesus at Rome who may have had restrictive views regarding 'clean' and 'unclean' foods."[3] Middendorf attempts to contextualize these discussions historically in "the transitional period of the early NT era, when the question as to whether the dietary and calendrical observances commanded and forbidden in the OT still remain in force or whether they have been fulfilled and/or transformed in and through the coming of Christ."[4] These three scholars represent a significant sampling of the most prevalent of interpretations of the exigence for Romans. It is, however, more likely that Paul is seeking to shape the identity of in-Christ gentiles in relation to Torah-informed praxis. He wants to advise them of the halakhic practices of the wider Christ-movement in which differing patterns of life are the norm. Jewish Christ-followers would have already been familiar with such differing halakhic practices. Thus, his concern is with the non-Jews among the group in Rome.[5]

This identity-driven context hints at my understanding of the identification of the weak and the strong. The consensus, however, is that the weak are primarily Jewish Christ-followers who (possibly along with some non-Jews) desire to follow a restrictive approach to communal life somewhat sourced in a strict interpretation of Torah (though restrictions on wine and meat are not required).[6] The strong are then understood

---

to 15:13. Toney (*Paul's Inclusive Ethic*, 50) contends that "the internal concerns of Rom 14:1—15:6 are broadened to include external concerns in Rom 15:7–13." Some of the other issues are discussed briefly below on page 202.

3. Longenecker, *Epistle to the Romans*, 1008.

4. Middendorf, *Romans*, 2.1420. He continues by asking: "If they have been fulfilled in Christ, *have some OT commandments now moved into the category of NT adiaphora*?" (emphasis original).

5. Nanos, "Question," 135. A creation of in-Christ gentiles practicing a Jewish way of life was one of the social implications of the gospel. The issues discussed in Romans 14–15 highlight the challenges associated with embodying such patterns of living. Mark Nanos reminds interpreters not to conflate Paul's resistance to non-Jews undertaking circumcision with the "practice of Jewish behavior by non-Jews"; these are two different categories. He was against the former identity transformation but was convinced that the patterns of life evident in his ancestral tradition, i.e., Jewish praxis, were crucial for a salient in-Christ social identity. This category distinction may prove useful as we navigate significant hermeneutical issues in Romans 14.

6. While, as is often pointed out, Torah does not restrict the consumption of meat or wine (14:2, 21), there is evidence that Jews chose to restrict the consumption of these items when they were of indeterminate origin. This was sometimes even extended to items which had been in the presence of non-Jews (likely because of the potential of inadvertent involvement in idolatrous practices). Daniel 1:8–16; Josephus,

primarily as gentiles, though with a few Jews like Paul who understand that since Christ is the end of the law (10:4), they are free to eat and drink everything, and that a commitment to honoring specific days is likewise no longer compulsory.[7] One problem with this approach is that the text does not distinguish the groups based on ethnicity; to read the issue as Jew versus gentile one has to fill in and smooth out the gaps in the text. Furthermore, as noted, even the food issues that are highlighted are not primarily delineated as Torah issues. Thus, since some gentiles also had "holiness discourse" with implications for food and drink, a wider cultural matrix may be in view.[8] This suggests then that the confusion was over the way gentile purity concerns are transformed within the Christ-following community as in-Christ gentiles share table fellowship with others who maintain different patterns of life.

In this sense, then, the consensus view needs further refinement. The claim that the weak were predominately Jewish since the matters here seem concerned with Torah observance is problematic. Three points make it more likely that the weak were those from non-Jewish cultural contexts who had previously gravitated towards monotheism, as either God-fearers or proselytes to Judaism. First, the in-Christ non-Jews in Rome were likely already drawn to Judaism and part of the broader

---

Life 14; see further Lo, "Identity Crisis," 4.

7. While Moo (*Romans*, 828–29) recognizes six different positions on this, Nanos's (*Mystery*, 110) argument that the weak are non-Christ-following Jews is the primary recent challenger to the consensus position just stated. I have deep sympathy for Nanos's position and recognize that it brings the broader synagogue community into the Christ-following community in important ways; however, 1:6–8 indicates the addressees are Christ-followers. (Note that his differentiation between the implied and encoded readers provides important corrections.) Second, it is not clear how non-Jewish semi-public synagogue members could affect the broader communal life of the public synagogue community to the degree that Romans 14–15 suggests. However, setting aside Nanos's claim about the weak does not preclude the idea that this community is still functioning *intra muros*. The presence of purity discourse suggests that this internal context is likely the setting. The comparative logic of κοινός (14:14) and καθαρός (14:20) strongly suggests a halakhic debate over differing social implications of Torah observance.

8. Ehrensperger ("Called," 94–95, 102, 108) shows that concerns about maintaining purity were evident among "peoples around the Mediterranean in the ancient world." Paul's instruction here thus mediates two holiness discourses, Jewish and non-Jewish, and seeks to provide a communal solution that makes explicit the nature of the transformation of gentile identity in Christ and the nature of the hospitality that emerges from this transformation. See below for specific examples of non-Jewish holiness discourse.

synagogue community prior to receiving the gospel. Second, non-Jewish adherents to Judaism may have been more enthusiastic for Jewish practices than some Jews; Cadbury called this group the over-converted.[9] Third, the communities of Christ-followers in Rome probably had a higher percentage of non-Jews than Jews. It would seem likely, therefore, that both the weak and the strong were predominately non-Jewish.

If these former God-fearers make up the group described as the weak, where did their interest in ritual purity and food impurity originate? As suggested above, their prior involvement with the synagogue community may have accounted for it. However, Ehrensperger offers another important context.[10] She contends that following purity codes and dietary restrictions was widespread in antiquity and not the exclusive domain of the Jews. Drawing on Schaefer's *Judeophobia*, the following examples are offered:[11] Sextus Empiricus notes, "a Jew or an Egyptian priest would prefer to die instantly rather than eat pork, while the taste of mutton is reckoned an abomination in the eyes of a Lybian, and Syrians think the same about pigeons and others about cattle."[12] Plutarch discusses the requirement of priests of Jupiter to abstain from even touching either flour or yeast, or raw flesh. And when the women of Eleusis celebrated the festival of the Haloa, they shared a common meal where everything could be eaten "except those forbidden in the Mysteries—pomegranates, apples, eggs, and fowls, and certain specified kinds of fish."[13]

Thus, Judaism was not unique in its concerns about purity and food. In this common arena, misunderstandings were likely to emerge. And Paul, as a bi-cultural mediator, steps into this arena and discusses κοινός and καθαρός in Rom 14:14, 20.[14] Additionally, the cultural associations from magical practices would reinforce the essentialism of foodstuff. Thus, one is left with a plausible setting in which a group of messianic gentiles might develop an approach to communal life from an admixture of their pre-Christ-following life along with their awareness of some Torah-informed communal practices. This development might have been aided by the absence, for a period of time, of at least some of

9. Cadbury, "Overconversion," 43–50.

10. Ehrensperger, *Paul at the Crossroads*, 94–95.

11. Schäfer, *Judeophobia*, 69–77.

12. Sextus Empiricus, *Pyr.* 111.24.223.

13. Plutarch, *Quaest. rom.* 109–10; 289c–290a.

14. See Ehrensperger, *Paul at the Crossroads*, 131–37; Tucker, "Paul in Bi-Cultural Perspective," 37–41.

the movement's Jewish leaders (depending on how one understands the effect of Claudius's decree).[15] Those leaders would thus not have been available to provide guidance for the way these in-Christ gentiles were to live within a Jewish movement, as a "Jewish-like group."[16]

In this reading of the text, the strong then are not those who see the food laws as no longer binding, or as a matter of indifference; rather, the strong had no problems eating things classified as κοινός (understood as unfit food or food of indeterminate origin).[17] They had decided to adhere to a looser halakhic stance than other group members. The strong then acted in faith while the weak could not come to see this more nuanced understanding of the situation and so were stumbling to the point of "ruin" (Rom 14:15). So, the weak's inability to participate in conviviality in the grey areas categorized as κοινός revealed their weak faith (not their desire to maintain a putative works-righteousness Torah observance over and against a group that wanted to live law-free, as good proto-Paulinists). Paul, as I will argue below, is creating a set of halakhically-informed practices for in-Christ gentiles based on existing diaspora Jewish debates concerning purity.

---

15. See discussion of Claudius on page 15. Since Claudius was advancing Roman identity, Roman concerns about food could also have played into these debates (Wallace-Hadrill, *Rome's Cultural Revolution*, 315–55).

16. See further on this group label in Nanos, "Question," 133–40. With regard to the context of the Christ-groups in Rome, as discussed earlier in this book, I see them as still in contact with the broader synagogue community, likely organized as semi-public synagogues. These were not particularly aligned with the Pauline Christ-movement with the exception of the "assembly" described in Rom 16:5 (cf. Rom 16:1, 4 ,5, 16, 23). The location of house-church gatherings, tenement, workshop, or other locations, while important, are not crucial to my argument, though the household discourse of προσλαμβάνω (14:1, 3; 15:7, 7) and οἰκέτης (14:4) may suggest that domestic structures of some sort are the primary context of the gathering. However, this does not preclude that the community was organized along the lines of a voluntary association of some sort. Further, the gathering/worship context is strongly suggested by the scriptural discourse found in 14:10c–12 and 15:9b–12. Thus, the problem Paul seeks to address is the differing identities reflected in opinions and practices that emerged during the communal meals associated with the gatherings of God's beloved in Rome. See Lo, "Identity Crisis," 4.

17. The suggestion below will be that κοινός refers to common foods, ones that emerge as a concern in the diaspora setting (and not specifically related to the details in Leviticus). Discussions about practices related to food of indeterminate origin relates to halakhic standards that developed to address situations when one could not tell whether food was impure. Paul may allude to something like this in 1 Cor 10:27.

So, in what follows I offer a constructive post-supersessionist reading of Paul's case for the continuation of Torah-informed praxis for
in-Christ gentiles. It responds first to the three interpretive moves that
reinscribe the traditional Paul of Paulinism, namely: (a) Paul is strong
and all things Jewish are *adiaphora*; (b) Paul's argument undermines the
continuation of Jewish praxis; and (c) Paul's solution was only a temporary accommodation. Then, second, I will build on David Rudolph's
argument that rather than setting aside the food laws in Rom 14:14, 20,
Paul expects there to be a continuation of Torah-informed praxis within
the community among those who remain different, especially among in-
Christ gentiles who continue to identify socially with the broader Jewish
community as a matter of calling.

Paul Is Strong and All Things Jewish are *Adiaphora*

Two particular claims are often made to support the first interpretive move in the Paul-of-Paulinism view described above. First, Paul is
viewed as an enlightened Christian thinker who is part of the strong in
faith. This means that the parochial concerns of Jewish life and practice
have been superseded in Christ and replaced by faith. Second, Paul does
not fully reject aspects of his (and other's) Jewish heritage; he allows for
Jewish practices to continue since they are not salvific, but they have been
relegated to the category of *adiaphora* and are seen as indifferent. While
these two claims may have something to commend them, and the text
could be understood this way, it also seems that these lines of reasoning
could be called into question.

Paul among the Strong

Paul clearly identifies with the strong in Rom 15:1, "We who are strong
ought to bear with the weaknesses of those not strong."[18] Often, it is
assumed that Paul accepts the position of the strong *in toto*, though in
14:3, 6, 22 he points out that neither side is completely justified. First,
one should not downplay the rhetorical purpose here, which is to get
the strong to carry the burdens of the weak.[19] Further, the diatribal ele-

18. Tatum ("To the Jew," 285) concludes that in 14:1 and 15:1, "Paul is *de facto*
defending the observance of the Law by Roman Christians."

19. Rodríguez, *If You Call*, 279–80. Paul's rhetorical use of "please our neighbor"

ments in these chapters suggest that Paul's identification is also related to a return to his debate with his gentile interlocutor from earlier in the letter.[20] The more important issue, however, is the assumption that Paul accepts the strong position in terms of practice. We will discover below that Paul does not require the weak to change their practice, just their attitude. More importantly, the strong are the ones required to change their practice. This suggests that Paul's halakhic stance is more generous than often thought.

Second, those who construe Paul to be identifying with the strong often infer that he thinks that the food laws have been set aside when he writes in 14:14, "no food is unclean in itself" (a likely allusion to Mark 7:15) and, in 14:20, "all food is clean" (cf. Mark 7:19).[21] These seemingly world-shattering claims are taken to indicate distance between the Christ-movement and the synagogue community and are thought to demonstrate that Paul sees no continuing relevance for Torah-based restrictions. This interpretation is based on the traditional reading of Mark 7:19b that sees in Jesus's teaching the end of dietary restrictions; however, as Rudolph has persuasively argued, what Jesus did there and what Paul is doing here is limiting them. Non-Jews do not have to follow these Israel-centric directives since cleanness is imputed by God's word. Rudolph's approach raises further issues with regard to the presence of κοινός (14:14) and καθαρός (14:20).[22] For Paul, like some other Jews, the status of cleanness/purity uncleanness/common is imputed by God's declaration and is *not ontological* (Exod 12:14–20). The defilement comes

---

echoes Lev 19:18; Mark 12:31. His earlier instruction in Rom 13:8 should be noted. The strong's identity performance is to be other-oriented.

20. The extensive presence of diatribe has been recognized by several scholars, e.g., Song, *Reading Romans*, 122. A non-Jewish interlocutor throughout the letter (seen in Thorsteinsson, *Paul's Interlocutor*, 165–94) should not be used to argue that the actual circumstances of the audience within the broader synagogue community are inaccessible to interpreters. Song (*Reading Romans*, 76) unsuccessfully critiques Stowers (*Rereading*, 100–4) for seeing an actual situation here. Cf. Stowers, *Diatribe*, 152–53; Tobin, *Paul's Rhetoric*, 97; Gadenz, *Called*, 175–78; Garroway, *Paul's Gentile-Jews*, 88–89, 187.

21. Reasoner (*Strong*, 16–17) rejects the idea that issues of Jewish practice are on debate here; this will be discussed below beginning on page 212. See, however, Rudolph, "Yeshua," 118, for an argument on Mark 7:19b that concludes that food laws are not made redundant for Jews here; rather there is an "*exemption* from the Leviticus 11 dietary laws . . . 'for gentiles.'"

22. See further below for the discussion of these two verses.

from the outside not the inside. So, Paul's identification with the strong is much more nuanced than sometimes claimed.

All Things Jewish Are Adiaphora

The rhetorical impact of Paul's argument in Rom 14:1—15:13 is often muted by placing the issues in the category of *adiaphora*, i.e., "indifferent things." Boyarin can serve as an example: "Keeping the Law was for Paul adiaphora; faith in Jesus was certainly not! Romans 14, especially if the 'weak' and the 'strong' are the law-abiding and the not-law-abiding, supports both halves of the proposition eloquently."[23] Deming concurs: "In one form or another, Paul treats many things as indifferents: social class, ethnic identity, gender, food, education, speaking in tongues, life and death, marriage, slavery, and circumcision."[24] At the end of his essay, he lists Rom 14:5, 6–8, 14–17, and 20 as relevant Pauline texts that support the idea that Paul was creating a taxonomy of categories in a manner similar to the Stoics.[25]

However, this seems to not be the case. The law was never *adiaphoron* for Paul, contra Strecker.[26] *Adiaphoron*, an "indifferent thing," is properly a category reserved for matters of personal choice that do not explicitly impact public actions. However, the issues Paul discusses in this section of his letter are matters of public action. First, Paul instructs the strong not to "judge" or "despise" the weak (14:1, 3), and similarly the weak are not to "judge" the strong (14:3).[27] The conflict thus seems to be a public one, especially when Paul details the disunity that result from these attitudes of judgment, evidenced from the pervasive κριν- word group in 14:4, 5, 10, 13. Further, Paul's anticipated resolution involves a public and mutual welcoming in 15:7 and worshiping in 15:6, 9–12.[28] However, the

---

23. Boyarin, *A Radical Jew*, 42.

24. Deming, "Paul," 388; see Stobaeus, *Ecl.* 2.7.5a; Diogenes Laertius, 7.101–2.

25. Deming, "Paul," 398; Engberg-Pedersen, "Everything," 22–38.

26. Strecker, "Befreiung," 480–84.

27. Rom 14:1—15:13 have become crucial for understanding the social setting in Rome; however, several interpreters question whether this is anything more than a general paraenesis which thus would not have a specific situation in view; see e.g., Oropeza, *Jews*, 144.

28. The formation of a doxological identity in these verses is discussed starting on page 221.

public nature of the conflict is not the only reason to reject the use of the category of *adiaphora* here.

Second, the debate is a matter of Israel's scriptural tradition. These practices are part of a symbolic universe that help Israel to embody their continuing covenantal identity. While the role of Torah within the Christ-movement, as we have seen, is itself a perplexing problem, Paul's gospel is not properly understood as "law-free." Instead, "circumcision-free" or "proselytism-free" would be more appropriate terms.[29] There are at least three ways Torah continues to be relevant. First, it serves a consultative role for walking in the ways of the Lord by the agency of the Spirit (Rom 8:4). Second, it provides a continuing pattern of life properly reserved for Jewish Christ-followers (1 Cor 10:32).[30] Third, it guides one when discerning which things do matter. Paul says as much when he writes, "and know his will and determine what is best because you are instructed in the law" (Rom 2:18).[31]

The overreliance on the category of *adiaphora* occurs because interpreters have a prior understanding of Paul that views him in a universalistic framework in which the social implications of the gospel are the same for both Jews and non-Jews. This raises some further questions: if food, wine, and days are not *adiaphora*, then why are those who avoid eating and drinking and venerate certain days described as "weak in faith"? Should Paul not see them as "strong in faith" and identify with them rather than the strong? How can Paul have a positive view of the weak if he refers to them with the disparaging moniker: "weak in faith"? Answers to these questions continue to divide interpreters in regards to Paul's relationship to Jewish patterns of life. But based on what we have uncovered throughout this book, it is quite probable that areas related to Jewish or Torah-informed praxis are not *adiaphora* for Paul.

Paul's Argument Undermines the Continuation of Jewish Praxis

John Barclay's work on Rom 14:1—15:13 has been and continues to be quite influential. He offers a nuanced approach to this passage and sees

---

29. See on this Nanos, "Myth," 4–5.

30. Bird, "Mark," 48. Bird, on the other hand, rejects the idea that the law is "*constitutive* for the identity, salvation and behaviour of believers."

31. See also Deming, "Paul," 403 n. 66.

Paul providing social space for the continuation of significant aspects of Jewish cultural identity within the Christ-movement. Near the end of his essay, however, he contends that there is a hidden (to Paul) implication in his argument. Barclay is worth quoting on this, since similar assertions are repeated so often in contemporary discussions on this passage: "In demanding this toleration, Paul subverts the basis on which Jewish law-observance is founded and precipitates a crisis of cultural integrity among the very believers whose law-observance he is careful to protect."[32] He further suggests that Paul's argument "introduces . . . a Trojan horse" into the community for those "who sought to live according to the law."[33] For Barclay, Paul ultimately weakens the place of Torah-informed praxis within the Christ-movement.

Paul's requirement for toleration, seen beginning in 14:15, is directed primarily towards the strong.[34] The renewed perspective on the kingdom in 14:17 as found in "righteousness, peace, and joy in the Holy Spirit" is also directed towards this group, who are called to "pursue what makes for peace and mutual upbuilding" (14:19). Thus, the strong are in a position of power and can exert social influence in a manner that the weak cannot. While Paul agrees with the statement that "all things are clean" understood within the ongoing Jewish debates concerning the declarative nature of cleanness (discussed below), the purity of the community is the issue. I would suggest that eating in a manner not aligned with the requirements of a righteous gentile is a "wrong" (κακός) that cannot be allowed to continue within the community (14:20). So, while Barclay does have a point that Paul requires the weak to not judge the strong, whether he also requires the weak to tolerate certain practices at odds with Torah observance is a different matter. On this issue, Barclay claims too much. Ultimately, the weak are not called to change their behavior; thus the subversion of continued law-observance, as construed by Barclay, is not an implication of Paul's argument.[35]

A couple of further comments are in order. First, Barclay's claim for "toleration" by the weak overlooks Paul's instruction to the strong to change their practice. His halakhah is actually quite similar to *mar'it 'ain*,

32. Barclay, "Undermine" 58–59.

33. Barclay, "Undermine" 58–59.

34. On the problems with tolerance as a pattern of life between Jews and gentiles, see Le Donne, *Near Christianity*, 167–88. His call for love, rather than mere tolerance of difference, comes close to Paul's instructions here.

35. Nanos, *Mystery*, 96–103.

according to Hedner Zetterholm, who cites Demai 6:2: "the principle according to which one must refrain from acts that are permitted but inappropriate because they may lead a less knowledgeable Jew to draw false conclusions and cause him or her to do something that is not permitted."[36] In theory the strong are correct that everything is clean (ontologically speaking), but in their day-to-day experience they are limited because of the damage their exercise of freedom might produce. This seems to support Jewish norms for the community, even for those technically not under Torah, i.e., the gentiles.

Second, Barclay takes for granted that the relation to the master mentioned in Rom 14:4 is the same for both Jews and non-Jews, even though this is not textually determined.[37] Paul writes, "Who are you to pass judgment on servants of another? It is before their own lord that they stand or fall. And they will be upheld, for the Lord is able to make them stand" (NRSV). The NRSV can be read in a misleading way as suggesting different masters are involved; however, as noted by Lee, "those who abstain and those who eat have the same master. Each servant has a different relationship with the master. Their identities are different, but both have the same status before the one Lord."[38] In 14:6–9, "the Lord" functions to unite those who continue to have different social identifications. The disparate practices that continue within the community are united under the Lordship of the Messiah. These practices, as seen above, are not *adiaphora*; they are undertaken as a way to honor the Lord. Paul, then, does not seem to undermine Jewish praxis by his instructions in these verses. Jews and non-Jews are equal in their relationship to the Lord but differences remain: "The identity derived from honoring the Lord does not abrogate ethnic-cultural identity, and one identity is not absorbed into another."[39] These are matters of living and dying, and thus crucial to one's in-Christ identity.

Paul's Solution Was a Temporary Accommodation

A theologically-bound identity detached from embodiment emerges because of an assumption that Paul thought Torah-informed praxis was the

---

36. Hedner Zetterholm, "Question," 96.

37. Lee, "Paul," 141–59.

38. Lee, "Paul," 152.

39. Lee, "Paul," 152.

problem. Sanders, as is well known, concluded concerning this passage: "[Paul] judged one form of behavior to be wrong. The wrong form was living according to the law."[40] Sanders, furthermore, doubts the possibility of Jews remaining Jews in a mixed community. And W. D. Davies, although he claims that "[i]n-Christ Jews remain Jews and Greeks remain Greeks" and "[e]thnic particularities are honoured," agrees with Sanders that this division could not be sustained, so that at best this was a temporary fix.[41] For Sanders, when there is a conflict, Jewish identity must be dispensed with.[42]

Theologically Bound Identity

First, Sanders has read into Rom 14:1—15:13 an ethnic demarcation that may not strictly be there. Second, his conclusion is the exact opposite of Paul's, who argued that the strong were the ones required to change their behavior. Notice, however, that the strong are not required to change their conviction. In 14:22, Paul writes to the strong, "the faith you have, have as your own conviction before God." Dunn takes this to support the theologically-bound-identity approach: "The 'stronger' the faith . . . the less dependent is it on observance of particular traditions; the 'weaker' the faith, the more dependent."[43] However, in 14:23, Paul turns to the weak and says, "he who doubts and eats is condemned if he eats." In other words, Paul does not want this group to change their behavior; he continues in 14:23 "because his eating is not from faith." This verse suggests Paul conceives of a Jewish praxis of faith that is a valid expression of an in-Christ social identity.

If the weak change their practice in order to get along with the strong, their actions proceed from a lack of faith, and, even more severely, emerge as sin (14:23c). Thus, if there is a theologically bound identity for Paul, it is expressed in various ways and may be described as a theologically bound open identity. His solution is not a mere accommodation to the lack of faith of one group in comparison to another. Rather, it reflects his contention that the gospel that is to the Jew first and then to

---

40. Sanders, *Paul, the Law,* 178.

41. Davies, "Paul," 23.

42. Sanders, *Paul, the Law,* 178.

43. Dunn, *Romans,* 2.827.

the non-Jew expects and embraces different social implications for each, since each relates differently to their master (14:4).

Imposition of the Temporary

My claim that Paul desires the strong to change their practice does raise several other concerns. For example, does not Paul's instruction here (directing the strong to conform to Jewish-like practices) go exactly against his earlier challenge to Peter in the so-called Antioch incident in Gal 2:11–14, where the latter was accommodating to those who held to a stricter approach to table fellowship? Against that concern, I would offer the following suggestions. First, the assumption that before the arrival of the "people from James" (v. 11), Peter had been eating food forbidden in Leviticus 11 is read into the text. At issue instead was the people with whom Peter was eating, not the food he was eating. Paul rebuked him for his solution: removing himself from the table, thus abandoning the in-Christ gentiles. Second, the Antioch incident sounds similar to Acts 11:1–3, where Peter is taken to the leaders in Jerusalem because he was going to see the foreskinned men and eating with them. The broader direction from Paul seems thus to consist in drawing all in-Christ peoples together into table fellowship, not adapting to halakhically instituted separations. Third, in the reading of Romans 14–15 being put forth here, Paul expects accommodation to those identifying with a Jewish way of life.[44] In this way, we find unity with Paul's thoughts in Galatians 2 when we understand that in both cases it is not Jewish dietary practices and whether they are abolished within the Christ-movement that is at issue, but equality among the identities of people who are and remain different in Christ.[45] This does not sound like a temporary communal practice that eventually goes away once people of different social identities come to realize that the only identity that matters is their universalistically understood (non-ethnic/social) theologically bound one.

This approach that validates the continuation of many aspects of differing identities in Christ may also be critiqued by an appeal to Paul's words in Gal 2:14 where he says to Peter "If you, though a Jew, live like a gentile and not like a Jew, how can you compel the gentiles to live like Jews?" However, this is likely the language of Peter and Paul's critics. Dunn

---

44. See Kinzer, *Postmisionary*, 83–84.

45. Willitts, "Paul, the Rabbi," 225–47.

picks up on this: "Paul was not using his own language (by that time Peter had ceased 'living like a Gentile'), but the language used against Peter earlier by the 'individuals from James.'"[46] Second, the phrase is likely ironic. Kinzer highlights this possibility, "Paul himself does not think that he and Peter live *like* Gentiles when they eat with Gentile Yeshua-believers. Yet Paul and Peter do live *with* Gentiles, in partnership and close association with them, without any intention of altering the distinct non-Jewish identity of these partners and associates."[47] So, Paul picks up the language of their critics to remind Peter that his actions are signaling a second-class citizenship for gentiles. If this becomes the norm in regards to table fellowship, then gentiles will be expected to transform their identity into a Jewish one. Third, the actual issue in 2:14 is not Peter's Jewish praxis or lack of it but the way newness of life had been experienced by the in-Christ gentiles. They have already experienced eschatological life as gentiles just like Peter experienced it as a Jew; neither social identity hindered Christ-followers from responding to God's call.[48] Furthermore, neither identity is incompatible with an ongoing life within the Christ-movement.

Ongoing Mission Not Temporary Fix

The strong are specifically required to change their practice. This is seen more explicitly in 1 Corinthians 8–10 generally and in 9:19–23 specifically, an earlier passage from Paul that addresses different table issues but offers similar solutions. Romans 14–15 cannot simply be a temporary fix because Paul sees existing identities as crucial for his ongoing mission to the nations (and, as we will see in the next chapter, for the future as well). Looking at 1 Cor 9:19–23 offers insights into the solution he supports in Romans 14–15.[49]

One of Paul's solutions to the problems of food offered to idols and civic engagements is mission as social identification. Paul writes in 1 Cor 9:19 that he is "free with respect to all"; however, he has also "made" himself "a slave to all." He acts in this way to "win more of them." Too often, this verse is read to suggest that Paul thinks he is free from Torah

---

46. Dunn, *Galatians*, 127–28.

47. Kinzer, *Postmissionary*, 84. See also Willitts, "Paul, the Rabbi," 225–47.

48. Nanos, *Mystery*, 355; Kinzer, *Postmissionary*, 85.

49. What follows builds on Tucker, *Reading 1 Corinthians*, 94–96.

observance, but the freedom in view here is, on the one hand, from becoming indebted to human masters and, on the other hand, from prioritizing his own safety or advantage in his interactions with others. This freedom, in turn, allows him to serve others as their apostle, as one who willingly gives up certain rights for his mission among the nations.

Paul then in 1 Cor 9:20–21 addresses his continuing social identification with those who are part of his ethnic group: "To the Jews I became as a Jew, to win Jews." The presence of "as" suggests to many interpreters that Paul had ceased to be a Jew, or that he only identified himself as such in certain missional situations. However, it is more likely that this refers to Paul's variety of practices as he relates to diaspora ethnic Jews generally, especially in the areas of hospitality and table fellowship, which is part of the larger context of 8:1—11:1. Paul then describes another group, "those under the law." If this simply referred to the Jews, it would be redundant, so Paul probably had something else is in view. It is quite likely that "under the law" refers to a subgroup identity, a group following a stricter halakhah possibly associated with the Pharisees.[50] Paul's experience as a Pharisee (Phil 3:5) would allow him to follow Pharisaic halakhah to reach this group with the gospel, even though he is "not under the law" (meaning the strict halakhot of this group).

The next group Paul brings up is "those outside the law." This terminology for gentiles emphasizes their sinfulness and thus their need for his mission (9:21; Gal 2:15). In discussing his approach to this group, Paul notes that he is "not free from God's law but" is "under Christ's law." In light of 1 Cor 7:17–20, where there is a calling in Christ for Jews to live as Jews, it seems likely that Paul would follow his own "rule" (7:17). Yet the phrase "Christ's law" has vexed interpreters. David Rudolph suggests that it *"refers to God's law (the law of Moses) in the hand of Christ as reflected in Christ's association with sinners."*[51] This interpretation fits well with Paul's hope to "win (κερδαίνω) those outside the law." This word is used five times in this section (9:19, 20 [x 2], 21, 22) suggesting that the crucial context here is mission. The Pharisees, in fact, used this term for "recruiting new members through table-fellowship and living among the masses."[52] This interpretation becomes even more likely when one

---

50. Tucker, *Remain in Your Calling*, 104.

51. Rudolph, *A Jew to the Jews*, 165, italics original; Gal 6:2.

52. Rudolph, *A Jew to the Jews*, 166.

considers Matt 23:15 and its description of a Pharisaic mission together with Paul's personal history claimed in Phil 3:8.

Paul's mission as social identification is further described in 1 Cor 9:22–23 when he writes, "to the weak I became weak, so that I might win the weak." The term "weak" is often thought to refer to those who are not in Christ. This would make sense in light of 9:23 where Paul says he does all of this "for the sake of the gospel." However, Paul's work of identity construal is broader than a one-time experience (1:18; Phil 2:12). In the present context the "weak" refers to a subgroup identity within the Christ-movement in Corinth for whom eating food offered to idols had "become a stumbling block" (8:7, 9). If the earlier discussion concerning "win" is considered, especially in light of Matt 18:15, then broader aspects of identity formation are part of Paul's "gospel" mission. This subgroup may also be those who were poor and disadvantaged, and therefore more impacted by eating restrictions. They could easily have been termed "weak" in light of Roman cultural expectations of strength (1 Cor 1:26–29). Paul socially identifies with this group by working "with his own hands" as a "tentmaker" in Corinth and by refusing to participate in Roman patronage (1 Cor 4:10, 12; Acts 18:3, 11, 18). It is likely that social identification with others is part of the imitation that Paul had in mind as he instructs the Corinthians to follow him as he follows Christ (1 Cor 11:1; 2 Cor 6:10; 8:9; Luke 4:13–14, 21). Concern for existing social identifications, whether they relate to ethnicity or socio-economic status, are crucial for Paul in his mission to the nations.[53] Any guidance he offers, whether in 1 Corinthians 8–10 or Romans 14–15, is more than a temporary accommodation. It is missionally significant and provides a basis for the continuation of Jewish identity within the Christ-movement. But one question remains: how can Jewish identity continue since Paul seems to set aside Torah-informed praxis via the rejection of the food laws in Rom 14:14, 20? It is to that question we turn next.

David Rudolph: Continuity in Torah-informed Praxis in Romans 14:14, 20

As has just been seen, Rom 14:1—15:13 continues to be a central passage in the ongoing debates concerning how best to understand Paul

---

53. In relation to economic inequality within the Christ-movement, see Tucker, "The Jerusalem Collection," 52–70.

and his placement within the various expressions of late Second Temple Judaism. Those who see him as removed from the broader synagogue community find in these chapters key phrases that support their contention that Paul no longer identified with his Jewish identity, nor expected other Christ-followers to do so. The three primary arguments for this were just addressed: Paul thought Jewish practices were *adiaphora*, he unintentionally undermined Torah by his instruction, and his solution was only a temporary accommodation until the inhabitants of Rome that he is writing to understood their theologically bound identity. However, two specific verses, Rom 14:14, 20, need specific attention because they seem to work against the arguments just presented. In Rom 14:14, it is thought that Paul is at his most un-Jewish when he writes: "I know and am persuaded in the Lord Jesus that nothing is *unclean* in itself; but it is *unclean* for anyone who thinks it *unclean*." Further, he appears to set aside Leviticus 10–11, when he writes in 14:20: "Do not, for the sake of food, destroy the work of God. Everything is indeed *clean*, but it is wrong for you to make others fall by what you eat."

John Barclay, as mentioned earlier, is one important example of this line of reasoning; he writes: "This [vv. 14, 20] constitutes nothing less than a fundamental rejection of the Jewish law in one of its most sensitive dimensions. . . . [T]his strong denial of the Scriptural distinction between 'clean' and 'unclean' food should not be watered down[;] . . . the certainty and candor with which Paul here expresses his freedom from the law is thus quite breathtaking. In principle, it appears, he could see no objection to eating shellfish, hare or pork. Do we have reason to doubt that his diet was sometimes as scandalously 'free' as his principles?"[54]

Barclay makes two argumentative claims here that require further discussion. First, he assumes "clean" and "unclean" has Israel's Leviticus 11 food laws in view. Second, he accepts the idea that Paul thought he was free from the law and could eat, at least from time to time, food otherwise restricted in Leviticus 11. However, what if one does not discount the idea that Paul continued to be Torah-observant, as he is described in Acts 21:17–26? What if his rule in all the assemblies, described in 1 Cor 7:17–24, that Jewish Christ-followers were to continue to live as Jews and non-Jewish Christ-followers were not to become Jews, guides Paul's argumentative logic here?[55] Do we end up with a different perspective on

54. Barclay, "Undermine" 50–51.

55. Though this doesn't preclude them from living halakhically-derived, Torah-informed lives (which starts to sound quite close to living in accord with the gospel;

Rom 14:14, 20? Perhaps a halakhically-oriented Paul would emerge, one who argues by Jewish ethical categories and in a manner similar to other Jewish writers during (or before and after) the period. If so, this would go a long way in addressing those who view Paul as bursting the bounds of Judaism with his mission to the nations.[56] David Rudolph has recently made a strong argument concerning the food laws in these verses, and we will rely on his work throughout this section.[57]

Leviticus Purity or κοινός

Romans 14:14, 20 are generally understood to be an annulment of the food laws with their distinction between "clean" and "unclean." This distinction comes from Lev 11:46–47 (which is part of the Leviticus 10–11 matrix on purity): "This is the law pertaining to land animal and bird and every living creature that moves through the waters and every creature that swarms upon the earth, to make a distinction between the unclean (ἀκαθάρτων) and the clean (καθαρῶν), and between the living creature that may be eaten and the living creature that may not be eaten." While Paul does use καθαρός "clean" in 14:20, he does not use ἀκάθαρτος "unclean" in 14:14, when he discusses what is "unclean." There he uses κοινός often translated with the English gloss "common." It is generally assumed, as has recently been argued by Matthew Thiessen, that ἀκάθαρτος and κοινός are synonyms, but is such a claim warranted?[58]

First, κοινός as a term to describe Israel's purity system is unattested in the LXX of the Pentateuch. It occurs first in 1 Macc 1:47, which describes some of the things that "many from Israel consented" (v. 43) to do: "To build altars and sacred precincts and shrines for idols, to sacrifice swine and other unclean (κοινά) animals" (1 Macc 1:47) and "But many in Israel stood firm and were resolved in their hearts not to eat unclean

---

ironically Gal 2:14 brings this to the fore, a verse often read with the exact opposite social implications than those being put forth here).

56. Novenson ("Paul's Former Occupation," 33) suggests that the word does not properly align with our contemporary term "Judaism"; rather, it is "the defense and promotion of Jewish customs by Jewish people."

57. The most accessible version of this is Rudolph, "Paul and the Food Laws: A Reassessment of Romans 14:13–23," 151–81, though some of what I draw on comes from a conference paper version of this essay.

58. Thiessen, *Contesting*, 131.

food (κοινά)" (1 Macc 1:62).[59] Thus, it is a late term, one that may describe those foods that did not fit clearly into the Leviticus 10–11 matrix. Leviticus 10:10, for example, reads: "You must distinguish between the holy (ἀγίων) and the common (βεβήλων), between the pure (καθαρῶν) and the impure (ἀκαθάρτων)."[60]

So, when the Maccabean use of the term is taken into consideration, rather than a Paul setting aside the Leviticus purity system, he may be understood as addressing a more narrowly focused area, those foods that are categorized as grey areas (i.e., foodstuff that might otherwise be deemed appropriate but are not because of other contextual considerations). In Rom 14:14, Rudolph suggests "impurish" as an alternative English gloss for what Paul was addressing.[61]

Second, the use of κοινός rather than ἀκάθαρτος may also relate to the close associations between certain foods and idolatrous practices.[62] The 1 Macc 1:47 passage clearly makes that connection as Isaac Oliver describes: "it could be that the author of 1 Maccabees considers the food prepared by any Gentile or Jewish renegade as κοινά and therefore defiling (in an offensive or moral sense), even if, technically, the food item is permitted for a Jew to eat. . . . We could add that the term came to be used to designate *any* food prepared by Gentiles."[63] So, the term κοινός comes to be used in certain halakhic situations for foods that do not fit the ἀκάθαρτος framework of Lev 10:10; 11:46–47. Further, since this framework did not technically apply to non-Jews, and in light of the truncated guidelines for them in Acts 15:19–31; 16:4, κοινός may have been used by Paul to describe several sub-categories of foods that are "unfit" or "impurish" or "of indeterminate origin" for various reasons: the manner in which it was slaughtered, or if it had been offered to idols.[64] Thus, those foods that would otherwise be acceptable are now deemed problematic. So, one does not see in these verses, as suggested by Barclay,

59. See also 4 Macc 7:6: "Eleazar, you are a priest who is worthy of the office. You didn't pollute your teeth; you didn't contaminate your stomach by eating the forbidden foods. Your stomach had room only for godly behavior and purity."

60. Milgrom, *Leviticus 1–16*, 616.

61. Rudolph, "Paul and the Food Laws," 12; this suggestion is only in the conference paper version.

62. Philo, *Spec. Laws* 2.41–53. Here he associates religious dietary practices with the observance of special days. Cf. Rom 14:5–6.

63. Oliver, *Torah*, 346–49.

64. See below on this starting on page 216.

the revocation of the food laws, rather the case-by-case application of the diverse ways differing Jewish-like groups might be seen as observant within the broader synagogue community.

Imputed Impurity

What about Barclay's second claim, that Paul thought he was free from the law and could eat, at least from time to time, food otherwise restricted in Leviticus 11? This is based on 14:14, "I know and am persuaded in the Lord Jesus that nothing is unclean in itself (δι' ἑαυτοῦ); but it is unclean for anyone who thinks it unclean." Paul's phrase δι' ἑαυτοῦ "in itself" may be his way of stating his perspective on the declarative nature of clean and unclean categorization. Paul, like other Jewish writers, thinks impurity and/or its antidote are not ontological categories; rather they are imputed by divine decree.[65] This non-ontological view is evident in the Torah: "For example, bread made with yeast is forbidden during the festival of unleavened bread but eaten during the rest of the year (Exod 12:14–20). The substance of the food does not change, only its designation as forbidden or permitted for Israel."[66] These categories are seen in a functional frame with impurity being imputed.[67] So, Paul's statement in 14:14, "nothing is unclean in itself" is not particularly breathtaking; it is a perspective that some connected with Israel's traditions would have shared, i.e., it is God's ordinance that affects the designation of clean/ unclean or pure/impure.[68] Thus, there is no claim being made here by Paul that the food laws have been made redundant; rather he is claiming that all of God's creation is good: "The LORD's is the earth and its fullness, the world and all those who live in it" (Ps 24:1).

Intentionality and Social Practice

So, Barclay's claim may be exaggerated with regard to Paul's putative un-Jewishness, but yet another phrase still needs attention. Paul writes in

65. Ehrensperger, "Called," 101.

66. Rudolph, "Paul and the Food Laws," 160, 177 n. 52. He also cites Yochanan ben Zakkai, see Pesiqta deRab Kahana 4:7; and Letter of Aristeas 147 as examples of others who see impurity via divine decree rather than ontology.

67. So Oliver, *Torah*, 242–51.

68. Ehrensperger, "Called," 101, 105–6.

14:14b, "it is unclean for anyone who thinks it unclean." This phrase is often taken to indicate a law-free approach. The primary issue here is what the person "thinks" is "unclean"; it is not about the Leviticus 10–11 standard. While I have already suggested the focus here is on κοινός and not the Leviticus framework, the idea of "intention" should not be seen as law-free; rather, it points to another halakhic approach, one in which intention (i.e., "who thinks it") determines practice.

Paul's claim in 14:14b relates to the implications that follow from an *a priori* decision to follow a certain course of action in regard to Torah observance. This phrase "thinks it unclean" is similar to Josephus's "choose to live according to it" (*Jewish Antiquities* 17.151), which describes those who participated in having the Roman eagle removed over one of the temple gates: "For Herod had caused such things to be made which *were contrary to the law*, of which he was accused by Judas and Matthias; for the king had erected over the great gate of the temple a large golden eagle, of great value, and had dedicated it to the temple. *Now the law forbids those that chose to live according to it*, to erect images or representations of any living creature."

These individuals had previously determined to live in a certain manner (i.e., in accordance with the law) and thus specific social implications emerged from that decision (i.e., images are forbidden). Thus, what might, at first glance, sound like a relativization by Paul of a certain lifestyle, actually is a revalorization of one: a prior determining obligates one to a certain course of action.[69] The claims of relative purity and the role of intentionality combine to offer a halakhic stance in which what is law for one is not necessarily law for another, but there are nonetheless social implications for all involved (though they might differ, as they do for in-Christ Jews and gentiles).[70]

---

69. The emphasis on intentionality is also seen in the purity system described in m. Hag. 2:5–7. The earlier idea that impurity itself is not ontological continues to be maintained since all is pure (2:7); however, the person's intention is paramount (2:5–6).

70. Schwartz ("Someone," 307–8) points to this in m. Qidd. 3:10: "If someone says to a woman 'I betrothed you' but she says 'you did not betroth me,' he is forbidden to marry her relations but she is allowed to marry his relations. If she says 'you betrothed me' but he says 'I did not betroth you,' he is allowed to marry her relations but she is forbidden to marry his relations." The man in this case could not marry one of her relations since, for him, he thinks he is betrothed; yet, she does not so she is free. If the roles are reversed, then he is free and she is not. Thus, the law's restrictions are situationally determined.

In a similar fashion, in Rom 14:20–23, Paul says that certain beliefs enjoin restrictions that might not otherwise accrue, even if another related party doesn't agree with the claim. So, even though the strong, in the way I read the text, think they can eat something from a grey area, or that impurity is imputed and not ontological, they still cannot do anything that, writes Schwartz, "might bring the weak to want to do something that they, the weak, think is forbidden to them—even though Paul, and the strong, believe that in fact there is no basis for the prohibition."[71] This is not the traditional law-free Paul who sought to break ties with late Second Temple Judaism; Barclay's assertion might need revision. Rather, as Rudolph describes Paul, he is

> a first-century halakhic pluralist who favored the Hillelite emphasis placed on personal intention when it came to purity issues. Seen in this way, Paul's statement in Rom. 14:14b—"it is unclean for anyone who thinks it unclean"—was not an expression of indifference toward ritual purity, but a claim consistent with the on-the-ground reality of a variegated first-century Judaism.[72]

Conclusion

So, what was uncovered in relation to Paul's guidance to the weak and strong? Romans 14–15 provides a basis for the continuation of Jewish identity within the Christ-movement. Paul is not arguing for a temporary accommodation by the strong, gentile Christ-followers towards the weak Jewish Christ-followers who still think they need to observe Torah. He is, rather, concerned with the purity of the community and argues for the continuation of difference with regard to an in-Christ identity. He calls for an end to any approach to communal life in which domination is evident. The result is the legitimation and maintenance of diversity within the Christ-movement, especially as it relates to Jewish or Torah-informed practice.

71. Schwartz, "Someone," 308.

72. Rudolph, "Paul and the Food Laws," 159. So, while Romans 14–15 does not have the focus on "conscience" that is in 1 Corinthians 8–10, Schreiner (*Romans*, 706) seems to miss the idea that it is "not mentioned" in Romans 14–15 (though he acknowledges it might be present to some extent).

In relation to 14:14, 20, what was discovered? First, Paul was not against the law or the Levitical framework; rather he was addressing a grey area described by a post-LXX perspective of κοινός. Second, he argued in Jewish ethical categories and was in agreement with some Second Temple writers, who by definition continued to be Torah-observant, and who viewed impurity in non-ontological ways. Third, he was not a radical Jew making breathtaking claims about the law when he brought to the fore the role of intentionality. All the claims in these verses can be understood *within* the diverse expressions of late Second Temple Judaism. Thus, we see a halakhically oriented Paul who called the weak only to not judge the strong. The strong, however, were called to change both their attitude and actions. Their view that (a) κοινός was a grey area and (b) nothing is ontologically impure, were areas of their faith, but (c) they needed to continue to respect the intentionality of the weak as a valid and abiding way of life within the Christ-movement.

We can close this chapter with a reminder from William S. Campbell. He believes that Romans 14–15 substantiates the claim that Jewish identity is not only compatible with an in-Christ one but that those who continue to identify via Torah-praxis should be welcomed and accepted without argumentation. Campbell thus reminds us that Paul was not only a champion of gentile identity in Christ but of Jewish identity as well.[73] This reading emerges when one recognizes that the institutional setting for interaction would be the broader synagogue community.[74] The continuation of relationships within the Christ-movement is more important than one's desire for a loose halakhah. The problem for these early followers of Christ was not a de-historicized, theological one; rather it came from the daily challenges of living in unity with those who were and who remained different.[75] Paul's rhetorical vision for them is one in which Christ-followers are to "pursue peace pleasing his neighbour for his good" in "a reconciling pattern of life even as Christ did not live to please himself (Rom. 15:2–3)."[76] Thus, Paul's mission is not concerned with erasing distinctions between Jews and gentiles, "but the enabling of

73. Campbell, *Unity*, 53.

74. Campbell, *Paul and the Creation*, 116.

75. Campbell, "Rule," 259; Nanos, *Mystery*, 85, 102, 114. For Ehrensperger (*Mutually Encouraged*, 181) "these chapters [are] to be linked both in structure and content to the issue that is central throughout the letter, the issue of the relationship of Jews and Gentiles . . . [they are] a prime example of the particularity of Paul's theology."

76. Campbell, "Let Us Maintain," 77.

all those who are called, whether from the nations or from Israel, to glorify God together in their transformed particular identities and in mutual recognition of their abiding differences (Rom. 15:7–13)."[77] The continuation of Jewish and gentile diversity in Christ is an enduring aspect of Campbell's work. It is to the glorifying of God together in Rom 15:7–13 that we now turn.

77. Campbell, *Unity*, 53.

9

A Doxological Social Identity

Introduction

THIS CHAPTER LOOKS AT the formation, in Rom 15:7–13, of a doxological social identity for in-Christ Jews and gentiles as each group in their abiding difference embodies the Messiah's welcome. My approach understands doxological identity as a future, possible social identity where Jews remain Jews in Christ and gentiles remain gentiles, worshipping together the God of Israel with the Davidic Messiah for the sake of the nations. In order to argue that this is Paul's vision for the future, I will briefly define doxological social identity. Then, I will address Joshua Garroway's recent challenge to the Messiah's service to the Jews. Next I will offer an Israel-centric reading of the citations in 15:9b–12 that challenges the tradition-fulfillment and gentile-inclusion approaches. I suggest that the chain of citations are best described as Paul's attempt to form a doxological identity among Israel and the nations, a vision of worship and welcome that subverts Rome's claims of power and glory.

Doxological Social Identity

A doxological social identity emerges from an awareness of and the value attached to one's membership in a group that embodies specific ritual and bodily worship practices that reinforce maximal distinctiveness from outgroup members over time. This definition builds on Tajfel and Turner's understanding of social identity, improved by Marco Cinnirella's idea of possible future social identities in which (a) groups/individuals project multiples of these identities, (b) in order to construe a variety of possible outcomes to assess the efficacy of either their formation or their maintenance, and (c) draw upon both past and present identities in their future-oriented (temporal-aspects) identity-constructions/visions. The definition further relies on Catherine Bell's work on ritual as activities that give tangible expression to beliefs, and the use of ritual for social control/community building (ritualization). This is how I view the function of Paul's argument in these verses.[1] A doxological identity, as I am describing it, is seen, for example, in 15:7 where the audience is expected to see themselves as those "welcomed" and "accepted" by the Messiah for the purpose of "God's glory." It is not merely a newly inscribed identity node but one that is made salient through worship and table fellowship practices. Both Jews and gentiles are encouraged to glorify the Lord together amid their existing (and future) social identities (15:10–11). Gorman picks up on this as well: "This powerful embodiment of welcome and worship, this community of Gentiles and Jews in mutual hospitality and in common glorification of God, is said in effect to be the very mission of Christ as the agent of God."[2] For Paul, existing identities are missionally significant; they are not an area of indifference.

Doxological Identity in Romans

The formation of a doxological identity has been a goal of Paul's throughout the letter to the Romans.[3] Ben Blackwell, rightly I think, has highlighted Paul's concern over the lack of the "glory of God" referred to in Rom 3:23. He suggests that Paul's focus on both the mortality and the shame that result from sin is rooted in his apprehension over the lack of God's glory that they indicate.[4] Dunn also sees glory as a "leitmotif" of the letter.[5] Thus, it is plausible to suggest that Paul had some concern

1. Tajfel and Turner, "Social Identity Theory," 7–24; Cinnirella, "Exploring," 227–48; Bell, *Ritual*, 89.

2. Gorman, *Becoming*, 292.

3. For concerns over a doxological identity in the broader cultural context, see Pickstock, *After Writing*, 45, who finds something similar in Plato, *Phaed.* 230.

4. Blackwell, "Immortal," 298. With regard to 3:23, Blackwell concludes that it "signifies the condition of corruption and mortality" (300).

5. Dunn (*Romans*, 2.534) notes "the glory of God as something man was made to share in, which he 'exchanged' and lost (1:23; 3:23), but which will always be the goal

over the Romans' misconstrual of the nature of glory. James Harrison has provided an appropriate framework for understanding the problem. He contends that Paul's glory discourse in Romans should be read against the backdrop of Roman questing for glory, especially as it was embodied in the Julio-Claudian rulers. In his understanding, the Roman Christ-followers had shifted their social identifications; they pursued glory as embodied by Roman imperial practices (Rom 1:23), which resulted, according to Paul, in not attaining God's glory (3:23). It is plausible that this competitive drive for glory at the expense of others and its concomitant cultural boasting contributed to the problems Paul addresses in Rom 14:1—15:13.[6]

Romans 15:7: Welcoming into a Doxological Identity

In 15:7, Paul writes, "Therefore, welcome (προσλαμβάνεσθε) one another (ἀλλήλους) just as the Messiah has welcomed you, for the glory of God." This discourse of welcoming began back in 14:1. The parallels between the verses are often noted by interpreters, but in 15:7 Paul broadens his rhetorical vision to all the members of community.[7] This mutual hospitality is one concrete way in which the Roman Christ-followers could express their shared identity in the context of their continuing differences. Nicolet-Anderson comes close to this conclusion by noting that "Differences are not erased, but they no longer function as what defines the believers in their most basic identity."[8] The Messiah's welcome here in

---

of the good man (2:7, 10), a goal made into a realistic hope by Christ's resurrection (5:2; 6:4)." He continues, "The point once again therefore seems to be the priority of Israel in God's purpose of salvation—the gospel of glory to Jew first as well as Gentile, the Gentile convert as entering into Israel's promised blessings."

6. Harrison, *Paul*, 269: for Paul, "glory was a gift of divine grace dispensed to his dependents through the dishonor of the crucified Christ who had become their *hilasterion*. Glory was democratised throughout the Body of Christ and its full expression postponed till the eschaton." On the competitive drive for glory, see, for example, Hunt ("Jesus Caesar," 264–66) who suggests that someone might be killed for treason for dishonoring the emperor or for assembling followers, but not for simply claiming to be king or emperor. Thus, dishonor is closely related to treason.

7. Miller, *Obedience*, 63; Hafemann, "Redemption," 207.

8. Nicolet-Anderson, *Constructing the Self*, 120. However, one wonders how one might construe a "most basic identity," and what would provide definitional affect for this.

15:7 becomes the model for the Roman Christ-follower's behavior "just as" (καθώς) it had earlier in 15:3.[9]

The doxological context is then made explicit: "for the purpose of the glory of God." The welcome of the other is an expression of one's participation in God's glory (and by extension a rejection of the competitive, honor-driven, approach evident in Roman civic life).[10] This becomes the new superordinate identity (those identified by God's glory) and goal (mutual welcome and worship) by which to organize communal life. Paul understands Jesus as Israel's Messiah and the use of the article (ὁ Χριστός) in v. 7 and in 15:3 (as well as in 9:5) indicates a close and continuing identification with Israel (15:8; 9:3–5).[11]

Romans 15:8–9: Christ's Service to Israel and the Nations

That brings us to Joshua Garroway who, by contrast, claims that 15:8 refers to Christ as the agent of circumcision for gentiles. Garroway rejects the traditional rendering of διάκονον . . . περιτομῆς as a "servant of the circumcision" and opts for Christ as the "agent of circumcision."[12] In this reading, Christ is "an agent who makes circumcision available to others," the one "removing the foreskin," not in the "physical circumstances" but the one who "facilitates the admission of Gentiles into the patriarchal covenant that has genital circumcision as its entrance requirement."[13] Christ has, in effect, circumcised non-Jews "by faith rather than by a knife" and this "fulfill[s] what God had promised to the patriarchs long ago."[14] Garroway's argument is further based on an intertextual discussion of Paul's use of διάκονος in his other writings. He contends that the phrase ἁμαρτίας διάκονος "servant/agent of sin" in Gal 2:17 supports his reading in Rom 15:8 since the Galatians phrase is not whether Christ becomes a "servant of sin" but one who *administers* it to others" by finding them

---

9. So similarly Miller, *Obedience*, 63; *pace* Moo, *Romans*, 875, who sees a causal link here.

10. Jewett, *Romans*, 1; his commentary has built much around this theme: "In the shameful cross, Christ overturned the honor system that dominated the Greco-Roman and Jewish worlds, resulting in discrimination and exploitation of barbarians as well as in poisoning the relations between the congregations in Rome."

11. So similarly Rudolph, *A Jew to the Jews*, 169 n. 246.

12. Garroway, *Paul's Gentile-Jews*, 119.

13. Garroway, *Paul's Gentile-Jews*, 119.

14. Garroway, *Paul's Gentile-Jews*, 119.

to be sinners.[15] In a similar fashion, in 2 Cor 3:6, Paul and Timothy are described as διακόνους καινῆς διαθήκης "servants of the new covenant." For Garroway this does not intimate serving the covenant, but rather "representing it, promoting it, and making it available to others."[16] This leads him to conclude that in Rom 15:8, "Paul calls Christ a διάκονον περιτομῆς, an 'agent of circumcision,' because in Paul's opinion Christ administers or 'serves up' circumcision to Gentiles."[17] Garroway's approach fits with the Paul within Judaism approach in which Christ is the focal point for gentiles. In what follows, however, I will suggest implications not only for gentiles but also for Jews in Rom 15:7–13.

In 15:8–9, Paul writes: "For I tell you that Christ has become (γεγενῆσθαι) a servant (διάκονον) of the Jews (περιτομῆς) on behalf of God's truth, so that the promises made to the patriarchs might be confirmed and, moreover, that the gentiles might glorify God for his mercy." Garroway's argument is based on the following evidence.[18] First, as described above, he rejects the idea that διάκονον . . . περιτομῆς refers to Christ as a "servant of the circumcision," based on his understanding of the use of the genitive in this phrase.[19] Second, he downplays the likelihood that circumcision functioned as a group label; in his view it, rather, refers to the rite. Third, he doubts that Jesus's earthly life bore rhetorical weight in Paul's argument nor did it fulfill any patriarchal promises.[20] Finally, he rejects the salience of the category of messianic servant as applied to Christ.[21] I will address the messianic (Davidic) servant idea and

15. Garroway, *Paul's Gentile-Jews*, 119–20.

16. Garroway, *Paul's Gentile-Jews*, 120.

17. Garroway, *Paul's Gentile-Jews*, 120.

18. Garroway, *Paul's Gentile-Jews*, 118.

19. While he acknowledges that in Rom 3:30 περιτομή is a group identity marker for the Jewish people and thus the traditional understanding is defensible, he, on the other hand, thinks that this understanding has significant grammatical difficulties associated with it. He references but does not debate the arguments by Williams ("Righteousness," 241–90) and Gaston (*Paul*, 133).

20. Garroway, *Paul's Gentile-Jews*, 118. His concern is more evident in the following: "how Christ's ministry among the Jews, if that is what Paul means when he calls Christ a 'servant of the circumcision,' would have fulfilled or confirmed any of the promises to the patriarchs remains unclear." Garroway points out that the content of the promises relate to the land, security, and a seed, not to a coming messianic servant (though he does acknowledge that this is evident in the prophets).

21. Further, Garroway (*Paul's Gentile-Jews*, 193 n. 9) points out that when this messianic identity is detailed, δοῦλος is used rather than διάκονος, as in 15:8. Ultimately, he is surprised that more interpreters have not noticed the problems connecting Christ

the promises (Israel's restoration for the sake of the nations) below in the exegesis of 15:9–12. I want to first address the type of genitive in 15:8, the use of circumcision as a group or social identity label, and then the role of Jesus's life in regards to reconciliation between Jews and gentiles. Finally, I will offer another way forward on the syntactical problem in 15:8–9a since it may further support Israel's continued covenantal identity.

Christ the Agent of Circumcision

The genitival relationship in the phrase διάκονον . . . περιτομῆς found in 15:8 is crucial to Garroway's argument. The objective reading is generally followed, in which case the phrase is construed to mean that those of the circumcision are the object of Jesus's service. Garroway instead understands it as a genitive of origin. In his reading, Christ has become an agent/servant of circumcision (see above). While this construal is possible, there is at least one verse in Romans that calls it into question. Romans 2:29 indicates that the Spirit is the agent of the circumcision, not Christ: "No, a person is a Jew who is one inwardly; and circumcision is circumcision of the heart, *by the Spirit*."[22] So Garroway's suggestion that 15:8 refers to Christ as the agent of circumcision runs afoul of 2:29.

Circumcision as a Group Identity

Paul's claim that Christ became a servant to the circumcision, understood as a circumlocution for the Jews, suggests that this term functions as a social-identity label. Garroway argues that it instead refers to the act of circumcision. Moo, in his discussion of that possibility, rightly I think, contends that "this [is] one of those many places where Paul refers to the distinctive Jewish rite as a way of denoting the Jews themselves."[23] Campbell, similarly, notes that "Paul does not use the term 'Israel' but prefers 'circumcision' despite all its ethnic connotations."[24] Then he concludes that "[s]ince for Paul circumcision is synonymous with Jewish identity (Christ became a servant to the circumcision, in 15:8) then Jewish identity is transformed in Christ and not obliterated or rendered obsolete, just

as a "servant of the circumcision" with "the promises to the patriarchs."

22. Barclay, *Paul*, 461.

23. Moo, *Romans*, 877.

24. Campbell, *Unity*, 66.

as in the case of the identity of those from the nations. A transformed Greek is still a Greek and a transformed Jew is still a Jew."[25]

Joel Marcus has put forth strong arguments that the term περιτομή was a "self-designation" of some in Rome, most likely of Jewish Christ-followers. Marcus's thesis is that the "weak" in Rome "called themselves 'the circumcision' and their opponents 'the foreskin,' and that the 'circumcision/uncircumcision' terminology in the letter reflects this sociological tension."[26] Romans 3:30 is a good example of the term being used as a social identity label: "since God is one, who will justify the circumcised by faith and the uncircumcised by faith."[27] In this way, as a social identity index for men, one's in-Christ identity, is further made salient by one's circumcision. This is far removed from the traditional view of Paul that sees a circumcised life for Jews as *adiaphora* (Gal 5:3).

Andrew Das disagrees and rejects Marcus's contention. He says that Marcus "ignores the use of 'circumcision' as a signal in Romans (4.9–12; 9.8) for Israel 'according to the flesh' (9.3–4)."[28] In this scenario, the label becomes a negative, outgroup identifier for those who had not positively responded to Christ's work, in contrast to those from the nations who had. Martin, however, in discussing Galatians, notes that the verb περιτέμνω and the noun περιτομή "refer either to an act, a state, or a practice" and that in 1 Cor 7:18–20, "Paul uses all three of these meanings in his discussion of circumcision."[29] This suggests that Das's critique of Marcus may not be as probative as it first seems. Furthermore, the reference to the state of being circumcised or uncircumcised in 1 Cor 7:18–20 supports the possibility that περιτομή is a group label in Rom 15:8.

It may be asked, however, whether "the circumcision" is a reference to Jesus's service to the Jews performed only during his ministry on earth. Matthew 15:24 seems to suggest so: "He answered, 'I was sent only to the lost sheep of the house of Israel.'"[30] In this reading, there is no ongoing service to the Jews after the resurrection. However, the perfect tense verb γεγενῆσθαι "has become" in Rom 15:8 suggests that there is, in fact, an

---

25. Campbell, *Unity*, 125.

26. Marcus, "Circumcision," 80.

27. Others may include: Rom 2:26–27; 3:30; 4:9; 15:8; Gal 2:7–9; Phil 3:3; Col 3:11; Eph 2:11. See Marcus, "Circumcision," 75–76. However, these uses, with the exception of Eph 2:11 whose authorship is disputed by some, are contested.

28. Das, "Praise," 97 n. 19.

29. Martin, "Apostasy," 451. See also Gen 17:14; 1 Macc 1:11–15, 52.

30. Tucker, "Matthew's Missional Particularism," 15–24.

ongoing service to the Jews. Moo elaborates: "Paul implies that Christ's ministry to Jews is not confined to his earthly life or sacrificial death, but continues even now, as the benefits of his death are appropriated by Jews."[31] However, there may be further service even beyond that.

Jesus's Life and a Call to Reconciliation

Garroway rejects the idea that Jesus's life effects reconciliation. He is convinced that, for Paul, reconciliation is purely a result of Christ's death and resurrection. He is correct to note the centrality of Jesus's death and resurrection, but his argument relies on the contested syntax of 15:8–9a and, most importantly, on the assumption that Jesus's life is irrelevant for Paul. However, Rom 14:13–18 offers an implicit allusion to Jesus's life, and 15:3–7 offers an explicit one in relation to reconciliation. This blunts the force of Garroway's claim.[32]

Constantineanu is quite convincing about the social significance of Christ's life. He notes: "The Roman Christians are to make the example of Jesus the paradigm for their life, seen practically in their self-denial, active love for their neighbour expressed as 'seeking their good,' and as living in harmony. Jesus as 'Christ did not please himself' but rather took upon himself the burdens of others, so they should renounce their own privileges for the sake of the other."[33] It is likely the case that Jesus's life did matter for Paul and not just his death. These three ideas: that the Spirit is the agent of circumcision rather than the Messiah, that the term "circumcision" functions as a group label, and that Rom 14:13–18 explicitly (and 15:3–7 implicitly) refer to Jesus's life and teaching as a model for reconciliation, combine to call into question Garroway's claim that Χριστὸν διάκονον γεγενῆσθαι περιτομῆς in 15:8 should be understood as "Christ is the agent of circumcision" for the letter's gentile addressees. Rather, the traditional idea that the Messiah has become a servant to the circumcision should be maintained, though with some refinements with regard to Israel's restoration and the implications for the nations. Before we turn to the extent and nature of the messianic fulfillment and the prominence of gentile inclusion in the citation chain (Rom 15:9–13), a syntactical issue in Rom 15:8–9a requires attention.

---

31. Moo, *Romans*, 877.

32. Garroway, *Paul's Gentile-Jews*, 118; Williams, "Righteousness," 225.

33. Constantineanu, *Social Significance*, 176. See Thompson, *Clothed with Christ*.

Romans 15:8–9a: Syntax and Israel's Covenantal Identity

The dominant understanding of the syntax of this passage views 15:8b and 15:9a as purpose clauses both of which are dependent on "Christ has become a servant" (15:8a). So, in this reading, Christ became a servant for the dual purpose of confirming the promises to the patriarchs and enabling the nations to glorify God. This view makes sense contextually but the awkward change in subject from "Christ" to "gentiles" and the need for an implied repetition of "in order" (εἰς τό) somewhat counts against it.[34] The second view sees the claims in 15:8b and 15:9 as dependent on "I say" in 15:8. So, this view understands Paul to say, I declare that Christ has become a servant and now the gentiles are glorifying God. This view fits the syntax of the passage more closely but does not explain the connection to Paul's instruction concerning mutual hospitality in 15:7.[35] Garroway is convinced his argument coheres with either of these two dominant approaches.[36]

Toney, however, offers a third way, one with which Garroway's approach might not fit. The main syntactical datum overlooked by the traditional solutions is that 9a does not require another "in order" (εἰς τό), as in 8b, to be construed as a result clause since this is accomplished by the "adverbial infinitive 'to glorify' (δοξάσαι)" in 9a.[37] Thus, the controlling assertion, as in the first view mentioned above, is "For I declare that Christ became a servant of the circumcised" (8a). But "Romans 15:9a is best understood as connecting the salvation of Gentiles as an *additional* result of God fulfilling his promises to the patriarchs."[38] It expresses this result in a subordinate clause that is parallel in meaning but not in structure to verse 8b. This analysis thus allows for a change in subject that is not ruled out by the syntax.[39]

This understanding makes sense in the context since both assertions describe unique implications of the Messiah's work. The result is

---

34. Toney, *Paul's Inclusive Ethic*, 109–11.

35. Barclay (*Paul*, 460 n. 25) takes it "as a second purpose of Christ's 'service' to the circumcision." Cf. Wagner, "Christ," 481–84; Engberg-Pedersen, *Paul*, 356–57.

36. Garroway, *Paul's Gentile-Jews*, 194–95 n. 17; Toney, *Paul's Inclusive Ethic*, 109–11.

37. Toney, *Paul's Inclusive Ethic*, 111.

38. Toney, *Paul's Inclusive Ethic*, 109.

39. Thanks to Laura Hunt for thinking through these syntactical issues with me and for helping to clarify the language.

that there are different implications that arise from the Messiah's service. First, as the servant to the circumcision, he confirms the promises made to the patriarchs. Second, this service to Jews, done on behalf of the nations, brings God's mercy to them who may then glorify God. Vanlaningham summarizes it this way: "there is a practical distinction between the intent of Christ's death for Israel and for Gentiles, suggesting that Israel does not just get folded into the predominantly Gentile Church."[40]

Romans 15:8–9a, therefore, offers evidence for suggesting that Israel's covenant identity continues within Paul's universalistic gospel discourse. Throughout the letter Paul highlights the priority of the Jewish people in salvation history, and these verses restate that theme (1:16; 2:9; 3:1–4; 9:4–5; 11:13–24).[41] Toney, rightly I think, concludes that Paul reminds these gentiles that service to the Jewish people benefits everyone.[42] The Roman congregation is being encouraged to follow the example of the Messiah. They are to become servants of the Jewish people, accepting different social identifications to the extent that as a group they cultivate practices of hospitality that allow for the continuation of the various expressions of Jewish identity so that they together might glorify God. Van Buren summarizes, saying that Paul "wanted his Gentile readers in Rome to see in Christ himself how they were to conduct themselves with respect to the Jewish people. The context of these verses is an exhortation to 'welcome one another,' the grounds for which is the assertion that Christ has welcomed you."[43]

This further suggests that Paul has been misread if he is thought to be seeking to remove the congregation in Rome from any connection to the broader synagogue community.[44] Two further claims to that effect need attention and will be addressed below. First, Garroway thinks his approach makes better sense of the fulfillment of the promises to the patriarchs (4:13–16 and 9:15–18). Second, he proposes that the citations are organized around the catchword "gentiles."[45] In order to discuss these ideas we will broaden the dialogue partners to include N. T. Wright, Michael Bird, and Colin Kruse.

---

40. Vanlaningham, "The Jewish People," 129.

41. So similarly Toney, *Paul's Inclusive Ethic*, 112, with a different emphasis.

42. Toney, *Paul's Inclusive Ethic*, 112.

43. van Buren, *Theology*, 347.

44. Watson, *Paul, Judaism*, 11.

45. Garroway, *Paul's Gentile-Jews*, 120–22.

Romans 15:8b Promises Fulfilled or Confirmed?

Romans 15:7–13 might appear supersessionist since the verses seem to claim that the promises to the patriarchs have already been fulfilled without remainder. The catena of scriptures cited have gentile inclusion into the people of God as their focus which in turn could suggest a displacement of Israel's covenantal identity.[46] For example, Michael Bird, following N. T. Wright's contention that Israel is summed up in Christ, asserts that "The net point is that God, by bringing Israel's covenantal history to its appointed climax in the Messiah, has opened the way for the Gentiles to join his renewed people."[47] This widely held view concludes that the prophetic promises have been fulfilled in Christ and that, while Israel's sociological identity continues, it is no longer properly understood as a covenantal identity, since in the new-covenant community ethnicity has no determinative value.[48]

However, in Rom 15:8b, Paul writes that Christ serves the Jewish people, "in order to *confirm* the promises made to the patriarchs (τὰς ἐπαγγελίας τῶν πατέρων)." Thus, the claim that the promises have been fulfilled without remainder is not exactly correct; the promises have been "confirmed" (βεβαιῶσαι).[49] Second, in-Christ Jews and gentiles are not the final fulfillment of Israel's restoration (though some sort of inauguration of this may be in view as these in-Christ gentiles join the elect remnant in Israel's history; Rom 9:15, 18–26).[50] Third, many assume that there is but one promise in view, the gentile inclusion detailed in Rom 4:13 and promised to Abraham in Gen 12:1–3 (cf. Rom 4:16; 9:4; 11:28). Pate is an example of this view: "Verses 8–9a state that Christ has fulfilled God's covenant promises to the patriarchs, which included in their purview the conversion of the Gentiles."[51] He also, in discussing Rom 4:13a,

---

46. This is an apt description of Wright's view ("Romans," 746–47). See the critique of Wright by Hafemann, "Redemption," 207.

47. Bird, *Romans*, 484. Hays (*Echoes*, 71–72) suggests mercy is the theme that holds this section together.

48. Zoccali, *Whom God*, 83.

49. Though Jewett (*Romans*, 892) points out there is evidence of semantic overlap here. With regard to βεβαιῶσαι in 15:8, the use of this word should be regarded as an affirmation of Israel's continued covenant identity not its annulment (so similarly Campbell, *Unity*, 78 with regard to 1:16–17).

50. Hafemann, "Redemption," 207; Witherington, *Romans*, 343 n. 70.

51. Pate, *Romans*, 280

notes that "the physical land of Israel is replaced by the kingdom of God in the hearts of his people (see Rom 14:17)."[52]

Here I will raise two points for consideration that suggest that more than the promise of gentile inclusion is in view. First, the promises here are plural and not singular, so at a minimum more than gentile inclusion is in view.[53] The fulfillment-only approach obliterates two of the promises, i.e., land and descendants, so that only the gentile inclusion promises remain. Yet, according to the Damascus Document and Jubilees, the promise of progeny and land continued to be salient for some Jewish writers: God "raised up for himself those called by name so as to leave a remnant for the *land* and in order to fill the face of the world with their offspring" (CD 2.11–12); "and I shall be with you and bless you because I will give all of this *land* to you and to your *seed*. And I will carry out my oath which I swore to Abraham, your father. And I will multiply your *seed* as the stars of the sky" (Jub. 24:[9a]10–11a).[54]

The threefold promise is restated in Sir 44:21, "And so the Lord made him a solemn promise that his *descendants* would be a blessing to the *world*; that their number would be countless, like the dust of the earth; that they would be *honored* more than any other people on earth; and that their *land* would extend from sea to sea, from the Euphrates to the ends of the earth" (see also Jub. 15:4–10). The inclusion of the nations, however, was of only occasional consideration: "They are to atone for all those in Aaron who volunteer for holiness, and for those in Israel who belong to truth, and for Gentile proselytes who join them in community" (1QS 5.6; but see Wisdom of Solomon 10–19). The Damascus Document doesn't consider gentiles at all but only speaks of how a member should properly relate to them: "No one should provoke his servant, his maid, or his employee on the Sabbath" (CD 11:12).

Second, the fulfillment approach assumes a stable referent for the patriarchs in Romans generally. While Abraham, Isaac, and Jacob are among them, both the Damascus Document and Jubilees include Noah as a patriarch, and in Jubilees the covenant established with Noah is being renewed with Abraham:

---

52. Pate, *Romans*, 101. See Wagner, *Heralds*, 309.

53. See on this the earlier discussion on Rom 9:4 in chapter 5, p. 123.

54. See also CD 1:7–8. The land also maintained pride of place: CD 2.11; cf. 1QS 8.9b–10a; Jub. 22:14; 24:10–11; 32:19.

And on that day the Lord made a covenant with Abram, saying: "To thy seed will I give this land, from the river of Egypt unto the great river, the river Euphrates, the Kenites, the Kenizzites, the Kadmonites, the Perizzites, and the Rephaim, the Pha-korites, and the Hivites, and the Amorites, and the Canaanites, and the Girgashites, and the Jebusites." And the day passed, and Abram offered the pieces, and the birds, and their fruit offerings, and their drink offerings, and the fire devoured them. And on that day we made a covenant with Abram, according as we had covenanted with Noah in this month; and Abram renewed the festival and ordinance for himself for ever. (Jub. 14:18–20)[55]

There may also be an implicit link with Moses if a violation of the patriarchal covenant meant a violation of the Torah of Moses: "But God called to mind the covenant of the forefathers" (CD 6.2).[56] So similarly, Sirach suggests God made Moses equal to the "holy ones," which likely refers to the patriarchs: "From Jacob's descendants the Lord raised up a godly man who won the favor of everyone, loved by God and people alike. This man was Moses, whose very memory is a blessing. The Lord made him as glorious as the angels and made his enemies fear him" (Sir 45.1–2). In the broader context, several of the patriarchs are described: Noah (44:17); Abraham (44:19); Isaac and Jacob (44:22–23). Fredriksen similarly concludes that in "15.8, Paul speaks of the fathers (plural), who include Jacob, Joseph, Moses, and many others who are not fathers of gen-tiles in the same way as Abraham." Thus, the exclusion of Moses among the patriarchs in Paul's thinking may need to be revisited by interpreters.[57]

So, I think that we should assume that Paul, if he remained in Judaism, implied the three-fold patriarchal promise when he spoke of "the promises," unless he clearly indicated otherwise. Even if one is not convinced by the above line of reasoning, Cranfield's expansive view of the promises should at least be considered, i.e., those "promises made to

55. See further Jubilees 6–7; CD 3.1–4.

56. See also CD 15.7–10a. This follows Heinsch, "Is Sauce for the Goose," 1–14. According to Jubilees, the covenant made between God and Noah (Gen 6:18; 9:8–17; Jub. 6:4), God and Abraham (Gen 15:18; 17:1–27; Jub. 14:18–20; 15:1–32), God and Isaac (Gen 17:19, 21; Jub. 15:19, 21), and God and Israel (Exod 19:5; cf. Jub. 6:11) is the same covenant, simply reinstated and the promises reaffirmed/made more explicit. And, as van Ruiten points out ("Covenant," 167–90), when the covenant is made with the particular patriarch, whether that be Noah, Abraham, Isaac, or Jacob, the covenant is made with their posterity as well, and the promises are reconfirmed (Gen 9:9–17; 17:1–27; Jub. 6:10, 17–19; 15:9, 11, 19, 28, 29; 22:15, 30).

57. Fredriksen, "Judaizing," 244 n. 28.

Abraham (Gen 12.7; 13.14–17; 17.4–8; 22.16–18; also the related promise in 21.12—cf. Rom 9.7f) and repeated to Isaac (Gen 26.3f) and to Jacob (Gen 28.13f)." However, as Cranfield also notes, Paul probably had in mind the wider "eschatological and messianic promises" as well: "2 Sam 7.12, 16, 28f; Isa 9.6f; Jer 23.5; 31.31ff; Ezek 34.23f; 37.24ff."[58] Even if one limits the referent to only those promises given to Abraham, Isaac, and Jacob, these are still more extensive than simply gentile inclusion. Furthermore, the syntax of 8–9a still suggests that the Messiah's service has different implications for Jews and gentiles.[59] Campbell then is likely closer to the mark when he points out that "an extension of Israel's privileges to gentiles (rather than a transfer of them away from Israel)" is in view.[60] In that case, Wright and Bird claim too much with regard to the fulfillment of the promises. For Paul, Israel's restoration for the sake of the nations still awaits the future. Or, as Hafemann put it: "The 'climax of the covenant' remains Israel's future restoration for the sake of the nations."[61]

Romans 15:9b–12:
Messiah, Gentiles, and Doxological Identity

Four biblical citations make up Rom 15:9b–12, and, as is often noted, they come from the Torah (Deut 32:42), the Writings (Ps 18:49 or 2 Sam 22:50), and the Prophets (Isa 11:10). Whether that was intended to be an inclusive testimony or a further substantiation of Rom 1:4 is unclear.[62] Paul begins the string of quotations with καθὼς γέγραπται; however, Black is undoubtedly wide of the mark when he argues that Paul is "clinching" his argument by an appeal to an unassailable "authority."[63] These are not proof texts; Paul's Israel-centric scriptural reasoning is more in line with the creative interpretive practices of first-century Judaism.[64] Paul cites Israel's scriptural tradition in this case to offer guidance about the type of

58. Cranfield, *Romans*, 2.464.

59. Matera, *Romans*, 323–24.

60. Campbell, *Unity*, 78.

61. Hafemann, "Redemption, 212–13.

62. Bird, *Romans*, 486. So similarly Hays, *Echoes*, 71, who notes this and also thinks these citations clinch Paul's argument. Hafemann ("Redemption," 208) notes these reflect a "comprehensive, canonical sweep."

63. Black, *Romans*, 173. Miller (*Obedience*, 72) seems to follow this approach to Paul's argumentation as well.

64. See Ehrensperger, "Paul and the Authority," 319.

"symbolic and social world" into which his audience is being socialized, one that differs from Roman imperial ideology.[65]

Colin Kruse, based on the presence of καὶ πάλιν in 15:10, 11, and 12, contends that these citations focus on the same thing: "the call of the Gentiles and their inclusion among the people of God."[66] However, the citations are about more than this; they provide a sequential argument that is concerned with more than the catchword ἔθνος. By looking at the citations in comparison with their original contexts, we will see that Paul's concern is with the restoration and redemption of Israel for the sake of the nations which results in the formation of a distinct doxological social identity for Jews and gentiles, one that is embodied in ritual practices of worship and welcome.[67] This decenters gentile identity in Christ since it is not a stand-alone identity. It only finds its salience in Israel's story: gentiles are actors on the Jewish stage, even if the Romans control the stage, props, and actors.[68]

Psalm 18:49 (2 Sam 22:50) in Romans 15:9bc

In 15:9bc, Paul has the Messiah declare: "Therefore I will praise you among the gentiles; I will sing the praises of your name." In the Psalm 18 context, David, the king, is blessing God for delivering him from his enemies and giving Israel victory over the nations.[69] This praise for God's covenant faithfulness to his promise to "David and his seed forever" is declared

---

65. So similarly Bird, *Romans*, 487. See Tucker, "Paul's Particular Problem," 407–24.

66. Kruse, *Romans*, 533. BDAG 752 categorizes the use of πάλιν in these verses as a "marker of a discourse or narrative item added to items of a related nature." I am not disagreeing that there is some relation between the items, just about the nature and identity of that relation. There is some sort of discourse development related to Israel's vocation that is overlooked by Kruse's claim which too quickly flattens out the rhetoric.

67. Hafemann ("Redemption," 208) is very close to this; for him it is a "call for the Gentiles to glorify God in fulfillment of his promises to the patriarchs."

68. See Tucker, "Gentile Christianity," 5 n. 24 and page 25 in this book. Bird (*Romans*, 486) gets close to what I am suggesting concerning these citations: "together they form a redemptive-historical mosaic that weaves together the narrative threads Paul has expounded across Romans, including God, Messiah, Israel, Gentiles, mercy, and glory."

69. The superscription attributes the psalm to "the Lord's servant, David," and 17:51 (LXX) indicates the speaker is God's anointed king. See Wagner, *Heralds*, 312.

among the nations (18:50). By putting these words on the lips of the Messiah, Paul aligns himself with later interpreters who read the earlier text eschatologically as a promise for future restoration of the house of David, a restoration that has begun in Christ.[70] This, then, contributes to the formation of a future, possible social identity. Barrett may have misread the evidence when he dismissed any interest in the "Davidic descent of Jesus" in this context.[71] While Wagner is correct to highlight the gentile aspect of the Messiah's mission in 15:9b, this doesn't preclude further political relevance for the Jews. He points to Ps 18:43–44a in which the gentiles, those strangers to God's people, now obey the Messiah who has arisen to rule them (Isa 55:12). So, the wider context of Psalm 18 suggests the Davidic discourse was part of Paul's framework, as earlier in Rom 1:3–4; it further suggests that this chain is about *more* than gentile inclusion. It is at the same time about God's mercy, the restoration of Israel, and the confirmation of God's promises. Israel's identity continues to be salient in Paul's mission to the nations.

Paul's mission to the nations proceeds in the service of the restoration of Israel (Rom 11:11–14, 25–32; 15:15–16, 31) and reinforces Israel's priority rather than its displacement (Rom 1:1–7, 11–17; 11:11–15, 25–29; 15:7–9). Talbert, in discussing the catena of citations, notes "that these scriptural quotations all are a support not of the fulfillment of the promises to the patriarchs but of the inclusion of the Gentiles through Christ."[72] In interpretations such as his, the inclusion of gentiles is seen as the focus, related to the promises either as a new event, or as a final fulfillment. The inclusion of the nations is better understood, however, as an expansion of the original promises to Israel, not as a final fulfillment of them. Most interpreters overlook the significance of the citation of Deut 32:43 in Rom 15:10 and its effect on any claim that gentiles are the focus of all the citations.[73]

---

70. That Messiah is the speaker is repeated among interpreters. Cranfield, *Romans*, 2.746. *Pace* Craigie, *Psalms 1–50*, 177, who thinks Paul does not draw out the Davidic significance of this psalm.

71. Barrett, *Romans*, 250.

72. Talbert, *Romans*, 321.

73. Starling (*Not My People*, 160) is one exception: a "reference to the Gentiles is present but confusingly expressed in the MT (possibly reflecting a disturbed textual tradition—hence the omission of 'Gentiles' altogether in the NRSV) but present in the LXX in a form that is the same as Paul's citation in Rom. 15:10." He also notes Fitzmyer (*Romans*, 706–7) as one who wrestles with this issue.

Deuteronomy 32:43 in Romans 15:10

In 15:10, Paul continues putting scripture on the lips of the Messiah by citing Deut 32:43, "And again he [the Davidic Messiah] says: Rejoice, O the nations, with his people."[74] The continuation of Israel's covenantal identity may be seen in the way Paul cites from the Song of Moses here, especially with the final phrase μετὰ τοῦ λαοῦ αὐτοῦ "with his people."[75] The citation in 15:10 is identical with what is found in the LXX and describes a directive in which the nations are now to worship with Israel (not on their own).[76] In other words, the referent for "his people" is Israel and not a reconstituted or redefined group of Christ-followers in which existing identities have been relativized. Doxological practices are to issue forth from among the nations and not just Israel. This has the effect of reminding the gentiles that God is still at work among the people of Israel. Thus, Wright's perspective that Israel's identity has been taken up in Christ to the extent that its unique covenantal identity and history have been absorbed into the life of the new-covenant community should be called into question (15:8). Witherington comes close to providing this critique: "The end result of recognizing God is still working with and for Jews and Jewish Christians should be that Gentiles praise God

---

74. Matera, *Romans*, 324.

75. Lincicum (*Paul*, 165) notes that "throughout Deuteronomy the LXX tends to translate *ad sensum* when referring to a 'people' or a 'nation,' using λαός for Israel and ἔθνος for Gentiles (within Deut 32 see λαός in 32:6, 9, 36, 43 and ἔθνος in 32:8[2x], 21 [2x], 28, 43; though HT has גוי in 32:8, 21, 28, 43 and עם in 32:6, 8, 9, 21, 36, 43)." Wagner (*Heralds*, 315) notes that the Song of Moses is integral to the argument of Romans: "Paul quotes Deuteronomy 32:31 in Romans 10:19 and subsequently alludes to the same text in Romans 11:11–14. Further echoes of the Song of Moses may be heard in Romans 9:14 (Deut 32:4) and possibly in Romans 11:1 (Deut 32:8–9). In addition, Paul quotes Deuteronomy 32:35 in Romans 12:19."

76. Seifrid, "Romans," 689: "The Messiah also speaks in the Song of Moses ('and again he says' [15:10]). Paul draws the second citation in the series from Deut. 32:43 LXX. The text of the MT is rather difficult. As it stands, it reads, 'Rejoice, nations, his people.'" Textual difficulties must have arisen rather early, since a Qumran fragment of Deuteronomy here reads, "Praise, heavens, his people" (1QDeuteronomyb). Targum Onqelos likewise shifts to "Praise, Gentiles, his people." The LXX plausibly presupposes a haplography, by which ʿim ("with") has been omitted, and supplies it to the text. Paul, in any case, follows the septuagintal reading: "Rejoice, Gentiles, with his people." So similarly, Whittle, *Covenant Renewal*, 137–38. Rodríguez (*If You Call*, 281 n. 63) notes "both here and in v. 11, 'his people' or 'the people' [*ho laos* (autou)] refers to Israel, God's chosen people, rather than people in general."

for his mercy on both Jews and themselves."[77] While one might quibble with Witherington's distinction between "Jews and Jewish Christians," his general insight is germane.

Paul's solution to the problem he began to address in Rom 14:1 concerning the weak and the strong is not to seek to remove the identity of one group or the other; rather, he casts a vision for a doxological identity (a future, possible social identity) in which the nations of the world are worshipping together with Israel. Esler provides further clarity:

> Paul illustrates and reinforces this point with a string of scriptural quotations that speak of the place of the non-Judeans in the broad scheme of salvation, with v. 10 (a verbatim quotation from the LXX of Deut. 32:43) being particularly interesting in its image of non-Judeans and Judeans rejoicing in unison, an image that clearly reveals the underlying ethnic division that Paul has just said (Rom. 15:6) he wants to see ended: 'Rejoice, foreign nations, with his people' (15:10).[78]

This vision, at the same time, subverts the empire which claimed that it was the Romans who had unified the disparate peoples of the world for Rome's eternal glory. Jupiter says: "Romulus, proud in the tawny hide of the she-wolf, his nurse, shall take up the line, and found the walls of Mars and call the people Romans after his own name. For these I set no bounds in space or time; but have given empire without end" (Virgil, *Aeneid* 1.275–79 [Fairclough, LCL]).

Psalm 117:1 in Romans 15:11

In 15:11, Paul cites Ps 117:1 as the Davidic Messiah continues to speak: "And again: Praise the Lord all you nations (τὰ ἔθνη); and praise him all the people (οἱ λαοί)." Kruse sees here only a reference to the nations praising the Lord. In his reading, the distinct identity of Israel has been lost.[79] However, the verse makes a distinction between the nations (τὰ ἔθνη) and the people, i.e., Israel (οἱ λαοί). Wagner, rightly I think, based on Paul's interpretation of Isa 65:1–2 in Rom 10:20–21, thinks that ἔθνη and λαοί are not "synonyms, but [are] references to distinct groups: Gentiles

---

77. Witherington, *Romans*, 344.

78. Esler, *Conflict*, 354

79. Kruse, *Romans*, 534. Matera (*Romans*, 324) recognizes that "all the peoples" in the original psalm referred to the gentiles and not to Israel.

and Israel, respectively."[80] Seeing οἱ λαοί as reference to Israel as God's people is consistent with Paul's reference to Israel as "his people" in 15:10. If this is the case, then 15:11 is a further statement for the formation of a doxological identity: Israel and the nations are to worship God together.[81] This psalm is part of the Hallel liturgical cycle (113–18 MT), which gives it an eschatological orientation and suggests it may have been part of Paul's broader restoration theology for Israel (as well as a future, possible social identity). Regardless, the citation of Ps 117:1 (along with its similarities with Ps 18:49) suggests the focus is on more than gentile inclusion. In other words, "gentiles" is not what holds these citations together; rather, it is the dual eschatological participation and roles of the Messiah and Israel for the sake of the nations.[82] Thus, Garroway and Kruse have missed the significance of the chain. It is about the continuing salience of Israel's identity and vocation within the Christ-following community and the benefits that accrue to the nations because of it.[83] This becomes even clearer in the final citation.

Isaiah 11:10 in Romans 15:12

In 15:12, Paul cites Isa 11:10: "And again Isaiah says: The root of Jesse (ἡ ῥίζα τοῦ Ἰεσσαί) will come, he who arises (ὁ ἀνιστάμενος) to rule the nations; in him will the nations hope."[84] Kruse continues to downplay any restoration nuance for Israel in this section. For him, the citation "speaks of the place of the Gentiles among God's people and serves well Paul's purpose of affirming the status of Gentile believers in the Roman communities."[85] One senses the ghost of Bultmann floating by as regards the dismissal of Davidic messianic discourse in Paul.

---

80. Wagner, *Heralds*, 314. But see, Shum, *Paul's Use*, 229–31.

81. So similarly Wagner, *Heralds*, 315.

82. So similarly Windsor, *Paul*, 98.

83. Donaldson (*Paul*, 194–95) misses the significance of the chain as well. Windsor (*Paul*, 98) rightly concludes that "[t]hese texts affirm Jewish pre-eminence in the Christ-believing community, and also associate this pre-eminence directly with abundant soteriological blessing for Gentiles."

84. On ῥίζα in BDAG 906: "that which grows from a root, *shoot, scion . . . the scion from Jesse.*"

85. Kruse, *Romans*, 534. He at least acknowledges that it was seen as messianic within Judaism: 1Q28b 5:20–29; 4Q11 frag. 9–14; 4Q285 frag. 5 are cited by him.

Before turning to the citation, one idea should be made more explicit. Joshua Jipp has recently brought to the fore the role of royal ideology in Paul's Christology, especially as it relates to the way he explicitly draws on the Davidic discourse. He points out three ideas that have contributed to the hesitancy among Pauline scholars to accept Davidic discourse in Paul. First, the Heitmüller/Bousset/Bultmann history-of-religions approach, which asserted a split between Jewish and gentile Christianity, with the latter only interested in Jesus as κύριος. Second, the ubiquitous nature of the term χριστός with no apparent significance, which led to it being seen as a name and not a title. Third, interpreters have often assumed that Jewish messianism is (and can only be) what is found in Psalms of Solomon 17–18. Since Paul does not sound like that, they reason, he cannot possibly be a messianist and has no interest in a Davidic Messiah.[86] I would agree with Jipp (and Willitts) that Paul, to the contrary, was a Davidic messianist; his use of the term "Christ" was more than as a name, and the Bultmannian framework should be set aside.[87]

Returning to the citation in Rom 15:12, we note, first, that Paul leaves off ἐν τῇ ἡμέρᾳ "in that day" from Isa 11:10. This suggests that he understands himself to be in the messianic time now, unlike the author of Psalms of Solomon, for whom the Davidic vision was still anticipated (17:21–44). Many argue that the Davidic vision of Psalms of Solomon 17 differs too much from Paul. Jipp, however, thinks Paul views Christ as "the Davidic king . . . the just ruler and righteous sufferer who calls upon God to see his righteousness and vindicate him." The letter as a whole, furthermore, "centers upon a messianic figure, and opens and concludes with direct references to the Messiah's Davidic heritage (Rom. 1:3–4; 15:7–12), including his role as innocently suffering at the hands of his enemies (Rom 15:3)."[88]

Second, the phrase, "the root of Jesse," suggests that Paul thinks the promise made concerning the Davidic Messiah in the past has been confirmed by 2 Sam 7:12–16. The "root of Jesse" is messianic in Rev 5:5, "Then one of the elders said to me, 'Do not weep. See, the Lion of the tribe of Judah, the Root of David, has conquered, so that he can open the scroll and its seven seals," and in Rev 22:16, "It is I, Jesus, who sent my

---

86. Jipp, *Christ*, 4–16. He is not alone in this; see also Novenson, *Christ*, 137–73; Whitsett, "Son of God," 661–81; Zetterholm, "Paul," 37–40; Bultmann, *Theology*, 1.128–32.

87. Willitts, "Matthew," 46–49, especially as it relates to the gentiles.

88. Jipp, *Christ*, 257.

angel to you with this testimony for the churches. I am the root and the descendant of David, the bright morning star." This individual member of the Davidic dynasty was to become the focal point of hope for the nations. Paul picks up on this and contends that Jesus is this hoped-for Davidic king.[89]

Third, the presence of "he who arises" (ὁ ἀνιστάμενος) is taken by many interpreters to be a reference to Christ's resurrection.[90] A rhetorical move that focuses on the resurrection here could only occur by the use of the LXX in contrast to the MT.[91] Daniel Kirk is generally helpful on the role of the resurrection in Romans, but goes awry concerning the identity-formation implications in this verse. He concludes that "the creation of a mixed people of God ruled by the resurrected Messiah vindicates God's faithfulness to the promises contained in Scripture."[92] Kirk, as well as Garroway's solution of hybrid gentile-Jews, argue for a fusion (and dissolution) of existing identities that seems foreign to what we have discovered in Paul.[93] The continuation of both Jewish and gentile identities is significant because it is a proleptic experience of the future rescue of both Israel and the nations.[94]

Fourth, in Paul's appropriation of Isaiah, the Davidic Messiah also "rules the nations." Wright correctly notes that "a risen Messiah 'ruling the nations' is, further, packed with explosive political implications, especially in a letter to Rome whose emperor claimed the nations."[95] This is not to argue that Paul expected the Messiah to subjugate the nations.[96]

The emperor, however, clearly did see himself as the ruler of the nations. Seneca, for example, has Nero state: "Have I of all mortals found favor with Heaven and been chosen to serve on earth as vicar of the gods?

---

89. Fitzmyer, *Romans*, 707–8.

90. Hafemann ("Redemption," 211) suggests that a future coming in glory of "the root of Jesse" is in view.

91. Wagner, *Heralds*, 319.

92. Kirk, *Unlocking*, 54.

93. Garroway, *Paul's Gentile-Jews*, 69. See my critique on these approaches in Tucker, *Remain in Your Calling*, 48, 53, 77, 88, 165 n. 18, 173, 185.

94. So somewhat similarly, Hafemann, "Redemption," 208. He describes these identities, somewhat provocatively, as "distinct but equal identities." This prolepsis suggests variegated ecclesiology is a likely implication of this section; social and eschatological identities have a present as well as future expression.

95. Wright, "Romans," 748.

96. So similarly Bird, *Romans*, 487. Though dealing with the Gospel of John, Hunt's insights are relevant here ("Jesus Caesar," 364–71).

I am the arbiter of life and death for the nations" (*De clemetia* 1.1.2).[97] Paul would disagree, as would the Pss. Sol. 17:34: "[The Lord's anointed] will show mercy to all the Gentiles [who come] before him with reverent fear."[98] Further, Wagner points out that Paul's purpose in 15:12 is "to show that scripture prophesies the inclusion of Gentiles in the worshipping community as a result of what God has done in and through Jesus Christ."[99] It may seem that Wagner disagrees with the argument being put forth here; however, he also notes that this verse was chosen because of its connection to "Isaiah's story of the eschatological restoration of Israel."[100] Paul sees God's work among the nations moving along this dual track. The doxological identity Paul ascribes here is quite different from that found in Roman imperial ideology (Rom 12:1; 13:1–7). For Romans, the τὰ ἔθνη were the "defeated nations," but for Paul, they were part of God's restoration of Israel, the consummation of his purposes in the world.[101]

Conclusion: Paul's Prayer, and Future, Possible Social Identities

By way of conclusion for this section, Paul's discursive ritualization offers this hope-filled prayer: "May the God of hope fill you with all joy and peace in believing, so that you may abound in hope in the power of the Holy Spirit" (Rom 15:13). Paul has just described the differing ways that the Messiah serves both Jews and gentiles by forming a doxological community of mutual welcome. In such a composite group, existing identities continue, though in differing and transformed ways. The future orientation of such a group is crucial in the formation of a doxological social identity.

Miroslav Volf suggests that "hope, in a Christian sense, is love stretching itself into the future."[102] The reference to "hope" in 15:12 is now reiterated in 15:13 and provides a framework for a future, possible social identity. Here leaders offer cognitive alternatives focusing on individual

---

97. Cited in Carter, *Roman Empire*, 84.

98. Wagner, *Heralds*, 320 n. 52.

99. Wagner, *Heralds*, 323.

100. Wagner, *Heralds*, 323.

101. Lopez, *Apostle to the Conquered*, 142, and her understanding of τὰ ἔθνη as the "defeated nations."

102. Volf, "Human Flourishing," 13.

and group perceptions of changing membership or, likely in this case, improving existing ones.[103] With regard to the problem of table fellowship in the Roman groups described in 14:1—15:6, Paul thinks that the formation of a superordinate identity, described here as a doxological one (being included in the glory of God, 15:7), provides a way to think and act differently with regard to welcoming those that are different with regard to conviviality. This results in a future social identity characterized by joy, peace, and hope by the agency of the Holy Spirit . . . which sounds a lot like what he described earlier in regards to the nature of life together in the kingdom of God: "For the kingdom of God is not food and drink but righteousness and peace and joy in the Holy Spirit" (14:17).[104]

103. Campbell, "All God's Beloved," 74: "Paul saw a need for Gentiles to recognize and relate positively to their Jewish neighbors."

104. Bird (*Romans*, 487) picks up on some of this: "Hope is the anticipation of future salvation (8:24), a hope of glory (5:5), amidst the futility and afflictions of this age (8:20; 12:12)."

10

Conclusion

THIS BOOK STARTED OUT with the statement that Paul was no supersessionist. We are now in a position to pull together the various findings from our investigation in order to determine if that statement stands. The introduction highlighted several interpretive moves that resulted in supersessionist readings of Romans. These were critiqued in various ways throughout the book. It was found that Paul maintained a christological exclusivism while at the same time he upheld an ecclesiological variegation in which differing social implications for Jews and gentiles emerge from the gospel.

Next, it was discovered that Paul works with a nuanced salvation-historical and Jewish-apocalyptic framework. Israel's story has an ongoing and future component to it, and even in the apocalyptic inbreaking of the Messiah, there is continuity between creation and new creation. This suggests a need for a revision in the way the two dominant frameworks are applied to Romans. It was also revealed that Paul thinks in covenantal terms, and his covenantal theologizing remains focused on Israel, though the nations are still in view secondarily. Thus, Israel's covenantal identity was found to continue even after the revealing of the Messiah. This insight was supported further by the idea that Paul thought the restoration of Israel included a political component that did not lose focus on the land. Furthermore, Paul was found to maintain a stable referent in his use of Israel-like terms throughout Romans; the distinction between Jews and non-Jews remained salient for him.

Finally, Paul saw a continuing role for Torah both within the Christ-movement and as a demarcator of the Jewish people. He also upholds Torah and Torah-informed praxis for Jewish and gentile Christ-followers, though in different ways for each group. Thus, the key hermeneutical moves that result in supersessionist readings of Romans have been addressed, and the way is cleared for future analyses that presume that Paul was not a supersessionist in Romans, and that include a future possible social identity of Israel and the nations worshipping the God of Israel in a sense of mutual welcome. However, before this work concludes I would like to highlight the significance of these findings for the contemporary ecclesial setting.

Three contemporary implications emerge from this monograph, even though it has concentrated primarily on Paul's first-century context. First, Jewish covenantal identity continues in Paul's universalistic gospel. This has been the animating research focus throughout this work. Paul maintains the importance of Jewish priority and resists early forms of Marcionism or gentile boasting. These identity issues were particularly germane for in-Christ gentiles since they were in a constant state of liminality at the intersection of Jewish, local, and Roman practices. Thus, Paul's rhetoric was directed towards gentiles and the invention of their social identity in Christ. This suggests that the Jew and gentile distinction should be taken more seriously in contemporary reflections on Paul's theologizing. Often, interpreters go to Romans looking for answers to theological problems, specifically sometimes to figure out the problem Paul had with Judaism, when, instead, the letter is written to address identity problems. Paul did not have a problem with Jewish patterns of life that needed fixing. His problems were in-Christ gentile identity salience and overidentification with the Roman empire.[1] The supersessionism evident in far too much contemporary scholarship can be overcome by reframing the letter as an occasional one written to gentiles still functioning within the broader synagogue community in Rome. This reconstruction can then add to the advances already attained by those engaged in Jewish and Christian interfaith dialogue.[2] While Paul will continue to be a "sticky point" for many of these discussions, the Paul-within-Judaism paradigm portrayed here offers new paths forward since the gospel does not have to be framed in such a way that Judaism serves as its foil.[3] Jewish covenantal identity has not been obliterated (Rom 11:1, 29). Therefore, messianic Judaism should be seen as a necessary and needed pattern of life within the contemporary ecclesial context.[4] Messianic Jews provide a vital

1. Fredriksen, *Paul*, 157–59. Hardin, *Galatians*. Elliott, *Arrogance*.

2. Kinzer, *Searching*.

3. Nanos and Zetterholm, *Paul with Judaism*.

4. Rudolph and Willitts, *Introduction to Messianic Judaism*.

link between Judaism and Christianity. Their presence in contemporary ecclesial settings serves as a reminder of God's covenantal faithfulness to Israel.[5]

Second, if Paul's contextualization of Torah as described here is on target, then interpreters would be wise to recognize that the everyday, lived experiences of these Christ-followers required a halakhic flexibility that is evident in Romans. Paul does not think Torah has been terminated, so there seems to be a need to re-frame the way Torah is applied or conceptualized in contemporary ecclesial settings. For example, Torah as a continual demarcator of the Jewish people should be maintained; otherwise Jewish identity is eviscerated of much of its core. Torah is also relevant to in-Christ gentiles but not in the same way as for Jews. In-Christ gentile males are as a rule not to be circumcised (thus becoming Jewish); however, the halakhic stance Paul takes with these "ex-pagan gentiles" is such that they would appear to outsiders as very Jewish-like.[6] This raises interesting identity-based questions today since in-Christ gentile identity is usually not thought to be connected to Jewish patterns of life. However, gentile identity in Christ is not a stand-alone identity; thus a closer posture of welcome towards Jews could renew gentile identity in Christ, especially as it relates to contemporary marginalized identity-based groups.[7] Torah itself is never a lone actor; the sphere in which it functions determines its effect.[8] This raises important challenges to the accepted view that those in Christ only fulfill Torah but do not "do" it. The close connection between the agency of the Spirit and the "second table" of commandments suggests much more continuity is in view for Paul.[9] Thus, some of the debates about what constitutes Christ's lordship may be missing Paul's point.[10] In Romans, Paul maintains the continuing validity of the law of Moses.

Third, this study reveals the need for a post-supersessionist hermeneutical approach. There are five key interpretive points that contribute to supersessionist readings. One of the most important ones

---

5. Rudolph, "Messianic Jews," 58–84. McDermott, *The New Christian Zionism*.

6. Fredriksen, *Paul*, 74.

7. Jennings, *The Christian Imagination*. Collins, *All But Invisible*. Rah, *The Next Evangelicalism*. Westfall, *Paul and Gender*.

8. Snodgrass, "Spheres," 93–113.

9. Fredriksen, *Paul*, 118.

10. Campbell, *Paul and the Creation*. Ehrensperger, *Paul and the Dynamics*. Tucker and Koessler, *All Together*.

relates to the standard salvation-historical and Barthian apocalyptic frameworks, since they often reinforce replacement theologizing.[11] The Jewish apocalyptic approach offers a better way forward since it maintains more continuity between creation and new creation.[12] Thus, Paul can be read as a figure of Second Temple Judaism.[13] All too often, the end result of Paulinist parallel studies is that scholars highlight the ideas of Jewish writers, and then Paul simply is thought to be their opposite.[14] Their approach reinforces the view that Paul should be seen in his Jewish context but without too much Jewishness.[15] The arguments put forth in this book related to the food laws, the land promise, the law of righteousness, and Davidic Messiah, and suggest, rather, that Paul fits comfortably within the diverse expressions of Jewish patterns of life in the mid-first century. This also means that when Paul cites passages from Israel's scriptural tradition, it should not be assumed that he has written gentiles into the promises that were originally given to historic Israel.[16] Romans 9:24–26 and 15:9–12 are two examples where the original referent remains. The same is true for Rom 4:13 where the land promise is often thought to have been reinterpreted and transcendentalized. Even there, as well as in 15:8, Paul maintains a hope for the confirmation of the patriarchal promises for the restoration of Israel for the sake of the nations. The way forward is a post-supersessionist canonical reading strategy that does not occlude Israel's story.[17] Soulen's metanarrative (creation, fall, Israel, redemption, and consummation) should form the basis of this transformed reading strategy.[18] The standard promise-fulfillment hermeneutic results in supersessionist outcomes and should be replaced by a promise-confirmation approach that allows for the expansion of referent but not to the degree that identities are dissolved.[19] One way to accomplish this is Boulton's model in which the earlier parts of the story

---

11. Wright, *Paul and the Faithfulness of God*. Watson, *Paul, Judaism*.

12. Harink, *Paul*. Reynolds and Stuckenbruck, *The Jewish Apocalyptic Tradition*.

13. Boccaccini and Segovia, *Paul the Jew*; Nanos, *Reading Paul*; Rudolph, *A Jew to the Jews*.

14. Barclay, *Paul*.

15. Blackwell, Goodrich, and Maston, *Reading Romans in Context*.

16. Watson, *Paul and the Hermeneutics*; Wright, *Climax*; Bird, *An Anomalous Jew*.

17. Sonderegger, *The Doctrine of God*, 407.

18. Soulen, *The God of Israel*.

19. Bock , "Scripture Citing Scripture," 255–76.

maintain their fundamental significance as the story continues.[20] Finally, since identity precedes theology, the tools of social identity theory need to be brought to bear.[21] This monograph allowed the insights from social identity theory to guide the reading strategy which resulted in a more concrete and social understanding of the lived experience of the early Christ-followers in Rome. Willie Jennings has noted that Christian theology missed the continuing significance of Jewish identity, and the results were disastrous for key aspects of the Christian tradition.[22] Social-scientific tools can help alert interpreters to the identity issues involved in order to correct some of the errors in the history of interpretation, often by exposing otherwise hidden presuppositions.[23] Existing identities continue to matter within the Christ-movement, and they should matter in our contemporary theology as well.

20. Boulton, "Supersession," 18–29.

21. Campbell, *Paul and the Creation*, 52; Tucker, *You Belong to Christ*; Tucker, *Remain in Your Calling*; Zoccali, *Reading Philippians*; Windsor, *Reading Ephesians and Colossians*.

22. Jennings, *The Christian Imagination*. See also Kinzer, *Postmissionary*, 27–49.

23. Clarke and Tucker, "Social History," 41–58; Ehrensperger, *Mutually Encouraged*, 5–42.

Bibliography

Aageson, James W. *Written Also for Our Sake: Paul and the Art of Biblical Interpretation.* Louisville: Westminster/John Knox, 1993.

Abasciano, Brian J. *Paul's Use of the Old Testament in Romans 9:1–9: An Intertextual and Theological Exegesis.* London: T. & T. Clark, 2005.

Achtemeier, Paul J. *1 Peter: A Commentary on First Peter.* Minneapolis: Fortress, 1996.

Adeyemi, Femi. *The New Covenant Torah in Jeremiah and the Law of Christ in Paul.* New York: Lang, 2006

Alkier, Stefan. "New Testament Studies on the Basis of Categorical Semiotics." In *Reading the Bible Intertextually,* edited by Richard B. Hays, Stefan Alkier, and Leroy Andrew Huizenga, 223–48. Waco, TX: Baylor University Press, 2009.

Avidov, Avi. *Not Reckoned Among Nations: The Origins of the So-Called "Jewish Question" in Roman Antiquity.* TSAJ 128. Tübingen, Germany: Mohr Siebeck, 2009.

Bachmann, Michael. *Anti-Judaism in Galatians? Exegetical Studies on a Polemical Letter and on Paul's Theology.* Grand Rapids: Eerdmans, 2008.

Badenas, Robert. *Christ the End of the Law: Romans 10.4 in Pauline Perspective.* Sheffield, UK: JSOT, 1985.

Barclay, John M. G. "'By the Grace of God I Am What I Am': Grace and Agency in Philo and Paul." In *Divine and Human Agency in Paul and His Cultural Environment,* edited by John M. G. Barclay and Simon J. Gathercole, 140–57. London: T. & T. Clark, 2006.

———. "'Do We Undermine the Law?': A Study of Romans 14.1—15.6." In *Pauline Churches and Diaspora Jews,* edited by John M. G. Barclay, 37–59. WUNT 275. Tübingen: Mohr Siebeck, 2011.

———. *Jews in the Mediterranean Diaspora from Alexander to Trajan (323 BCE–117 CE).* Edinburgh: T. & T. Clark, 1996.

———. *Paul and the Gift.* Grand Rapids: Eerdmans, 2015.

———. "Unnerving Grace: Approaching Romans 9–11 from The Wisdom of Solomon." In *Between Gospel and Election,* edited by Florian Wilk and J. Ross Wagner, 91–109. WUNT 257. Tübingen: Mohr Siebeck, 2010.

Barrett, C. K. *The Epistle to the Romans.* Peabody, MA: Hendrickson, 1991.

Barth, Karl. *Church Dogmatics.* Translated by G. W. Bromiley. Edinburgh: T. & T. Clark, 1956–69.

———. *Epistle to the Romans.* Translated by E. Hoskyns. Oxford: Oxford University Press, 1933.

Battle, John A., Jr. "Paul's Use of the Old Testament in Romans 9:25–26." *Grace Theological Journal* 2 (1981) 115–29.

Baur, F. C. *The Church History of the First Three Centuries.* Translated by Allan Menzies. London: Williams & Norgate, 1878.

Beale, G. K. *A New Testament Biblical Theology: The Unfolding of the Old Testament in the New.* Grand Rapids: Baker, 2011.

Beale, G. K., and Benjamin L. Gladd. *Hidden But Now Revealed: A Biblical Theology of Mystery.* Downers Grove, IL: InterVarsity, 2014.

Bell, Catherine M. *Ritual: Perspectives and Dimensions.* New York: Oxford University Press, 1997.

Bell, Richard H. *Provoked to Jealousy: The Origin and Purpose of the Jealousy Motif in Romans 9–11.* WUNT 2.63. Tübingen: Mohr (Siebeck), 1994.

Bernat, David A. *Sign of the Covenant Circumcision in the Priestly Tradition.* Atlanta: Society of Biblical Literature, 2009.

Bird, Michael F. *An Anomalous Jew.* Grand Rapids: Eerdmans, 2016.

———. *Evangelical Theology.* Grand Rapids: Zondervan, 2013.

———. "Mark: Interpreter or Peter and Disciple of Paul." In *Paul and the Gospels: Christologies, Conflicts, and Convergences,* edited by Michael F. Bird and Joel Willitts, 31–61. London: T. & T. Clark, 2011.

———. *Romans.* The Story of God Bible Commentary. Grand Rapids: Zondervan, 2015.

Bjoraker, Bill. "'To the Jew First . . .': The Meaning of Jewish Priority in World Evangelism." *International Journal of Frontier Missions* 21 (2004) 110–16.

Black, Matthew. *Romans.* NCB. Grand Rapids: Eerdmans, 1984.

Blackwell, Ben C. "Immortal Glory and the Problem of Death in Romans 3.23." *JSNT* 32 (2010) 285–308.

Blackwell, Ben C., John Goodrich, and Jason Maston, eds. *Reading Romans in Context: Paul and Second Temple Judaism.* Grand Rapids: Zondervan, 2015.

Boccaccini, Gabriele, and Giovanni Ibba, eds. *Enoch and the Mosaic Torah: The Evidence of Jubilees.* Grand Rapids: Eerdmans, 2009.

Boccaccini, Gabriele, and Carlos A. Segovia, eds. *Paul the Jew: Rereading the Apostle as a Figure of Second Temple Judaism.* Minneapolis, Fortress, 2016.

Bock, Darrell. "Scripture Citing Scripture." In *Interpreting the New Testament Text: Introduction to the Art and Science of Greek Exegesis,* edited by Darrell Bock and Buist M. Fanning, 255–76. Wheaton, IL: Crossway, 2006.

Bockmuehl, Markus N. A. *Jewish Law in Gentile Churches: Halakhah and the Beginning of Christian Public Ethics.* Edinburgh: T. & T. Clark, 2000.

———. *Revelation and Mystery in Ancient Judaism and Pauline Christianity.* WUNT 2.36. Tübingen: J.C.B. Mohr, 1990.

Boulton, Matthew. "Supersession or Subsession? Exodus Typology, the Christian Eucharist and the Jewish Passover Meal" *Scottish Journal of Theology* 66 (2013) 18–29.

Boyarin, Daniel. *Border Lines: The Partition of Judaeo-Christianity.* Philadelphia: University of Pennsylvania Press, 2004.

———. *A Radical Jew: Paul and the Politics of Identity.* Berkeley: University of California Press, 1997.

Brewer, Marilynn B., and Michael D. Silver. "Group Distinctiveness, Social Identification, and Collective Mobilization." In *Self, Identity, and Social Movements,* edited by Sheldon Stryker, Timothy J. Owens, and Robert W. White, 153–71. Minneapolis: University of Minnesota Press, 2000.

Brindle, Wayne A. "'To the Jew First': Rhetoric, Strategy, History, or Theology?" *BSac* 159 (2002) 221–33.

Brueggemann, Walter. *The Land: Place as Gift, Promise, and Challenge in Biblical Faith.* Philadelphia: Fortress, 1977.

Bultmann, Rudolf. *Theology of the New Testament.* London: SCM, 1952.

Burge, Gary M. *Jesus and the Land: The New Testament Challenge to "Holy Land" Theology.* Grand Rapids: Baker, 2010.

Burke, Trevor J. *Adopted into God's Family: Exploring a Pauline Metaphor.* Nottingham, UK: Apollos, 2006.

Burnett, David. "'So Shall Your Seed Be': Paul's Use of Genesis 15:5 in Romans 4:18 in Light of Early Jewish Deification Traditions." *Journal for the Study of Paul and His Letters* 5 (2015) 211–36.

Byrne, Brendan. *Romans.* Collegeville, MN: Liturgical, 1996.

Cadbury, Henry. "Overconversion in Paul's Churches." In *The Joy of Study: Papers on New Testament and Other Related Subjects Presented in Honor of Frederick Clifton Grant*, edited by Sherman E. Johnson, 43–50. New York: Macmillan, 1951.

Campbell, Constantine R. *Basics of Verbal Aspect in Biblical Greek.* Grand Rapids: Zondervan, 2008.

Campbell, Douglas. *The Deliverance of God: An Apocalyptic Rereading of Justification in Paul.* Grand Rapids: Eerdmans, 2013.

Campbell, William S. "'All God's Beloved in Rome!': Jewish Roots and Christian Identity." In *Celebrating Romans: Template for Pauline Theology: Essays in Honor of Robert Jewett*, edited by Sheila E. McGinn and Robert Jewett, 67–82. Grand Rapids: Eerdmans, 2004.

———. "Covenantal Theology and Participation in Christ: Pauline Perspectives on Transformation." In *Paul and Judaism: Crosscurrents in Pauline Exegesis and the Study of Jewish-Christian Relations*, edited by Reimund Bieringer and Didier Pollefeyt, 41–60. LNTS 463. London: T. & T. Clark, 2012.

———. "Differentiation and Discrimination in Paul's Ethnic Discourse" *Transformation* 30 (2013) 157–68.

———. "Divergent Images of Paul and His Mission." In *Reading Israel in Romans: Legitimacy and Plausibility of Divergent Interpretations*, edited by Cristina Grenholm and Daniel Patte, 186–208. Harrisburg, PA: Trinity, 2000.

———. "'Let Us Maintain Peace' (Romans 5:2): Reconciliation and Social Responsibility." In *The Bible in Church, Academy, and Culture: Essays in Honour of the Reverend Dr. John Turdo Williams*, edited by Alan P. F. Sell, 58–80. Eugene, OR: Pickwick, 2011.

———. *The Nations in the Divine Economy: Paul's Covenantal Hermeneutics and Participation in Christ.* Minneapolis: Fortress, 2018.

———. *Paul and the Creation of Christian Identity.* London: T. & T. Clark, 2006.

———. "Paul, Anti-Semitism, and Early Christian Identity Formation." In *Paul the Jew: Reading the Apostle as a Figure of Second Temple Judaism*, edited by Gabriele Boccaccini and Carlos Segovia, 301–40. Minneapolis, MN: Fortress.

———. *Paul's Gospel in an Intercultural Context: Jew and Gentile in the Letter to the Romans.* Frankfurt am Main: Lang, 1991.

———. "'A Remnant of Them Will Be Saved' (Rom 9:27): Understanding Paul's Conception of the Faithfulness of God to Israel." *The Journal of the Jesus Movement in its Jewish Setting* 2 (2015) 79–101.

———. "Romans III as a Key to the Structure and Thought of Romans." In *The Romans Debate*, edited by Karl P. Donfried, 251–64. Peabody, MA: Hendrickson, 1991.

———. "The Rule of Faith in Romans 12:1—15:13." In *Pauline Theology*, Vol. 3, edited by D. M. Hay and E. Johnson, 259–86. Minneapolis: Augsburg Fortress, 1995.

———. *Unity and Diversity in Christ: Interpreting Paul in Context: Collected Essays*. Eugene, OR: Cascade, 2013.

Carraway, George. *Christ Is God Over All: Romans 9:5 in the Context of Romans 9–11*. LNTS 489. London: Bloomsbury, 2015.

Carson, D. A. "Mystery and Fulfillment: Toward a More Comprehensive Paradigm of Paul's Understanding of the Old and the New." In *Justification and Variegated Nomism*, Vol. 2, *The Paradoxes of Paul*, edited by D. A. Carson, Peter T. O'Brien, and Mark A. Seifrid, 393–436. Grand Rapids: Baker, 2004.

———. "Pauline Inconsistency: Reflections on 1 Corinthians 9.1–23 and Galatians 2.11–14." *Churchman* 100 (1986) 6–45.

Carter, Warren. *The Roman Empire and the New Testament: An Essential Guide*. Nashville: Abingdon, 2006.

Casey, Maurice. *From Jewish Prophet to Gentile God*. Louisville: Westminster/John Knox, 1991.

Castelli, Elizabeth A. "Romans." In *Searching the Scriptures*, Vol. 2, *A Feminist Commentary*, edited by Elisabeth Schüssler Fiorenza, 272–300. New York: Crossroad, 1994.

Charlesworth, James Hamilton. "Wright's Paradigm of Early Jewish Thought: Avoidance of Anachronism?" In *God and the Faithfulness of Paul: A Critical Examination of the Pauline Theology of N. T. Wright*, edited by C. Heilig, J. T. Hewitt, and M. Bird, 207–34. Tübingen: Mohr Siebeck, 2016.

Christiansen, Ellen Juhl. *The Covenant in Judaism and Paul: A Study of Ritual Boundaries as Identity Markers*. Leiden: Brill, 1995.

Ciampa, Roy E. "Deuteronomy in Galatians and Romans." In *Deuteronomy in the New Testament*, edited by M. J. J. Menken and Steve Moyise, 99–117. LNTS 358. London: T. & T. Clark, 2007.

———. "The History of Redemption." In *Central Themes in Biblical Theology*, edited by Scott J. Hafemann and Paul R. House, 254–308. Grand Rapids: Baker, 2007.

Cinnirella, Marco. "Exploring Temporal Aspects of Social Identity: The Concept of Possible Social Identities." *European Journal of Social Psychology* 28 (1998) 227–48.

Clarke, Andrew D., and J. Brian Tucker. "Social History and Social Theory in the Study of Social Identity," In *T. & T. Clark Handbook to Social Identity in the New Testament*, edited by J. Brian Tucker, and Coleman A. Baker, 41–58. London: Bloomsbury T. &T. Clark, 2014.

Cohen, Shaye J. D. Review of *Contesting Conversion: Genealogy, Circumcision, and Identity in Ancient Judaism and Christianity*, by Matthew Thiessen. *CBQ* 75 (2013) 379–81.

———. *Why Aren't Jewish Women Circumcised? Gender and Covenant in Judaism*. Berkley, CA: University of California Press, 2005.

Collins, John J. *The Invention of Judaism: Torah and Jewish Identity from Deuteronomy to Paul*. Oakland, CA: University of California Press, 2017.

Collins, Nate. *All But Invisible: Exploring Identity Questions at the Intersection of Faith, Gender & Sexuality*. Grand Rapids: Zondervan, 2017.

Concannon, Cavan W. *"When You Were Gentiles": Specters of Ethnicity in Roman Corinth and Paul's Corinthian Correspondence.* New Haven: Yale University Press, 2014.

Constantineanu, Corneliu. *The Social Significance of Reconciliation in Paul's Theology: Narrative Readings in Romans.* LNTS 421. London: T. & T. Clark, 2010.

Conway, Kevin P. *The Promises of God: The Background of Paul's Exclusive Use of "epangelia" for the Divine Pledge.* BZNW 211. Berlin: De Gruyter, 2014.

Coppins, Wayne. *The Interpretation of Freedom in the Letters of Paul: With Special Reference to the "German" Tradition.* WUNT 2.261. Tübingen, Germany: Mohr Siebeck, 2009.

Cosgrove, Charles H. "Did Paul Value Ethnicity?" *CBQ* 68 (2006) 268–90.

Cottrell, Jack. *Romans.* Joplin, MO: College, 2005.

Craigie, Peter C. *Psalms 1–50.* WBC. Waco, TX: Word, 1983.

Cranfield, Charles. E. B. *A Critical and Exegetical Commentary on the Epistle to the Romans.* ICC. 2 vols. Edinburgh: T. & T. Clark, 1975.

Cranford, Michael. "Abraham in Romans 4: The Father of All Who Believe." *NTS* 41 (1995) 71–88.

Crisler, Channing L. *Reading Romans as Lament: Paul's Use of Old Testament Lament in His Most Famous Letter.* Eugene, OR: Pickwick, 2016.

Cromhout, Marcus. "Israelite Ethnic Identity Responding to the Roman *Imperium* in Revelation." In *T. & T. Clark Handbook to Social Identity in the New Testament,* edited by J. Brian Tucker and Coleman A. Baker, 527–50. London: Bloomsbury/T. & T. Clark, 2014.

Cunningham, Philip. "Paul's Letters and the Relationship between the People of Israel and the Church Today." Paper presented at the New Perspectives on Paul and the Jews Conference, Katholieke Universiteit, Leuven, 2009.

D'Angelo, Mary R. "Roman 'Family Values' and the Apologetic Concerns of Philo and Paul: Reading the Sixth Commandment." *NTS* 61 (2015) 525–46.

Das, A. Andrew. *Paul and the Jews.* Peabody, MA: Hendrickson, 2003.

———. *Paul, the Law, and the Covenant.* Peabody, MA: Hendrickson, 2001.

———. "'Praise the Lord, All You Gentiles': The Encoded Audience of Romans 15.7–13." *JSNT* 34 (2011) 90–110.

———. *Solving the Romans Debate.* Minneapolis: Fortress, 2007.

Davies, Glenn N. *Faith and Obedience in Romans: A Study in Romans 1–4.* Sheffield, UK: Sheffield, 1990.

Davies, W. D. *The Gospel and the Land: Early Christianity and Jewish Territorial Doctrine.* Berkeley: University of California Press, 1974.

———. "Paul and the People of Israel." *NTS* 24 (1977) 4–39.

Davis, Stephan K. *The Antithesis of the Ages: Paul's Reconfiguration of Torah.* Washington, DC: Catholic Biblical Association of America, 2002.

Deming, Will. "Paul and Indifferent Things." In *Paul and the Greco-Roman World,* edited by J. Paul Sampley, 384–403. Harrisburg, PA: Trinity, 2003.

———. *Paul on Marriage and Celibacy: The Hellenistic Background of 1 Corinthians 7.* Cambridge: Cambridge University Press, 1995.

Dodd, C. H. *The Epistle of Paul to the Romans.* New York: Harper and Brothers, 1932.

Doering, Lutz. "The Reception of the Book of Exodus in the *Book of Jubilees.*" In *The Book of Exodus: Composition, Reception, and Interpretation,* edited by Thomas B. Dozeman, Craig A. Evans, and Joel N. Lohr, 485–510. Leiden: Brill, 2014.

Donaldson, Terence L. "'The Field God Has Assigned': Geography and Mission in Paul." In *Religious Rivalries in the Early Roman Empire and the Rise of Christianity*, edited by Leif E. Vaage, 109–37. Waterloo, Ontario: Published for the Canadian Corp. for Studies in Religion/Corporation Canadienne des Sciences Religieuses by Wilfrid Laurier University Press, 2006.

———. "'Gentile Christianity' as a Category in the Study of Christian Origins." Paper presented at SBL Annual Meeting, San Francisco, CA, 2011.

———. "Jewish Christianity, Israel's Stumbling and the *Sonderweg* Reading of Paul." *JSNT* 29 (2006) 27–54.

———. *Jews and Anti-Judaism in the New Testament: Decision Points and Divergent Interpretations*. Waco, TX: Baylor University Press, 2010.

———. *Judaism and the Gentiles: Jewish Patterns of Universalism (to 135 CE)*. Waco, TX: Baylor University Press, 2007.

———. *Paul and the Gentiles: Remapping the Apostle's Convictional World*. Minneapolis: Fortress, 1997.

———. "Paul within Judaism: A Critical Evaluation from a 'New Perspective' Perspective." In *Paul within Judaism: Restoring the First-Century Context to the Apostle*, edited by Mark D. Nanos and Magnus Zetterholm, 277–301. Minneapolis: Fortress, 2015.

———. "Supersessionism and Early Christian Self-Definition." *The Journal of the Jesus Movement in its Jewish Setting* 3 (2016) 1–32.

Donfried, Karl P. *The Romans Debate*. Peabody, MA: Hendrickson, 1991.

Duff, Paul B. *Moses in Corinth: The Apologetic Context of 2 Corinthians 3*. Supplements to Novum Testamentum 159. Leiden: Brill, 2015.

Dunn, James D. G. *The Epistle to the Galatians*. BNTC 9. Grand Rapids: Baker Academic, 1993.

———. "The Jew Paul and His Meaning for Israel." In *A Shadow of Glory: Reading the New Testament after the Holocaust*, edited by Tod Linafelt, 201–15. London: Routledge, 2002.

———, ed. *Paul and the Mosaic Law*. Grand Rapids: Eerdmans, 2001.

———. *Romans. 1–8*. WBC. Dallas, TX: Word, 1988.

———. *Romans. 9–16*. WBC. Dallas, TX: Word, 1988.

———. *The Theology of Paul the Apostle*. Grand Rapids: Eerdmans, 1998.

Dunne, John Anthony. "Suffering and Covenantal Hope in Galatians: A Critique of the 'Apocalyptic Reading' and Its Proponents." *SJT* 68 (2015) 1–15.

Eastman, Susan G. "Israel and the Mercy of God: A Re-Reading of Galatians 6:16 and Romans 9–11." *NTS* 56 (2010) 367–95.

Eco, Umberto. *Semiotics and the Philosophy of Language*. Bloomington, IN: Indiana University Press, 1984.

Ehrensperger, Kathy. "'Called to be Saints': The Identity-Shaping Dimension of Paul's Priestly Discourse in Romans." In *Reading Paul in Context: Explorations in Identity Formation. Essays in Honour of William S. Campbell*, edited by Kathy Ehrensperger and J. Brian Tucker, 90–112. LNTS 428. London: Bloomsbury/T. & T. Clark, 2010.

———. "Narratives of Belonging: The Role of Paul's Genealogical Reasoning." *Early Christianity* 8 (2017) 373–92.

———. "Paul and the Authority of Scripture: A Feminist Perspective." In *As It Is Written: Studying Paul's Use of Scripture*, edited by Stanley E. Porter and Christopher D. Stanley, 291–319. Atlanta: SBL, 2008.

———. *Paul and the Dynamics of Power: Communication and Interaction in the Early Christ-Movement.* London: T. & T. Clark, 2007.

———. *Paul at the Crossroads of Cultures: Theologizing in the Space-Between.* London: Bloomsbury, 2013.

———. "The Pauline Ἐκκλησίαι and Images of Community in Enoch Traditions." In *Paul the Jew: Rereading the Apostle as a Figure of Second Temple Judaism*, edited by Gabriele Boccaccini and Carlos A. Segovia, 183–216. Minneapolis: Fortress, 2016.

———. *That We May Be Mutually Encouraged: Feminism and the New Perspective in Pauline Studies.* London: T. & T. Clark, 2004.

———. "To Eat or Not to Eat—Is That the Question? Table Disputes in Corinth." In *Decisive Meals: Table Politics in Biblical Literature*, edited by Nathan MacDonald, Luzia Sutter Rehmann, and Kathy Ehrensperger, 134–50. London: Bloomsbury, 2013.

Eisenbaum, Pamela Michelle. *Paul Was Not a Christian: The Real Message of a Misunderstood Apostle.* New York: HarperOne, 2009.

Elliott, Neil. *The Arrogance of Nations: Reading Romans in the Shadow of Empire.* Paul in Critical Contexts. Minneapolis: Fortress, 2008.

———. "The Letter to the Romans." In *A Postcolonial Commentary on the New Testament Writings*, edited by Fernando F. Segovia and R. S. Sugirtharajah, 194–219. London: T. & T. Clark, 2009.

———. *The Rhetoric of Romans: Argumentative Constraint and Strategy and Paul's Dialogue with Judaism.* Minneapolis: Fortress, 2007.

Engberg-Pedersen, Troels. "'Everything is Clean' and 'Everything That is Not of Faith is Sin': The Logic of Pauline Casuistry in Romans 14.1—15.13." *Paul, Grace and Freedom Essays in Honour of John K. Riches*, edited by Paul Middleton, Angus Paddison, and Karen J. Wenell, 22–38. London: T. & T. Clark, 2009.

———. *Paul and the Stoics.* Louisville, KY: Westminster John Knox, 2000.

Esler, Philip F. *Conflict and Identity in Romans: The Social Setting of Paul's Letter.* Minneapolis: Fortress, 2003.

Eysenck, Michael W. *Principles of Cognitive Psychology.* Hove, UK: Psychology, 2001.

Fitzmyer, Joseph A. *Romans: A New Translation with Introduction and Commentary.* New York: Doubleday, 1993.

Forman, Mark. *The Politics of Inheritance in Romans.* Cambridge: Cambridge University Press, 2011.

Foster, Robert B. *Renaming Abraham's Children: Election, Ethnicity, and the Interpretation of Scripture in Romans 9.* WUNT 2.421. Tübingen: Mohr Siebeck, 2016.

Fredriksen, Paula. *Augustine and the Jews: A Christian Defense of Jews and Judaism.* New York: Doubleday, 2008.

———. "How Jewish Is God? Divine Ethnicity in Paul's Theology." *JBL* 137 (2018) 193–212.

———. "Judaism, the Circumcision of Gentiles, and Apocalyptic Hope: Another Look at Galatians 1 and 2." *JTS* 42 (1991) 532–64.

———. "Judaizing the Nations: The Ritual Demands of Paul's Gospel." *NTS* 56 (2010) 232–52.

———. "Mandatory Retirement: Ideas in the Study of Christian Origins Whose Time Has Come to Go." In *Israel's God and Rebecca's Children: Christology and Community in Early Judaism and Christianity. Essays in Honor of Larry W.*

Hurtado and Alan F. Segal, edited by David B. Capes et al., 25–38. Waco, TX: Baylor University Press, 2007.

———. *Paul the Pagans' Apostle*. New Haven: Yale University Press, 2017.

———. "The Question of Worship: Gods, Pagans, and the Redemption of Israel." In *Paul within Judaism: Restoring the First-Century Context to the Apostle*, edited by Mark D. Nanos and Magnus Zetterholm, 175–201. Minneapolis: Fortress, 2015.

Fruchtenbaum, Arnold. "To the Jew First in the New Millennium: A Dispensational Perspective." In *To the Jew First: The Case for Jewish Evangelism in Scripture and History*, edited by Darrell L. Bock and Mitch Glaser, 189–216. Grand Rapids: Kregel, 2008.

Gadenz, Pablo T. *Called from the Jews and from the Gentiles: Pauline Ecclesiology in Romans 9–11*. Tübingen: Mohr Siebeck, 2009.

Gard, Daniel L. "The Church's Scripture and Functional Marcionism." *CBQ* 74 (2010) 209–24.

Garroway, Joshua D. *Paul's Gentile-Jews: Neither Jew nor Gentile, But Both*. New York: Palgrave Macmillan, 2012.

Gaston, Lloyd. *Paul and the Torah*. Vancouver: University of British Columbia Press, 1987.

Gathercole, Simon J. *Where Is Boasting? Early Jewish Soteriology and Paul's Response in Romans 1–5*. Grand Rapids: Eerdmans, 2002.

Gaventa, Beverly Roberts. *Apocalyptic Paul: Cosmos and Anthropos in Romans 5–8*. Waco, TX: Baylor University Press, 2013.

———. "Questions about *Nomos*, Answers about *Christos*: Romans 10:4 in Context." In *Torah Ethics*, edited by Susan J. Wendel, 121–34. Grand Rapids: Eerdmans, 2016.

———. "Thinking from Christ to Israel: Romans 9–11 in Apocalyptic Context." In *Paul and the Apocalyptic Imagination*, edited by Ben C. Blackwell, John K. Goodrich, and Jason Maston, 239–55. Minneapolis: Fortress, 2016.

———. *When in Romans: An Invitation to Linger with the Gospel According to Paul*. Grand Rapids: Baker, 2016.

Givens, Tommy. *We the People Israel and the Catholicity of Jesus*. Minneapolis: Fortress, 2014.

Glenny, W. Edward. "The 'People of God' in Romans 9:25–26." *BSac* 152 (1995) 42–59.

Goodrich, John K. "From Slaves of Sin to Slaves of God: Reconsidering the Origin of Paul's Slavery Metaphor in Romans 6." *BBR* 23 (2013) 509–30.

———. "Sold under Sin: Echoes of Exile in Romans 7.14–25." *NTS* 59 (2013) 476–95.

———. "Until the Fullness of the Gentiles Comes In." *Journal for the Study of Paul and his Letters* 6 (2016) 5–32.

Gorman, Michael J. *Becoming the Gospel: Paul, Participation, and Mission*. Grand Rapids: Eerdmans, 2015.

Gregory, Bradley C. "Abraham as the Jewish Ideal: Exegetical Traditions in Sirach 44:19–21." *CBQ* 70 (2008) 66–81.

Grieb, A. Katherine. *The Story of Romans: A Narrative Defense of God's Righteousness*. Louisville: Westminster John Knox, 2002.

Grindheim, Sigurd. "Election and the Role of Israel." In *God and the Faithfulness of Paul: A Critical Examination of the Pauline Theology of N. T. Wright*, edited by Christoph Heilig, J. Thomas Hewitt, and Michael F. Bird, 329–46. Tübingen: Mohr Siebeck, 2016.

Hafemann, Scott J. *Paul, Moses, and the History of Israel: The Letter/Spirit Contrast and the Argument from Scripture in 2 Corinthians 3*. Peabody, MA: Hendrickson, 1996.

———. "The Redemption of Israel for the Sake of the Gentiles," In *Introduction to Messianic Judaism*, edited by David J. Rudolph and Joel Willitts, 206–13. Grand Rapids: Zondervan, 2013.

Hagner, Donald. "Paul as a Jewish Believer—According to his Letters." In *Jewish Believers in Jesus: The Early Centuries*, edited by Oskar Skarsaune and Reidar Hvalvik, 96–120. Peabody, MA: Hendrickson, 2007.

———. "Paul's Quarrel with Judaism." In *Anti-Semitism and Early Christianity: Issues of Polemic and Faith*, edited by Craig A. Evans and Donald A. Hagner, 128–50. Minneapolis: Fortress, 1993.

Hakola, Raimo. "Social Identities and Group Phenomena in Second Temple Judaism." In *Explaining Christian Origins and Early Judaism: Contributions from Cognitive and Social Science*, edited by Petri Luomanen, Ilkka Pyysiäinen, and Risto Uro, 259–76. Leiden: Brill, 2007.

Halpern-Amaru, Betsy. *Rewriting the Bible: Land and Covenant in Post-Biblical Jewish Literature*. Valley Forge, PA: Trinity, 1994.

Hardin, Justin K. "Equality in the Church." In *Introduction to Messianic Judaism*, edited by David J. Rudolph and Joel Willitts, 224–34. Grand Rapids: Zondervan, 2013.

———. *Galatians and the Imperial Cult: A Critical Analysis of the First-Century Social Context of Paul's Letter*. Tübingen: Mohr Siebeck, 2012.

———. "'If I Still Proclaim Circumcision' (Galatians 5:11a): Paul, the Law, and Gentile Circumcision." *Journal for the Study of Paul and his Letters* 3 (2013) 145–63.

Harink, Douglas. *Paul among the Postliberals: Pauline Theology beyond Christendom and Modernity*. Grand Rapids: Brazos, 2003.

Harrington, Daniel J. *Paul on the Mystery of Israel*. Collegeville, MN: Liturgical, 1992.

Harrison, James R. *Paul and the Imperial Authorities at Thessalonica and Rome: A Study in the Conflict of Ideology*. WUNT 273. Tübingen: Mohr Siebeck, 2011.

Hays, Richard B. *The Conversion of the Imagination: Paul as Interpreter of Israel's Scripture*. Grand Rapids: Eerdmans, 2005.

———. *Echoes of Scripture in the Letters of Paul*. New Haven: Yale University Press, 1989.

Hedner Zetterholm, Karin. "Alternative Visions of Judaism and Their Impact on the Formation of Rabbinic Judaism." *Journal of the Jesus Movement in Its Jewish Setting* 1 (2014) 127–53.

———. *Jewish Interpretation of the Bible: Ancient and Contemporary*. Minneapolis: Fortress, 2012.

———. "The Question of Assumptions: Torah Observance in the First Century." In *Paul within Judaism: Restoring the First-Century Context to the Apostle*, edited by Mark D. Nanos and Magnus Zetterholm, 79–103. Minneapolis: Fortress, 2015.

Heinsch, Ryan. "Is Sauce for the Goose, Sauce for the Gander? Evaluating Models and Methods in Galatians 4:21–31." *Canadian-American Theological Review* 5 (2016) 1–14.

———. "What Does Hagar Have to Do with Mount Sinai and Jerusalem: Critical Spatial Theory and Identity in Galatians." Paper presented at the Annual Meeting of the SBL, Boston, MA, 27 November 2017.

Hill, Craig C. "Romans." In *The Oxford Bible Commentary*, edited by John Barton and John Muddiman, 1083–1108. Oxford: Oxford University Press, 2001.

Horbury, William. "The Gifts of God in Ezekiel the Tragedian." In *Messianism among Jews and Christians*, edited by William Horbury, 91–109. 2nd ed. London: Bloomsbury/T. & T. Clark, 2016.

Horner, Barry E. *Future Israel: Why Christian Anti-Judaism Must Be Challenged.* Nashville: B&H, 2007.

Horrell, David G. *Becoming Christian: Essays on 1 Peter and the Making of Christian Identity.* London: Bloomsbury, 2013.

———. "Pauline Churches or Early Christian Churches? Unity, Disagreement, and the Eucharist." In *Einheit der Kirche im Neuen Testament*, edited by A. Alexeev et al., 185–203. WUNT 218. Tübingen: Mohr Siebeck, 2008.

Hsieh, Nelson S. "Abraham as 'Heir of the World': Does Romans 4:13 Expand the Old Testament Abrahamic Land Promises?" *MSJ* 26 (2015) 95–110.

Hubing, Jeff. *Crucifixion and New Creation: The Strategic Purpose of Galatians 6.11–17.* London: Bloomsbury/T. & T. Clark, 2015.

Hübner, Hans. *Law in Paul's Thought.* Edinburgh: T. & T. Clark, 1984.

Hultgren, Arland J. *Paul's Letter to the Romans: A Commentary.* Grand Rapids: Eerdmans, 2011.

Hunt, Laura J. "Alien and Degenerate Milk: The Role of the Semiotic Object and Cultural Units in 1 Peter 2:1-3 for Elucidating Social Identity Formation in the Letter." Paper presented at the Annual Meeting of the SBL, Boston, MA, 20 November, 2017.

———. "Jesus Caesar: A Roman Reading of John 18:28—19:22." PhD diss., University of Wales Trinity Saint David, 2017.

Hvalvik, Reidar. "Jewish Believers and Jewish Influence in the Roman Church until the Early Second Century." In *Jewish Believers in Jesus: The Early Centuries*, edited by Oskar Skarsaune and Reidar Hvalvik, 179–216. Peabody, MA: Hendrickson, 2007.

———. "'To the Jew First and Also to the Greek': The Meaning of Romans 1:16b." *Mishkan* 10 (1998) 1–8.

Irons, Charles Lee. *The Righteousness of God A Lexical Examination of the Covenant-Faithfulness Interpretation.* WUNT 2.386. Tübingen: Mohr Siebeck, 2014.

Isaac, Munther. *From Land to Lands, from Eden to the Renewed Earth: A Christ-Centred Biblical Theology of the Promised Land.* Carlisle, UK: Langham, 2015.

Jennings, Willie James. *The Christian Imagination: Theology and the Origins of Race.* New Haven: Yale University Press, 2010.

Jewett, Robert. "The Law and the Coexistence of Jews and Gentiles in Romans." *Int* 39 (1985) 341–56.

———. *Paul the Apostle to America: Cultural Trends and Pauline Scholarship.* Louisville: Westminster/John Knox, 1994.

———. *Romans: A Commentary.* Minneapolis: Fortress, 2007.

Jipp, Joshua. *Christ Is King Paul's Royal Ideology.* Minneapolis: Fortress, 2015.

———. "Rereading the Story of Abraham, Isaac, and 'Us' in Romans 4." *JSNT* 32 (2009) 217–42.

Johnson-Hodge, Caroline E. *If Sons, Then Heirs: A Study of Kinship and Ethnicity in the Letters of Paul.* Oxford: Oxford University Press, 2007.

———. "The Question of Identity: Gentiles as Gentiles—But Also Not—in Pauline Communities." In *Paul within Judaism: Restoring the First-Century Context to the Apostle*, edited by Mark D. Nanos and Magnus Zetterholm, 153–73. Minneapolis: Fortress, 2015.

Kaiser, Walter C., Jr. "Leviticus 18:5 and Paul: 'Do This and You Shall Live' (Eternally?)." *JETS* 14 (1971) 19–28.

Kamell, Mariam J. "Sirach and Romans 4:1–25." In *Reading Romans in Context*, edited by Ben C. Blackwell, John K. Goodrich, and Jason Maston, 66–72. Grand Rapids: Zondervan, 2015.

Kamudzandu, Israel. *Abraham as Spiritual Ancestor: A Postcolonial Zimbabwean Reading of Romans 4.* Leiden: Brill, 2010.

———. *Abraham Our Father: Paul and the Ancestors in Postcolonial Africa.* Minneapolis: Fortress, 2013.

Käsemann, Ernst. *Commentary on Romans.* Translated by Geoffrey William Bromiley. Grand Rapids: Eerdmans, 1980.

———. "The Faith of Abraham in Romans 4." In *Perspectives on Paul*, edited by Ernst Käsemann, 79–101. Philadelphia: Fortress, 1971.

Keck, Leander E. *Romans.* Nashville: Abingdon, 2005.

Keener, Craig S. *Romans: A New Covenant Commentary.* Eugene, OR: Cascade, 2009.

Kinzer, Mark. *Postmissionary Messianic Judaism: Redefining Christian Engagement with the Jewish People.* Grand Rapids: Brazos, 2005.

———. *Searching Her Own Mystery: Nostra Aetate, the Jewish People, and the Identity of the Church.* Eugene, OR: Cascade, 2015.

Kirk, J. R. Daniel. *Unlocking Romans: Resurrection and the Justification of God.* Grand Rapids: Eerdmans, 2008.

Kooten, George H. van. "Philosophical Criticism of Genealogical Claims and Stoic Depoliticization of Politics: Greco-Roman Strategies in Paul's Allegorical Interpretation of Hagar and Sarah (Gal 4:21–31)." In *Abraham, the Nations, and the Hagarites Jewish, Christian, and Islamic Perspectives on Kinship with Abraham*, edited by Martin Goodman, Geurt Hendrik van Kooten, and J. van Ruiten. 361–86. Leiden: Brill, 2010.

Koperski, Veronica. *What Are They Saying about Paul and the Law?* New York: Paulist, 2001.

Korner, Ralph J. "*Ekklēsia* as a Jewish Synagogue Term: Some Implications for Paul's Socio-Religious Location." *The Journal of the Jesus Movement in Its Jewish Setting* 2 (2015) 53–78.

———. "The *Ekklēsia* of Early Christ-Followers in Asia Minor as the Eschatological New Jerusalem: Counter-Imperial Rhetoric?" In *Urban Dreams and Realities in Antiquity: Remains and Representations of the Ancient City*, edited by Adam Kemezis, 455–99. Mnemosyne Supplements: History and Archaeology of Classical Antiquity 375. Leiden: Brill, 2015.

———. *The Origin and Meaning of* Ekklēsia *in the Early Jesus Movement.* Leiden: Brill, 2017.

Krauter, Stefan. *Studien zu Röm 13,1–7.* WUNT 243. Tübingen: Mohr Siebeck, 2009.

Kruse, Colin G. *Paul, the Law, and Justification.* Peabody, MA: Hendrickson, 1997.

———. *Paul's Letter to the Romans.* Grand Rapids: Eerdmans, 2012.

Le Donne, Anthony. *Near Christianity: How Journeys along Jewish-Christian Borders Saved My Faith in God.* Grand Rapids: Zondervan, 2016

Lee, Jae Won. "Paul and Ethnic Difference in Romans." In *They Were All Together in One Place: Toward Minority Biblical Criticism*, edited by Randall C. Bailey, Tatsiong Benny Liew, and Fernando F. Segovia, 141–59. Semeia Studies 65. Atlanta: SBL, 2009.

Levenson, Jon D. *Inheriting Abraham: The Legacy of the Patriarch in Judaism, Christianity, and Islam*. Princeton: Princeton University Press, 2012.

———. "The Universal Horizon of Biblical Particularism." In *Ethnicity and the Bible*, edited by Mark G. Brett, 143–69. Biblical Interpretation Series 19. Leiden: Brill, 1996.

Lewis, Robert Brian. *Paul's "Spirit of Adoption" in its Roman Imperial Context*. LNTS 545. London: Bloomsbury, 2016.

Liebengood, Kelly. *Reading 1 Peter after Supersessionism*. Eugene, OR: Cascade, forthcoming.

Lincicum, David. "F. C. Baur's Place in the Study of Early Christianity." In *The Rediscovery of Jewish Christianity from Toland to Baur*, 137–66. History of Biblical Studies 5. Atlanta: SBL, 2012.

———. "Genesis in Paul." In *Genesis in the New Testament*, edited by Maarten J. J. Menken, and Steve Moyise, 99–116. London: Bloomsbury/T. & T. Clark, 2012.

———. *Paul and the Early Jewish Encounter with Deuteronomy*. WUNT 2.284. Tübingen: Mohr Siebeck, 2010.

Livesey, Nina E. *Circumcision as a Malleable Symbol*. WUNT 2.295. Tübingen: Mohr Siebeck, 2010.

Lo, Lung-kwong. "Identity Crisis Reflected in Romans 14:1—15:13 and the Implications for the Chinese Christians' Controversy on Ancestral Worship." In *SBLSP*, 1–32. Atlanta: SBL, 2002.

Lodge, John G. *Romans 9–11: A Reader-Response Analysis*. Atlanta: Scholars, 1996.

Longenecker, Bruce W. "On Israel's God and God's Israel: Assessing Supersessionism in Paul." *JTS* 58 (2007) 26–44.

———. "Salvation History in Galatians and the Making of a Pauline Discourse." *Journal for the Study of Paul and his Letters* 2 (2012) 65–87.

———. *The Triumph of Abraham's God: The Transformation of Identity in Galatians*. Nashville: Abingdon, 1998.

Longenecker, Richard N. *The Epistle to the Romans: A Commentary on the Greek Text*. NIGTC. Grand Rapids: Eerdmans, 2015.

———. *Introducing Romans: Critical Issues in Paul's Most Famous Letter*. Grand Rapids: Eerdmans, 2011.

Longman, Tremper. *Genesis*. The Story of God Bible Commentary. Grand Rapids: Zondervan, 2016.

Lopez, Davina C. *Apostle to the Conquered: Reimagining Paul's Mission*. Paul in Critical Contexts. Minneapolis: Fortress, 2008.

Luomanen, Petri. "Ebionites and Nazarenes." In *Jewish Christianity Reconsidered: Rethinking Ancient Groups and Texts*, edited by Matt Jackson-McCabe, 81–118. Minneapolis: Fortress, 2007.

Macaskill, Grant. *Union with Christ in the New Testament*. Oxford: Oxford University Press, 2013.

Magda, Ksenija. *Paul's Territoriality and Mission Strategy: Searching for the Geographical Awareness Paradigm behind Romans*. WUNT 2.266. Tübingen: Mohr Siebeck, 2009.

Magee, Gregory S. "Paul's Gospel, the Law, and God's Universal Reign in Romans 3:31." *JETS* 57 (2014) 341–50.

Marcus, Joel. "The Circumcision and the Uncircumcision in Rome." *NTS* 35 (1989) 67–81.

Martin, Dale B. "The Promise of Teleology, the Constraints of Epistemology, and Universal Vision in Paul." In *St. Paul among the Philosophers*, edited by John D. Caputo and Linda Alcoff, 91–108. Bloomington, IN: Indiana University Press, 2009.

Martin, Troy. "Apostasy to Paganism: The Rhetorical Stasis of the Galatian Controversy." *JBL* 114 (1995) 437–61.

Marttila, Tomas. *The Culture of Enterprise in Neoliberalism Specters of Entrepreneurship*. New York: Routledge, 2013.

Martyn, Louis J. *Galatians*. New York: Doubleday, 1997.

Matera, Frank J. *Romans*. Grand Rapids: Baker Academic, 2010.

McComiskey, Thomas Edward. *Hosea*. Grand Rapids: Baker, 1992.

McDermott, Gerald R., ed. *The New Christian Zionism: Fresh Perspectives on Israel & the Land*. Downers Grove, IL: InterVarsity, 2016.

McFarland, Orrey. "Whose Abraham, Which Promise? Genesis 15.6 in Philo's *De Virtutibus* and Romans 4." *JSNT* 35 (2012) 107–29.

McGowan, Andrew. "Ecclesiology as Ethnology: The Church in N. T. Wright's *Paul and the Faithfulness of God*," in *God and the Faithfulness of Paul: A Critical Examination of the Pauline Theology of N. T. Wright*, edited by Christoph Heilig, J. Thomas Hewitt, and Michael F. Bird, , 583–602. Tübingen: Mohr Siebeck, 2016.

Merkle, Ben L. "Romans 11 and the Future of Ethnic Israel." *JETS* 43 (2000) 709–21.

Mermelstein, Ari. *Creation, Covenant, and the Beginnings of Judaism: Reconceiving Historical Time in the Second Temple Period*. Leiden: Brill, 2014.

Meyer, Paul W. "Romans 10:4 and the 'End' of the Law." In *The Divine Helmsman: Studies on God's Control of Human Events. Presented to Lou H. Silberman*, edited by J. L. Crenshaw and S. Sandmel, 59–78. New York: KTAV, 1980.

Middendorf, Michael P. *Romans 1–8*. Saint Louis: Concordia, 2013.

———. *Romans 9–16*. Saint Louis: Concordia, 2016.

Milgrom, Jacob. *Leviticus 1–16*. AB 3. New York: Doubleday, 1991.

Miller, James C. *The Obedience of Faith, the Eschatological People of God, and the Purpose of Romans*. Atlanta: SBL, 2000.

Mininger, Marcus A. *Uncovering the Theme of Revelation in Romans 1:16—3:26 Discovering a New Approach to Paul's Argument*. WUNT 445. Tübingen: Mohr Siebeck, 2017.

Mitchell, Margaret. "Gentile Christianity." In *The Cambridge History of Christianity. Vol. 1, Origins to Constantine*, edited by Margaret M. Mitchell and Frances M. Young, 103–24. Cambridge: Cambridge University Press, 2006.

Moo, Douglas J. *The Epistle to the Romans*. Grand Rapids: Eerdmans, 1996.

———. "The Law of Christ as the Fulfillment of the Law of Moses: A Modified Lutheran View." In *Five Views on Law and Gospel*, edited by Greg L. Bahnsen, 319–76. Grand Rapids: Zondervan, 1996.

Morales, Rodrigo Jose. *The Spirit and the Restoration of Israel: New Exodus and New Creation Motifs in Galatians*. WUNT 2.282. Tübingen: Mohr Siebeck, 2010.

Mounce, Robert H. *Romans*. Nashville: Broadman & Holman, 1995.

Moxnes, Halvor. *Theology in Conflict: Studies in Paul's Understanding of God in Romans*. Leiden: Brill, 1980.

Nanos, Mark D. "'Broken Branches': A Pauline Metaphor Gone Awry? (Romans 11:11–36)," In *Between Gospel and Election: Explorations in the Interpretation of Romans 9–11*, edited by F. Wilk and J. R. Wagner, 339–76. Tübingen: Mohr Siebeck, 2010.

————. "'Callused', Not 'Hardened': Paul's Revelation of Temporary Protection until All Israel Can Be Healed." In *Reading Paul in Context: Explorations in Identity Formation Essays in Honour of William S. Campbell*, edited by Kathy Ehrensperger and J. Brian Tucker, 52–73. London: Bloomsbury/T. & T. Clark, 2010.

————. "'The Gifts and the Calling of God are Irrevocable' (Romans 11:29): If So, How Can Paul Declare that 'Not All Israelites Truly Belong to Israel' (9:6)." *Studies in Christian-Jewish Relations* 11 (2016) 1–17.

————. "Images of Jews and Judaism in Paul's Letter to the Romans: Challenging Translation Decisions That Subvert Paul's Message." Washburn University King Lecture. Topeka: Washburn University Press, 2010.

————. "Introduction." In *Paul within Judaism: Restoring the First-Century Context to the Apostle*, edited by Mark D. Nanos and Magnus Zetterholm, 1–29. Minneapolis: Fortress, 2015.

————. "The Jewish Context of the Gentile Audience Addressed in Paul's Letter to the Romans." *CBQ* 61 (1999) 283–304.

————. "A Jewish View." In *Four Views on the Apostle Paul*, edited by Michael F. Bird, 159–93. Grand Rapids: Zondervan, 2012.

————. *The Mystery of Romans: The Jewish Context of Paul's Letter*. Minneapolis: Fortress, 1996.

————. "The Myth of the 'Law Free' Paul Standing between Christians and Jews." *Studies in Christian-Jewish Relations* 4 (2009) 1–22.

————. "Paul and Judaism: Why Not Paul's Judaism?" In *Paul Unbound: Other Perspectives on the Apostle*, edited by Mark D. Given, 117–60. Peabody, MA: Hendrickson, 2010.

————. "Paul and the Jewish Tradition: The Ideology of the *Shema*." In *Celebrating Paul: Festschrift in Honor of Jerome Murphy-O'Connor, O.P., and Joseph A. Fitzmyer, S.J.*, edited by Peter Spitaler, 62–80. Washington, DC: The Catholic Biblical Association of America, 2011.

————. "Paul's Non-Jews Do Not Become Jews, But Do They Become 'Jewish'?: Reading Romans 2:25–29 within Judaism, Alongside Josephus." *The Journal of the Jesus Movement in its Jewish Setting* (2014) 26–53.

————. "Paul's Relationship to Torah in Light of His Strategy 'to Become Everything to Everyone' (1 Corinthians 9:19–23)." In *Reading Corinthians and Philippians within Judaism: Collected Essays of Mark D. Nanos, Vol. 4*, edited by Mark D. Nanos, 52–92. Eugene, OR: Cascade, 2017.

————. "The Question of Conceptualization: Qualifying Paul's Position on Circumcision in Dialogue with Josephus's Advisors to King Izates." In *Paul within Judaism: Restoring the First-Century Context to the Apostle*, edited by Mark D. Nanos and Magnus Zetterholm, 105–52. Minneapolis: Fortress, 2015.

————. *Reading Paul within Judaism*. Eugene, OR: Cascade, 2017.

————. *Reading Romans within Judaism*. Eugene, OR: Cascade, 2017.

————. "Romans," In *The Jewish Annotated New Testament: New Revised Standard Version Bible Translation*, 253–86, edited by Amy-Jill Levine and Marc Zvi Brettler. Oxford: Oxford University Press, 2011.

Nanos, Mark D., and Magnus Zetterholm, eds. *Paul within Judaism: Restoring the First-Century Context to the Apostle*. Minneapolis: Fortress, 2015.

Naselli, Andrew David, and J. D. Crowley. *Conscience: What It Is, How to Train It, and Loving Those Who Differ*. Wheaton, IL: Crossway, 2016.

Neutel, Karin. *A Cosmopolitan Ideal: Paul's Declaration 'Neither Jew nor Greek, Neither Slave nor Free, nor Male and Female' in the Context of First-Century Thought.* LNTS 513. London: Bloomsbury, 2016.

Nicolet-Anderson, Valérie. *Constructing the Self: Thinking with Paul and Michel Foucault.* WUNT 2.324. Tübingen: Mohr Siebeck, 2012.

Noort, Ed. "Abraham and the Nations." In *Abraham, the Nations, and the Hagarites: Jewish, Christian, and Islamic Perspectives on Kinship with Abraham,* edited by Martin Goodman, Geurt Hendrik van Kooten, and J. van Ruiten. 3–32. Leiden: Brill, 2010.

Novak, David. "The Covenant in Rabbinic Thought." In *Two Faiths, One Covenant? Jewish and Christian Identity in the Presence of the Other,* edited by Eugene Korn and John Pawlikowski, 65–80. Lanham, MD: Rowman & Littlefield, 2005.

Novenson, Matthew V. *Christ among the Messiahs: Christ Language in Paul and Messiah Language in Ancient Judaism.* New York: Oxford University Press, 2012.

———. *The Grammar of Messianism: An Ancient Jewish Political Idiom and Its Users.* New York: Oxford University Press, 2017.

———. "The Messiah ben Abraham in Galatians: A Response to Joel Willitts." *Journal for the Study of Paul and His Letters* 2 (2012) 97–104.

———. "Paul's Former Occupation in *Ioudaismos.*" In *Galatians and Christian Theology: Justification, the Gospel, and Ethics in Paul's Letter,* edited by Mark W. Elliott et al., 24–39. Grand Rapids: Baker, 2014.

———. "The Self-Styled Jew of Romans 2 and the Actual Jews of Romans 9–11." In *The So-Called Jew in Paul's Letter to the Romans,* edited by Rafael Rodriguez and Matthew Thiessen, 133–62. Minneapolis: Fortress, 2016.

Oliver, Isaac W. "The 'Historical Paul' and the Paul of Acts: Which is More Jewish?" In *Paul the Jew: Rereading the Apostle as a Figure of Second Temple Judaism,* edited by Gabriele Boccaccini and Carlos A. Segovia. 51–80. Minneapolis: Fortress, 2016.

———. *Torah Praxis after 70 CE: Reading Matthew and Luke-Acts as Jewish Texts.* WUNT 2 355. Tübingen: Mohr Siebeck, 2013.

Oropeza, B. J. *Jews, Gentiles, and the Opponents of Paul: Apostasy in the New Testament Communities.* Eugene, OR: Cascade, 2012.

Ortlund, Dane Calvin. *Zeal without Knowledge: The Concept of Zeal in Romans 10, Galatians 1, and Philippians 3.* London: T. & T. Clark, 2012.

Osborne, Grant R. *Romans.* Downers Grove, IL: InterVarsity, 2004.

Oswalt, John N. *The Book of Isaiah Chapters 40–66.* Grand Rapids: Eerdmans, 2006.

Paget, James Carleton. "The Definition of the Terms *Jewish Christian* and *Jewish Christianity* in the History of Research." In *Jewish Believers in Jesus: The Early Centuries,* edited by Oskar Skarsaune and Reidar Hvalvik, 22–52. Peabody, MA: Hendrickson, 2007.

Pate, C. Marvin. *Romans.* Grand Rapids: Baker, 2013.

Patte, Daniel. *Ethics of Biblical Interpretation: A Reevaluation.* Louisville: Westminster John Knox, 1995.

Pickstock, Catherine. *After Writing: On the Liturgical Consummation of Philosophy.* Oxford: Blackwell, 1998.

Porter, Stanley E. *The Letter to the Romans: A Linguistic and Literary Commentary.* Sheffield, UK: Sheffield Phoenix, 2015.

Quesnel, Michel. "La figure de Moïse en Romains 9–11." *NTS* 49 (2003) 321–35.

Rah, Soong-Chan. *The Next Evangelicalism: Releasing the Church from Western Cultural Captivity*. Downers Grove, IL: InterVarsity, 2009.

Räisänen, Heikki. *Paul and the Law*. Philadelphia: Fortress, 1986.

Rapa, Robert Keith. *The Meaning of "Works of the Law" in Galatians and Romans*. New York: Lang, 2001.

Reasoner, Mark. "Romans 9–11 Moves from Margin to Center, from Rejection to Salvation: Four Grids for Recent English-Language Exegesis." In *Between Gospel and Election: Explorations in the Interpretation of Romans 9–11*, edited by Frank Schleritt, J. Ross Wagner, and Florian Wilk, 75–89. WUNT 257. Tübingen: Mohr Siebeck, 2010.

———. *Romans in Full Circle: A History of Interpretation*. Louisville: Westminster John Knox, 2005.

———. "The Salvation of Israel in Romans 9–11." In *The Call of Abraham: Essays on the Election of Israel in Honor of Jon D. Levenson*, edited by Joel S. Kaminsky and Gary A. Anderson, 256–79. Notre Dame, IN: University of Notre Dame Press, 2013.

———. *The Strong and the Weak: Romans 14.1—15.13 in Context*. SNTSMS 103. Cambridge: Cambridge University Press, 1999.

Revell, Louise. *Roman Imperialism and Local Identities*. Cambridge: Cambridge University Press, 2009.

Reynolds, Benjamin E., and Loren T. Stuckenbruck, eds. *The Jewish Apocalyptic Tradition and the Shaping of New Testament Thought*. Minneapolis: Fortress, 2017.

Rhyne, C. Thomas. *Faith Establishes the Law*. Chico, CA: Scholars, 1981.

Richardson, Peter. "Early Synagogues as Collegia in the Diaspora and Palestine." In *Voluntary Associations in the Graeco-Roman World*, edited by John S. Kloppenborg and Stephen G. Wilson, 90–109. London: Routledge, 1996.

Richardson, Peter, and Paul W. Gooch. "Accommodation Ethics." *TynBul* 29 (1978) 89–142.

Richter, Daniel S. *Cosmopolis: Imagining Community in Late Classical Athens and the Early Roman Empire*. Oxford: Oxford University Press, 2011.

Ridderbos, Herman. *Paul: An Outline of His Theology*. Grand Rapids: Eerdmans, 1997.

Rock, Ian E. "Another Reason for Romans—A Pastoral Response to Augustan Imperial Theology: Paul's Use of the Song of Moses in Romans 9–11 and 14–15." In *Reading Paul in Context: Explorations in Identity Formation Essays in Honour of William S. Campbell*, edited by Kathy Ehrensperger and J. Brian Tucker, 74–89. LNTS 428. London: T. & T. Clark, 2010.

———. *Paul's Letter to the Romans and Roman Imperialism: An Ideological Analysis of the Exordium (Romans 1:1–17)*. Eugene, OR: Pickwick, 2012.

Rodríguez, Rafael. *If You Call Yourself a Jew: Reappraising Paul's Letter to the Romans*. Eugene, OR: Cascade, 2014.

Rodríguez, Rafael, and Matthew Thiessen, eds. *The So-Called Jew in Paul's Letter to the Romans*. Minneapolis: Fortress, 2016.

Roetzel, Calvin. "Διαθῆκαι in Romans 9,4." *Bib* 51 (1970) 377–90.

———. "Paul and *Nomos* in the Messianic Age." In *Reading Paul in Context: Explorations in Identity Formation: Essays in Honour of William S. Campbell*, edited by Kathy Ehrensperger and J. Brian Tucker, 113–27. London: T. & T. Clark, 2013.

Rosner, Brian S. *Paul and the Law: Keeping the Commandments of God*. Downers Grove, IL: InterVarsity, 2013.

Ross, Allen P. *Recalling the Hope of Glory: Biblical Worship from the Garden to the New Creation*. Grand Rapids: Kregel, 2006.

Rudolph, David J. *A Jew to the Jews: Jewish Contours of Pauline Flexibility in 1 Corinthians 9:19–23*. WUNT 2.304. Tübingen: Mohr Siebeck, 2011. (2nd ed. Eugene, OR: Pickwick, 2016.)

———. "Messianic Jews and Christian Theology." *Pro Ecclesia* 14 (2005) 58–84.

———. "Paul and the Food Laws: A Reassessment of Romans 14:13–23." Paper presented at the Third Nangeroni Meeting, Rome, Italy, June 2014.

———. "Paul and the Food Laws: *A Reassessment of Romans 14:14, 20*." In *Paul the Jew: Rereading the Apostle as a Figure of Second Temple Judaism*, edited by Gabriele Boccaccini and Carlos A. Segovia, 151–81. Minneapolis: Fortress, 2016.

———. "Paul's 'Rule in All the Churches' (1 Cor 7:17–24) and Torah-Defined Ecclesiological Variegation." *Studies in Christian-Jewish Relations* 5 (2010) 1–24.

———. "Yeshua and the Dietary Laws: A Reassessment of Mark 7:19b." *Kesher* 16 (2003) 97–119.

———. "Zionism in Pauline Literature: Does Paul Eliminate Particularity for Israel and the Land in His Portrayal of Salvation Available for All the World?" In *The New Christian Zionism*, edited by Gerald R. McDermott, 167–94. Downers Grove, IL: InterVarsity, 2016.

Rudolph, David J., and Joel Willitts, eds. *Introduction to Messianic Judaism: Its Ecclesial Context and Biblical Foundations*. Grand Rapids: Zondervan, 2013.

Ruiten, Jacques T. A. G. M. van. *Abraham in the Book of Jubilees: The Rewriting of Genesis 11:26—25:10 in the Book of Jubilees 11:14—23:8*. Leiden: Brill, 2012.

———. "The Covenant of Noah in Jubilees 6.1–38." In *The Concept of the Covenant in the Second Temple Period*, edited by Stanley E. Porter and Jacqueline C. R. De Roo, 167–90. Leiden: Brill, 2003.

Runesson, Anders. "Inventing Christian Identity: Paul, Ignatius, and Theodosius I." In *Exploring Early Christian Identity*, edited by Bengt Holmberg, 59–92. WUNT 226. Tübingen: Mohr Siebeck, 2008.

———. "Jewish and Christian Interaction from The First to the Fifth Centuries." In *The Early Christian World*, edited by Philip F. Esler, 244–64. New York: Routledge, 2017.

———. *The Origins of the Synagogue: A Socio-Historical Study*. 2nd ed. Stockholm: Almqvist & Wiksell, 2001.

———. "Paul's Rule in All the *Ekklēsiai*." In *Introduction to Messianic Judaism*, edited by David J. Rudolph and Joel Willitts, 214–23. Grand Rapids: Zondervan, 2013.

———. "Placing Paul: Institutional Structures and Theological Strategy in the World of the Early Christ-believers." *SEÅ* 80 (2015) 43–67.

———. "The Question of Terminology." In *Paul within Judaism: Restoring the First-Century Context to the Apostle*, edited by Mark D. Nanos and Magnus Zetterholm, 53–77. Minneapolis: Fortress, 2015.

Ruzer, Serge. "Paul's Stance on Torah Revisited: Gentile Addresses and the Jewish Setting." In *Paul's Jewish Matrix*, edited by Thomas G. Casey and Justin Taylor, 75–97. Rome: Gregorian and Biblical, 2011.

Rydelnik, Michael. "The Relationship of Messianic Jews to the Church and the People of Israel." Paper presented at the Biblical Studies Conference Messianic Judaism History, Theology, and Education 2009, Denver Seminary, Denver, CO.

Sanday, William, and Arthur C. Headlam. *A Critical and Exegetical Commentary on the Epistle to the Romans*. ICC. Edinburgh: T. & T. Clark, 1902.

Sanders, E. P. *Paul: The Apostle's Life, Letters, and Thought*. Minneapolis: Fortress, 2015.

———. *Paul, the Law, and the Jewish People*. Philadelphia: Fortress, 1983.

Schäfer, Peter. *Judeophobia: Attitudes toward the Jews in the Ancient World*. Cambridge: Harvard University Press, 1997.

Schliesser, Benjamin. *Abraham's Faith in Romans 4: Paul's Concept of Faith in Light of the History of Reception of Genesis 15:6*. Tübingen: Mohr Siebeck, 2007.

Schmidt, Karl L. "ἔθνος." In *TDNT* 2:369–72.

Schnelle, Udo. *Apostle Paul: His Life and Theology*. Grand Rapids: Baker Academic, 2005.

Schreiner, Thomas R. *40 Questions about Christians and Biblical Law*. Grand Rapids: Kregel, 2010.

———. *The Law and Its Fulfillment: A Pauline Theology of Law*. Grand Rapids: Baker, 1993.

———. *Romans*. BECNT. Grand Rapids: Baker, 1998.

Schwartz, Daniel R. "Someone Who Considers Something," In *Paul's Jewish Matrix*, edited by, Thomas G. Casey and Justin Taylor, 293–309 Rome: Gregorian and Biblical, 2011.

Scobey, David. "Exterminating Gestures: On Linking the Coercive and Discursive Moments of Power." *Center for Research on Social Organization* 471 (1992) 1–24.

Scott, James M. *Adoption as Sons of God: An Exegetical Investigation into the Background of* ΥΙΟΘΕΣΙΑ *in the Pauline Corpus*. WUNT 2.48 Tübingen: Mohr, 1992.

———. "'And Then All Israel Will Be Saved' (Rom 11:26)." In *Restoration: Old Testament, Jewish, and Christian Perspectives*, edited by James M. Scott, 489–527. Leiden: Brill, 2001.

———. *Paul and the Nations: The Old Testament and Jewish Background of Paul's Mission to the Nations with Special Reference to the Destination of Galatians*. WUNT 84. Tübingen: Mohr, 1995.

Sechrest, Love L. *A Former Jew: Paul and the Dialectics of Race*. London: T. & T. Clark, 2009.

Seifrid, Mark A. *Christ, Our Righteousness: Paul's Theology of Justification*. Downers Grove, IL: InterVarsity, 2000.

———. "Romans." In *Commentary on the New Testament Use of the Old Testament*, edited by G. K. Beale and D. A. Carson, 607–94. Grand Rapids: Baker, 2007.

Sherman, Steven J., David L. Hamilton, and Amy C. Lewis. "Perceived Entitativity and the Social Identity Value of Group Membership." In *Social Identity and Social Cognition*, edited by Dominic M. Abrams and Michael A. Hogg, 80–110. Oxford: Blackwell, 1999.

Shulam, Joseph, and Hilary Le Cornu. *A Commentary on the Jewish Roots of Romans*. Baltimore: Messianic Jewish, 1998.

Shum, Shiu-Lun. *Paul's Use of Isaiah in Romans: A Comparative Study of Paul's Letter to the Romans and the Sibylline and Qumran Sectarian Texts*. WUNT 2.156. Tübingen: Mohr Siebeck, 2002.

Siker, Jeffrey S. *Disinheriting the Jews: Abraham in Early Christian Controversy*. Louisville: Westminster/John Knox, 1991.

Skarsaune, Oskar. *In the Shadow of the Temple: Jewish Influences on Early Christianity*. Downers Grove, IL: InterVarsity, 2002.

Sloan, Robert B. "Paul and the Law: Why the Law Cannot Save." *NovT* 33 (1991) 35–60.

Snodgrass, Klyne R. "Justification by Grace—to the Doers: An Analysis of the Place of Romans 2 in the Theology of Paul." *NTS* 32 (1986) 72–93.

———. "Spheres of Influence: A Possible Solution to the Problem of Paul and the Law." *JSNT* 32 (1988) 93–113.

Sonderegger, Katherine. *Systematic Theology*. Vol. 1, *The Doctrine of God*. Minneapolis: Fortress, 2015.

Song, Changwon. *Reading Romans as a Diatribe*. New York: Lang, 2004.

Soulen, R. Kendall. *The God of Israel and Christian Theology*. Minneapolis: Fortress, 1996.

———. "'They Are Israelites': The Priority of the Present Tense for Jewish-Christian Relations." In *Between Gospel and Election: Explorations in the Interpretation of Romans 9–11*, edited by Frank Schleritt, J. Ross Wagner, and Florian Wilk, 497–504. WUNT 257. Tübingen: Mohr Siebeck, 2010.

Sprinkle, Preston M. *Law and Life: The Interpretation of Leviticus 18:5 in Early Judaism and in Paul*. WUNT 2.241. Tübingen: Mohr Siebeck, 2007.

Stanley, Christopher D. *Arguing with Scripture: The Rhetoric of Quotations in the Letters of Paul*. London: T. & T. Clark, 2004.

———. "'Neither Jew nor Greek': Ethnic Conflict in Graeco-Roman Society." *JSNT* 64 (1996) 101–24.

———. "Paul the Ethnic Hybrid? Postcolonial Perspectives on Paul's Ethnic Categorizations." In *The Colonized Apostle: Paul through Postcolonial Eyes*, edited by Christopher D. Stanley, 110–26. Minneapolis: Fortress, 2011.

Staples, Jason. "What Do the Gentiles Have to Do with 'All Israel'? A Fresh Look at Romans 11:25–27." *JBL* 130 (2011) 371–90.

Starling, David I. *Not My People: Gentiles as Exiles in Pauline Hermeneutics*. BZNW 184. Berlin: De Gruyter, 2011.

Stegemann, Ekkehard. "Coexistence and Transformation: Reading the Politics of Identity in Romans in an Imperial Context." In *Reading Paul in Context: Explorations in Identity Formation Essays in Honour of William S. Campbell*, edited by Kathy Ehrensperger and J. Brian Tucker, 3–23. LNTS 428. London: T. & T. Clark, 2010.

Stendahl, Krister. "Qumran and Supersessionism—and the Road Not Taken." In *The Bible and the Dead Sea Scrolls*, edited by James H. Charlesworth, 397–405. Waco, TX: Baylor University Press, 2006.

Stowers, Stanley Kent. *The Diatribe and Paul's Letter to the Romans*. Chico, CA: Scholars, 1981.

———. *A Rereading of Romans: Justice, Jews, and Gentiles*. New Haven: Yale University Press, 1994.

Strecker, Georg. "Befreiung und Rechtfertigung: zur Stellung der Rechtfertigungslehre in der Theolodie des Paulus." In *Rechtfertigung: Festschrift für Ernst Käsemann zum 70. Geburtstag*, edited by Johannes Friedrich, Wolfgang Pöhlmann, and Peter Stuhlmacher, 479–508. Tübingen: Mohr, 1976.

Stuckenbruck, Loren T. "Some Reflections on Apocalyptic Thought and Time in Literature from the Second Temple Period." In *Paul and the Apocalyptic Imagination*, edited by Ben C. Blackwell, John K. Goodrich, and Jason Maston, 137–55. Minneapolis: Fortress, 2016.

Tait, Michael, and Peter Oakes, eds. *The Torah in the New Testament: Papers Delivered at the Manchester-Lausanne Seminar of June 2008.* London: T. & T. Clark, 2009.

Tajfel, Henri. "Social Categorization, Social Identity and Social Comparison." In *Differentiation between Social Groups: Studies in the Social Psychology of Intergroup Relations,* edited by H. Tajfel, 61–76. London: Academic, 1978.

Tajfel, Henri, and John C. Turner. "An Integrative Theory of Intergroup Conflict." In *The Social Psychology of Intergroup Relations,* edited by W. G. Austin and S. Worchel, 33–47. Monterey, CA: Brooks/Cole, 1979.

———. "The Social Identity Theory of Intergroup Behaviour." In *Psychology of Intergroup Relations,* edited by S. Worchel and W. G. Austin, 7–24. 2nd ed. Chicago: Nelson-Hall, 1986.

Talbert, Charles H. *Romans.* Macon, GA: Smyth & Helwys, 2002.

Tanner, J. Paul. "The New Covenant and Paul's Quotation from Hosea in Romans 9:25–26." *BSac* 162 (2005) 95–110.

Tapie, Matthew A. *Aquinas on Israel and the Church: The Question of Supersessionism in the Theology of Thomas Aquinas.* Eugene, OR: Pickwick, 2014.

Tatum, Gregory. "Law and Covenant in *Paul and the Faithfulness of God.*" In *God and the Faithfulness of Paul: A Critical Examination of the Pauline Theology of N. T. Wright,* edited by Christoph Heilig, J. Thomas Hewitt, and Michael F. Bird, 311–27. Tübingen: Mohr Siebeck, 2016.

———. "Putting Galatians in its Place." PhD diss., Duke University, 1997.

———. "'To the Jew First' (Romans 1:16): Paul's Defense of Jewish Privilege in Romans." In *Celebrating Paul: Festschrift in Honor of Jerome Murphy-O'Connor, O.P., and Joseph A. Fitzmyer, S.J.,* edited by Peter Spitaler, 275–86. Washington, DC: Catholic Biblical Association of America, 2011.

Thielman, Frank. "The Coherence of Paul's View of the Law: The Evidence of First Corinthians." *NTS* 38 (1992) 235–53.

———. *From Plight to Solution: A Jewish Framework for Understanding Paul's View of the Law in Galatians and Romans.* Leiden: Brill, 1989.

———. *Paul & the Law: A Contextual Approach.* Downers Grove, IL: InterVarsity, 1994.

Thiessen, Matthew. *Contesting Conversion: Genealogy, Circumcision, and Identity in Ancient Judaism and Christianity.* New York: Oxford University Press, 2011.

———. *Paul and the Gentile Problem.* New York: Oxford University Press, 2016.

———. "Paul's So-Called Jew and Lawless Lawkeeping." In *The So-Called Jew in Paul's Letter to the Romans,* edited by Rafael Rodriguez and Matthew Thiessen, 59–83. Minneapolis: Fortress, 2016.

Thompson, Michael. *Clothed with Christ: The Example and Teaching of Jesus in Romans 12.1—15.13.* Sheffield, UK: JSOT, 1991.

Thornhill, A. Chadwick. *The Chosen People: Election, Paul, and Second Temple Judaism.* Downers Grove, IL: InterVarsity, 2015.

Thornton, Dillon T. "Sin Seizing an Opportunity through the Commandments: The Law in 1 Tim 1:8–11 and Rom 6–8." *Horizons in Biblical Theology* 36 (2014) 142–58.

Thorsteinsson, Runar M. *Paul's Interlocutor in Romans 2: Function and Identity in the Context of Ancient Epistolography.* Stockholm: Almqvist & Wiksell, 2003.

Thorsteinsson, Runar, Matthew Thiessen, and Rafael Rodríguez. "Paul's Interlocutor in Romans: The Problem of Identification." In *The So-Called Jew in Paul's Letter to the*

Romans, edited by Rafael Rodríguez and Matthew Thiessen, 1–37. Minneapolis: Fortress, 2016.

Thurén, Lauri. *Derhetorizing Paul: A Dynamic Perspective on Pauline Theology and the Law.* Harrisburg, PA: Trinity, 2002.

Ticciati, Susannah. "The Nondivisive Difference of Election: A Reading of Romans 9–11." *Journal of Theological Interpretation* 6 (2012) 257–78.

Tobin, Thomas H. *Paul's Rhetoric in Its Contexts: The Argument of Romans* Peabody, MA: Hendrickson, 2004.

Toews, John E. *Romans.* Scottdale, PA: Herald, 2004.

Tolmie, Francois. *Narratology and Biblical Narratives: A Practical Guide.* Eugene, OR: Wipf & Stock, 2012.

Tomson, Peter J. *Paul and the Jewish Law: Halakha in the Letters of the Apostle to the Gentiles.* Minneapolis: Fortress, 1990.

Toney, Carl N. *Paul's Inclusive Ethic: Resolving Community Conflicts and Promoting Mission in Romans 14–15.* WUNT 2.252. Tübingen: Mohr Siebeck, 2008.

Townsend, Philippa. "Who Were the First Christians? Jews, Gentiles, and the *Christianoi.*" In *Heresy and Identity in Late Antiquity*, edited by Iricinschi, Eduard, and Holger M. Zellentin, 212–30. Tübingen: Mohr Siebeck, 2008.

Trebilco, Paul R. *Self-Designations and Group Identity in the New Testament.* Cambridge: Cambridge University Press, 2012.

Tucker, J. Brian. "Children of Israel." In *Dictionary of the Bible and Western Culture*, edited by Mary Ann Beavis and Michael J. Gilmour, 85–86. Sheffield, UK: Sheffield Phoenix, 2012.

———. "Diverse Identities in Christ according to Paul: The Enduring Influence of the Work of William S. Campbell." *Journal of Beliefs and Values* 38 (2017) 139–52.

———. "'Gentile Christianity' as a Category in the Study of Christian Origins: A Response to Terence Donaldson." Paper presented at SBL Annual Meeting, San Francisco, CA, 2011.

———. "The Jerusalem Collection, Economic Inequality, and Human Flourishing: Is Paul's Concern the Redistribution of Wealth, or a Relationship of Mutuality (or Both)?" *Canadian Theological Review* 3 (2014) 52–70.

———. "Matthew's Missional Particularism and the Continuation of Gentile Social Identity." *Canadian-American Theological Review* 5 (2016) 15–24.

———."Paul and the Three Grammars of Identity in Romans." Paper presented at SBL Annual Meeting, San Antonio, TX, 2016.

———. "Paul between Supersessionism and Pluralism." In *The Future Restoration of Israel*, edited by Stanley E. Porter and Alan E. Kurschner, forthcoming. Eugene, OR: Cascade, 2018.

———. "Paul in Bi-Cultural Perspective—A New Paradigm." *Journal of Beliefs and Values* 34 (2013) 374–77.

———. "Paul within or without Judaism: That is the Question." *Journal of Beliefs and Values* 36 (2015) 37–41.

———. "Paul's Economics of Neighbor-Love in Romans 13." Paper presented at Old Testament and New Testament and Economics Colloquium at The Land Center for Cultural Engagement, Southwestern Baptist Theological Seminary, Fort Worth, TX, 2017.

———. "Paul's Eschatological Anthropology: Systematic or Situational?" *Journal of Beliefs and Values* 37 (2016) 120–22.

———. "Paul's Particular Problem—The Continuation of Existing Identities in Philemon." In *T. & T. Clark Handbook to Social Identity in the New Testament*, edited by J. Brian Tucker, and Coleman A. Baker, 407–24. London: Bloomsbury, 2014.

———. *Reading 1 Corinthians*. Cascade Companions. Eugene, OR: Cascade, 2017.

———. *Remain in Your Calling: Paul and the Continuation of Social Identities in 1 Corinthians*. Eugene, OR: Pickwick, 2011.

———. "The Role of Moses in the Formation of an in Christ Social Identity for Gentiles in Corinth." Paper presented at SBL Annual Meeting, San Antonio, TX, 2016.

———. *You Belong to Christ: Paul and the Formation of Social Identity in 1 Corinthians 1–4*. Eugene, OR: Pickwick, 2010.

Tucker, J. Brian, and John Koessler. *All Together Different*. Chicago: Moody, 2018.

Tucker, J. Brian, and Coleman A. Baker, eds. *T. & T. Clark Handbook to Social Identity in the New Testament*. London: Bloomsbury, 2014.

van Buren, Paul Matthews. *A Theology of the Jewish-Christian Reality*. Part 2, *A Christian Theology of the People of Israel*. Lanham, MD: University Press of America, 1995.

Vanlaningham, Michael G. *Christ, the Savior of Israel: An evaluation of the Dual Covenant and* Sonderweg *Interpretations of Paul's Letters*. Frankfurt am Main: Lang, 2012.

———. "The Jewish People according to the Book of Romans," In *The People, the Land, and the Future of Israel: Israel and the Jewish People in the Plan of God*, edited by Darrell L. Bock and Mitch Glaser, 117–32. Grand Rapids: Kregel, 2014.

Vickers, Brian. "The Kingdom of God in Paul's Gospel." *The Southern Baptist Journal of Theology* 12 (2008) 52–67.

Visscher, Gerhard H. *Romans 4 and the New Perspective on Paul: Faith Embraces the Promise*. New York: Lang, 2009.

Vlach, Michael J. *Has the Church Replaced Israel? A Theological Evaluation*. Nashville: B&H Academic, 2010.

———. "The Kingdom of God in Paul's Epistles." *MSJ* 26 (2015) 59–74.

———. "What Does Christ As 'True Israel' Mean for the Nation Israel? A Critique of the Non-Dispensational Understanding." *MSJ* 23 (2012) 43–54.

Volf, Miroslav. "Human Flourishing." In *Renewing the Evangelical Mission*, edited by Richard Lints, 13–30. Grand Rapids: Eerdmans, 2013.

Wagner, J. Ross. "The Christ, Servant of Jew and Gentile: A Fresh Approach to Romans 15:8–9." *JBL* 116 (1997) 473–85.

———. *Heralds of the Good News: Isaiah and Paul "in Concert" in the Letter to the Romans*. Leiden: Brill, 2002.

———. "'Not from the Jews Only, But Also from the Gentiles': Mercy to the Nations in Romans 9–11." In *Between Gospel and Election*, edited by Florian Wilk and J. Ross Wagner, 417–31. WUNT 257. Tübingen: Mohr Siebeck, 2010.

Wallace, David R. *Election of the Lesser Son: Paul's Lament-Midrash in Romans 9–11*. Minneapolis: Fortress, 2014.

Wallace-Hadrill, Andrew. *Rome's Cultural Revolution*. Cambridge: Cambridge University Press, 2010.

Watson, Francis. "Constructing an Antithesis: Pauline and Other Jewish Perspectives on Divine and Human Agency." In *Divine and Human Agency in Paul and His Cultural Environment*, edited by John M. G. Barclay and Simon J. Gathercole, 99–116. London: T. & T. Clark, 2006.

———. "The Law in Romans," In *Reading Paul's Letter to the Romans*, edited by Jerry L. Sumney, 93–107. Atlanta: SBL, 2012.

———. *Paul and the Hermeneutics of Faith*. London: T. & T. Clark, 2004.

———. *Paul, Judaism, and the Gentiles: Beyond the New Perspective*. Grand Rapids: Eerdmans, 2007.

———. "The Two Roman Congregations: Romans 14:1—15:13." In *The Romans Debate: Revised and Expanded Edition*, edited by Karl P. Donfried, 203–15. Peabody, MA: Hendrickson, 1991.

Wenham, Gordon J. *Genesis 16–50*. WBC. Dallas, TX: Word, 1994.

Westerholm, Stephen. *Israel's Law and the Church's Faith: Paul and His Recent Interpreters*. Grand Rapids: Eerdmans, 1988.

———. *Perspectives Old and New on Paul: The "Lutheran" Paul and His Critics*. Grand Rapids: Eerdmans, 2004.

Westfall, Cynthia Long. *Paul and Gender: Reclaiming the Apostle's Vision for Men and Women in Christ*. Grand Rapids: Baker, 2016.

Whitsett, Christopher G. "Son of God, Seed of David: Paul's Messianic Exegesis in Romans 1:3–4." *JBL* 119 (2000) 661–81.

Whittle, Sarah. *Covenant Renewal and the Consecration of the Gentiles in Romans*. SNTSMS 161. Cambridge: Cambridge University Press, 2014.

———. "Jubilees and Romans 2:6–29: Circumcision, Law Observance, and Ethncity." In *Reading Romans in Context*, edited by Ben C. Blackwell, John K. Goodrich, and Jason Maston, 46–51. Grand Rapids: Zondervan, 2015.

Williams, Sam K. "The 'Righteousness of God' in Romans." *JBL* 99 (1980) 241–90.

Willitts, Joel. "Context Matters: Paul's Use of Leviticus 18:5 in Galatians 3:12." *TynBul* 54 (2003) 105–22.

———. "Davidic Messiah in Galatians: Clearing the Deck for a Study of the Theme in Galatians." *Journal for the Study of Paul and his Letters* 2 (2012) 143–61.

———. "Isa 54,1 in Gal 4,24b–27: Reading Genesis in Light of Isaiah." *ZNW* 96 (2005) 188–210.

———. "Jewish Fish (ΙΧΘΥΣ) in Post-Supersessionist Water: Messianic Judaism within a Post-Supersessionistic Paradigm." *HTS Theologiese Studies/Theological Studies* 72 (2016) 1–5.

———. "Matthew and *Psalms of Solomon's* Messianism: A Comparative Study in First-century Messianology." *BBR* 22 (2012) 27–50.

———. "Paul and Jewish Christians in the Second Century." In *Paul and the Second Century*, edited by Michael F. Bird and Joseph R. Dodson, 140–68. London: T. & T. Clark, 2011.

———. "Paul, the Rabbi of Messianic Judaism: Reading the Antioch Incident within Judaism as an Irreducibility Story." *Journal for the Study of Paul and his Letters* 6 (2016) 225–47.

Wilson, Todd A. *The Curse of the Law and the Crisis in Galatia: Reassessing the Purpose of Galatians*. WUNT 2.225. Tübingen: Mohr Siebeck, 2007.

———. "The Supersession and Superfluity of the Law? Another Look at Galatians." In *Introduction to Messianic Judaism*, edited by David J. Rudolph and Joel Willitts, 235–44. Grand Rapids: Zondervan, 2013.

Windsor, Lionel J. *Paul and the Vocation of Israel: How Paul's Jewish Identity Informs His Apostolic Ministry, with Special Reference to Romans*. BZNW 205. Berlin: De Gruyter, 2014.

——. *Reading Ephesians and Colossians after Supersessionism Christ's Mission through Israel to the Nations.* NTAS. Eugene, OR: Cascade, 2017.

Witherington, Ben. *Paul's Letter to the Romans: A Socio-Rhetorical Commentary.* Grand Rapids: Eerdmans, 2004.

Woolf, Greg. "Afterword: The Local and The Global in the Graeco-Roman West." In *Local Knowledge and Microidentities in the Imperial Greek World,* edited by Tim Whitmarsh, 189–200. Cambridge: Cambridge University Press, 2010.

Wright, N. T. *The Climax of the Covenant Christ and the Law in Pauline Theology.* Minneapolis: Fortress, 1992.

——. "Justification by (Covenantal) Faith to the (Covenantal) Doers: Romans 2 within the Argument of the Letter." In *Doing Theology for the Church: Essays in Honor of Klyne Snodgrass,* edited by Rebekah Ann Eklund and John E. Phelan Jr., 95–108. Eugene, OR: Wipf and Stock, 2014.

——. "The Law in Roman 2." In *Paul and the Mosaic Law,* edited by J. D. G. Dunn, 131–50. Tübingen: Mohr Siebeck, 1996.

——. *The Letter to the Romans.* NIB 10. Nashville: Abingdon, 2002.

——. *The New Testament and the People of God.* London: SPCK, 1992.

——. *Paul and the Faithfulness of God.* London: SPCK, 2013.

——. "Paul and the Patriarch: The Role(s) of Abraham in Galatians and Romans." In *Pauline Perspectives: Essays on Paul, 1978–2013,* edited by N. T. Wright, 554–92. Minneapolis: Fortress, 2013.

——. "Paul in Current Anglophone Scholarship." *ExpTim* 123 (2012) 367–81.

——. *Paul in Fresh Perspective.* Minneapolis: Fortress, 2005.

Zetterholm, Magnus. *Approaches to Paul: A Student's Guide to Recent Scholarship.* Minneapolis: Fortress, 2009.

——. "Paul and the Missing Messiah." In *The Messiah: In Early Judaism and Christianity,* edited by Magnus Zetterholm, 33–56. Minneapolis: Fortress, 2007.

——. "'Will the Real Gentile-Christian Please Stand Up!' Torah and the Crisis of Identity Formation." In *The Making of Christianity: Conflict, Contacts, and Constructions: Essays in Honor of Bengt Holmberg,* edited by Magnus Zetterholm and Samuel Byrskog, 373–93. Winona Lake, IN: Eisenbrauns, 2012.

Zoccali, Christopher. "'And so All Israel Will Be Saved': Competing Interpretations of Romans 11.26 in Pauline Scholarship." *JSNT* 30 (2008) 289–318.

——. "Children of Abraham, the Restoration of Israel and the Eschatological Pilgrimage of the Nations: What Does It Mean for 'in Christ' Identity." In *T. & T. Clark Handbook to Social Identity in the New Testament,* edited by J. Brian Tucker, and Coleman A. Baker, 253–71. London: Bloomsbury/T. & T. Clark, 2014.

——. "Paul and Social Identity in 1 Corinthians." *Journal of Beliefs and Values* 34 (2013) 105–14.

——. *Reading Philippians after Supersessionism.* NTAS. Eugene, OR: Cascade, 2017.

——. *Whom God Has Called: The Relationship of Church and Israel in Pauline Interpretation, 1920 to the Present.* Eugene, OR: Pickwick, 2010.

Index of Ancient Sources

OLD TESTAMENT/ HEBREW BIBLE

Genesis

1:31	39
6:18	233n56
9:8–17	233n56
9:9–17	233n56
12:1–3	231
12:1	79n80
12:2–3	76, 95
12:2	80n84
12:3	74, 78, 130n73, 145
12:7	73, 74, 76, 78, 79, 79n80, 80n84, 234
12:12	80n84
13:14–17	80n84, 234
13:15–17	79n80
13:15	73
13:17	73
15:4	80n84
15:5	45
15:6	90
15:7–8	79n80
15:7	73
15:18–21	73
15:18	127n59, 233n56
17:1–27	233n56
17:2	127n59
17:4–8	234
17:5	82
17:8	73, 79n80
17:9–14	45
17:11	71
17:12	49n95
17:14	46, 49, 227n27
17:16	80n84
17:19	80n84, 136, 233n56
17:20	136
17:21	136, 233n56
18:8	80n84
18:10	138
18:14	138
21:12	136, 234
22:16–18	80n84, 234
22:17–18	78, 145
22:17	45
22:18	95
25:1–4	45, 136
25:6	136
25:13–14	45
25:19–26	45
26:1–5	79n83
26:3–5	127n59
26:4	45
26:5	78n75
28:14	136
32–34	119n18
32:28	45n82
32:32	119n18
35:10–11	45n82
35:11–12	79n83
37:28	45
49:10	21n81

Exodus

1:1	46n82
1:12	46n82
1:22	46n82
2:24	127n59
3:13–16	130n70
4:22–23	125
4:24–26	46
6:4–5	127n59
12:14–20	203, 216
12:25	128
14:19–20	126
14:24	126
16:7	125
16:10	126
18:5	187n60
19	126
19:5–6	128
19:5	126
19:10–11	46n83
20	127
20:8–11	86n7
24	126
24:7–8	127n59
24:12–18	126
25–31	128
31:18	128
33:13	21n81
33:18	126

Leviticus

5	163
8:1–5	163
10–11	213, 214, 215, 217
10:10	215
11	203n21, 209, 216
11:46–47	214, 215
12:3	49n95
18:5	155, 156, 162, 163, 165, 168, 168n72, 169
19:18	93, 202n19
26:2–13	78n73
26:41	53n117
26:42	127n59

Numbers

16:17–21	175
20:15	130n70
26:55	130n70

Deuteronomy

1:8	130n70
4:19	21n81
6:4	100
7:6	34
8:3	130n70
8:16	130n70
8:17	170
8:18	130n70
9:1	79
9:4	170
9:5	130n70
10:16	52, 53n114, 53n117, 54
11:23	79
12:2	79
24:1	110n99
24:8–9	49n96
26:17–19	57
30	167, 168n72, 170
30:6	53n114, 54, 167
30:11–14	168
30:12–14	163, 165, 167, 170
30:12	170
30:13	170
30:14	170
30:15–20	78n73
31:3	79
31:27–29	193
32:4	237n75
32:6	237n75
32:8–9	237n75
32:9	237n75
32:21	151
32:31	237n75
32:35	237n75
32:36	237n75
32:42	234
32:43	237, 237n75, 237n76, 238

Joshua

22:7	128

1 Kings

4:7	187n60
6:13	46n82
12:1	187n60

2 Kings

3:6	187n60
17:34	45n82

1 Samuel

3:20	187n60
4:5	187n60
18:6	187N60

2 Samuel

5:5	187n60
7:12	234, 240
7:16	234
8:15	187n60
10:17	187n60
22:50	234
23:5	127n59

1 Chronicles

1:32	45
16:13–22	71n35
16:15	127
16:17	127

2 Chronicles

36:13	193

Ezra

2:70	187n60
6:14	46n82

Nehemiah

1:2	46n82
9:29	163

Psalms

18	235, 236
18:43–44a	236
18:49	234, 239
19:1	126
24:1	216
105:1	71n35
105:47	193n91
117:1	238, 239
119:18	113

Isaiah

11:10	99, 130, 234, 239, 240
17:3	46n82
17:9	46n82
27:9	126, 152, 189, 190n77
28:16	38
41:8–9	95
41:8	71
45:4	75
45:6	75
49:3	95
49:6	57, 71, 95, 134n87
51:2	62n2
54:1	79, 145
54:3	79
59:20–21	126, 152, 189, 190n77
59:20	187
59:21	11, 12, 71, 187
61:9	71n35
65:1–2	238

Jeremiah

4:4	52n113, 53, 53n117
9:25–26	52n113, 53
23:5	234
26:27	193n91
31	193
31:31–34	90
31:31	65, 193
31:33	11, 193, 194

Jeremiah (continued)

31:34	193
38:7–8	193n91
38:33	53n114
39:32	46n82

Ezekiel

2:3–4	193
4:4–9	52n113
11:19	122
20:11	163
20:13	163
20:21	163
36:8–12	77
36:22–38	78n73
36:24–29	90
36:26	122
36:27	12, 90
36:36–37	56n127
37:24–28	78n73
44:7	53n114

Daniel

1:8–16	198n6
6:2	207
9:7	187n60
9:11	187n60

Hosea

1–2	149, 150
1:10	140, 150
2:23	140, 141, 150
9:25–26	145
11:1	125

Habakkuk

2:4	162

Zephaniah

3:19	193n91
8:7–8	193n91
10:6	193n91

Haggai

2:5–7	217n69

Zechariah

14:9	100

Malachi

3:24	187n60

✢

APOCRYPHA

Tobit

1:3–6	187n60
1:10–12	21n81
13:3	46n82

Judith

4:12	21n81

Wisdom of Solomon

10–19	232

Sirach Prologue

1:1	41

Sirach

24:23	89
31:5	64n12
31:10	64n12
44:17	233
44:19	233
44:20	78n75
44:21	74, 77, 80n84
44:22–23	233
45:1–2	233
51:12	46n82

1 Maccabees

1:11–15	21n81, 227n28

1:47	214, 215	1:25	125
1:52	227n28	6–7	233n55
1:62	215	6:4	233n56
2:51–53	78n75	6:10	233n56
5:45	187n60	6:17–19	233n56
5:63	187n60	14:18–20	233, 233n56
		15:1–32	233n56
2 Maccabees		15:4–10	232
15:9	41	15:14	49n95
		15:19	233n56
		15:21	233n56
2 Esdras		15:30–32	136
4:23	21n81	15:33	49n96, 50n102
9:7	21n81	16:28	78n75
		19:11–12	45
		22:14	77, 232n54
4 Maccabees		22:15	77, 233n56
7:6	215n59	22:30	233n56
		23:10	78n75
✧		24:10–11	232n54
		32:19	232n54
		50:9	187n60

PSEUDEPIGRAPHA

		Liber Antiquitatum Biblicarum	
Aristeas		22:1	187n60
313	89		
		Odes of Solomon	
2 Baruch		11:1–3	56
51:1–16	99		
57:2	78n75	**Psalms of Solomon**	
		14:1–2	78n73
1 Enoch		14:9–10	78n73
5:7ab	77	17–18	99, 240
90:37–38	63n8	17:4	99
		17:21–44	240
4 Ezra		17:30–31	99
7:28–29	97n39	17:32	99
		17:34	242
Jubilees		17:42	99
1:1–3	126		
1:1	127	**Testament of Joseph**	
1:17	129	20:5	187n60
1:22–24	53n117		
1:23	49n95, 52n113	**Testament of Naphtali**	
		8:7–9	92, 96

Testament of Simeon

7:2	21n81

✛

NEW TESTAMENT

Matthew

1:3	121n30
1:5	121n30
1:6	121n30
5:17–19	13
5:17	161
15:24	227
18:15	212
19:3–9	110n99
23:15	212

Mark

7:15	203
7:19	203
7:19b	203, 203n21
12:31	202n19

Luke

4:13–14	212
4:21	212

John

5:24	175n11

Acts

3:25–26	71
11:1–3	209
13:49	95
15	58
15:19–31	215
15:21	96
15:29	14
16:4	215
17:1–2	36
18:2–4	17
18:2	17, 97

18:3	212
18:4	97
18:5–6	97
18:11	212
18:12	17
18:18	212
21:17–26	76, 213
21:21	51
21:24	122, 128
21:29	97
22:19	38n53
28:21–22	15n50
28:30	36

Romans

1–5	103
1–4	28, 35, 46, 58
1:1–7	236
1:1	1, 192
1:2	34, 59, 158
1:3–4	39n55, 80n84, 97, 236, 240
1:3	98, 120, 121, 130
1:4	56n127, 234
1:5–7	107
1:5–6	18
1:5	1, 3, 25, 56, 57
1:6–8	199n7
1:7	83, 84n104
1:9	56n127
1:11–17	236
1:11–12	56
1:13–15	87
1:13–14	107
1:14	38
1:16–17	41n63, 231n49
1:16	33, 38, 40, 69, 159, 230
1:16c	33, 34, 38
1:17	41n63, 42
1:18—3:20	102n55, 157n16
1:18—2:29	31
1:18–32	28
1:23	222n5, 223
1:26–27	99
1:30	31
1:32	176n18

2	46
2:7–29	45, 222n5
2:9–11	44
2:9–10	34, 94
2:9	230
2:10	222n5
2:12	88, 89, 90, 94
2:13–17	102n58
2:13	88, 94
2:14	88
2:17–29	47, 48, 49, 55n126, 56
2:17	18, 19, 30, 37n43, 47
2:18	205
2:20	88
2:21–22	50, 99
2:23	30
2:25—3:2	57
2:25–27	50
2:25	51, 52
2:25a	50, 51
2:26–27	54, 227n27
2:26	103
2:27	89
2:28—3:2	60
2:28–29	12, 47, 52n111, 53, 54, 64n10, 122, 132n80
2:28	55, 81n84, 131n78
2:29	53n117, 54, 55, 194n95, 226
3:1–8	35
3:1–4	230
3:1–2	34, 35n31, 52, 54, 56, 57, 78n73, 89, 123, 127
3:1	54
3:2	54, 57
3:3–4	195
3:3	118
3:4	43
3:8	51n107
3:9	32, 43
3:10–20	72n37
3:12	43
3:13–14	134
3:19–21	97

3:19–20	106
3:19	43, 88, 95, 106n75, 108
3:20–22	158, 165, 165n56
3:20	40, 43, 120, 158
3:21–31	109, 166
3:21–26	44, 64
3:21–22	33n18, 40, 163, 165
3:21	41, 41n63, 42, 58, 59, 69, 158, 159, 160
3:22–23	43
3:22	10, 29, 39, 40, 42, 43, 44, 60, 64, 89
3:23	43, 146, 222, 222n4, 222n5, 223
3:25	41n63
3:26	40, 41n63, 84n104
3:27	31
3:28	40, 58, 163, 165
3:29–30	100
3:29	21n81
3:30	52, 84n104, 225n19, 227, 227n27
3:31	51n107, 58, 59, 60, 95, 99, 101, 109, 158
4	42, 59, 62, 65, 66, 70, 71, 84, 102n56, 127, 129, 145, 194n95
4:1–12	82n94
4:1–8	62n1
4:1–4	82n94
4:1	37, 62n2, 63, 80n84
4:4–5	90
4:5–8	82n94
4:6	40
4:9–18	62n1
4:9–12	82n94, 227
4:9–10	70, 227n27
4:10	78
4:11–17	138n95
4:11–13	64
4:11–12	12, 66, 71n36, 84

Romans (continued)

4:11b–12	62, 66, 67, 68, 70, 71, 80, 84
4:11b	67
4:12	67, 68, 69
4:13–17	81n87
4:13–16	230
4:13	62, 66, 72, 73, 76, 78, 79, 81, 128, 163, 165, 231, 247
4:13a	231
4:14	78, 94, 95, 128, 163, 165
4:15	72n37
4:16–17	83, 84n104
4:16	62, 66, 71, 78, 80, 81, 82, 83, 95, 96, 128, 163, 165, 231
4:17–18	71n36, 77
4:17	80
4:18	81
4:19–25	62n1
4:20	128
4:23–24	59
5–6	112n109
5:1	84n104
5:2	31, 222n5
5:3	31
5:5	242n104
5:8	106n73
5:11	31
5:20–21	106n75
5:20	102, 102n55, 159
6	105n69, 107
6:1	51n107
6:4	222n4
6:14–15	13n42, 87, 94, 102, 104, 105, 106
6:14	98, 108
6:15	51n107
6:16	108
7	105n69, 107, 109n91, 111
7:1–13	102n55
7:1–6	109, 110n99, 111, 112n109
7:1–4	99

7:1–2	110
7:1	18, 51n107, 98, 107
7:3	110
7:4	13n42, 87, 102, 104, 111, 112
7:4a	109
7:5–6	112n109
7:5	111, 112n109, 159
7:6	13n42, 87, 91, 102, 104, 109, 110, 111, 112, 157n16
7:6ab	109
7:6b	112n109
7:6c	109
7:7–8:4	159
7:7–25	90
7:7–23	109n91
7:7	56n131, 109, 159
7:9–10	90
7:10	94, 101
7:12	96, 101, 104, 158
7:13–20	109n91
7:14–8:11	91
7:14	91, 158
7:24–8:1	158
8	176
8:1–4	109, 111
8:1	107
8:2–4	91, 167
8:2	106
8:3–4	91, 166
8:3	59n142, 120
8:4–5	98
8:4	101, 111
8:7	94, 101, 111
8:9	12, 91
8:13	122
8:15	125
8:17–23	10n29
8:18–25	9n27
8:20	243n104
8:23	125
8:24	243n104
9–11	30, 35n33, 39, 44, 64n13, 98, 104n63, 107n85, 114, 117, 118, 124,

	149, 163, 166, 173, 175, 176, 184, 188, 190, 194, 195	9:15	118n17, 231
9:1—11:36	82n91	9:18–26	231
9–10	171	9:20–23	193
9	66, 114, 115, 116, 117, 122, 142, 150, 170	9:22–29	143
		9:22–23	143, 144, 145
		9:22	143
9:1–29	139, 152	9:23	143
9:1–6	145	9:24–26	71n36, 116, 138n95, 139, 140, 143, 146, 149, 193, 247
9:1–5	44, 116, 117, 119n17, 139		
9:1–3	117, 123	9:24	138, 140, 141, 143, 144, 145, 149, 150
9:2–5	131n78		
9:2	118, 131	9:25–29	143
9:3–5	224	9:25–26	140, 143, 144, 145, 146
9:3–4	121, 150, 227		
9:3	12, 119, 124	9:25	141, 142, 143
9:4–5	32, 34, 37, 56, 117, 123, 125, 131, 195, 230	9:26	141, 142
		9:27–29	144
		9:27	46n82, 145, 151
9:4	11, 12, 56n131, 76, 89, 121, 123, 124, 125, 138, 145, 231, 232n53	9:30—10:21	152
		9:30—10:14	154, 168
		9:30—10:8	102n55
		9:30—10:4	108n85, 160, 167n65
9:5	66, 68, 98, 121, 129, 130	9:30–33	159
		9:30–31	21n81
9:6–29	141, 143	9:30	84n104, 143
9:6–13	45, 121	9:31	96, 170
9:6–9	116, 131, 134, 139, 194n95	9:32–33	159
		9:32	84n104, 155, 170
9:6–7	81	9:33	38
9:6	12, 64n10, 68, 131, 131n78, 132, 133, 134, 139, 175, 184n42, 186	10	152n141
		10:1	30n8, 150, 158
		10:2–4	158, 165, 165n56
		10:2	157
9:7–16	134n86	10:3	156, 158, 168, 170
9:7–12	12n37	10:4	13, 26, 59, 98, 102, 104, 153, 154n2, 155, 156, 157, 158, 159, 162, 167n65, 168, 169, 170, 199
9:7–8	138		
9:7	135, 137, 141		
9:8	128, 137, 138, 227		
9:9–13	128		
9:9	138	10:5–8	107n85, 156, 157, 158, 163, 165n56
9:10–23	139n102		
9:10–13	141	10:5–6	26, 154, 155, 162, 168, 169
9:11	173n5		
9:13	193, 194	10:5	163, 164, 165, 166, 167, 168, 169
9:15–18	230		

Romans (continued)

10:6–8	170
10:6	84n104, 162, 163, 164, 165, 167, 168
10:12–13	44
10:12	10, 29, 39, 40, 43, 44, 60, 64, 89, 142n109, 146
10:13	7, 30n8, 190
10:18	122, 137
10:19	88, 151, 237n75
10:20–21	238
10:20	164
11	171, 172, 173, 176, 186n50
11:1–36	149, 150
11:1–32	143
11:1–24	192
11:1–11	56n131
11:1–10	173
11:1–5	12n40
11:1–2	119
11:1	12, 32, 44, 71, 107, 118, 124n45, 150, 172, 174, 175n9, 184, 190, 195, 237n75, 245
11:2	131, 150
11:5–6	32, 173
11:5	131, 150, 173n5, 175, 190
11:6	32
11:7–10	80
11:7	139, 150, 151, 173, 173n5
11:10	173
11:11–36	151, 173
11:11–32	178
11:11–30	81n88
11:11–24	151, 192, 195
11:11–15	236
11:11–14	188, 236, 237n75
11:11–12	37
11:11	32, 32n16, 75n59, 106, 131n78, 174, 179, 182, 186, 190
11:12	151, 174, 187, 188
11:13–32	30
11:13–24	230
11:13–14	31, 147
11:13	18, 23, 36, 87, 150, 167n65, 179, 182
11:14	32n16, 150, 151, 187, 189, 190
11:15	32n16, 37, 71n34, 151, 174, 175, 188
11:16	32, 122, 175, 176
11:17–24	8n23, 32, 125, 151, 177, 178
11:17–19	178
11:17	148, 178, 179, 180, 182, 183, 188
11:18	31, 180, 184
11:19	32, 181, 182, 183
11:20–23	193
11:20	118, 181, 183
11:20b–21	31
11:21–24	151
11:21	89, 182
11:22	181, 182, 183
11:23–24	183, 184
11:23	118, 184n42, 187, 189n71
11:24	186
11:25–36	151
11:25–32	101, 236
11:25–29	236
11:25–27	135n90, 142n110, 185, 195
11:25–26	12, 31, 44, 149, 188
11:25	151, 183n41, 187, 188, 189, 193
11:25b	191
11:26–27	129
11:26	7, 12, 30n8, 32n16, 34, 174, 184, 185, 185, 186, 187, 189, 192
11:26a	32
11:27	11, 12, 71, 126, 126n58, 193, 194
11:28–29	12, 32, 32n16, 34, 125, 194, 196

11:28	68, 124, 130, 189, 231
11:28b–29	44, 172, 195
11:29	12, 32, 34, 176n18, 195, 245
11:30–36	33
11:30–33	32
11:30–32	37, 189n71, 192
11:30–31	188
11:30	151
11:31	191
11:33–36	119n17, 124
12:1–21	31
12:1–2	58n134, 63, 242
12:3–8	7, 44
12:3	31
12:12	243n104
12:19	237n75
13:1–7	83n102, 242
13:8–10	56n131, 91, 93n28, 99, 104, 109, 111, 111n101, 166n61
13:8	92, 166
13:9	92, 166
13:10	92
13:13	176n18
13:18	202n19
14–15	38n51, 39, 59n139, 83, 98, 111, 170, 198n5, 199n7, 209, 210, 212, 218, 218n72, 219
14:1—15:13	197, 197n2, 204, 204n27, 205, 208, 212, 223
14:1—15:6	56n131, 198n2, 243
14	198n5, 204
14:1–6	86
14:1	30, 201n16, 202n18, 204, 223, 238
14:2	44, 198n6
14:3–4	30
14:3	3, 201n16, 202, 204
14:4	27, 201n16, 204, 207, 209
14:5	3, 44, 83, 204
14:6–9	207
14:6–8	204
14:6	202
14:10	204
14:10c–12	201n16
14:13–23	214n57
14:13–18	228
14:13	204
14:14–17	204
14:14	197, 199n7, 200, 202, 203, 212, 213, 214, 215, 216, 219
14:14b	217
14:15	201, 206
14:17	64, 206, 231, 243
14:19	206
14:20–23	218
14:20	27, 197, 199n7, 200, 202, 203, 204, 206, 212, 213, 214, 219
14:21	198n6
14:22–23	98, 104n64
14:22	202, 208
14:23	83, 84n104, 98, 208
14:23c	208
15	75n59
15:1	55, 202, 202n18
15:2–3	219
15:3–7	228
15:3	130, 224, 240
15:5–13	100
15:6	204, 238
15:7–13	12, 27, 185, 220, 221, 225, 231
15:7–12	240
15:7–9	236
15:7	3, 18, 130, 201n16, 204, 222, 223, 224, 229, 243
15:8–13	33, 154
15:8–9	12n37, 225, 226, 228
15:8–9a	226, 228, 230

Romans (continued)

15:8	12, 75, 99, 128, 131, 224, 225, 225n21, 227, 227n27, 229, 231n49, 233, 237, 247
15:8a	229
15:8b	229, 231
15:9–13	228
15:9–12	27, 204, 226, 247
15:9	229
15:9a	229
15:9b–12	201n16, 221, 234
15:9b	236
15:9bc	235
15:10–11	222
15:10	32, 75, 235, 236n73, 237, 238, 239
15:11	235, 238, 239
15:12	99, 130, 235, 239, 240, 242
15:13	242
15:15–16	18, 236
15:16	36, 107
15:23–26	3
15:24	183n41
15:27	151, 188
15:30–32	192
15:31	236
16:3–16	118n15
16:3–5	147, 148
16:3	97
16:4	20n76, 55, 201n16
16:5	201n16
16:7	120n26
16:11	120n26
16:16	201n16
16:21	120n26
16:21	201n16
16:25–26	59
16:26	4, 25

1 Corinthians

1:22	46n82
1:26–29	212
3:16	76
3:23	22n83
4:10	212
4:12	212
4:16	53n114
6:9–11	176n18
6:19	76
7:5	92
7:17–24	3, 7n22, 24, 67, 154, 213
7:17–20	211
7:17–19	57
7:17–18	14, 122
7:17	47, 211
7:18–20	227
7:18	47, 52
7:19	3, 14, 47, 52, 78n73, 113n110, 176n18, 177
7:19b	113
7:20	14, 122
7:39	110n99
8:1—11:1	211
8–10	210, 212, 218n72
8:7	212
8:9	212
9:19–23	3, 36, 210
9:19–21	116
9:19	210, 211
9:20–21	211
9:20	86, 94, 99, 122, 211
9:21	13n44, 47, 104, 211
9:21–23	212
9:22	211
9:23	212
10:1–11	88
10:1	130
10:11	115
10:18	37, 121, 133, 137
10:27	201n17
10:32	205
11:1	53n114, 212
11:25	126n58
12:2	147
14:7	44n76
14:33b–35	148

15:3–4	88
15:23	22
16:1–4	3

2 Corinthians

3	55n126
3:6	126n58, 225
3:7–11	159, 159n28
3:7–9	116
3:13	126n55
3:14–16	116
3:14	126n58
3:15	87
3:16	65, 91
6:10	212
6:16	76
8:9	212
11:22	71, 121
11:24	97

Galatians

1:8–9	110n95
1:15–16	23
2	209
2:1–10	58
2:7–9	227n27
2:11–14	51, 209
2:11	209
2:14	209, 210, 213n55
2:15	86, 211
2:16	157n16
2:17	224
2:18	58
2:19	157n16
2:21	157n16
3	194n95
3:6–18	58
3:8	130n73
3:10–12	163
3:10	110n95
3:11–12	107n85, 156, 164
3:11	157n16, 164
3:12	162, 164, 169
3:13	110n95
3:15–18	153
3:15	126n58
3:16	81

3:17	126n58
3:21	157n16
3:22	157n16
3:23—4:7	159, 159n28
3:23–25	103n62, 157n16
3:23	94
3:28	37n42, 64, 130n73
4:4–5	94
4:21–31	88
4:21	94
4:27	79
5:2–3	51n105
5:2	57
5:3	49n96, 227
5:4	157n16
5:11–12	51n105
5:15	157n16
5:18	94
5:19–23	176n18
5:24	22
6:2	13n44, 99, 104, 211n52
6:12–13	51n105
6:13	49n96
6:15	10, 113n110
6:16	64n10, 116, 133, 133n85, 137, 194n95

Ephesians

2:11	227n27
2:12	64n10
2:13	12n37
2:17	12n37
4:17	21n81

Philippians

2:12	212
3:3	54n121, 142n109, 194n95, 227n27
3:5	46n82, 49, 211

Colossians

2:11–13	106n73
2:11	54n121

Colossians (continued)

3:8	212
3:11	227n27

1 Thessalonians

1:6	53n114
2:14–17	116
2:14	53n114

2 Thessalonians

2:3–4	76

1 Timothy

1:5	156

2 Timothy

2:8	130

Hebrews

7:11–17	97n39
11:22	46n82

James

5:1–6	50n101

1 Peter

2:4–10	

Revelation

2:14	46n82
5:5	240
22:16	130, 240

✦

DEAD SEA SCROLLS

1Q28b

5.20–29	239n85

1QH

4.17–26	90
18.20	52n113

1QpHab

11.13	52n113

1QS

4.20	90
5.5	52n113, 53n114
5.6–7	52n113
5.6	232
8.9b—10a	232n53
9.11	97n39
11.7–19	90

4Q11

Frag. 9–14	239n85

4Q285

Frag 5	239n85

4Q504

4.3.11	52n113

CD

2.11–12	232
2.11	232n54
3.1–4	233n55
3.8–16	187n60
3.13–14	134
6.2	233
11.12	232
15.5	187n60
15.7–10a	233n56

✦

RABBINIC WRITINGS

Yoma

286	78n75

Qiddushin

3:10   217n70
4:14   78n75

Shabbat

7:2   86n7

Sanhedrin

10:1–3   187n60

Sifre on Deuteronomy

6:4 (Piska 31)   100

✧

GRECO-ROMAN WRITINGS

Appian
The Civil Wars

2.26.99   20n75
2.28.107   20n75

Arrian
Discourses of Epictetus

4.8.17–20   55n126

Cassius Dio
Roman History

51.20.6–8   21n78
60.5.2   17n62
60.6.7   17n56

Josephus
Jewish Antiquities

1.18   88
1.21   88
1.26   88
1.29   88
1.33–34   88

1.122–53   62n2
1.148–49   62n2
1.158   62n2
11.169   62n2
14.255   62n2
17.151   217
17.159   89n14
20.17–48   50n98
20.34–50   54n120
20.96   50n98

Against Apion

2.150   89
2.151   89
2.175   96

Jewish War

2.463   24n97, 50n98
5.380   62n2
7.41–62   24n97
7.45   50n98

The Life

14   198n6

Pausanias
Description of Greece

8.40.2   179

Philo
On the Life of Abraham

5–6   78n75
60–61   78n75
275   78n75

On the Migration of Abraham

16.92   52n113
89–93   54n120

On The Embassy to Gaius

1.156   96

On the Life of Moses

2.12   89

Questions and Answers on Exodus

2.2   54n120

Questions and Answers on Genesis

3.46–52   53n114

On Dreams

2.127   97

On The Special Laws

1.51   54n120
1.6   53n114
1.66.305   52n113
1.345   88, 89

Pliny

Natural History

3.20.136–37   21n79

Plutarch

Amatorius

750 E   157

Res Gestae Divi Augusti

3.25–33   21n80

Seneca

Apolocyntosis

9.5   17n62

Ad Polybium de consolatione

8.2   17n61
11.6   17n61

Suetonius

Claudius

3.2   17n62

11.2   17n62
25.4–5   17n57
25.4   15n50

Tacitus

Annals

12.52   17.59

Germania

39   23n91

Virgil

Aeneid

1.275–79   238

᪐

EARLY CHRISTIAN WRITINGS

Ignatius

To the Magnesians

10.2–3   22n83

Irenaeus

Against Heresies

36.2   6n16

Justin Martyr

Dialogue with Trypho

47   22n83
135   133n83
135.3   6n16

Paulus Orosius

Seven Book of History Against the Pagans

7.6.15

Index of Modern Authors

Aageson, James W., 134
Abasciano, Brian J., 64, 132
Achtemeier, Paul J., 64
Adeyemi, Femi, 87
Alkier, Stefan, 119
Avidov, Avi, 25

Bachmann, Michael, 79n82
Badenas, Robert, 87n10, 157,
    157n17, 157n18, 159n26,
    161, 161n37, 168n74,
    169n77, 169n78
Barclay, John M. G., 11n36, 47n86,
    47n87, 50n100, 59n139,
    66n20, 70n32, 72n37, 75n61,
    81n89, 81n90, 82n94, 82n95,
    83n103, 96n37, 107n85,
    118n12, 166n62, 180n31,
    206, 206n32, 206n33, 207,
    213, 213n54, 215, 226n22,
    229n35, 247n14
Barrett, C. K., 33, 33n20, 132,
    132n80, 134, 160, 160n34,
    161, 161n35, 236, 236n71
Barth, Karl, 9n28, 119n20
Battle, John A., Jr., 145, 145n119
Baur, F. C., 20, 74, 74n55
Beale, G. K., 75n61, 140, 140n104
Bell, Catherine M., 222n1
Bell, Richard H., 138n95
Bernat, David A., 45n79
Bird, Michael F., 4n12, 91, 91n16,
    96n37, 133n84, 181n35,
    182, 182n38, 205n30, 230,
    231, 231n47, 234, 234n62,
    235n65, 235n68, 241n96,
    243n104, 247n16

Bjoraker, Bill, 36n34
Black, Matthew, 234, 234n63
Blackwell, Ben C., 222, 222n4,
    247n15
Boccaccini, Gabriele, 87n10, 247n13
Bock, Darrell, 247n19
Bockmuehl, Markus N. A., 87n10,
    186, 186n54, 186n55
Boulton, Matthew, 146n127, 248n20
Boyarin, Daniel, 20n73, 65n15, 122,
    122n39, 204, 204n23
Brewer, Marilynn B., 22n85
Brindle, Wayne A., 35n33, 37n41,
    37n46
Brueggemann, Walter, 73, 73n49
Bultmann, Rudolf, 239, 240, 240n86
Burge, Gary M., 72, 72n44, 72n45,
    73, 73n46, 73n47, 73n48,
    76n67, 79
Burke, Trevor J., 125, 125n51
Burnett, David, 80n84
Byrne, Brendan, 37, 37n45

Cadbury, Henry, 200, 200n9
Campbell, Constantine R., 124n48
Campbell, Douglas, 48n90
Campbell, William S., 3n8, 3n9,
    11n35, 11n36, 12n39, 19n69,
    33, 34n21, 36n38, 37, 37n43,
    39n54, 40n58, 47, 48n88,
    53n116, 54n121, 58n137,
    59n139, 63n8, 64n13, 65n14,
    78n76, 80, 80n85, 81, 81n87,
    82, 82n92, 83, 83n103, 84,
    86, 86n8, 95, 95n33, 109n91,
    113n110, 133n85, 137,
    138n95, 139n101, 140n106,

Campbell, William S. (*continued*) 146, 146n125, 159n28, 164, 165, 165n54, 165n55, 165n58, 177, 177n21, 178, 178n22, 178n23, 180, 180n32, 183, 184n42, 196, 196n101, 196n103, 219, 219n73, 219n74, 219n75, 219n76, 220, 226, 226n24, 227n25, 231n49, 234, 234n60, 243n103, 246n10, 248n21

Carraway, George, 44n78

Carson, D. A., 86, 86n6

Carter, Warren, 242n97

Casey, Maurice, 22, 22n88, 22n89, 85, 85n3

Castelli, Elizabeth A., 123, 123n40

Charlesworth, James Hamilton, 9n26

Christiansen, Ellen Juhl, 76n68, 125n50, 126n57, 127, 127n60, 127n61, 127n62, 129n67

Ciampa, Roy E., 34n25, 167, 167n67

Cinnirella, Marco, 222n1

Clarke, Andrew D., 2n5, 248n23

Cohen, Shaye J. D., 46n83, 49, 49n97

Collins, John J., 51, 51n103, 51n104

Collins, Nate, 246n7

Concannon, Cavan W., 147n131

Constantineanu, Corneliu, 228, 228n33

Conway, Kevin P., 75n60, 138, 138n98, 139n99, 139n100

Coppins, Wayne, 110, 110n93, 110n94, 110n95, 110n96, 110n98, 111, 111n104

Cosgrove, Charles H., 118n15

Cottrell, Jack, 12n40, 65n17

Craigie, Peter C., 236n70

Cranfield, Charles. E. B., 13n45, 40, 41n61, 42, 42n67, 65, 69n27, 80n86, 83n101, 106, 106n79, 119, 119n20, 132, 133n83, 143n113, 158, 159n24, 234, 234n58, 236n70

Cranford, Michael, 65, 65n18

Crisler, Channing L., 119n18

Cromhout, Marcus, 63n5

Cunningham, Philip, 31, 32n13, 32n14, 32n16, 33n17

Das, A. Andrew, 14n47, 18, 18n65, 87n10, 145n120, 178n24, 227, 227n28

Davies, Glenn N., 82n98, 87n10, 164, 164n51, 168n74, 170, 170n79, 170n80, 170n81

Davies, W. D., 72, 72n38, 72n38, 72n40, 73, 79, 208, 208n41

Davis, Stephan K., 160n30

Deming, Will, 92n23, 204, 204n24, 204n25, 205n31

Dodd, C. H., 131, 132n79

Doering, Lutz, 126n54

Donaldson, Terence L., 5n14, 13n43, 19, 20, 20n74, 21, 21n78, 22n87, 23, 23n90, 23n93, 24, 24n95, 50n98, 63n6, 63n8, 64, 65n14, 75n58, 142n109, 191, 191n80, 239n83

Donfried, Karl P., 14n47

Dunn, James D. G., 5n15, 28, 28n3, 36, 36n37, 37n48, 52n109, 52n111, 63n8, 87n10, 102n58, 103n58, 122n36, 125n52, 129n69, 132, 132n81, 138n96, 143n114, 146, 146n124, 157, 157n19, 158, 158n20, 159, 159n27, 178n25, 208, 208n43, 209, 210n46, 222, 222n5

Dunne, John Anthony, 9n29

Eco, Umberto, 119n21

Ehrensperger, Kathy, 3n9, 5n15, 37n47, 39n54, 62n3, 63n8, 75n56, 76n64, 113n110, 123, 123n40, 123n41, 123n42, 133n85, 137, 137n91, 137n93, 144n116, 151n137, 161n39, 184, 184n43, 199n8, 200, 200n10, 200n14, 216n65, 216n68, 219n75, 234n64, 246n10, 248n23

Eisenbaum, Pamela Michelle, 7, 7n19
Elliott, Neil, 20n75, 28n2, 30, 30n9, 30n10, 49n94, 245n1
Engberg-Pedersen, Troels, 204n25, 229n35
Esler, Philip F., 11n36, 39, 39n55, 65n15, 78n76, 137n92, 138n95, 160, 160n31, 160n32, 179n28, 181, 181n33, 238, 238n78
Eysenck, Michael W., 63n4

Fitzmyer, Joseph A., 34n26, 37n46, 40n58, 53n117, 68, 68n24, 80n84, 132, 132n82, 138n96, 175, 175n9, 175n11, 236n73, 241n89
Forman, Mark, 73, 73n49, 73n50, 73n51, 77n71,
Foster, Robert B., 15, 16n55, 17n59, 46n83, 82n96, 115, 115n1, 115n2, 116, 116n3, 116n4, 116n5, 116n6, 116n7, 116n8, 117, 117n9, 117n10, 117n11,
Fredriksen, Paula, 3n9, 22n85, 47n87, 50n98, 75n58, 93n28, 140, 140n103, 233, 233n57, 245n1, 246n6, 246n9
Fruchtenbaum, Arnold, 36n34

Gadenz, Pablo T., 18n66, 63n6, 203
Gard, Daniel L., 147n129
Garroway, Joshua D., 22n88, 51n107, 106n73, 203n20, 224, 224n12, 224n13, 224n14, 255, 225n15, 225n16, 225n17, 225n18, 225n20, 225n21, 226, 228, 228n32, 229, 229n36, 230, 230n45, 239, 241n93
Gaston, Lloyd, 225n19
Gathercole, Simon J., 28, 28n4, 64n12, 103n60
Gaventa, Beverly Roberts, 9n29, 10n31, 123n43, 153, 153n1, 186n53

Givens, Tommy, 119n20, 120n27, 120n28, 120n29, 132n79, 132n80
Gladd, Benjamin L., 75n61
Glenny, W. Edward, 145n121
Goodrich, John K., 112n105, 185, 185n48, 186, 186n56, 188, 188n67, 189, 189n72, 189n74, 191, 191n82, 192, 192n86, 193n94
Gorman, Michael J., 222, 222n2
Gregory, Bradley C., 77n70
Grieb, A. Katherine, 29n6, 64n13
Grindheim, Sigurd, 189n70

Hafemann, Scott J., 92n25, 100, 100n51, 112, 112n107, 166n61, 223n7, 231n46, 231n50, 234, 234n61, 234n62, 235n67, 241n90, 241n94
Hagner, Donald, 112n109, 157n16
Hakola, Raimo, 22n84
Halpern-Amaru, Betsy, 79n79, 127n63
Hardin, Justin K., 7n22, 159n28, 245n1
Harink, Douglas, 7, 7n19, 176n15, 196n101, 247n12
Harrington, Daniel J., 32n16
Harrison, James R., 76n65, 223, 223n6
Hays, Richard B., 82n95, 146n128, 149, 149n135, 231n47, 234n62
Hedner Zetterholm, Karin, 24n97, 86n7, 87n10, 108n85, 111n99, 166, 166n63, 207, 207n36
Heinsch, Ryan, 76n66, 223n56
Hill, Craig C., 173, 173n6
Horbury, William, 77n71
Horner, Barry E., 133n84
Horrell, David G., 21n77, 64n10
Hsieh, Nelson S., 76, 77, 77n69, 77n70
Hubing, Jeff, 10n32
Hübner, Hans, 87n10

Hultgren, Arland J., 34, 34n26, 42,
　42n66, 52n113, 58n138, 92,
　92n24, 161n38
Hunt, Laura J., 17n61, 21n80,
　22n86, 22n88, 64n10,
　119n21, 223n6, 229n39
Hvalvik, Reidar, 15n49, 34n22,
　34n24, 35n28, 35n33

Ibba, Giovanni, 87n10
Irons, Charles Lee, 41n63
Isaac, Munther, 72, 72n40, 72n41,
　72n42, 72n43, 73, 79

Jennings, Willie James, 6, 246n7,
　248, 248n22
Jewett, Robert, 35n28, 37n48,
　38n50, 40n59, 56n131,
　82n94, 92, 92n21, 121,
　121n34, 129n69, 167n65,
　178n25, 224n10, 231n49
Jipp, Joshua, 70n32, 99n45, 129n69,
　240, 240n86, 240n88
Johnson-Hodge, Caroline E., 81n87,
　83n101

Kaiser, Walter C., 167, 167n68
Kamell, Mariam J., 77n70
Kamudzandu, Israel, 63n9, 74n53
Käsemann, Ernst, 33n19, 67, 67n22,
　81n91,
Keck, Leander E., 35, 35n31, 91,
　91n18, 123, 124, 124n44,
　124n45, 124n46, 159,
　159n25, 164, 164n52
Keener, Craig S., 188n65
Kinzer, Mark, 7n21, 37n47, 71n34,
　119n23, 120n30, 122n38,
　131, 131n76, 131n77, 173n5,
　175, 175n12, 176, 176n13,
　176n14, 176n15, 176n16,
　182n36, 195n99, 209n44,
　210, 210n47, 210n48, 245n2,
　248n22
Kirk, J. R. Daniel, 241, 241n92
Kooten, George H. van, 74n54
Koperski, Veronica, 87n10

Korner, Ralph J., 17n60, 19n71,
　24n97, 148, 148n132, 173n2
Krauter, Stefan, 83n102
Kruse, Colin G., 34, 34n27, 35n28,
　40n59, 87n10, 92, 92n19,
　159, 159n28, 160n29,
　160n30, 230, 235, 235n66,
　238, 238n79, 239, 239n85

Le Donne, Anthony, 206n34
Lee, Jae Won, 207
Levenson, Jon D., 67, 75n57
Lewis, Robert Brian, 74n57
Liebengood, Kelly, 64n10
Lincicum, David, 74n55, 82n93,
　237n75
Livesey, Nina E., 69n28, 70n31
Lo, Lung-kwong, 199n6, 201n16
Lodge, John G., 12n38
Longenecker, Bruce W., 8n23,
　14n46, 78n75,
Longenecker, Richard N., 14n47,
　19n70, 64n10, 67, 68n23,
　81n91, 118n15, 126n55,
　127n59, 128, 128n65,
　128n66, 129n69, 178n25,
　182n38, 188, 197, 198n3
Longman, Tremper, 45n81
Lopez, Davina C., 20n75, 21, 21n79,
　242n101
Luomanen, Petri, 23n90

Macaskill, Grant, 11n33, 11n34,
　76n66
Magda, Ksenija, 33n20, 36n34
Magee, Gregory S., 100, 100n48
Marcus, Joel, 227, 227n26
Martin, Dale B., 121, 121n31, 130,
　130n71
Martin, Troy, 227, 227n29
Marttila, Tomas, 62
Martyn, Louis J., 10n32
Matera, Frank J., 18n68, 158n23,
　160, 160n33, 234n59,
　237n74
McComiskey, Thomas Edward,
　145n18
McDermott, Gerald R., 246n5

McFarland, Orrey, 83n98
McGowan, Andrew, 135n90
Merkle, Ben L., 185n50
Mermelstein, Ari, 77n72
Meyer, Paul W., 87n10, 167, 167n65
Middendorf, Michael P., 41, 41n63,
    43, 44, 44n75, 44n76, 44n77,
    47, 47n86, 56n127, 69,
    69n26, 69n27, 70, 70n29,
    109n91, 119n20, 126n58,
    130n70, 180n31, 187n59,
    188n63, 191n84, 198, 198n4
Milgrom, Jacob, 215n60
Miller, James C., 223n7, 224n9,
    234n63
Mininger, Marcus A., 55n126
Mitchell, Margaret, 20n74
Moo, Douglas J., 34n22, 35n28,
    37n48, 40n59, 54n118, 59,
    59n142, 68, 69n25, 81n88,
    82n93, 83n103, 102n58,
    102n58, 110n93, 119n20,
    120, 120n25, 134, 134n89,
    144, 144n117, 160n30, 161,
    161n36, 168n73, 169n75,
    191, 191n84, 199n7, 224n9,
    226, 226n23, 228, 228n31
Morales, Rodrigo Jose, 77n72
Mounce, Robert H., 33, 33n19,
    138n97
Moxnes, Halvor, 70n29
Nanos, Mark D., 2n2, 3n9, 4n12,
    14n48, 14n49, 15n50, 18,
    18n67, 19n72, 20n75, 21n82,
    24n97, 27, 35n32, 36, 36n35,
    36n36, 36n40, 48, 48n90,
    48n92, 50n98, 51n105,
    52n110, 53, 53n114, 53n117,
    55, 55n124, 55n125, 55n26,
    56, 56n130, 57, 57n133,
    57n134, 60n146, 78n74,
    83n99, 83n100, 85, 85n2,
    85n3, 93n28, 100, 100n47,
    100n49, 102n56, 103n58,
    107, 107n82, 108, 108n88,
    122n35, 131n78, 132n81,
    133n82, 133n85, 134n86,
    134n87, 151n139, 161n39,

173n5, 175, 176n13, 177n20,
    178, 179, 179n26, 179n27,
    179n29, 182, 182n37, 183,
    183n40, 183n41, 184,
    184n43, 184n44, 184n45,
    194n97, 196n102, 197n1,
    198n5, 199n7, 201n16,
    205n29, 206n35, 210n48,
    219n75, 245n3, 247n13

Naselli, Andrew David, 118n14
Neutel, Karin, 82n96
Nicolet-Anderson, Valérie, 223,
    223n8
Noort, Ed, 79n79
Novak, David, 65n19
Novenson, Matthew V., 9n27,
    48n93, 63n8, 66n20, 97n39,
    214n56, 240n86

Oakes, Peter, 87n10
Oliver, Isaac W., 3n9, 215, 215n63,
    216n67
Oropeza, B. J., 204n27
Ortlund, Dane Calvin, 167n65
Osborne, Grant R., 35, 35n30
Oswalt, John N., 79, 79n81

Paget, James Carleton, 20n76
Pate, C. Marvin, 156, 156n11,
    156n12, 231, 231n51,
    232n52
Patte, Daniel, 173n3
Pickstock, Catherine, 222n3
Porter, Stanley E., 181, 181n34,
    182n39

Quesnel, Michel, 118, 118n17

Rah, Soong-Chan, 246n7
Räisänen, Heikki, 87n10
Rapa, Robert Keith, 87n10
Reasoner, Mark, 9n27, 42, 42n69,
    142n110, 192n89, 193,
    193n92, 194, 194n96,
    203n21
Revell, Louise, 25n98
Reynolds, Benjamin E., 247n12

Rhyne, C. Thomas, 59, 59n141,
    59n144, 59n145, 60, 87n10
Richardson, Peter, 19n72, 85, 86n4
Richter, Daniel S., 25n99
Ridderbos, Herman., 5, 5n14
Rock, Ian E., 16, 16n51, 16n53, 17,
    17n57, 17n60, 18n63, 74n53,
    192n85
Rodríguez, Rafael, 19n69, 48, 48n89,
    48n91, 106n72, 106n73,
    107n83, 107n84, 108n86,
    174n7, 202n19, 237n76
Roetzel, Calvin, 12, 13n45
Rosner, Brian S., 59, 59n143, 87n10,
    91, 91n17, 92, 92n20,
    92n22, 93, 93n26, 93n27,
    104, 104n66, 105, 105n68,
    105n69, 105n70, 105n71,
    105n72, 106, 106n73,
    106n74, 106n76, 107,
    107n81, 108n87, 108n89,
    112, 112n106, 154, 154n5,
    155n6, 156, 156n14, 157n16,
    162, 162n41, 162n42, 166,
    166n62
Ross, Allen P., 126n53
Rudolph, David J., 3n9, 7n21,
    9n27, 20n76, 27, 36n39,
    51, 51n106, 73, 73n52, 74,
    74n55, 76, 76n63, 76n67,
    77, 77n71, 78, 79n83, 84,
    125n49, 130n74, 131n75,
    155n6, 188, 188n68, 188n69,
    195, 195n98, 195n100, 202,
    203, 203n21, 211, 211n51,
    211n52, 212, 214, 214n57,
    215, 215n61, 216n66, 218,
    218n72, 224n11, 245n4,
    246n5, 247n13
Ruiten, Jacques T. A. G. M. van.,
    45n80, 233n56
Runesson, Anders, 3n9, 19, 19n69,
    19n70, 19n71, 22n83, 24n94,
    24n96, 24n97, 149, 149n133,
    176n18
Ruzer, Serge, 86, 86n9, 87n12, 91n15
Rydelnik, Michael, 54n118

Sanday, William, 133, 133n84,
    134n87
Sanders, E. P., 56, 56n131, 65,
    65n16, 65n17, 86, 86n5,
    87n10, 102, 102n56, 102n57,
    208, 208n40, 208n42
Schäfer, Peter, 200n11
Schliesser, Benjamin, 62n1
Schmidt, Karl L., 137, 137n92,
    137n94
Schnelle, Udo, 110n97
Schreiner, Thomas R., 37n48, 87n10,
    105n67, 106n79, 108n90,
    129n69, 143n115, 156,
    156n9, 156n10, 168, 168n73,
    170, 174, 175n9, 175n10,
    175n11, 218n72
Schwartz, Daniel R., 217n70, 218,
    218n71
Scobey, David, 62
Scott, James M., 38n49, 125n50,
    187, 187n60, 187n61, 188,
    188n62, 188n63, 193n91
Sechrest, Love L., 122, 122n39,
    137n92, 137n94
Segovia, Carlos A., 247n13
Seifrid, Mark A., 112n108, 146n126,
    237n76
Sherman, Steven J., 22n84
Shulam, Joseph, 106n78
Shum, Shiu-Lun, 239n80
Siker, Jeffrey S., 71n36
Silver, Michael D., 22n85
Skarsaune, Oskar, 133n83
Sloan, Robert B., 110n97
Snodgrass, Klyne R., 26, 86, 86n9,
    87, 87n10, 94n31, 94n32,
    98n41, 101, 101n53, 102n54,
    102n58, 103, 103n59,
    103n60, 103n61, 106n72,
    111, 111n100, 111n101,
    111n104, 157n16, 170,
    170n82, 246n8
Sonderegger, Katherine, 119n20,
    247n17
Song, Changwon, 203n20

Soulen, R. Kendall, 5n15, 35, 35n29, 124, 124n47, 152, 152n140, 247, 247n18

Sprinkle, Preston M., 156, 156n13, 162, 163, 163n43, 166, 166n62, 167, 167n66, 168

Stanley, Christopher D., 23n90, 28n2, 38n49, 146n123, 149n135

Staples, Jason, 192n94

Starling, David I., 64n10, 79n82, 236n73

Stegemann, Ekkehard, 2n6

Stendahl, Krister, 9

Stowers, Stanley Kent, 28n3, 48n90, 55n126, 56, 56n128, 56n29, 108n86, 158n22, 203n20

Strecker, Georg, 204, 204n26

Stuckenbruck, Loren T., 11n33, 247n12

Tait, Michael, 87n10

Tajfel, Henri, 2, 2n3, 121n33, 221, 222n1

Talbert, Charles H., 236, 236n72

Tanner, J. Paul, 145n121

Tapie, Matthew A., 6n16, 9n26

Tatum, Gregory, 28, 28n1, 29n5, 35n32, 36, 36n41, 37n46, 47, 47n85, 57n132, 58, 58n135, 58n136, 60, 86n7, 88, 88n13, 154, 154n3, 157, 157n16, 202n18

Thielman, Frank, 16, 16n52, 17n60, 87n10, 102, 102n55, 102n56, 111n103

Thiessen, Matthew, 3n9, 19n69, 48, 48n89, 49, 49n95, 49n96, 50, 50n99, 50n101, 50n102, 51, 52n112, 79n82, 82n97, 174n7, 214, 214n58

Thompson, Michael, 228n33

Thornhill, A. Chadwick, 64n10, 139n102

Thornton, Dillon T., 101n53

Thorsteinsson, Runar M., 19n69, 47n87, 48, 48n89, 52n110, 174n7

Thurén, Lauri, 101, 101n52

Ticciati, Susannah, 123n43

Tobin, Thomas H., 64n13, 203n20

Toews, John E., 119, 119n19, 169, 169n76, 169n77

Tolmie, Francois, 147n130

Tomson, Peter J., 87n10, 110n99

Toney, Carl N., 198n2, 229, 229n34, 229n36, 229n37, 229n38, 230, 231n41, 231n42

Townsend, Philippa, 22, 22n87

Trebilco, Paul R., 37n42, 38, 38n52, 38n53

Tucker, J. Brian, 2n2, 2n4, 2n5, 2n6, 2n7, 3n8, 7n19, 7n21, 8n24, 10n30, 11n34, 13n44, 16n54, 18n64, 24n96, 30n10, 31n11, 34n21, 39n57, 46n82, 63n9, 64n10, 104n65, 113n110, 118n13, 130n70, 130n72, 130n73, 133n85, 147n131, 159n28, 161n39, 180n30, 200n14, 210n49, 211n50, 212n53, 227n30, 235n65, 235n68, 241n93, 246n10, 248n21, 248n23

Turner, John C., 2, 2n3, 121n33, 221, 222n1

van Buren, Paul Matthews, 230, 230n43

Vanlaningham, Michael G., 7n19, 158n22, 189n71, 190n77, 191, 191n80, 191n84, 192, 192n88, 230, 230n40

Vickers, Brian, 64n10

Visscher, Gerhard H., 70n32, 77n71, 102n56

Vlach, Michael J., 6n17, 54n118, 64n11, 75n61, 176n17

Volf, Miroslav, 242, 242n102

Wagner, J. Ross, 59, 59n140, 141n108, 149, 149n134, 149n35, 151, 151n138, 164n50, 232n52, 235n69, 236, 237n75, 238, 239n80,

Wagner, J. Ross (*continued*)
239n81, 241n91, 242,
242n98, 242n99, 242n100
Wallace, David R., 118, 119n17,
124, 187
Wallace-Hadrill, Andrew, 201n15
Watson, Francis, 19, 19n70, 48n88,
53, 53n115, 54, 55, 55n124,
65n15, 87n10, 97, 97n38,
108n85, 155, 155n7, 155n8,
156, 166n60, 166n62,
172, 172n1, 173, 173n5,
177, 177n19, 178, 178n24,
178n25, 197, 197n2, 230n44,
247n11, 247n16
Wenham, Gordon J., 79, 79n80
Westerholm, Stephen, 87n10, 155n6
Westfall, Cynthia Long, 246n7
Whitsett, Christopher G., 240n86
Whittle, Sarah, 12n39, 48n93, 128,
128n64, 128n65, 237n76
Williams, Sam K., 225n19, 228n32
Willitts, Joel, 5n14, 9n26, 9n27,
20n73, 79n82, 163, 163n44,
163n45, 163n46, 164,
164n47, 164n48, 164n49,
209n45, 210n47, 240,
240n87, 245n4
Wilson, Todd A., 87n10, 103n62,
107n80, 108n90, 109,
109n91, 109n92, 110n95,
111n102, 111n03, 166,
167n64
Windsor, Lionel J., 48, 48n90, 54,
54n120, 54n121, 54n122,
55n124, 58n134, 70, 70n30,
70n33, 71, 71n35, 81n86, 86,
86n9, 94n30, 95n34, 106,
106n75, 106n77, 120n24,
133n82, 133n85, 138n95,
155n6, 158, 158n21, 158n22,
161, 162, 162n40, 162n41,
165, 165n56, 165n57,
177n20, 190n78, 239n82,
239n83, 248n21

Witherington, Ben, 231n50, 237,
238, 238n77
Woolf, Greg, 23n91
Wright, N. T., 8n25, 9n26, 11n36,
12n39, 29, 29n7, 29n8, 30,
41n63, 47n86, 54n119,
63n9, 64n10, 65n17, 66n20,
70n32, 72n37, 74n55,
75n61, 81n87, 100, 100n50,
102n58, 118, 118n16,
120n29, 122n35, 128,
128n65, 132n80, 133n84,
135n90, 141, 141n107, 142,
143n112, 145n121, 146,
146n128, 150n136, 153,
154, 154n2, 154n4, 167,
167n69, 168n71, 174n8,
176, 176n17, 185, 185n46,
186, 186n52, 186n57, 187,
188, 188n64, 188n66, 189,
189n70, 189n73, 189n75,
193, 193n93, 194, 194n95,
196n101, 230, 231, 231n46,
234, 237, 241, 241n95,
247n11, 247n16

Zetterholm, Magnus, 2n2, 23n92,
240n86, 245n3
Zoccali, Christopher, 3n7, 8n24,
12n38, 37, 37n47, 54n121,
70n32, 75n58, 78n76, 82n93,
121n32, 132n80, 133n85,
140, 140n105, 142n109,
165n59, 168n72, 185,
185n47, 185n51, 188n69,
190, 190n76, 190n78, 191,
191n79, 191n81, 191n83,
191n84, 192, 192n85,
192n87, 192n90, 231n48,
248n21

Printed by BoD™in Norderstedt, Germany